THE WAITE G

JAVA

PRIMER PLUS

SUPERCHARGING
WEB APPLICATIONS WITH THE JAVA
PROGRAMMING LANGUAGE

PAUL M. TÝMA, GABRIEL TOROK, TROY DOWNING

WAITE GROUP PRESS™
A Division of Sams Publishing
Corte Madera, CA

Publisher Mitchell Waite
Editor-in-Chief Charles Drucker

Acquisitions Editor Jill Pisoni

Editorial Director John Crudo
Managing Editor Kurt Stephan
Content Editor Scott Calamar
Copy Editor Merilee Eggleston
Technical Reviewer Gary L. Craig

Production Director Julianne Ososke
Production Manager Cecile Kaufman
Interior and Cover Design Sestina Quarequio
Production Tom Debolski
Illustrations Pat Rogondino
Cover Illustration © Rafael Lopez/Stockworks

Printed in the United States of America
96 97 98 99 • 10 9 8 7 6 5 4 3 2 1

Library of Congress Cataloging-in-Publication Data

Tyma, Paul.
    Java primer plus / Paul Tyma, Gabriel Torok, Troy Downing.
        p.   cm.
    Includes index.
    ISBN 1-57169-062-X
    1. Object-oriented programming (Computer science)   2. Java (Computer program language)
3. Multimedia systems.   4. World Wide Web (Information retrieval system)   I. Torok, Gabriel, 1967-
II. Downing, Troy.   III. Title.
QA76.64.T96   1996
005.1--dc20
                                                                                95-51487
                                                                                CIP

Dedication

To my mother and father: thanks for everything.

—Paul Týma

To my mother and father: thanks for all your help and support.

—Gabriel Torok

I dedicate this to my mother, Kathleen Downing: thanks for all of your help and support.

—Troy Downing

Message from the
Publisher

WELCOME TO OUR NERVOUS SYSTEM

Some people say that the World Wide Web is a graphical extension of the information superhighway, just a network of humans and machines sending each other long lists of the equivalent of digital junk mail.

I think it is much more than that. To me the Web is nothing less than the nervous system of the entire planet—not just a collection of computer brains connected together, but more like a billion silicon neurons entangled and recirculating electro-chemical signals of information and data, each contributing to the birth of another CPU and another Web site.

Think of each person's hard disk connected at once to every other hard disk on earth, driven by human navigators searching like Columbus for the New World. Seen this way, the Web is more of a super entity, a growing, living thing, controlled by the universal human will to expand, to be more. Yet, unlike a purposeful business plan with rigid rules, the Web expands in a nonlinear, unpredictable, creative way that echoes natural evolution.

We created our Web site not just to extend the reach of our computer book products but to be part of this synaptic neural network, to experience, like a nerve in the body, the flow of ideas and then to pass those ideas up the food chain of the mind. Your mind. Even more, we wanted to pump some of our own creative juices into this rich wine of technology.

TASTE OUR DIGITAL WINE

And so we ask you to taste our wine by visiting the body of our business. Begin by understanding the metaphor we have created for our Web site—a universal learning center, situated in outer space in the form of a space station. A place where you can journey to study any topic from the convenience of your own screen. Right now we are focusing on computer topics, but the stars are the limit on the Web.

If you are interested in discussing this Web site or finding out more about the Waite Group, please send me email with your comments and I will be happy to respond. Being a programmer myself, I love to talk about technology and find out what our readers are looking for.

Sincerely,

Mitchell Waite

Mitchell Waite, C.E.O. and Publisher

200 Tamal Plaza
Corte Madera CA 94925
415 924 2575
415 924 2576 fax

Internet email:
support@waite.com

Website:
http://www.waite.com/waite

CREATING THE HIGHEST QUALITY COMPUTER BOOKS IN THE INDUSTRY

Waite Group Press
Waite Group New Media

Come Visit
WAITE.COM
Waite Group Press
World Wide Web Site

Now find all the latest information on Waite Group books at our new Web site, **http://www.waite.com/waite**. You'll find an online catalog where you can examine and order any title, review upcoming books, and send email to our authors and editors. Our ftp site has all you need to update your book: the latest program listings, errata sheets, most recent versions of Fractint, POV Ray, Polyray, DMorph, and all the programs featured in our books. So download, talk to us, ask questions, on **http://www.waite.com/waite**.

The New Arrivals Room has all our new books listed by month. Just click for a description, Index, Table of Contents, and links to authors.

The Backlist Room has all our books listed alphabetically.

The People Room is where you'll interact with Waite Group employees.

Links to Cyberspace get you in touch with other computer book publishers and other interesting Web sites.

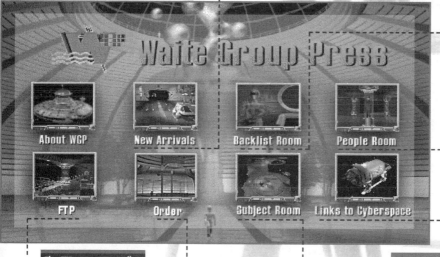

The FTP site contains all program listings, errata sheets, etc.

The Order Room is where you can order any of our books online.

The Subject Room contains typical book pages that show description, Index, Table of Contents, and links to authors.

World Wide Web:

COME SURF OUR TURF—THE WAITE GROUP WEB

http://www.waite.com/waite
Gopher: gopher.waite.com
FTP: ftp.waite.com

About the Authors

Paul Týma is president of preEmptive Solutions, Inc., an Internet technologies consulting firm specializing in Java™. He holds a B.S. and an M.S. in computer science, and is currently pursuing his Ph.D. at Syracuse University. His dissertation research is in the areas of object-oriented language design and distributed computing environments. When he's not working, doing research, or writing, you'll find Paul sleeping.

Gabriel Torok is vice president of preEmptive Solutions, Inc. He is also a professional software engineer and a graduate of Cleveland State University. He has programmed numerous VAX/VMS and Microsoft Windows applications and has been interested in Java since its release. Besides programming, Gabe enjoys traveling, skiing, biking, and good conversation.

Troy Downing is a research scientist, programmer, and Web administrator at New York University's Media Research Lab. Troy is also an adjunct faculty member in the Information Technology division of NYU, teaching classes on WWW development. Troy has been a primary force in WWW development at the Lab and has recently turned his focus to Java, porting many of the Media Research Lab's efforts to a Java platform. Troy regularly gives talks on Java development at NYU and local special interest groups. When he's not sitting in front of a computer terminal, you will find Troy making silly faces at his daughter Morgan, racing mountain bikes, or perfecting his latest batch of homebrew.

Contents

Table of Contents

Acknowledgments

The authors would like to thank Bill Leach, Gary Craig, Nataraj Nagaratnam, and Doug Lea for their merciless criticisms, tireless quibbling, and insightful advice, all of which helped make this a better book. Additional thanks go out to Scott Calamar and Kurt Stephan, whose perspicacious edits and peculiar suggestions made the final draft a joy. Troy would also like to thank New York University and the Media Research Lab.

A final thanks to all the folks out on comp.lang.java and the mailing list that preceded it for always seeming to ask the questions we were going to. And, of course, thanks to the Java team for answering them.

Preface

Welcome to *Java™ Primer Plus*. We're confident that this is the most comprehensive guide to learning the Java programming language available. If you're in a bookstore right now trying to decide on what book is right for you, we appreciate that you are taking a closer look—we know you have a lot of choices. Continue reading this introduction, but when you see a reference to a section of the book that really interests you, go there. That's the only way to really get a feel for how this book is designed. We think you'll like what you read, and you'll agree that this book is your best bet for learning and using Java.

Who Are You?

Well, needless to say, you are someone interested in learning more about Java. This book is labeled as an intermediate to advanced text. From looking at the comprehensive object-oriented programming chapters and the advanced topics section, it's easy to see why. On the other hand, the book starts out at a calm pace. No significant knowledge of any programming is assumed. If you are an advanced C or C++ programmer, you have a jump on the game and you'll be able to skim the earlier chapters. If you are a novice, don't fret: this book is designed to hand-hold you at first, then does its best to try to keep up as you get flying.

What Does This Book Contain?

This book has all you need to start programming Java right away. More importantly, it keeps you learning by exploring Java's object-oriented features and covering advanced topics. The chapters are placed so that they lead you into programming at the core of Java and gradually introduce you to more advanced concepts throughout the book.

Chapter 1: Introducing Java™

As with most introductory chapters, this one lets you figure out where you are and why. It introduces the design ideas behind Java and what influenced them. If you're wondering what all the excitement is about, here's where you'll find out.

Chapter 2: The Java™ Model

Hard and fast, this chapter steps you through how Java works, how its compiler fits in, and how Java works with the World Wide Web. The chapter then moves on to the security issues behind Java and lets you know the lengths that the designers went to make sure Java is safe.

Chapter 3: Interfacing to the Web

This chapter gives you an introduction to the Web and HTML. In addition, by using some prebuilt Java applets, it shows you how to infuse your Web pages right away. If you've never seen Java in action before, this chapter will give you a grand glimpse.

Chapter 4: Designing Java™ Programs

Here you'll learn about the high-level aspects of designing Java programs. From naming conventions to applets to an introduction to object-oriented programming, you'll hit the ground running.

Chapter 5: Data and Variables

If you're new to computer languages, this chapter will walk you through how Java stores and uses data. You'll also start to see how Java code is developed and how to use its advanced `Math` functions.

Chapter 6: Everything Is under Control

This chapter walks you through Java's control structures. This includes iteration, conditional statements, and flow control. This is definitely a nuts-and-bolts review of Java's syntax.

Chapter 7: Arrays and Strings

Java implements these data types unlike most any other language. This chapter will guide you through examples on how to use them—effectively.

Chapter 8: Designer Methods

This chapter is really the start of your move into the object world. Important notions regarding Java's class and method design are discussed. The chapter then moves into designing applets and letting you know why they work the way they do. You'll also get an introduction to multithreading, mouse control, and graphics.

Chapter 9: Objects

Java's pure object-oriented design takes over with full force from here on out. You'll explore object-oriented programming in Java with no holds barred.

Chapter 10: Object-Oriented Superpowers

This chapter delves into Java's advanced object-oriented design features. It covers Java's core object-oriented methodologies and walks you through examples to solidify the concepts. This chapter is designed to get you thinking about how to correctly design your programs using OO concepts.

Chapter 11: Exceptions and Debugging

With Java's advanced features, finding and handling bugs in your programs have never been easier. This chapter will step you through setting up your own error-handling facilities, and gives you an introduction to tracking elusive bugs.

Chapter 12: Java™ vs. C/C++

This chapter is tailor-made for C and C++ programmers. It provides you with a quick reference to using what you already know and applying it to Java.

Chapter 13: Graphics and Sound

Java's capabilities for multimedia are impressive. This chapter will cover the most important aspects of creating graphics and sound in Java. In addition, it discusses common graphics techniques such as double buffering and clipping, and how they are implemented in Java.

Chapter 14: By a Thread

Java incorporates the concept of running simultaneous processes. This chapter will explain the basics of this concept and move you into working with your own multithreading programs.

Chapter 15: The Net Works

This chapter walks you through setting up a full client-server application using Java's built-in functionality. You'll see the design of an application that allows for worldwide communication and how to adapt what you learn to your own applications.

Chapter 16: Native Methods: Interfacing to C

This chapter reveals the way you can interface C code to Java programs. This feature provides a means to access hot functions written in C to enhance your Java.

Chapter 17: Data Structures

This chapter introduces the classic data structure Java provides, and designs two new ones. Data structures are the pinnacle example of reusability within the OO methodology.

Chapter 18: The Future

Where are Java and the Internet headed? This chapter discusses some of the issues behind the design of Java and where it might be going.

Appendix: Java™ APIs

The section gives you a quick reference to Java's built-in API packages. The functionality in these packages is largely responsible for Java's comprehensive set of features. You'll find this section an invaluable reference guide as your journey through Java programming progresses.

System and Software Requirements

Well, if you know anything about Java, you probably know that your options for computing machinery are wide open. Java runs on a variety of platforms and more are on the way. The CD-ROM in the back of this book contains the Java compiler for several architectures/operating systems. It's always best to check for the latest releases at http://java.sun.com (the official Java site). You'll probably also want to secure a World Wide Web browser capable of running Java. The newest release of Netscape is always a good choice (Chapter 3 gives you more details on this).

The CD-ROM

The CD-ROM included with this book contains the example code from every chapter. It is organized by directories named after the chapters. From there the file names should be self-explanatory. You'll also find a directory with several versions of the Java binaries (many thanks to Sun Microsystems for allowing us to put them there). In general, the code is there for you to play with and mangle at your discretion. As with most things, the best way to learn Java is to jump in and work with it yourself. Each directory should have a read me file to give a better explanation of what's there, and be sure to check out the read me at the root level of the CD-ROM for a general explanation of CD contents, organization, etc.

Go Pour Yourself a Cup

You're now well-armed to start using Java! If you're new to programming, start at the beginning and don't stop until you reach the end. If you're a seasoned veteran, then jump to the sections that most interest you and be amazed at what Java can do.

Now, go get yourself some Java!

PART I:
Introduction

Introducing
Java™

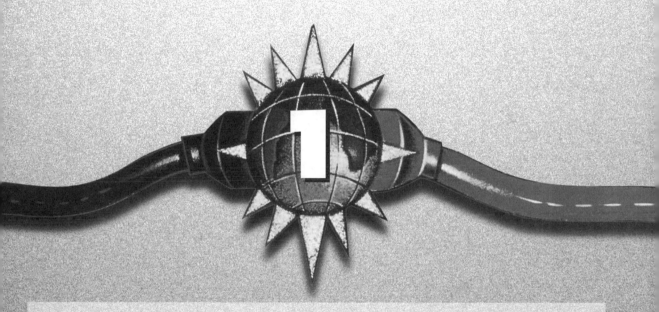

You will learn about the following in this chapter:

- What Java™ is and where it came from
- The ideas behind object-oriented programming
- What features set Java apart from most computer languages
- Why HotJava™ was popular and why it may fizzle
- How to compile and run Java programs

Maybe you didn't realize it, but the only thing the programmers of the world have ever really wanted is one of those little tricorder devices from Star Trek. Not because they look neat or because they make that rather hollow whirring sound. Not even because the most seemingly brainless crew member (you know him, the one destined to get vaporized) can look at it, hit the "commence-whirring" button, and provide a full report about the bone composition of the gruesome creature behind the next rock. What's great about the tricorder is that whenever the crew gets into a mess, the engineer always suggests reconfiguring one of those gadgets into the exact thing they need to solve all their immediate problems. Through the decades those things have been reliably converted into anything from a single-shot freeze ray to a dual-slice toaster oven. In other words, the beauty of the tricorder is not what it is but what you can turn it into.

Programming languages of the past came close to being what programmers asked for, but didn't quite cut it. The C, C++, Pascal, etc., languages all provided an immense amount of general purpose functionality, again, not because of what they were but because of what you could turn them into. But as we enter this age of the Internet, it has become easier to find application areas in which these languages fall short.

We have waited a long time, but it's been worth it; Java™ is here. By learning from the mistakes and shortcomings of its predecessors, the Java language is the most complete and easy to learn programming language available. It includes a more comprehensive list of features than any previous language. It has pure object-orientation, security, internetworking, architecture independence, and multithreading, to name but a few of its niftiest features. Finally, in the age of Internet, the programmers of the world have found their tricorder.

What Is Java™?

Well, besides being an island in Indonesia and a reference to coffee, Java is a new programming language developed by Sun Microsystems. What sets Java apart is its well-thought-out design and its comprehensive set of features, which are not found in any other popular programming language.

Something Borrowed

Java's design is a result of research done on scads of different languages that were developed in academic and industrial settings. It borrowed the best features of these languages to form an easy-to-learn and object-oriented language. So in essence, a lot of Java's design is not new; many other languages in recent years have had its well-designed structure and usually some semblance of its advanced features. These languages including Self, Smalltalk, ODL, etc., varied in levels of programming difficulty but all purporting the same next generation programming language ideals as Java. Unfortunately, their commercial success has been questionable (with the notable exception of Smalltalk, which is now coming on strong). This isn't because the languages are in some way worse than Java; mostly it is because they have failed to offer a solid reason for industry to use them. In other words, companies already had C, C++, and many other good solutions. For them to switch to a new language, there would have to be a darn good reason. Switching is not a trivial thing; serious amounts of retraining and retooling of people, machines, and existing code must be done.

The Gimmick

So the next question is, what is Java's ace in the hole that will cause acceptance by the industry at large? You'll be happy to know it has more than one. First of all, Java was developed and is supported by Sun Microsystems. Having such a prominent company backing a language is certainly a plus. An immediate campaign to encourage Java education is underway.

Okay, so Java has a solid support base and will hopefully have a small legion of knowledgeable programmers. Is this enough reason for industry to make the switch? Maybe not, but never fear. The big sell is in that Java can do things just not possible in any conventional language. First and foremost is its ability to *infuse* World Wide Web pages. To infuse a Web page with Java code is to bring true power, interactivity, and live content to what would otherwise be static page.

Current Web pages are just a display of information. You can sometimes type in something (e.g., a search string) and get a response, but the page itself is static data—nothing is going on. But Java changes all that. Java-infused pages can contain live action video, networked games, animations, sounds, etc. The possibilities are endless. Get ready for an industry starving for Java programmers.

 Object-Oriented Programming

Java is purely object-oriented. If you are new to object-oriented programming or even programming in general, you are probably wondering what it's all about. First off, if you are a novice programmer, you aren't in bad shape, since you can learn object-oriented programming from the start and won't be bogged down by shaking off bad habits. If you are an experienced programmer, consider that comparatively few people have programmed in a purely object-oriented language. For those C++ programmers out there quietly smirking with an air of superiority, smirk again. C++ is not purely object-oriented. It is a hybrid-language—in other words, you can certainly do things outside the tight restrictions of the object-oriented paradigm. In any event, experienced programmers need only take another look at how they approach their effort. All of your coding skills will move to the object world just fine; it's your design skills that need some attitude adjustment.

What's It All About?

So just what is this mystical object-oriented programming all about? Don't worry, as you plod through these pages, the ideas will be surreptitiously implanted into your brain. You'll need to rethink your way of programming to truly take advantage of Java's strengths. Object-oriented programming is to some degree looking at programming from a different angle than you may be used to. Basically, you create objects in your running program; they can be rectangles, bank balances, anything. They are analogous to the things you have already included in any program you have ever written. The difference is that you are accustomed to having them and using them as you see fit. In other words, you have a rectangle and you decide to draw it on the screen.

Object-oriented programming doesn't allow you such apparently reckless operations upon your elements (actually, you can still do whatever you like, just be prepared to organize things a bit better). In an object-oriented program you can also have a rectangle, but now that rectangle is its own object. (Don't get too worried, just move your thinking to the real world. Your computer is an object, so is your monitor, and chances are so is your favorite burger restaurant—so why not that rectangle?). The difference between non-object and object-oriented programming (OOP) is that in OOP you don't draw the rectangle. What you do is send the rectangle a message that you would like it to be drawn and it goes off and draws itself! Figure 1-1 shows the results.

The key here is that objects know all about themselves and how to act upon themselves. Therefore, you are relieved of the burden of knowing how to draw rectangles or circles or anything. Each object knows how to draw itself.

If you have had object-oriented programming experience, then moving to Java will be nothing less than a joy because of its clean implementation. If you have never programmed using an object-oriented language, don't fret. The code doesn't change much;

FIGURE 1-1

Rectangles

you just need to start visualizing how each object will be put together—i.e., what that rectangle needs to know about itself.

So What?

Good point. So what? Why is looking at rectangles, bank balances, or space invaders as their own objects any better than the old way? Actually, there are a slew of reasons and more are invented every day, but two of the most important are *encapsulation* and *reuse*.

Encapsulation

With encapsulation, once you have defined your object, you only let the outside world access the parts of it that they absolutely need to. For one thing, this prevents anyone from relying on how you put your object together. So if you want to change the way your rectangle draws itself, go ahead. Since no one knew how it did it before, your changing it won't affect anyone.

For a simple example, assume Mr. Jones orders a pepperoni pizza every day at 5 p.m., and it's your job to deliver it. Unfortunately, your pizza shop and Mr. Jones are located on exactly opposite sides of the most notorious pizza-stealing area in the city. A foolish move on your part would be to make public that you will always take Cheese Street through that part of town. This is initially foolish because since the nefarious pizza thieves have access to this information, they will likely set up an ambush. Secondly, the police may realize the danger of your situation and spend a lot of time and money posting guards along Cheese Street to insure your safety. You've created a war zone on Cheese Street!

Then one dark day, you decide to take ExtraCheese Street. You upset the thieves and police alike. Now, because everyone feels deceived, the thieves are going to be extra nasty and the police will likely pull their protection, since they can't keep trying to guess which way you will go.

The best tactic would have been not to publish your route. This way, if one street starts getting dangerous, you can change it at will. The overall goal of your mission is still completed (i.e., getting Mr. Jones his pizza), but your means can change and no one gets particularly upset. When applied to programming, this level of hiding increases your flexibility and prevents anyone from forming unreasonable dependencies on your objects. In other words, you promise to provide a service, but how you get it done is your business. That way, if you need or want to change your methodology later, go ahead; your promise will still be good.

Reuse

A second important advantage of OOP is reuse. Since you have designed your program elements as objects, they are in and of themselves complete for their intended usage. In other words, your rectangle has all it needs to keep track of itself (width, height), and it even knows how to perform operations on itself (calculate area, draw itself). Therefore, if you ever write another program that requires a rectangle (chances are you will; once you write one rectangle program you're bound to write another—they are quite addicting), you can literally pluck out this rectangle design and reuse it for your next program.

If you currently find yourself loudly ranting about how you can already do this in your favorite non-object-oriented language, rant again. Sometimes it's possible, but usually in languages like C or Pascal you find yourself making assumptions about your rectangle code. You end up having pieces of the code dealing with your rectangle scattered across your program. Removing all the code associated with your rectangle usually ends up stealing lines from many different functions, which gets messy and may spur legions of syntax errors. Don't misread this; it is certainly possible to design your code in a non-object-oriented language so that later you can easily pluck out pieces for reuse elsewhere. But usually you don't. That's the biggest difference with object-oriented programming—it guides you to a better design.

With all its organization, OOP makes programming easier. By isolating the distinct pieces of your program, you know right where to go for changes or fixes. You'll also be able to depend on a solid way of interfacing with those pieces. It's a sure thing: you're going to love OOP.

Java's Features

What is meant by "features"? For this purpose, the focus is on any advantage Java has over whatever language you are currently using. Java's hook into the Web and its inherent superiority over many conventional languages have already been discussed. Above and beyond all that, it includes several other goodies:

> Java provides a four-level security system to keep its programs well behaved. Gone are the days when code can nose its way into another program's memory space or corrupt data.

- Java provides built-in *multithreading*. The short story is that Java programs can be designed to do several things at once. This topic is covered in depth in Chapter 14.

- Java has built-in internetworking capabilities. This functionality allows you to immediately start using the Internet as a means of accessing multiple computers. Networked games, distributed applications, or advanced Net surfing has never been easier.

- Java has its own garbage collection features. Programmers in many environments are quite familiar with wayward memory pointers or memory leaks. Java prevents these disasters from happening in the first place. All the memory management is taken care of for you.

- Java incorporates advanced exception handling facilities. Exceptions (analogous to runtime program errors) are no longer things that stop your program cold with an accompanying disturbing error message. Now you can design your programs to recover from unexpected events and fix the problem on the fly or just exit gracefully. In either case, exception handling is under your control.

- Java professes architecture independence. What this means is that if you write a game in Java on your home computer, that game is immediately (and that does mean right this minute) runnable on any other computer architecture. No more porting of code from one machine to another. Programs written on a Macintosh can run on Intel machines, and so on.

These features can usually be found piecemeal in other systems. However, rarely is such a solid collection of useful (and generally pretty slick) features seen all in one package.

What Is HotJava™?

If you've been closely following Internet-related industry (or in the past few months glanced at the front cover of any publication whose title starts with "Cyber"), you have probably at least heard of HotJava™. So, if Java is a programming language, then is HotJava a hot programming language? Not even close. Actually, HotJava is the first showboat application developed in Java. It is a World Wide Web browser. A WWW browser is a program that allows you to peruse or surf the Web, bringing up text, images, and whatnot from all over the world. This blatant accessibility to vast amounts of data is usually touted as a way for great minds to share great ideas. Yeah, well, that's a nice ideal, but as any Web surfer will tell you, the Web is just as happy to supply you with anything from academic treatises to up-to-the-minute sports scores to stock quotes to the latest hot game demo. Figure 1-2 shows three browsers.

HotJava, Netscape, and Mosaic

Compared to Competition

Keep in mind that besides the similarity between their names, Java and HotJava are very different things. Java is a programming language and HotJava is an application written in that language. This is not exactly a symbiotic relationship. HotJava is only discussed here because of its importance in the early stages of exposing Java to the world. HotJava's future is uncertain.

HotJava is by no stretch of the imagination the only way to cruise the Web. At its birth, it was a competitor (of sorts) with the Netscape and Mosaic WWW browsers, among others. Remember the difference between Web pages with and without Java code. To be fair, for standard (no Java code) Web viewing, HotJava was a bit rudimentary compared to its competition. It did not support many of the advanced features found in the other browsers. For pages without Java code, HotJava was way behind the pack.

But, HotJava had a hook. At its inception, it was the only *Java-aware* browser available. What that means is that HotJava was the only browser that could understand and run Java programs across the Web. This is, in effect, the only way to make Web pages come alive.

Supercars

As far as standard Web browsing (i.e., no Java code) is concerned, you have a Lamborghini and a Ferrari (Netscape, Mosaic, etc.) and then you have HotJava, basically a beat-up Yugo with one bad cylinder. The only catch is this Java-aware thing. As it turns out, that happens to be a pretty significant little feature. So in effect, it's more like a beat-up Yugo that happens to have a rocket launcher mounted on top. Granted, the big boys will buzz by you in your Yugo like there is no tomorrow, at least right up until the road leads to some Java code. It's right about then that the little old rocket launcher lights up, clearing a path in the road for the putt-putting Yugo. So next thing you know, people realized that Ferraris were cool, but rocket launchers were cooler (especially since they were something new).

Hence, the Internet community started seeing a disproportionate number of Yugos (er…HotJava users) on the road.

What Sun Microsystems plans to do with the HotJava browser seems to be one of life's little uncertainties. They would need a solid commitment to bring HotJava up to par with its competitors in other areas of browsing. Overall, that doesn't seem likely, but more importantly, it doesn't matter. Netscape and others are already licensing the Java technology so their browsers will become Java-aware—they are mounting rocket launchers on their vehicles, too. Pretty soon, you'll have your choice of which supercar you would like to use to buzz around the Web while still having the optional rocket launch feature. So choose your car and hit the road. If you happen to run into a little Java code, fear not; just hit that little red button.

The Net

If it wasn't for the Internet, the world would be a seriously different place. Possibly more interesting than the physical makeup of the Internet is what it gives us. It provides near effortless access to unlimited information. Read that again; small sentence, big words. That sentence is one of the closest things to science fiction that has ever become a reality. This super connection of great information resources has snowballed, and will continue to do so. Overall, the computers that are heedlessly tacked onto the Net at random points have not done anything too amazing except act as vehicles for you, the curious Net surfer. Java is just more icing on the cake. Before Java, the Internet was pure information. Java adds boundless functionality to that equation.

The single most important reason for Java's success is the amazing functionality it adds to the World Wide Web. The good news is that it is unique in this ability and it's sure to rocket Java onto the screens of programmers everywhere. The bad news is that Java is much more than a Web page enhancer and it will be a challenge to get those same programmers to realize it. Anything you can do in C, C++, or Pascal, you can do in Java. In fact, with its clean design and solid object-orientation, you can usually get things done faster and better. In other words, less milk, more cookies.

Mastering the Web

The infusion of Java into the Web is going to quickly become the rage. Don't think that the excitement will end at Web pages with animation and sound. Serious applications are going to take advantage of this ability to propagate code and data. Some of the examples in this book provide some pretty impressive functionality for such small pieces of code. And that code will run without modification on any modern machine. Boy, this is going to be big.

Initially, you're bound to see a lot of interesting distributed games popping up. Not bad; open your browser, type in a network address, and bang—you are looking down a 3D hallway and some guy from Australia is aiming a big, ugly gun at you. After that, businesses around the Net will realize the potential they have for Web interaction. They can provide program demos, distributed applications, and hot Web pages. The Web is definitely the place to be.

Applications Spanning the Net

Because of Java's commitments of architecture independence and networking, creating networked applications is easier than ever. The network could be a local area network or the Internet. Note that the World Wide Web in this context is really only one piece of the puzzle. Java can use a network for communication between program entities to allow computers around the world to cooperate in solving problems. With all of Java's built-in features and its disposition to reusing its code, the upcoming wave of applications will be staggering.

Security

It's hard to speak of the Internet without addressing security issues. The first thing to note is that the designers of Java were well aware of the risks with an environment such as Java and went to great lengths to keep it secure. Security permeates every aspect with how Java is built, from its language design to its built-in security functions. It is well prepared. Chapter 2 will give you a detailed look at Java's security implementation and hopefully give you the warm and fuzzies. Keep in mind, the designers knew that Java's security was key to its success, and they addressed this problem aggressively.

Using the Compiler

Given that Java is maturing at a rapid rate and that it lives on a multitude of different machines, a concise lesson in compiling Java programs is impossible. However, the general methodology dictates you name all your Java files with a .java suffix. For the supplied compiler, your files should reside in plain ASCII text format. In other words, you can use the editor of your choice, such as emacs, vi, or any plain vanilla editing package.

After creating your text code file, you need to compile it. As distributed with Java, the compiler is named javac and is used as follows:

```
javac myprogram.java
```

A successful compile will result in no response except for the creation of the runnable code in files with the suffix .class.

This should be a relatively standard method on most machines. As Java continues to gain popularity, massively overhelpful tools will appear, making your compiling experience a more pleasant if not a more confusing one.

Using the Runtime

Running your programs is almost as simple. If your application is built for a Web page, then you just need to pull up the page it resides on and see what happens. Chapter 3 discusses the aspects of infusing Web pages from the Web side of things.

Standalone applications can be run from the command line with

```
java myprogram
```

This command attempts to run a file called myprogram.class, which was generated by the compile from the previous section. Notice that the suffix (.class) is not included for the interpreter to find it. In fact, if you do include the suffix, the interpreter will complain that it can't find the file you are talking about. So if you correctly invoke the interpreter, your program will begin executing. As with compilation, you can expect much friendlier methods of programming, running, and testing Java programs in the near future.

Summary

Hopefully this introduction gave you a solid feel for where Java is coming from and maybe where it's headed. The next chapter gets a little deeper into how Java does some of its wondrous tricks. After that, you will quickly move into designing and coding your own Java applications. Another thing Java has over many other languages is that it's fun to use and learn. You will be able to do so many things amazingly fast. Chapter 3 is designed to have you infusing your Web pages even before you write your first line of code. So, boot up the system and get going!

The Java™ Model

You will learn about the following in this chapter:

- How Java exists in the Web and on its own
- Where the Java compiler fits in
- The pluses and minuses of interpreted Java
- How a just-in-time compiler works
- How Java gives the Web dynamically enhanced capabilities
- The design of Java's four-level security system

As you continue your journey through this book, you'll see the amazing array of features that were designed into Java. Java is basically a conglomeration of some of the best features found in many different modern languages. Scads of languages have popped up in recent years with advanced features, but they never saw commercial success. This is usually because no one wants to throw out all their current code (written in C, C++, Fortran, etc.) and move to a new language. There would have to be a darn good reason.

Hopefully, Java is that reason. The designers of Java examined many languages and gleaned the brightest ideas to implement into Java. On top of that, Java has abilities such as architecture independence and Web infusion that set it apart from its predecessors. This chapter will give you an insight into how Java works its voodoo. Throughout its compiler and its runtime, Java is complete.

Double Life

Java has two lives—one in the World Wide Web and one as a standalone computer language. Miniapplications written in Java that run inside Web pages are called *applets*. Applets bring Web pages to life and are guaranteed to bring Java into the limelight, turning tons of people into Java-ites. This is a wonderful place for Java to start; this medium will solidify Java in the industry.

Java also runs as a standalone development environment. In other words, it can run normal programs doing anything you want just as well or better than C, C++, Pascal, etc.

Considering the Web's popularity in universities, new computer graduates will soon be Java savvy. As if by osmosis, the industry will find itself with a multitude of Java programmers (old hands at Web jockeying) and realize their talents can be used for real applications. The battle between C++ and Java should be interesting. Java is new, sexy, and in many ways better. C++ owns the object-oriented hill and doesn't want to move.

Like most other programs, Java code offers two opportunities for scrutiny—when it is compiled, and when it is run.

The Compiler

After you have written a program in Java, the fun really starts. Writing the program likely took painstaking hours of your creativity and skill, but the steps the compiler and runtime environment take to get it to work safely, efficiently, and seamlessly make it look as if you were twiddling your thumbs. Okay, maybe that's an exaggeration, but teams of smart people spent countless months implementing the Java environment.

A big selling point for Java is its architecture independence. This means that a compiled Java program can run on any computer. That's a nasty bit of news, since anybody who has even come close to programming a computer knows that a compiler (and supporting programs) turns the computer language (Java, FORTRAN, C, C++, Pascal, etc.) ultimately into something the computer can understand. Usually that something is the computer's machine language. The problem is that machine languages are vastly different in different machines. So the big question is, how does the Java compiler turn your Java program into a language that any machine, anywhere, can understand? Precisely the question the designers asked.

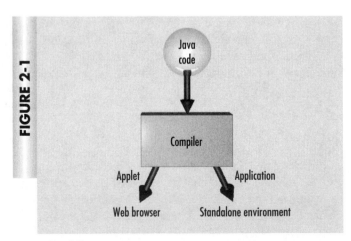

FIGURE 2-1

Java life

Giving Speeches

Consider giving a speech conveying some key ideas to a ten-member international delegation. Assume that each of the ten delegates is from a different country and that they all only speak their own language. To continue to tailor this example, also assume that you are a master linguist and can speak eleven languages. Coincidentally, you can speak each of the delegate's languages in addition to English (none of the delegates speaks English). Besides firing the person who set up this talk, what could you do? Obviously, you could perform your speech ten times, once in each language. Unfortunately, during each recital, nine of the delegates would probably be rather bored, and your speech would take ten times too long.

A better solution would be to hire ten translators. You do not need extremely diverse translators; all you need is a translator for each delegate who can translate English to the language of that delegate. Now you can give your speech in English, and the translators will do the work as far as getting the final message to the delegates. In fact, giving the speech in English means you are really giving the speech to the translators, not the delegates. You are interested in making sure the translators understand what you are talking about so they can effectively convey the meaning to the intended recipients.

The method Java uses to solve its problem of speaking to many possible architectures is similar. It is a common practice to compile computer languages to some intermediate representation before translating them all the way down to a specific machine's language. That way, the front end of the compiler can be standard across machines. In other words, much like your single speech in English, only one effort is needed to convert your message to some intermediate form that can later be easily translated to the final language. In this case, the final language is the machine languages of many different types of architectures.

Above, your speech went from ideas to English, and finally into the language of the delegate. English was the intermediate language used for transmission of the ideas. What about in Java? What is Java's intermediate language? It is basically a generic assembly language. It doesn't typically correspond to any one machine's low-level language, but tends to be a representation that would be easily convertible to any and all.

Java's Own Intermediate Language

The Java designers had the advantage that they were converting Java into an intermediate language that they created (and were still creating). This gave them a great deal of flexibility. If you could add words to English as you saw fit, you could probably get your ideas across quicker and things overall would just be funner (er…more fun). With this ability, they were able to add functionality as problems arose. At this level, they could also perform security checks on the code, since they knew exactly what it was going to do. This is really where Java's first level of security checks come into play. The compiler can watch what the code is intending to do and complain loudly if anything goes awry. Figure 2-2 shows the conceptual move.

FIGURE 2-2

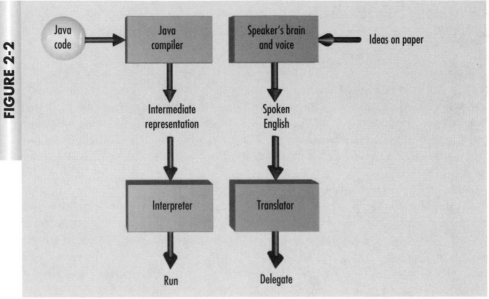

Java to IR

Java calls its intermediate form a *bytecode* representation. This is because the intermediate language is set as byte-sized codes indicating its different commands. Optimizing and outputting the intermediate or bytecode representation is about as far as the Java compiler goes.

The actual look of the bytecodes is of most interest to developers of Java system software. However, it's quite likely all Java programmers will encounter actual bytecodes at one point or another. Often, peeking at the bytecodes can provide a lot of information for tracking bugs and wayward code. Figure 2-3 is an example of a Java program and the bytecodes it is compiled into. The figure shows a simple piece of Java code on the left, and its intermediate representation on the right. The compiler was the vehicle to convert the left side into the right side.

See Java Run

You already know that the Java compiler converts Java code into its intermediate bytecode representation. And you know that the bytecodes are the things that actually get run. Well, there are a few more details on how that's going to happen. So, assume now you've written the most important Java program ever created. You compile it and have in your hands (or at least on your hard disk) a file that contains the bytecodes generated from your Java program. There are now two ways your code can run—either interpreted or just-in-time compiled.

It's up to Interpretation

Interpreted bytecodes are executed by an interpreter (that makes sense). An interpreter is a program that will read in the bytecodes and execute the operation each indicates. In other words, if a bytecode (remember, a bytecode is basically an instruction) indicates that two numbers should be added together, the interpreter will do just that. An interesting point here is that an interpreter is a program in its own right. You also know that the byte-codes are the result of the compile of a Java program. Therefore, when you run the interpreter to run your bytecodes, effectively, you are running a program to run your program. It certainly seems odd to have this extra level. Why can't you just run the bytecodes? If you remember, the bytecodes are not in the computer's language.

The interpreter is analogous to the translators in the international delegation example discussed earlier. Each machine will have its own interpreter (translator) that examines every bytecode command and tells the machine how to do it. This is exactly how you would expect the delegate's translators to operate—as you speak, they will translate every word (as best as translation allows) into the delegate's language. If the translators are not extremely fluent in both languages, they will take extra time to think in between hearing one language and saying the other. Also, some languages rely on word ordering and other factors that could delay the translation. Much in the same way, interpretive computer languages are traditionally slow. One reason is the program running a program paradigm; this extra level of abstraction adds overhead to your program's execution.

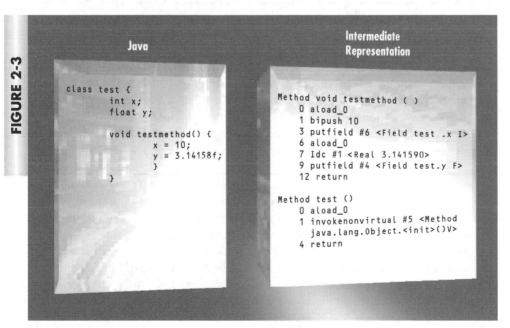

FIGURE 2-3

Java and bytecodes

Compiling Just-In-Time

The other method by which Java programs will execute is within a *dynamic* or *just-in-time* compiled environment. This method works in a different way than an interpretive one. When a bytecode program is executed, the first thing that actually happens is that a just-in-time (JIT) compiler begins. The JIT compiler reads in all the bytecodes and translates them directly into the machine language of the current machine without actually executing any of them.

Once that process is done, the JIT compiler ends and passes control to the machine language version of the bytecodes. Now the machine language version starts running, but the "program running a program" paradigm of the interpreter is not present. It's just the machine language version of your original Java program—converted to bytecodes—then converted to machine language—running on its own. This is much faster than the execution in the interpretive environment.

Just-In-Time Delegation

Extend this to the international delegation example. Now you can assume that you give your speech with only the translators in the room. They all judiciously scribe your words. Then, when you are done, they sit down and take great care in converting the entire text to their target language (i.e., they are performing the JIT compile). Since the delegates aren't breathing down their necks, they have more time to consider using features of their target language in order to better convey your original meaning. When the conversion is finished, they hand the final product to the delegate for review.

The delegates can now read your speech start to finish, not bothered by pauses the translators needed during the interpreted translation. Several bonuses exist for both the delegates and Java programs. First of all, everything happens faster; since the final product is in the final target language (the native tongue of the delegate and the machine language of the specific computer), all time-consuming elements regarding translation are in the past. Now all they have to deal with is using the information provided.

Secondly, once this final target language has been created, both the computer and the delegates can continuously refer to it if they need to. For the delegates in the interpreted environment, if they forgot something you said, they may have to ask the translator to ask you to reiterate what you said and have the translators retranslate it. You should be well aware that computer programs tend to use many sections of code multiple times. Once it has been compiled, that's it; it stays compiled. From now on, there is no further need to translate from bytecodes to machine language. That's all been done.

Figure 2-4 shows the schematic of the two techniques discussed. Unfortunately, JIT compiling does have several disadvantages, too. To begin with, it's much harder to implement. Of course, you as a Java user don't care too deeply about how hard it was to originally implement Java, but the designers sure did. Also, there is a pause, a big long one, right

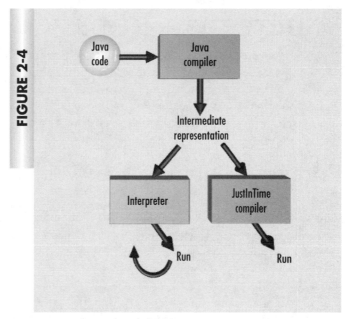

FIGURE 2-4

Just-In-time compiled

as execution begins. This is when the JIT compile takes place. This is analogous to the time it took the translators to efficiently convert your speech into the target language. The delegates were off somewhere waiting for the translators to return with the final version.

As far as Java JIT compiling is concerned, it's possibly a morbid bit of luck that byte-codes will often be sent over a network to the target execution machine. This is lucky for JIT compiling, since network transmission times are still painfully slow compared to most computer operations. Therefore, the eternity it takes for the bytecodes to get to your machine over a network will likely overshadow any time it takes for the JIT compile to complete.

In the End

In the end, JIT compiling will generally be better for running Java programs than interpreting. Most of the time, you will be at the mercy of your browser or runtime environment as to which method will be used. No problem; as they say in the art world, a little interpretation won't kill you. A final note is that since the same Java program could run on fast and slow machines alike, trying to gauge the speed of running code could get ugly (proper timing is important in many applications, such as games). Having your code sometimes be interpreted and sometimes JIT compiled will only exacerbate the problem. Count on timing algorithms popping up as one of Java's pet influences.

Where Java Runs

Okay, so now you know that after you write some Java code, the compiler will churn it into Java bytecodes. You know how it could run, but where will it run? In other words, was the code written as an applet to run across the World Wide Web, or is it a standalone application? Don't worry about looking for buried clues to find the answer to that question; designing an applet and a standalone program is notably different, and it's hard to mix them up.

Forever Changing the Web

As was said, Java code that is designed to exist within a Web page is called an applet. Be a bit careful about that limiting definition, since the applet may start in the Web page but can do much more. Many applets bring up an additional window on your screen or attempt connection to a server somewhere else on the Net. In other words, saying that Java applets can "jump off the page" is literally true.

The bytecodes sit in the directories of the user's home page along with all the images, sounds, and other supporting paraphernalia. Initially, they're just more data that needs to be sent across the Net when the page is brought up. As was discussed in Chapter 1, your browser needs to be Java-aware in order for it to understand and subsequently begin executing the bytecodes. The model of this process is illustrated in Figure 2-5.

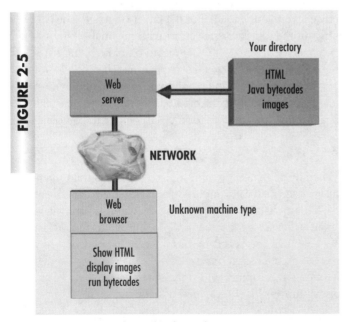

FIGURE 2-5

From one machine to the other

The browser itself has a bytecode interpreter (or maybe a JIT compiler) built into it. It will interpret the bytecodes and effectively run the program. Since the browser is already running on what is to you a foreign, unknown architecture, it has smarts enough to know how to execute the commands inside the bytecodes to get the job done on that particular machine.

On-the-Fly Updates

One of the most amazing abilities of Java-aware browsers is their ability to extend the abilities on the fly. This gives them the ability to adapt to new types of information dynamically—i.e., you don't have to wait until the next release comes out; updates can be done as needed. For example, today there are many different image formats, including JPEG and PCX. A new one could be invented tomorrow that surpasses all the rest (call it BES, since it's the best). Browser companies all over the world will be scrambling to incorporate this technology in the next release of their browser. To not have it would be to fall behind the competition.

But Java-aware browser companies can sit tight, because their browsers can be updated automatically. In fact, likely the first time the browser user attempts to retrieve an image in the new BES format, the browser will not only retrieve the image, it will also end up retrieving a Java program that knows how to display BES images. From then on, the browser is all set and ready to display BES images. Java browsers could be updated dynamically and immediately. Other browsers will be updated in their next release, which could be months away.

This ability to dynamically update features could be taken far beyond simple Web pages. Updates to software and implementation of new protocols can all be done dynamically as you link to the Net. Since you have Java running on your machine, this is all possible.

Standalone Programs and the APIs

Apart from running on Web pages, Java programs can run the same way you run any other program, from a command prompt, an icon in a windowing system, or whatever. In other words, anything you've made in other programming languages you can make in Java.

What makes Java attractive for developing new applications is the vast API library that comes with it. API stands for Applications Program Interface. The library is basically a repository of different functions that Java already knows how to do. Some of these abilities are rather impressive. Simply by using these APIs you can set up network connections, draw graphics, and perform disk I/O. Even the ability to create applets is actually part of the API library. A full list of the APIs is listed in the Appendix. Expect to become familiar with that section.

Tidy Memory

Java's secure design relieves the programmer of some traditional programming woes. In an effort to secure programs and just to make programming that much more of a joy, Java keeps a sharp eye on memory usage. It's not that your program is limited in its memory usage, it's just that Java is sure to watch that your code only uses what it asked for. All memory references in Java are checked for validity. In reality, the programmer no longer explicitly allocates memory (as in C's `malloc`, etc.). The programmer expresses what he or she wishes to do, and Java takes care of the underlying memory representations. This parental attitude keeps things in check. You can have what you ask for, but always ask, don't try to take.

Java's *garbage collection* facilities are quite comprehensive. Garbage collection (in this context) is the act of the Java runtime cleaning up any memory you are no longer using. It makes that memory available for reuse. When you are done using the memory you had, Java will take care of cleaning it up for you. No more explicit deallocation of memory (as in C)—big brother Java is looking out for you. How does it know when you are done with some memory? The implementation of the garbage collector is discussed in Chapter 10, but for now just think of it as being the same as how a thermos knows how to keep its contents hot or cold—it just knows.

 Security

Since its inception, no discussion of Java has occurred without security issues entering the fray. No wonder; consider the mad scenario that actually takes place. You log into the Net, naively bring home some code from who-knows-where that does who-knows-what and involuntarily run it. This seems about as safe as wading into the water so you can cast your line closer to where the piranha are (don't worry, the piranha will be closer soon).

A virus is not, per se, the greatest threat. This isn't because it's impossible, but because the Java environment is just too tasty for other types of beasties—especially Trojan horses. As with the original Trojan horse, this danger is concealed by an unobtrusive covering. You could download a perfectly harmless animation that also contains code that tries to wipe clean your hard drive. The designers of Java spared no expense in addressing these problems.

To some degree, the reason Java exists today is because of its security needs. The original idea was to use C++ in this environment, but the designers found it had just too many security holes. Java eliminates the holes and provides a four-level security defense system to prevent such danger.

The Language

As mentioned, the Java language has been designed with security in mind. As a general rule, any activities that allowed for uncontrolled system access were ruled out of the language specification. Given Java's close relationship to C, the differences are evident and understandable. Most notably, Java allows the programmer no ability to touch actual memory pointers.

The compiler enforces the restrictions of the language specification. Java checks that you are using things as they are supposed to be used. If you declare to Java that you want to draw a circle to the screen, but then covertly try to scrape it into the hard drive, Java will be around asking a few questions. However, there is a cost to all this safety. The time Java spends checking for improprieties is time not spent running the safe parts of your program. Luckily, Java is designed to spend as little time as necessary to ensure a safe environment, so the overall impact on performance isn't huge. Note that even if the speed concerns were monumental, the *safety checks* would still have to be there. Without Java's comprehensive attention to security, implementation of such a global environment would be just too dangerous. Make no mistake, there was some compromise between security and speedy runtime.

Bytecode Verification

The designers continued their search for loopholes in security and took into account all possibilities. Figure 2-6 shows a problem.

The fact is that the only place you have any real control over a Java application is when it is running on your machine. Even if the designers went to buckets of trouble to be sure the compiler will not generate any risky code, who's to say some bad person out there didn't write their own compiler? In addition, since the bytecodes have traversed an unsecure Internet, who's to say they haven't picked up any evil tendencies along the way? It was clear; compiler security was just not enough.

This level of security is implemented in the runtime environment (i.e., browser). Code is checked along the way to ensure its validity and to protect against unscrupulous activity. In general, things are checked to be sure they are doing what they are supposed to do. Figure 2-7 shows where this verification occurs.

FIGURE 2-6

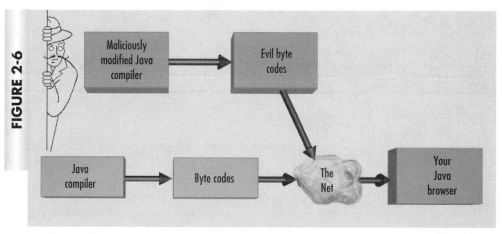

Bad people

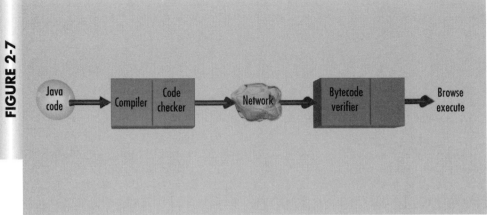

FIGURE 2-7

First two levels of security

Java's bytecodes are well designed for this task. Unlike most assembly languages, the Java bytecodes convey a good deal of type information. This allows the verifier to check many things it otherwise couldn't. All in all, these two security levels shield your machine from running malicious code.

Class Loading

After bytecode verification, the code hits the class loader. Magical and wondrous things happen in the class loader. The class loader ensures a distinction between built-in classes and those that come across the Net. In general, this means that internally, the runtime categorizes pieces of code according to where they came from. Assumedly, programs you run right from your own environment are pretty safe; after all, you have them on your hard drive—why would you keep nasty code around? Code coming in from foreign and hostile lands is watched a little closer. No matter what, all code runs through the previous two security checks. This step gives a more concerted decision as to what code can do based upon where it came from.

Off-Limits Resources

The final level of security comes from system resource protection. The simple rule is that Java programs can't change the system (erase hard drives, etc.). Of course, it's more complicated than that, but that's the goal. Once a piece of code has passed all the above guards and is now running on your system, it can still cause implicit security problems.

When imported code attempts access to controlled system resources (disks, etc.), the runtime starts making decisions as to what to do. This may involve coming to you, the user, and asking what you think. In any case, malicious code will have a serious challenge to get by Java's defenses.

 Summary

This chapter introduced you to how Java is set up. You should now have a good feel for what's going on within a Java system. Knowledge of this high-level design is crucial for creating any sort of efficient Java applications. It should also give you an idea of what type of applications may or may not be well suited to Java. In the long run, the list of applications poorly suited to be developed in Java will be small. Java's abilities to run inside or outside of the Web, seamlessly interact across the Net, or stay right on your machine make it a most powerful development system. However, the good news is that it's only going to get better.

The next chapters will begin your journey through the trenches of interfacing Java with the Web. First, by using the prebuilt applets in the system, you'll get a shot at seeing how it works before you even have to program. All you'll need is the background on how to interface these applets to your Web page. From then on you'll be knee deep into Java programming. Once you get going, you won't be able to stop—Java is just too much fun.

Questions

1. Why is Java compiled into an intermediate representation? Isn't this only doing half the job that is needed?

2. What separates a Web page with Java applets from one without?

3. What other ways could dynamically extending the capabilities of Java browsers be utilized? In other words, like the BES image format, what other types of enhancements could be implemented on the fly?

4. When might it not be worth it to just-in-time compile bytecodes as opposed to just running them interpretively?

5. Why is Java's garbage collection facility so comprehensive? C has none and Java has a highly complex system; why this difference?

6. If Java's security system wasn't so adamant about protecting memory, what sort of security holes would this open up?

7. The bytecode verifier protects against modified Java compilers that produce illegal code. How else could illegal code enter a browser from the source?

8. Why is Java a viable contender to be a primary general purpose language (such as C++)? In other words, why would a company choose Java over C++ and why would a company choose C++ over Java?

Interfacing to
the Web

You will learn about the following in this chapter:

- The details of operating the HotJava Web browser
- What the Java Appletviewer is
- The details of operating the Netscape Java-enhanced Web browser
- Some basic HTML tags
- The HTML you need to get Java going
- How to use Java's supplied applets

Apart from being an interesting, powerful, object-oriented language, Java is also one of the best ways to distribute interesting, dynamic, and interactive applications over the World Wide Web. Java-capable browsers are new to the Internet, but if you want to be able to experience the really exciting applications that are now being developed on the Web, you need a browser that can execute Java applets.

The first such browser was developed at Sun Microsystems. The HotJava browser has built-in Java support as well as the capability of handling most of the non-"Netscape-enhanced" HTML code that you are likely to see on Web pages. The main problem with the early releases of the HotJava browser was that they didn't handle all of the Netscape extensions properly. This is not meant to imply that the Java development team missed the boat; it's just that they had more important things to work on, like developing the Java language and creating development tools for Java programmers.

Luckily, Netscape Communications, Inc., licensed the Java interpreter technology to include in the next generation of the Netscape Web browsers. This means that a larger population of Web citizens will have the ability to view applications that are written in Java. Once the Web community starts to see how exciting client-side applications can be, there is sure to be a huge demand for Java-content-rich Web sites. Actually, there was incredible interest in Java generated by the publicly available beta versions of Netscape Navigator 2.0.

This chapter will familiarize you with interfacing your Java applications to the Web. It will start with a guided tour of the HotJava and Netscape browsers, cover basic Web navigation, and go on to explain how a Java applet is bound to an HTML page. Finally it will provide a quick overview of HTML that should leave you well prepared to browse the Web, place your compiled Java applications in the appropriate places for Web access, and create HTML pages that are linked to applets.

Java, the Browser

The HotJava browser was created at Sun Microsystems as a Web interface to allow anyone to execute compiled Java accessed over the Internet. The browser has most of the basic functionality that you would expect of a Web browser with the added bonus of being able to download and execute Java applets. The HotJava browser has a basic set of navigation and control tools that include a text window for entering URL information; a series of pull-down menus for printing documents, viewing HTML source code, and other operating parameters; and a series of navigation buttons for moving forward or backward between URLs, and stopping execution of an applet. At this point, a few definitions might be in order:

- **URL** Universal Resource Locator. This is a basic canonic form for an Internet service address. The general form of a URL is type://machine.dom[port]/ path/file. So, the URL to the Java home page is http://java.sun.com, or the URL to the Netscape file archive site is ftp://ftp.netscape.com/pub.

- **Applet** An applet is an executable program that was compiled from Java source code. The main difference between an applet and a standalone Java application is that an applet is intended to run in a Web browser and is normally included in an HTML document.

- **HTML** The HyperText Markup Language. This is the basic description language of a Web page. Normally, a Web page is written in HTML and includes tags that point to images, applets, or other URLs.

Figure 3-1 shows a typical HotJava session. The major features are numbered and explained below.

1. Title field. This field lists the title of the document that you are currently viewing. Figure 3-1 shows the HotJava home page.

2. File menu. The File menu lists a number of options that allow you to open a new window, open an alternate URL, reload the current URL, save the current document, print the current document, view the HTML source of the current document, close the current window, and exit the HotJava browser.

3. Options menu. The Options menu allows you to set certain preferences that affect the look or operation of the browser. This menu allows you to change the font or color of the document window, configure security parameters, set up proxies and other properties, flush the cache, and start an activity/progress monitor.

4. Navigate menu. The Navigate menu is used for basic document navigation. It allows you to move forward and backward through URLs, jump to your default home page, list a history of URLs

FIGURE 3-1

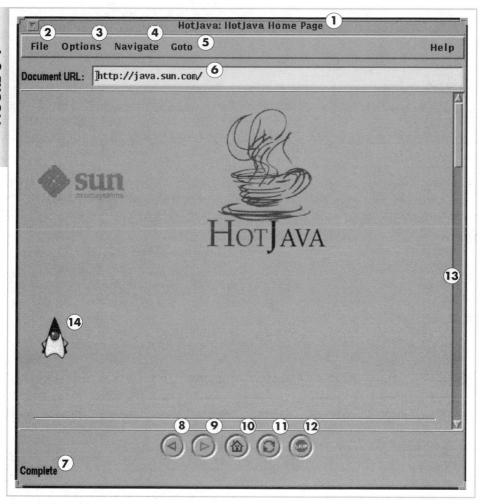

The HotJava browser

that you have visited, add items to a hotlist, show items in your hotlist, and find information in a document.

5. **Goto menu.** The Goto menu is a list of URLs that you want to be able to jump to quickly and easily. There is an Add Current option that will add the current document to your goto list. All documents that you add using this mechanism are listed below the Add option. By selecting one of these URLs, the HotJava browser attempts to connect to the selected service.

6. **URL window.** This field lists the current URL. You may change the contents in this window (by typing in a new Web address) and press the return key to jump to another URL.

7. **Status.** The current status of the HotJava browser is listed here. Normally, the names of documents and applets that are being downloaded are listed here as they are being accessed. The status of these connections is continuously updated until the entire document has been loaded, or the operation has been aborted.

8. **Previous button.** Jumps to the previous URL.

9. **Next button.** Jumps to the next URL, if you have gone back to a previous URL.

10. **Home button.** This will take you to the default home page for your browser.

11. **Reload button.** This will reload the current document.

12. **Stop button.** This will stop a URL from downloading but will not normally stop the execution of an applet once it has been loaded and has started running. It will, however, keep an applet from running if you hit the stop button before the applet has begun.

13. **Scroll bar.** This is used to scroll through a document that doesn't fit in a single window.

14. **Duke.** Here is the friendly Java mascot. You'll probably run into Duke often if you spend much time surfing Sun's Java site.

Accessing a URL

A URL can take many forms, depending on the type and location of service you want. This section will discuss two main forms of URLs and leave it up to the myriad of HTML books on the market to deal with the rest.

One of the simplest ways to access a service on the Internet with your Web browser is to type the URL for the service into the text field at the top of the browser's window. Normally, if you want to access something on the Internet, the URL will take the form http://machine.domain/path/document.html.

Here, machine.domain is the Internet address of the service you wish to access, and path/document.html is the path and file name of the document you are interested in. If you want to access local files, the best way to list the URL is file:/path/document.html. Here, it is assumed that the file is located on the same machine that you are running your browser on. Path is the exact or relative path to the files, and document.html is the file name.

Usually, the "file" URL is useful for browsing documentation on your local machine that is in HTML format, or for debugging HTML pages and Java applets locally without the need to use an intermediary server.

The Appletviewer

The Java development team has been concentrating more on improving the Java API and development tools, rather than on the HotJava browser. Consequently, when the prebeta and beta1 versions of the Java Developer's Kits were released, they were no longer compatible with the HotJava browser, and the HotJava browser wasn't updated to handle the new applet format. This made it difficult to run Java applets over the Web, so in the interim, they released an applet viewer that does just what you'd think it would—it runs applets.

The Appletviewer doesn't work as a Web browser. The Appletviewer takes a URL as an argument, but rather than displaying the entire HTML page, it just looks for imbedded applet tags, loads those applets, and runs them in their own windows. The good part of this is that it gives you a vehicle to test your Java applets, but the downside is that you have no idea what your applet will look like once it is placed in a window with the rest of the HTML document that it is imbedded in.

The Appletviewer is run from the command line and is followed by the URL, or file name of an HTML document that contains <APPLET> tags. For example, if you typed the following at a command prompt:

```
appletviewer http://found.cs.nyu.edu/downing/javajabber.html
```

this command would start the Appletviewer, try to find the document referenced by the URL, and look for imbedded applets in the HTML page. If any are found, they are downloaded and executed.

The Appletviewer has a single pull-down menu that allows you to restart an applet, display the HTML tag that loaded the applet, reload the applet, and quit the application. It's a very simple and compact mechanism for viewing applets, but it's not particularly useful for surfing the Web.

Netscape

Netscape has the largest market share in the Web browser market. Much of this is due to Netscape's aggressive approach to extending the somewhat limited capabilities of HTML. Netscape was one of the first browsers that could parse HTML 3.0, but even that wasn't a rich enough language for Web page development, so Netscape extended the language. In other words, Netscape has its own extensions to HTML that allow users to create much more visually intriguing Web pages. The fact that Netscape has such a large share of the browser market means that the time you spend creating "Netscape-enhanced" Web pages is worth it—chances are your pages will be viewed mostly by the huge number of people using the Netscape Web browser.

Keeping with this philosophy of pushing the technology envelope in Web documents, Netscape has licensed the Java execution environment to include it in their latest line of Web browsers. This almost certainly guarantees that a huge portion of the Internet population will be able to download, run, and interact with Java applications on the Web. This is very important if you want to devote time and money to developing killer Web applications and are not sure if it will pay off. What's the use of developing a killer app if nobody can see it?

The following is a brief tour of the Netscape browser (shown in Figure 3-2).

1. **Document title.** This lists the title of the current document.

2. **File menu.** The File menu allows you to open new windows, jump to new URLs, open local files, save the current document, e-mail the current document URL and/or its contents, print the current document, close the current window, or exit the program.

3. **Edit menu.** The Edit menu allows you to cut/paste/copy objects or text from the current document. It also allows you to search for information in the current document.

4. **View menu.** The View menu allows you to reload the current document, load images associated with the current document, refresh the window, or view the HTML source code for the current document.

5. **Go menu.** The Go menu allows you to quickly jump to the previous or next URL, view a listing of the URLs that you have visited, and easily jump to a listed URL.

6. **Bookmarks menu.** The Bookmarks menu allows you to create markers to certain URLs and easily jump to these URLs (actually any page can be bookmarked as long as it was not the result of an HTML form submittal).

7. **Options menu.** The Options menu allows you to change your preferences, including how the browser looks and functions.

8. **Directory menu.** The Directory menu allows easy access to URLs that Netscape Communications think would be of interest to their users. This includes the What's New, What's Cool, and Net Directory pages.

9. **Back button.** Jumps to the previous URL.

10. **Forward button.** Jumps to the next URL (if you've used the Back button.)

11. **Home button.** Jumps to the default home page.

12. **Reload button.** Reloads the current document.

13. **Images button.** Loads images in current document.

14. **Open button.** Displays a dialog box to enter a URL. Jumps to the specified URL.

15. **Print button.** Prints the current document.

16. **Find button.** Searches for text in current document. Basically, matches a text string that you supply to the entire document and stops when it finds the first occurrence of the string.

17. **Stop button.** Halts downloading of the current document or images in the current document.

18. **URL window.** Displays the current URL. May also be used to enter or change a URL. Press the return key while in this window to jump to the listed URL.

19–23. **URL buttons.** These jump to certain services that are commonly accessed by Netscape users.

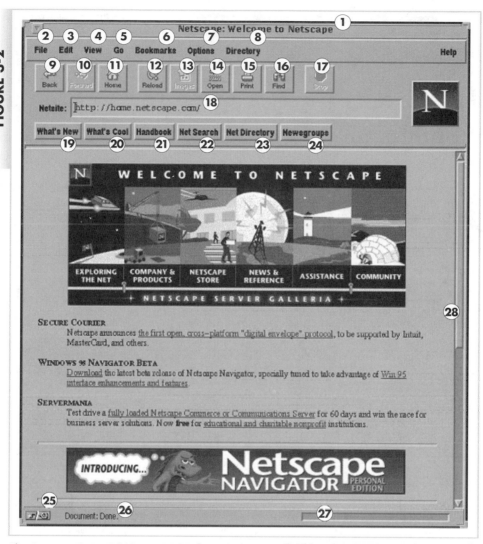

The Netscape Web browser

24. Newsgroups button. This allows you to configure and read Usenet newsgroups with the browser.

25. Secure icon. This key is broken when your Internet transactions are not secure and is in one piece during secure transactions. Basically, any Internet transactions to services that support the Netscape security protocols will cause the icon to appear as a complete key.

26. Document status. Lists status of current document while loading. Also lists the URLs of hyperlinks within the current document.

27. Progress indicator. Graphic display shows progress while downloading and formatting documents.

28. Scroll bar. Used to scroll through documents that don't fit in a single screen.

Installing the Netscape Navigator

This section will explain briefly how to install the Navigator on your computer.

1. Download the software. The easiest way for most people to get a copy of the Netscape Navigator is to download it over the Internet using the File Transfer Protocol (FTP). Netscape currently makes their software available free of charge to educational, research, and not-for-profit institutions. If you do not fit into one of these categories, you should purchase a copy from your local software retailer. The FTP site is at ftp://ftp.netscape.com/. Download the version that matches your system (Mac, Windows, or various flavors of UNIX).

2. Unpack the files. If you downloaded the software using FTP, the resulting file is in a compressed format. The UNIX versions are compressed tar files, the Windows versions are zipped self-extracting archives, and the Macintosh version is a binhexed Stuffit archive. On a UNIX box, you would extract the files by using a command such as

```
zcat filename.tar.Z | tar xvf -
```

Replace `filename.tar.Z` with the actual name of the file that you downloaded. The command `zcat` will effectively uncompress the file and send the results to standard out. This is then piped through `tar`, which extracts the component files from the data stream.

To extract the Windows version, simply execute the file from either a DOS prompt or the Run menu. You do this by typing the name of the file, which will probably end with .exe. Once this is run, it will automatically expand itself into its component files.

To extract the Macintosh version, you will need a decompression utility that understands .hqx and .sit file types. A common shareware utility that will do both of these for you is Stuffit Expander. This can be found at many public archives that carry Macintosh shareware.

3. Install the software. In UNIX, there are a number of ways that you can do this. The simplest way is to simply move the netscape executable to a directory where you normally keep your executable files. Often this is something like /usr/local/bin but is site dependent. Then it is necessary to deal with the moz20.car file. One of the files that was extracted when you unpacked

the Netscape distribution was moz20.car. This is a compressed file of Java classes that is needed by the Netscape Navigator in order to run Java applets. There are a few approaches to making it available to the browser. One way is to copy it into your local .netscape directory relative to your home directory. The other way is to add an entry to your CLASSPATH environment variable that points to the directory containing this file. This second way is preferable, since it is more economical to have users on your system modify a path variable than make multiple copies of this file in their home directories.

The Windows installation is a little more straightforward. From the Run menu in Windows, run the file called setup.exe in the .netscape directory that your files were decompressed in. This will start an installation program that will ask you a few questions about where you want things put, and then install the software on your system. Once this is complete, you should have a Netscape icon in the group directory that you specified during installation ready to be launched.

The Macintosh installation is trivial. After unpacking the installation, you will have a resulting file called something like Netscape Installer. Simply double-click on this file, click on the Easy Install button, and it will take care of the installation for you. The only thing left to do is to delete the archive and installation files afterward, if you choose to.

Well, that wasn't so hard. The important thing to note when installing Netscape on a UNIX box is that the CLASSPATH *must* contain an entry that points to the directory containing the moz20.car file (unless you have a local copy in .netscape, of course.)

Overview of the HyperText Markup Language

The HyperText Markup Language (HTML) is the basic description language that Web pages are built with. HTML is a language that allows you to insert graphics in documents, format text, and create hyperlinks to other documents. The current version of HTML is 3.0. Most Web browsers support HTML 2.0 and a few of the HTML 3.0 additions.

The intent here is not to demonstrate the entire HTML vocabulary, but rather to provide enough information to allow you to understand how it is used to format documents and insert Java applets in Web documents.

The basic atom of HTML is a tag. An HTML tag is a text string surrounded by angle brackets. Normally there is a begin and an end tag that surround optional text, graphics, or other document elements. The end tag has the same name as the begin tag, but the text is preceded with a forward slash. For example:

```
<TAG1 ... > ... </TAG1>
```

Some HTML tags allow optional parameters that are listed in the beginning tag marker after the tag name.

```
<TAG1 option option ... > ... </TAG1>
```

Basic HTML Tags

The following are the most common HTML tags that you are likely to encounter. These are tags that are used for basic formatting and inserting objects in a document. Since this is not a complete discussion of HTML tags, not every parameter is listed.

<HTML>...</HTML> These tags are normally the very first and last elements of an HTML document; they delimit its beginning and ending points. Not all browsers require this tag at present, but it's generally good style to use it.

<HEAD>...</HEAD> The <HEAD> tag is used to delimit HTML header information. Valid items that may appear between a begin and end <HEAD> tag are document title, META information, and certain text that specifies author and organization information.

<TITLE>...</TITLE> The text that appears between these tags is listed as the title to the document. The document title appears at the very top of the Netscape and HotJava browsers.

<BODY>...</BODY> The <BODY> tags delimit the body of the document. Basically, if it's not part of the head, then it's part of the body. Netscape allows a few interesting options that can be included in the <BODY> tag. These options follow the word BODY in the beginning tag, but not in the end tag. The first is the BACKGROUND option. The BACKGROUND option allows you to specify an image that will be used as the background for your document. The image may be specified as a local file, or as a URL. Example:

```
<BODY BACKGROUND=wallpaper.gif> ... </BODY>.
```

You may also specify RGB color values as options in the <BODY> tag. You can set the color of the background, the default text color, the color of untouched hyperlinks, and the color of hyperlinks to places that have already been visited. The option names are BGCOLOR, TEXT, LINK, and VLINK. The RGB value is listed as a series of hexadecimal numbers corresponding to red, green, and blue (in that order). Each color has an 8-bit range (from 00 to FF). The color black would be represented as 000000, white as FFFFFF, and orange as somewhere around FFCC33. If you are interested in using colors in your <BODY> tags, there is a very useful table of colors and RGB values at http://www.phoenix.net/~jacobson/rgb.html. Thanks to Doug Jacobson for putting this chart on the Net.

Hexadecimal

A system of numbering that uses 16 as the base rather than 10. So, when you run out of numbers (after 9), letters are used. For example, numbers 1–16 would look like: 1,2,3,...,9,A,B,C,D,E,F,10. Hexadecimal notation is used often in computer applications.

The following example sets the background image to cool.gif, sets the text color to white, and sets the color of hyperlinks to blue:

```
<BODY BACKGROUND=cool.gif TEXT=FFFFFF LINK=0066CC>
```

<A HREF=...> ... </A> The anchor tag. This tag is used to create hyperlinks in an HTML document. The HREF is set to a local file or a URL. Everything that appears between the tags (including images) is made "hot." In other words, the user may click on any of the text and/or images between these tags to jump to the item specified in the HREF option. Example:

```
<A HREF=http://www.mrl.nyu.edu/downing>Jump to Troy's page</A>
```

In the previous example, the phrase "Jump to Troy's page" would appear as a hyperlink because it appears between the <A ...> and </A> tags. Selecting this link would cause your browser to jump to the URL http://www.mrl.nyu.edu/downing.

<P>...</P> This is used to separate paragraphs in a document.

**
** This causes a line break in a document.

<HR> This will draw a horizontal line in an HTML document.

These are just some of the basic tags, and should be all you need to understand how a document is formatted in HTML. If you are interested in reading more on HTML, there are a number of good, comprehensive books on writing HTML on the market. One such book, *HTML Web Publisher's Construction Kit* (Waite Group Press, ISBN 1-57169-018-2), was written by one of the authors of this book, and should include most of the information you would want on HTML.

The <APPLET> Tag

Okay, how is a Java applet included in an HTML document? This is done via an <APPLET> tag. When a Java-capable Web browser loads an HTML page that contains an <APPLET> tag, the browser figures out the name of the applet and where it is located before downloading the main applet class and supporting files that the applet will need in order to run. Once the applet is loaded, the browser starts the applet, and voila, you have an applet executing in an HTML document.

Here is the basic format of the <APPLET> tag:

```
<APPLET code=MyApplet.class
        codebase = http://myserver.com/mydirectory/
        width = 100
        height = 100
        align = center >
        <PARAM name = name1 value = value1>
        <PARAM name = name2 value = value2>
        <PARAM ... >

        <BLOCKQUOTE>
        Extra text, that can include standard HTML tags...
        This text will be displayed
        while the applet is loading...
        </BLOCKQUOTE>
</APPLET>
```

All right, let's take that apart. The first part is obvious; APPLET is the name of the tag. The parameters included in the beginning tag are as follows:

- **code.** This is the name of the applet that you want to run. The name corresponds to the name of the class that extends the Applet class in the applet. This may not make sense at this point in the book, but the short explanation is that this is the name of the main file of your applet.

- **codebase.** This is used to specify the base URL of the applet. The browser can find your applet by appending the class name that was specified in the code attribute to the URL specified in the codebase attribute. So, in the above example, the browser would try to load the applet from the URL http://myserver.com/mydirectory/MyApplet.class. The browser also uses the codebase to find other classes that the applet may depend on, but are not listed directly in the <APPLET> tag.

- **width.** The width attribute works in a similar fashion to the width attribute in an <IMG> tag. This is used to specify how much of the window the applet will take up. The width can be defined in two ways, either as a number that will be interpreted as the number of pixels, or as a number followed by a "%". In this case, the width will be interpreted as a percentage of the currently visible browser window.

- **height.** This attribute works in exactly the same fashion as the width attribute.

- **align.** This attribute is also similar to the attribute in the <IMG> tag of the same name. It specifies where the applet will be placed on the screen. Valid values for this tag are "left," "right," and "center."

The next interesting part of the <APPLET> tag is the <PARAM> tag. This tag only makes sense between a beginning and ending <APPLET> tag. The <PARAM> tag is used to send parameters to the applet. Parameters are listed as name/value pairs. This is a useful way of supplying applets with different data and parameters, rather than hardcoding the data into the applet itself. One example would be an animation applet. The applet could be written in a fashion that expected a parameter to be passed that specifies the names of the images to be used in the animation. This way, one applet could be used to run many different animations. There can be an arbitrary number of <PARAM> tags used in an applet, or none at all.

The final part of the <APPLET> tag is just plain old HTML text. This text is displayed while an applet is loading, and will also be displayed on a browser that doesn't understand the <APPLET> tag. This is due to the fact that most browsers will ignore tags that they don't understand, but once they get to the text part, it will be treated as standard HTML.

Making a Precompiled Applet Work for You

Finally, let's take a look at a simple applet that is on one of the applet demo pages at java.sun.com (the main Web server for the Java development team). This particular applet is probably one of the first animation applets that has been written for Java. The name of the applet is ImageLoopItem, and it can be found at http://java.sun.com/applets/applets/ImageLoop/index.html.

This applet is a simple example of parameterizing the data that it needs to run. The applet gets the name of the images, the number of images, and timing parameters all from <PARAM> tags in the HTML page. The neat thing about this is that you can use this applet without ever doing any Java programming; all you need to do is pass the right parameters to run your animation. So, rather than seeing an animation of Duke waving his hands at you, you can show an animation of yourself making silly faces. Let's take a look at the <APPLET> tag:

```
<APPLET code = ImageLoopItem
        codebase=http://java.sun.com/applets/applets/ImageLoop/
        width = 80
        height = 90>
        <PARAM name=nimgs value=10>
        <PARAM name=img value=duke>
        <PARAM name=pause value=1000>
</applet>
```

In the previous code, the name of the applet is ImageLoopItem. ImageLoopItem is an applet that grabs a number of images specified with the nimgs parameter. The base name of the images is specified with the img parameter, and a pause time (in milliseconds) is specified with the pause parameter.

If you were to write your own tag that referenced this applet but specified a different set of images, you would essentially have your own animation running on the page of your choice, rather than just having Duke wave at you. See Figure 3-1 for an image of Duke at rest. Basically, just create a set of images, put them on your machine somewhere that can be accessed through a URL, change the values of the parameters accordingly, and you're in business.

Summary

Java is not going to replace HTML. HTML is the means for describing a page that may contain Java applets. Java will, however, replace certain HTML objects with better, more exciting, dynamic elements that just can't be duplicated in HTML alone.

A rich Web page should contain a certain amount of HTML, (actually *must* contain some HTML), and interspersed Java applets. The HTML is the basic formatting substrate, and the applets are displaying images, displaying animations, giving the user interaction opportunities that are unheard of in plain vanilla HTML implementations.

Now that you know how an applet is included in a page, and basically what a browser needs to know in order to grab an applet, the next step is writing your own applets.

The next sections will familiarize you with basic Java structure and syntax and get you started writing your own Java applications and applets to be included in Web pages. It won't be long before you have the ability to create useful, exciting content as standalone applications or applications distributed on the information superhighway.

Questions

1. How do you load a URL with the HotJava and Netscape browsers?

2. What happens when a document containing an <APPLET> tag is selected in a Java-aware Web browser? What happens if the browser doesn't recognize the <APPLET> tag?

3. What tags are allowed between the <HEAD> and </HEAD> tags in an HTML document?

4. How many arguments can be passed to a Java applet using <PARAM> tags?

Exercises

1. Write an HTML page that includes an applet in a local directory, and a second applet on a remote server.

2. Write an HTML page that contains several applets that are displayed next to each other.

3. Write an HTML page that contains an applet that takes up the entire browser window, even after you change the size of the window.

PART II:
Programming in Java™

Designing Java™ Programs

You will learn about the following in this chapter:

- How Java defines comments
- How Java structures its code
- How to design your code in high-level packages
- How to import Java's prebuilt functionality
- How object-oriented programming works
- How to start coding classes in Java
- The basics of writing applets
- The basics of standalone applications

he years Java spent in development allowed its designers time to analyze a lot of computer languages. This analysis let them pinpoint different languages' strong points and decide on a suitable implementation for Java. It's quite evident from Java's syntax that the designers had an affinity for the C and C++ languages' straight-to-the-point implementation. Many C/C++ constructs are present verbatim in Java, and many others have only minor modifications. Their design was further influenced by the commitment to a language that was object-oriented, architecture independent, and secure.

This chapter will overview the organization of Java programs. You'll also get your first look at Java's syntax, high-level structure, building Java applets, and standalone programs. That's a pretty big order for one chapter; then again it's a pretty big chapter. Hopefully, this discussion will set the stage to let you see where you (and Java) are headed.

Details, Details, Details

Before you go diving head first into Java programming, it would be nice to know a few details about what Java code looks like. Don't expect any rocket science just yet; here you'll just become familiar with a few of the syntax notions Java uses.

Comments Appreciated

Designating text as a comment instructs the compiler to ignore it. Therefore, you can include comments within your code to serve as an explanation to help future readers of your code more easily understand what your code is doing. As with any programming language, comments within your Java code are vital to making your code readable. On top of that, when you write some rather stupendous code, it's kind of nice to toot your own horn a bit within the comments (all under the guise of trying to increase code readability). Sparing no expense, the Java designers have implemented three different kinds of comments for your commenting pleasure.

Two of the comment styles are identical to C++'s implementation:

```
// This line is commented out.
/* So is this */
```

The first style consists of starting the line with two slashes. Once the compiler encounters two slashes, it will ignore the rest of the line. Note that legal Java code can start the line, then be followed by two slashes and a comment, as in

```
Java code (not ignored by compiler); // This is ignored
```

The second style of commenting has a begin and an end delimiter. The slash-asterisk instructs the compiler that a comment has begun. The compiler will then ignore all text until it reaches the closing asterisk-slash. Unlike the slash-slash comment style, this comment style can span several lines.

```
/* comment starts
      My Java Program
      Paul Tyma
   comment ends */
```

The third style of commenting is really a flavor of the slash-asterisk type but includes an additional power. This style looks like this:

```
/** Comment goes here */
```

You'll notice the only difference to be an additional asterisk at the start of the comment. This type of commenting is only allowed in front of legal Java declarations. You'll soon know what is and is not a Java declaration. In any event, using this type of comment style allows you to later run a program called javadoc, supplied with the Java distribution. This program is smart enough to extract these comments and create external documentation with them. For now, you will only see and will probably only use the first two styles.

Blocks

Java code is organized into blocks (or sections). You specify the beginning and end of a block using curly braces.

```
{
// Java block of code
 }
```

Regardless of how much code is within the curly braces, it is considered a block of Java code. As you will see, blocks are usually used to designate some code to be related to a preceding command or declaration. Every executable statement in Java will be within one or more blocks.

Separation

As in C, Java uses the lowly semicolon to indicate the end of a statement. Statements in Java are a many splendored thing. To be more specific, a statement is a sequence of symbols (characters, numbers, etc.) that describe a complete and specific operation. Indentation, newlines, and/or pages of blank space have no effect on the compiler that is in search of the end to a given statement. The only thing that will tell it that a statement is over is a semicolon.

```
statement1; statement2;
statement3;
```

If you forget one, the compiler will be sure to let you know.

The Whole Package

Java has several levels of hierarchy for code organization, the highest of which is the *package*. A package is intended as a grouping of related classes. Consider writing a graphics package that is to supply an entire set of graphics functions to be used by other programmers. In your package you would include code to draw lines, circles, rectangles, etc. Programmers wanting to use your comprehensive drawing package would assume it would provide them with all the basic graphics functions. They would also assume that code to compute a bank balance would probably not be present in your package since bank balances have little to do with graphics (or do they?). In any case, a package is intended to be organized as a logical grouping, whether that be graphics, I/O, or data structures.

Designing Packages

It is Sun's request (and already a warmly accepted standard) that you follow the convention of naming your packages with a reversal of your Internet domain name. If you don't have such an affiliation, you could use your name, alias, or some permutation. There is no solid restriction for picking package names, but if everyone followed Sun's suggested standards, life sure would be swell. The package statement should always be the first statement of your code and follow the form

```
package packagename ;
```

Some examples of standard package names for your graphics package would be

```
package COM.preemptive.graphics;
package Tyma.Paul.graphics;
package MIL.airforce.CAD.tools.graphics;
```

continued on next page

continued from previous page

```
package UK.stonehenge.graphics;
package EDU.syr.cat.graphics;
```

The periods in the name are separators allowing you to further organize the hierarchy of your code. Beyond the company or personal name, you could specify departments, directories, or groups. You will assuredly be writing many packages in your work with Java, and this convention will help you keep them straight. This convention also helps distinguish between packages of different origin that may have the same name for low-level functions. A spreadsheet package created by XYZ Corp. could conceivably contain a rectangle function. In light of the fact that your graphics package would also likely contain a rectangle function, deciding which rectangle function the compiler should use can come from the package specification.

Figure 4-1 shows an overview of Java's organizational hierarchy. Packages are broken down into classes and interfaces. Both of these concepts will be addressed thoroughly later, but for now, think of them again as logical, distinct package elements. For the graphics example, each graphics primitive (e.g., line, rectangle, circle) would have its own class within the package. The next level in the hierarchy is methods and data. These are all specific elements pertaining to each class.

The package concept is deep-seated within the Java design. Any classes you develop will always be within a package. It's not your choice; Java includes a no-name package that

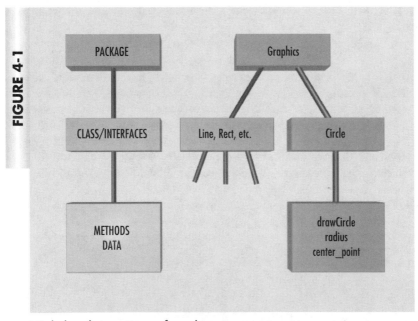

FIGURE 4-1

High-level overview of package organization

is used as a catch-all for any class created without a specific package association. For any large project, it is a smart move to decide early on how your packages will be defined and named. It will help you organize your code more efficiently.

The Importing Business

One of the reasons Java is so powerful out-of-the-box is because of its well-designed prebuilt packages. Extremely useful tasks such as graphics, networking, and threading are all prebuilt and there for the taking. Accessing this vast functionality is as easy as using the import statement. This statement makes classes from other packages available and takes the form

```
import packagename.classname ;
import packagename.* ;
```

The first form specifies to import a specific class from a package. The second specifies to import all classes (using the asterisk as a wildcard) from a package. Few programs can be written without importing at least some of the prebuilt packages Java provides. A full list of these packages is available in the Appendix, and it would probably give you a better feel for this discussion if you took a quick glance there now.

Using Import

To continue the graphics example, assume your graphics package is complete and you wish to actually use it to write a CAD program. You will need to import your graphics package and possibly additional prebuilt packages:

```
import java.io.FileInputStream;
import COM.preemptive.graphics.*;
```

The first line imports the java.io.FileInputStream class. The java.io prebuilt package has a wide variety of input/output classes; here only one specific class is imported, giving you some functionality in reading files. The next line imports your graphics package and makes it available to this namespace (i.e., you can call your rectangle function with no worries about the compiler finding it or choosing the wrong one). The asterisk on the end of the COM.preemptive.graphics.* string specifies to bring in all packages/classes under that heading, whereas the java.io.FileInputStream specifier tells the compiler to only get that specific class and not to worry about the rest of the java.io classes.

If the compiler generates a nasty message claiming it cannot locate a class you are referencing (and your spelling happens to be impeccable), the import statements are the first place to look. The functionality your code requires will dictate what packages you will need to import. You must first become familiar with the prebuilt packages that are available to you in order to know exactly what to import. Initially, the code examples, the API Appendix, and trial and (compiler) error will be your guide.

Straight Up

Besides importing, you can access the prebuilt classes another way. If you do not need the whole package (or any significant part of it), you may specify the entire package name inside your actual code. In other words, if you only need a rectangle, instead of importing the entire `COM.preemptive.graphics.*` package as seen above, you could instead type `COM.preemptive.graphics.rectangle` directly in your code, completely bypassing the usage of an explicit import. This method is kind of an on demand type of importing. Examples in subsequent chapters will further illustrate this technique.

Classes and Objects

As said many times before, Java's entire design is based on object-oriented principles. These concepts are so deeply rooted that several of them must be considered even before any code can be written. The notions of classes and objects are well-known object-oriented principles, and Java uses them along the same lines as C++ and many other object-oriented languages.

Everything about a Thing

You can think of a *class* as a template that describes everything about some element in your program. In principle, and especially in Java, classes are defined as wholly complete descriptions of some object (i.e., thing). The buzzword definition states that the class describes the *state* and *behavior* of some set of objects, the state representing current features of the object (i.e., data) and the behavior representing the functionality built into the object.

This whole notion of objects shouldn't be too peculiar; you live in a world full of objects. Consider creating a list of features that would help you classify automobiles (did you notice the use of the word classify in that sentence—this is getting suspicious). Logical things you'd like to keep track of could be price, engine size, interior space, etc. These are all elements that are common to any automobile, yet the specific values could vary widely from one automobile to the next.

For the graphics package example, there would likely exist a circle class. Note that the circle class itself is really not an actual circle on the screen somewhere, it's more of a list of features about any possible circle—i.e., a template. What do all circles have in common? At a minimum, they all have a radius and a center point. Therefore, in your class definition you can create data variables that will hold the radius and the center point for each circle. So far, C programmers should see this as an analogy to C's `struct`, and Pascal programmers to a `record`.

Classes in Java Go Far

As you can see from Figure 4-2, these analogies aren't far off. All three constructs are ways of structuring data; however, as you will see, classes take that concept much further in order

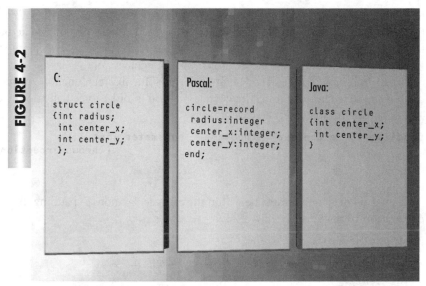

FIGURE 4-2

```
C:                    Pascal:                Java:

struct circle         circle=record          class circle
{int radius;            radius:integer        {int center_x;
 int center_x;          center_x:integer;      int center_y;
 int center_y;          center_y:integer;     }
 };                   end;
```

Structuring data in C, Pascal, and Java

to promote many more object-oriented principles. The general form for a Java class definition is

```
[modifiers] class classname [extends parentname]
                                    [implements interfacename
                                    [, interfacename ] ]
        { // class block
        }
```

This statement encompasses an entire *class definition block,* which begins with the `class` statement and surrounds the block with the curly braces. Everything that happens in Java really happens inside of classes. No code is allowed to exist outside the guards of a class (or interface) definition. This concept is often intriguing to experienced programmers seeing the Java language for the first time. Few languages are built upon such a purely object-oriented foundation.

Quite often the primary modifier found in front of the `class` keyword is the `public` modifier. A simplified definition is that this modifier allows your class to be accessed by the outside world. Without it, usage of your class has certain restrictions. For now, just expect to see the `public` modifier in many of the examples. It will be explained at greater depth in later chapters.

Methods for Behavior

The class concept was designed to describe everything about some type of thing. This concept also extends to "What to do with the thing?" For the circle example, you only need to think about what a programmer would want to do with a circle once the radius and center point values have been decided. First off, it would certainly be nice to actually draw the circle. Classes accommodate this functionality by implementing *methods* into the class. In other words, methods are created to define the behavior of the class.

A method is a sequence of code that performs some discrete function pertinent to the class. The circle class can use a drawCircle method in order to actually do the drawing. The general form for a method definition is

```
[modifiers] returntype methodname ( parameter_list )
                                              [throws exception_list]
                    { ...
                    }
```

A method declaration must be within the class declaration. Expanding the circle class declaration from above:

```
public class circle {
   int radius;
   int center_x;
   int center_y;

/* Constructor Method */
   circle(int r, int cx, int cy) {
           radius = r;
           center_x = cx;
           center_y = cy;
           }

/* Method to draw the circle */
   void drawCircle(Color theColor)
     {
         /* code to draw the circle of color _theColor */
     }

}
```

The first method added is just called `circle` (followed by some parameters). It is a special kind of method called a *constructor*. Constructor methods are used as initializers. Later chapters will give you a much harder look at constructors; at this point realize that constructors are special in that they do not have a return type and they must be named the same as the class they are in. Although using constructors for initialization is vital, most methods you create will not be constructors.

In front of the `drawCircle` method declaration is the `void` modifier. Each method you declare must specify what type of value it will return to its caller (except, of course, for constructors). You designate this by a type name in front of the method name; common types are `int`, `float`, or `void`. The somewhat special case of `void` indicates the method will return nothing to its caller. Methods have a wide variety of standard possible return types. As illustrated in Figure 4-3, a method to calculate a factorial would want to return

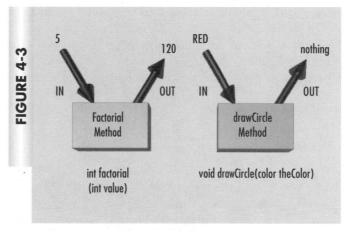

Calling into and out of a method

an integer (the result of the calculation) to its caller, whereas the method that draws a circle on the screen really has nothing to inform its caller about and could commonly return **void**. The circle would actually get drawn on the screen, but (besides possibly a status value indicating it was drawn successfully) there is no real information the caller needs to know.

The *parameter list* is the list of variables delimited by parentheses following the method name and is somewhat the converse of the return value. It's a list of what the caller must send to the method, or more accurately, what the method needs to know to successfully perform its task. The factorial example needs to know for what value to calculate the factorial, and the **drawCircle** example needs to know what color you want your circle.

When Methods Go Bad

Where applicable, method declarations must include the keyword **throws**. It is placed behind the parameter list but in front of the method body and is followed by its corresponding **exception_list**. The format is

```
void myMethod( parameter_list ) throws exception_list
```

The exception list (amazingly) lists all the exceptions that can occur within that method. For now you can think of exceptions as basically just runtime errors. So, in effect you are declaring what runtime errors could occur in that method (bet you didn't know you have psychic powers). Well, keep in mind that you do not always need the **throws** keyword and an exception list. For example, the **drawCircle** method presented earlier did not have a **throws**. It all depends on the operations your method is performing.

It would just be good, clean, fun to say no exceptions ever happen and never use the keyword. However, you will soon become knee-deep in using Java's built-in API libraries (see Appendix), which were designed to be quite studious about declaring what exceptions (and havoc) they produce. The bad part about all that is that if you use something that declares its possible exceptions, you will need to declare them too. The examples throughout the book will include throws as needed, and Chapter 11 will give you more than you wanted to know about this subject. Your own coding will be forcibly directed (somewhat like a figure skater down a bobsled track) by compiler errors telling you what to include in your method's **throws**.

Creating Things

After all this discussion about creating classes, you must remember that a class definition is only a template. The class definition for a circle is not actually a circle, it's only a template for creating a circle. In order to create circles, you must *instantiate* this class. Instantiation is basically telling the compiler, "Create one of the circle things for me." Each instantiation of a class is called an *object* in that class. All objects that were instantiations of a class have all the data elements and methods defined within that class. From here you can make as many circles as you like just by instantiating the class multiple times.

As you can see in Figure 4-4, from one template you can create many instances of what that template represents. They are all the same kind of thing, but may have some differing internal values.

FIGURE 4-4

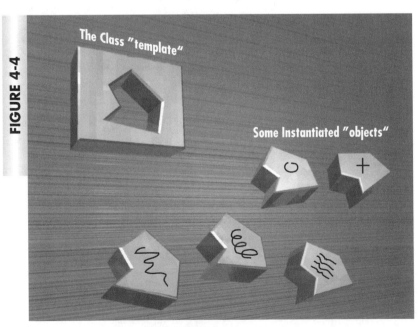

The class template and created objects

Objects

Most classes you define will be as support classes for some main class. What this means is that the classes in and of themselves can't do much. Only one class will be running the show, and it will instantiate instances of your support classes, pulling them into the action. Until that happens, these support classes are relatively helpless. For example, the `circle` class below could be used by a CAD program that uses it to make circles (i.e., `circle` is a support class for the CAD program). Note though, that you run the CAD program that uses the `circle` class, not the other way around.

Making Things Happen

Let's define several circles (i.e., objects of the circle class) and see how they are used. Here's a code example:

```
/* the circle class */
public class circle {
  int radius;
  int center_x;
  int center_y;

  circle(int r, int cx, int cy) {
          radius = r;
          center_x = cx;
          center_y = cy;
          }

  void drawCircle(Color theColor)
     {
          /* code to draw the circle of color 'theColor' */
     }
}




       .
       .
       .
// code in some other class/method
// (in a CAD program, Paint program, etc.)
circle of_friends;                 // declare the objects
circle I_run_in;

of_friends = new circle(5,10,10); // instantiate the objects
I_run_in = new circle(6,20,10);

of_friends.drawCircle(Color.red); // call their methods
I_run_in.drawCircle(Color.blue);
       .
       .
       .
```

There are two instantiations of the circle class in this code segment, a circle `of_friends` and a circle `I_run_in`. The declaration statement

```
circle of_friends;
```

declares an object of type `circle`. After this statement, `of_friends` still does not actually exist as a circle; you have merely told the compiler that you will be instantiating a circle with the name `of_friends` at some later point. The `new` statement in the succeeding statement is where the actual instantiation will take place when the program runs. The `new` statement is aptly named, as it does just that—creates a new thing—in this case, a new circle.

After the `new` keyword is a call to the constructor that was defined earlier. So, in essence, the whole `new` statement creates a new circle object and calls its constructor with the parameters. For the first circle, it is defined with a radius of 5 and a center point of (10,10). If you look up the original constructor code, you'll see that the constructor assigns the input parameters to the variables declared in the class. After the `new` statement, a new `circle` object exists. Mind you, it is not drawn anywhere; it is just defined (as far as a radius and center point) within the running program. In other words, it's now ready to be acted on (in this program's case, it will soon be acted on in the form of drawing it).

Drawing Circles

Following the instantiations, the program actually uses the circles by calling the `drawCircle` method for both circles. The syntax dictates the method call as

```
objectname.methodname ( parameter_list ) ;
```

The object name that precedes the method name (separated by a period) indicates which circle the `drawCircle` method should be applied to. You can think of this as calling the method "within the context" of the indicated object. So the first `drawCircle` call is within the context of or pertaining to the object `of_friends`. The `drawCircle` method will use the values within the object (i.e., radius and center point) to determine how to draw the circle. In other words, you already said that the object existed by just being instantiated and having the constructor set its radius and center point. The `drawCircle` method will use these previously set values and perform the details of putting a circle on the screen with those parameters. Only the color is specified while calling `drawCircle`.

This exemplifies the difference between object-oriented and non-object-oriented programming. In non-object-oriented languages, the command "print Fred" tells the print command to go find Fred and print him. In object-oriented languages, the command "print Fred" tells Fred to go and find out how to print himself.

In practice, the classes you define will have many methods, and you will often instantiate multiple objects from each class. You can see now where object-oriented got its name. All code and organization is focused on objects and their manipulation. C++ allowed for this model but didn't enforce it, which diminished its return. The fact that C++ compilers can compile C programs is a testament to this defect. Java's object-oriented design will quickly (and forcibly) organize the way you program. After all, you live in a world full of objects; your way of thinking is already working for you.

Mother of All Applets

There are two main arenas in which Java programs will initially exist. First and most visible will be within the browsers of the World Wide Web—HotJava, Netscape, and soon others will support Java-infused WWW pages. This should prove to be the industry's initial love affair with Java. Web pages that come alive are sure to be the rage of the Internet in no time. Java applications that run within the confines of a browser are dubbed *applets*, i.e., little applications.

The second area Java applications will surface will be as standalone programs; this is the way programmers are used to having their code run. Initially, the servers for distributed WWW games and search engines will popularize this Java environment. However, the industry will quickly see the value of Java as a viable distributed language, and full-scale distributed applications are soon to be on the horizon. If all this makes you salivate, welcome to the club.

Setting Up the Skeleton

Almost all of the intricate details of interfacing a WWW page and a Java applet have been done for you with Java's prebuilt packages (APIs). For the most part, you just need to access the provided functionality; however, in order to do this you must first define a class of your own.

The class you create must be one that the browser (i.e., HotJava, Netscape, etc.) knows how to access. Java has the tools for you to do this built in to its **java.applet** package. Within the **java.applet** package you will find a prebuilt class confusingly named **Applet**. Pardon this weirdness; the whole identifier is **java.applet.Applet**, where **java.applet** is the package and **Applet** is the class.

Subclassing

In order to actually create an applet, your class must *subclass* this prebuilt class. Subclassing is an object-oriented technique that lets you extend a class (also called creating a child class) modeled after the parent class. The child class has all the parent's functionality plus any more you choose to give it. Figure 4-5 shows an example of a subclassing hierarchy reusing the **circle** example. The child class is **filledcircle**.

The **circle** class has as its data elements the **radius** and **center_point** values and methods of **drawCircle** and **eraseCircle**. The subclass **filledcircle** has a new data element of **filltype**. You can assume this element pertains to what sort of design the circle is filled with—i.e., it may be solid, thatched, or some other pattern. This data element doesn't pertain to the parent **circle** class and therefore only exists in filled circles. However, a filled circle still needs a **radius** and **center_point**. Welcome to the wonderful world of subclassing—because **filledcircle** is a subclass of **circle**, it will *inherit* the data elements of its parent. So in actuality, every filled circle will have all three data elements: **radius**, **center_point**, and **filltype**.

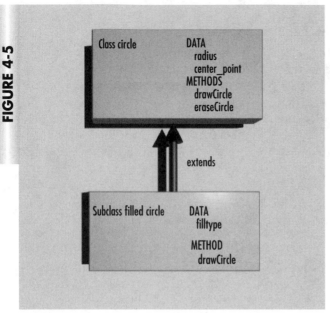

FIGURE 4-5

Subclassing `circle`

This concept of inheritance extends to methods too. Assuming the method to erase a circle is adequate for both types of circles—i.e., it performs some indiscriminate annihilation of circles (filled and unfilled alike) from the screen. The `circle` class's `eraseCircle` method can be inherited by the subclass to provide that service.

On the other hand, drawing a filled and unfilled circle are two very different operations. Therefore, every filled circle will use the `filledcircle` class's `drawCircle` method and every unfilled circle will use the `circle` class's method. The `filledcircle` class's `drawCircle` method *overrides* the `circle` class's method for filled circles only. In actuality, there are two `drawCircle` methods that do essentially different operations. Initially, it seems confusing to have methods that are named the same but in actuality do different things. This is the wrong way to view this. This goes back to printing Fred or Fred printing himself. It's not that there are several ways to draw circles, it is more that every circle knows how to draw itself. Programmers' burdens are lessened, since whenever they want a circle to be drawn, all they must do is tell the specific circle object to draw itself, and the circle itself will handle the details.

Subclassing Applet

Now that you have a feel for subclassing, let's amble back to finishing your first applet. Remember that your applet's class will subclass the Java Applet class. The common skeleton code for a Java applet that extends the Applet class is

```
import java.applet.Applet;          // import Applet class
import java.awt.Graphics;           // import Graphics class

public class MyJavaApp extends Applet          // subclass Applet
        {
         // more code
        }
```

You should already know what the first two lines are doing. Two classes are being imported, `java.applet.Applet` and `java.awt.Graphics`. These are classes from Java's prebuilt packages that are being made available to this applet. The `java.applet.Applet` is the entire reason your code is allowed onto a Web page, so it's an absolute must. The `java.awt.Graphics` provides your code the ability to put things on the page. So unless you are writing some type of undetectable stealth applet, this class is pretty much required too. The next statement is the class declaration. The class `MyJavaApp` is being defined as an extension/child of the `Applet` class (i.e., the class that was imported in the import statement). This example is the skeleton of what's needed for an applet to interface with a browser. What goes inside the class is the code that will add life to your Web page.

Defining the Methods

The methods defined for the applet have a few restrictions, since the class is a child of the `Applet` class. The bare minimum is that your class must contain at least two methods, called `init` and `paint`. In actuality you are overriding the `Applet` class with these two methods (`Applet` itself has an `init` and a `paint`), but you need to in order to get anything done. Recalling the code from before:

```
import java.applet.Applet;
import java.awt.Graphics;

public class MyJavaApp extends Applet {

        public void init()                 // define init method
          {
          // init code
          }
        public void paint(Graphics g)      // define paint method
          {
          // paint code
          }
        }
```

The `init` and `paint` methods should always be in any applet code you put together and must be defined exactly as above. Simply from the names you should be getting an idea of what these methods will do. The `init` method is the place you put code to tell the browser what to do initially when executing your applet. Usually this is the place for initializing variables or setting up your window on the Web page. The `init` method is executed only once and is the first code within your applet to actually be executed.

The **paint** method is executed whenever your area needs repainting. This can occur at several times:

- Immediately after running **init**, your window will need to be painted for the first time.

- In a windowing system, whenever the user covers your applet (likely with some foul nondistributed application) and subsequently uncovers it.

- Whenever the user scrolls your applet onto the screen.

- Whenever the browser is resized and the positioning of your applet changes.

The calling of the **init()** and **paint(Graphics g)** methods is automatic, so you don't have to be concerned about how to call them, the browser will do all that for you. As outlined above, it is more important that you understand when they will be called.

To make the above code actually do something, only a few statements are still needed:

```
import java.applet.Applet;
import java.awt.Graphics;

public class MyJavaApp extends Applet
        {
        // initialize the window
        public void init()
          {
          resize(120,100);                 // resize the window
          }

        // Draw some stuff!
        public void paint(Graphics g)
          {
          // put something on the screen
          g.drawString("My Java Applet!", 10, 20);
          g.fillRect(10,40,110,50);
          }
        }
```

The **resize** statement in the **init** method tells the browser to initially resize this applet's window (i.e., space on the Web page) to a new size of 120 by 100. Resizing your window initially is always a good idea, as the default size could vary given the different browsers and implementations your applet may end up running on. The paint function calls two methods; one draws the string "My Java Applet!" inside the window at coordinates 10,20. It then draws a filled rectangle under the words. The parameter **Graphics g** passed to the **paint** method is the object that represents your applet's window on the Web page. As in the example, all graphics functions must be prefixed with this object name (**g** in this case) to direct their efforts to your window. Later you'll see why it might be necessary to draw to an invisible window, but for now your applets will only need the main window.

Incorporating this applet in an empty Web page produces the result in Figure 4-6.

FIGURE 4-6

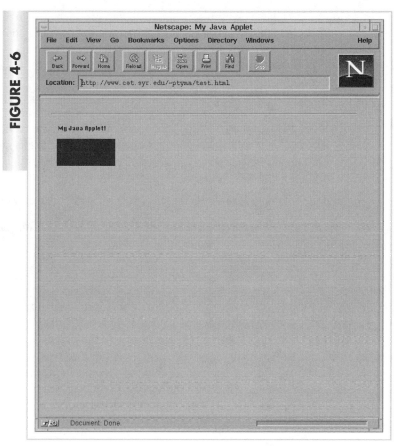

My Java Applet!

Put this code together with the interfacing instructions of Chapter 3, and you can already experiment with a wide variety of possibilities. The Appendix lists additional methods that are already being imported to this applet via the `import java.awt.Graphics` statement. In other words, they are already at your disposal for experimentation.

 # Standalone Applications

Experienced programmers will initially feel a little more at home writing standalone Java programs. Applets, as outlined above, are not really start-to-finish programs. They are more a group of methods made available to the browser for execution. In effect, the browser is the main program and your class is merely a nuisance, granted execution subject to the browser's potentially evil whims and desires. Standalone programs, on the other hand, are complete programs. They run from start to finish wholly under your control—Java's true power will be shown in this field of applications. The center of their execution is in a method that all standalone programs must have, named `main`. C and C++ programmers should be chomping at the bit by now, since this concept is in line with C/C++'s organization.

The Main Method

The main method is the place that the program will start to run, and (barring any unforeseen calamities) it's also where the program will end. In the meantime, `main` can send execution off into many other classes to get things done, but `main` is the method in charge. The skeleton for a standalone program looks like this:

```
public class MyStandAlone {                    // define class

    public static void main (String args[])    // declare main
    {
    // code
    }
}
```

This class definition is bit more qualified than the applet declaration. That makes sense, since this code is actually defining a start-to-finish program. First off, notice there are no import statements. They're not included here because this example won't do enough to really warrant them. However, any class besides an empty one will usually require some of the functionality found in the supplied prebuilt packages. As your applications become more complex, your usage of the prebuilt packages will become second nature.

The class definition in this code is called `MyStandAlone` and is somewhat different from the applet example. There is no extension (i.e., explicit subclassing) this time because `MyStandAlone` is not a child of any other class. The `main` method is treated just like any other method, except it is the magic entry point for execution. Every standalone program is required to have a `main` declared exactly as above in order for the runtime environment to know where to start running the program. The modifiers `public static void` are required for any `main` method. The endless permutations of method modifiers is stifled for the case of the `main` method. It must always be declared `public static void`.

The `main` method also has a set input parameter, which is shown above as `String args[]`. This parameter is also unchangeable and is a vehicle for the user who is running your program to pass it arguments. This could be a number, file name, URL address, etc. It could be anything your program needs to know that you wouldn't want to hardcode. The slight catch is that regardless of the type of the data, it will be initially interpreted as a `String` type and must be dealt with accordingly.

Hello World

The code example for the applet cannot be completely transferred to an analogous standalone application—at least not easily. Remember the standalone application is going to run right from the command line; there is no assumption of an existing graphical environment as in the applet case. Note that it's well within the power of Java to set up a graphical environment. In fact, this would be a seamless operation for any architecture Java currently runs on. However, for now the code is a bit sticky and beyond the scope of the current discussion. Instead, let's just look at the analogous version without the rectangle, i.e., printing the message.

```java
public class MyStandAlone {

 public static void main (String args[])
  {
   System.out.println("My Java Application!");
  }

}
```

The output of this program would be just as you expect: immediately after running it, "My Java Application!" would be printed and then the program would end. The statement that actually does the printing is rather complex for performing such a simple task. The `System` class defines many system functions that hide any architecture-specific details. It also includes several data elements, one of which is the `out` class variable. This is a static data element that points at the system's output stream, usually your screen. The command is calling the `println` method, within the context of the system's `out` variable (in other words, you're asking the `out` stream to figure out how to print to itself), in order to print the string "My Java Application!". This may seem a bit pretentious for such a simple command, but this organization helps keep consistency across many functions. Additional `System` class features can be found in the Appendix.

Summary

In this chapter you saw the building blocks of coding in Java and the high-level requirements for making applets and standalone applications. You also looked at an overview of object-oriented structures and where they fit into coding in Java. Hopefully, this introduction has provided you with enough information to get the feel for coding in Java and its overall code structure.

Java's number one rule is "Everything is a class." That is, of course, unless it is something within a class or is a collection of classes. In any case, the concept of classes is at the root of Java's design. Don't underestimate their power or importance; classes and objects, if used for good, are concepts with sincere potential.

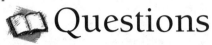

Questions

1. Label each of the following items with the Java hierarchical element that most suits it—package, class, or object.

   a. A dog
   b. A job application
   c. A train engine
   d. A dog whose name is Spot
   e. A human anatomy chart
   e. A collection of rubber stamps

2. Name three possible subclasses for a hypothetical class building.

3. What values would likely be needed by a method that calculates the payment on a loan?

4. Besides resizing, what are other possible tasks that might be placed in an applet's `init` method?

5. What is the difference between a standalone application and an applet?

Exercises

1. Design a class to describe a "bird".

2. Create a class hierarchy with the bird class at the top, and create at least two logical child classes.

3. Write an applet that puts five nonoverlapping rectangles on the screen.

4. Extend this chapter's graphics package example by formally defining the classes that would likely be found within it.

Data and Variables

5

You will learn about the following in this chapter:

- How Java specifies its built-in data types
- How to use integer, floating point, and character values
- How to effectively utilize Java's operators
- How to create mathematical expressions in Java
- What instance and local variables are
- How Java defines its operator precedence
- How to use Java's Math class

The manipulation of data is the lifeblood of any program. Using data cleverly can reduce your program's storage requirements and increase performance. Java's structure for implementing data types is relatively straightforward, and programmers of any popular programming language should swiftly relate its concepts to ones they know. However, it is important to know that Java does contain some subtle differences in its data storage and manipulation facilities. Some of these arise from its challenges of architecture independence and security; others were simply design decisions made by its creators.

This chapter covers all Java's built-in data types and their usage. It provides examples of commonly used mathematical expressions and functions. It also covers Java's built-in math class, which affords programmers a comprehensive set of useful "ready to go" functions. This information should give you a solid foundation to begin coding increasingly complex programs in the Java language.

Java's Data Types

Java's data types have some unique features and restrictions that are not found in any other language design. These elements are likely present in part to keep the language safe to run on any architecture. The construction of a language's standard data types is rather important information. It will help you design your code to make better use of memory and be sure you never run into an overflow. So if your code stubbornly won't add in that 129th interest payment, the first thing to do is check the data types.

Java's Built-in Types

Java divides its built-in types into four main categories: integer, floating point, character, and Boolean. It's somewhat uncommon to encounter a modern programming language that doesn't include these standard types. As you'll see, there are also subcategories further dividing these categories. The final selection of available data types should be sufficient to make programmers of many different languages feel right at home.

A side note to any highly object-oriented readers: the built-in data types presented here are not objects. However, you should know that you can intentionally use some Java built-in wrapper classes to make objects out of them. A discussion of that ability appears later in the chapter. This object/non-object existence of data types is a slight detraction from some purely object-oriented language methodologies. Nonetheless, this is Java's implementation, and both methodologies will be discussed.

Integer

The integer type is divided into four sizes. Practically, this means that the various flavors of integers have different ranges of legal values they can store. Figure 5-1 illustrates the categories.

This arrangement standardizes definitions of integers, which is vital given Java's existence across multiple platforms. The reason several different sizes are available is for flexibility

FIGURE 5-1

	Bits/Width	Legal Range of Values
byte	8	−127 to 128
short	16	−32767 to 32768
int	32	−2147483647 to 2147483648
long	64	~−9.223e18 to ~9.223e18

Types of integers

between need, speed, and memory usage. Byte representations will be the most economical as far as memory requirements and should be the fastest (or tied for the fastest) for processing and calculations on any architecture. However, it's certainly not uncommon for a programmer to need variables that can hold greater than the value 128. Picking an integer type that is too small for your needs is an infamously stealthy program bug.

Declaring integer variables is more or less identical to C or C++, with the notable absence of some of C/C++'s variable modifiers, such as **unsigned**, etc. This similarity extends even to the point of allowing initializers in the declaration.

```
int a,b,c=99;
```

This statement declares integer variables **a**, **b**, and **c**. It also initializes the value of **c** to 99 during declaration. The statement does not, however, specifically initialize the variables **a** and **b**. Especially with Java's multiplatform existence, initializing your variables before usage is always a good idea.

In the above declaration, **int** could have been replaced with **byte**, **short**, or **long** according to the desired size of the variable. Note that the result of an expression that uses only integer variables will always be either **int** or **long**. The result will be **long** if any of the operands are **long**; in all other cases the result is **int**. Expressions cannot result in a **byte** or **short** answer regardless of the presence of these types in the expression (i.e., multiplying a **short** and a **byte** results in an **int**).

Integer literals can be expressed in several ways in Java. The following code sets each variable to the decimal value 79.

```
d = (int)79.4;    // assume d is an integer variable, this will
                  // truncate (i.e. cast) to 79
e = 79;           // usual form (79 assumed by compiler to be int)
f = 79L;          // 'L' converts 79 to a long (f should be long)
g = 0x4f;         // hexadecimal conversion
h = 0117;         // octal conversion
```

Note that the value for **h** is 0117. A leading zero indicates to the compiler that the number is in base 8 (octal) format. The compiler will always assume a literal value to be 32 bits wide unless it is evidently larger (i.e., outside the range of **int** in Figure 5 1) or explicitly cast otherwise (as with variable **f** above). Most application programmers will typically use the form of variable **e** above. However, Java provides the other forms for convenience in dealing with various types of data (the octal form is gaining massive popularity in the PDP-11 community).

Floating Point

Java's floating point numbers have two possible representations: **float** and **double**. The **float** data type is 32 bits wide and the **double** is 64 bits wide. The **double** data type is just as it seems, a more precise or larger **float**. They are declared as

```
float a;
double b;
```

In theory, a floating point variable cannot hold a perfect integer. If you assign a `float` variable to 1, it's actually stored as 1.0 with trailing zeros up to the level of precision. If you only need an integer, then only use an integer—they are faster and guaranteed to be what you expect. Computers still don't claim to do perfect floating point math, and you never know what computer burp lurks at the tenth significant digit past 1.0 . Some legal assignments to floating point variables are

```
a = 2;        // casts an int to float (a is float)
b = 3.44e5;   // 3.44 x 10^5 (b is double)
a = 4.0f;     // trailing 'f' indicates to treat 4 as float
b = 4d;       // trailing 'd' indicates to treat 4 as double
```

As with the `long` (i.e., `0L`) indicator for integer variables, you can specify `F` (or `f`) and `D` (or `d`) to force a literal as a `float` or `double`, respectively. If no specification is given to a floating point number, then `double` is the default (the compiler will nag if you try to assign a floating point number to a `float` variable without a cast).

The Java language's floating point implementation closely follows the IEEE 754 standard for binary floating point arithmetic. What's that? Well the Institute for Electronics and Electrical Engineers is a group of undeniably smart people who have developed at least 754 different standards by now, this one pertaining to a well-designed plan for arithmetic operations upon floating point numbers.

This standard includes some amazing features; for one, there is no such thing as a floating point arithmetic error. This is not to say that "divide by zero" just goes away; instead this error is no longer discriminated against because of its mathematical beliefs (its occurrence is no longer an error). Java has adopted this standard to also accommodate values that have no real numerical representation (representationally challenged values) such as infinity. Java uses `Inf` to indicate a signed infinity.

```
f = 9.3f / 0;  // trailing f indicates float value
```

After this statement, `f` would equal `Inf` and no exception would be generated. Having infinity as a value in one of your variables is, to say the least, a situation that calls for a bit of caution. You will have to be careful in developing your code and be aware of this implementation.

Another nonrepresentable value is `NaN`, which is an acronym for "Not a Number." This is used for calculations that result in nonmeaningful values. Dividing `Inf` by `Inf` results in `NaN`. Overall `NaN` is a nasty creature. Any comparison involving `NaN` (e.g., `3 < NaN`) is false, except for `NaN != somenumber,` which is always true. The primary exposure you will have to `NaN` will be as a "mathematical virus"; you will want to find out why you got it and how you can get rid of it.

Character

Java keeps a clear distinction between its character type and what is defined as a string of characters. The character type holds single character values (not strings). As another step toward architectural (and global) uniformity, Java uses the Unicode character set, which includes everything from the Cyrillic alphabet to several thousand Hangul syllables and, of course, every character appearing in this book. A character is defined as a 16-bit unsigned integer. It is possible to sneak around the compiler and use the character type as an actual unsigned numerical value. However, any expression involving only integer and/or character types will return an integer result—even if the expression is to "add" two characters. Overall, it's likely best to use integers as integers and characters as characters.

Character variables are defined with the keyword `char`:

```
char a,b,c;
```

Assignments are typically done as

```
me = 'u';
```

After that statement, the variable `me` will contain the character "u." Seasoned programmers are quite accustomed to this everyday, wanton confusion. When you need to set a character variable to a nonvisible or system character, things become slightly more obfuscated. Figure 5-2 displays strings assigned to nonvisible characters for assignments.

For example, assigning a carriage return to the `me` variable would look like this:

```
me =   '\r';
```

The value "\r" is actually two physical characters, but the compiler watches for backslash sequences and interprets them according to Figure 5-2. Any character literal starting with

FIGURE 5-2

English	Unicode designation	Character string
Backspace	BS	\b
Backslash	\	\\
Carriage Return	CR	\r
Double Quote	"	\"
Form Feed	FF	\f
Horizontal Tab	HT	\t
Single Quote	`	\'
Unicode Character	0x####	\u####

Character assignments for nonvisible characters

a backslash is under immediate suspicion by the compiler—that is why you are required to use "\\" in order for the compiler to actually assign a single backslash.

Boolean

"True or false" largely sums up this data type. The Boolean type can only hold one of these two values. Optimally, this would be represented in a computer system as a single bit, as this is all the memory required to hold these possible values. The Boolean values `true` or `false` are not numbers in any way and cannot be cast to any numeric type. C/C++ programmers should heed that idea; none of the magic tricks of using Booleans as numerics are available. In Java, Boolean values are not numbers. Not even sometimes. They are defined as expected:

```
boolean a,b;
```

Boolean literals are actually the words `true` and `false`. These are reserved Java keywords and may not be used for variable names, etc. Many familiar operators don't work on Boolean data types:

```
a = true + false;      // Error!
```

This statement generates a compiler error. There is no way to add truth values (i.e., two wrongs don't make a right, and in fact, they don't even make a wrong). Later we'll cover standard Java operators that work on straight Boolean values, but it's worth mentioning here how non-Boolean types can produce Boolean values. Any *relation*, as defined with Java's relational operators, returns a Boolean value. For example:

```
(3 < 5)        // returns 'true'
(4 == 5)       // returns 'false'
```

This extends to the point of forming Boolean assignment statements:

```
boolean boovar;
int foovar1, foovar2;

foovar1 = 10;
foovar2 = 99;

boovar = (foovar1 <= foovar2);      // 'true' in this case
```

After this code segment, `boovar` would be true because `foovar1` is less than or equal to `foovar2`. Along with their strong presence in conditional statements, Boolean values/variables are often used as flags that mark the occurrence of some event.

More on Assignments

Several interesting points arise through the use of assignment statements and declarations initializers within Java. Java affords programmers (actually C did too, but Java continues the tradition) the ability to perform several tricks using the assignments and initializers. The following statement initializes all three variables to ten:

```
a = b = c = 10;
```

This works because of the phenomenon that the assignment statement itself actually returns a value. So for the above example, the breakdown is

```
a = (b = (c = 10));
a = (b = 10);          // c is now 10
a = 10;                // b is now 10
```

The parentheses are used above to clarify what is happening, but in actuality the statements are still valid Java syntax. This trick can be used within expressions when you wish to have a side effect of assigning a variable.

Initializers can also be perverted into various forms. The following initialization is legal:

```
int a = 10;
int b = a * 2;
```

This is fine and even occasionally useful, but you must be wary of forward referencing initialization variables. If the above two statements had their order reversed, a compiler error would be born.

Java's Built-in Types as Objects

Java includes prebuilt classes to be able to define many of the standard data types as objects. An integer object is inherently different from a simple integer variable. For example, you cannot use an equal sign to assign a value, and the + operator will not add integer objects (C++ programmers will note that Java does not support overloaded operators). Considering that it is a true object, this shouldn't be any great surprise. Objects are only acted upon by methods. The prebuilt classes for each data type include many methods to perform those everyday needs you may have for your data type objects. Here is some code for comparison; this code focuses on integers, but relatively equivalent facilities exist for most of the built-in types.

```
int normal_int;          // normal int definition
Integer object_int;      // 'Integer' specifies integer
                         //   object

normal_int = 5;          // normal assignment
object_int = new Integer(5); // must instantiate objects
                         //   this also inits object
                         //   to 5

normal_int = normal_int + 1; // add one

// perform 'add one' for int object

object_int = new Integer(object_int.intValue() + 1);
```

That's ugly to say the least. As with any objects, the integer object must be instantiated before usage. This includes an instant initialization. The **add one** statement is quite complex for such a trivial operation. The `intValue` method is called to retrieve the `int` value of the object. The result is added to 1. The code then creates a new integer object with the new value. The original integer object is now orphaned and will be swept up by the garbage collector on its next pass. That's perfectly okay, since you are no longer interested in it; you're only interested in the new incremented integer object. This certainly seems like a lot of running around to just manipulate some numbers. Well, types as objects do have their purpose, but speed (in coding *and* running) is not one of them.

Often you will have to use data type objects to take playful advantage of some of Java's prebuilt data structures such as `Stack` or `hashTable`. These prebuilt data structures leniently accept any objects as elements, but only true objects. Generally, your usage of built-in data types will not be as objects. Using normal data types as objects is more of a necessity than a pleasure.

 # Operators

Anyone familiar with the operators in C/C++ will have no problem using Java's. All (seemingly) normal operators found in any popular programming language are there: +, - , * , /, along with C/C++'s bit twiddling ANDs, ORs, etc. Java does add a few operators of its own, which are discussed below.

The Master List

Table 5-1 represents a master list of the built-in arithmetic and Boolean operators in Java. In general, operators with the same precedence level will be evaluated from left to right in the given expression.

Precedence Level	Operator	Example Usage	Example Result	Description
1	()	(5)	5	groups expressions
2	++	++5 or 5++	6	increment by 1 (or 1.0)
2	--	--5 or 5--	4	decrement by 1 (or 1.0)
2	!	!true	false	Boolean negation
2	~	~95	-96	bitwise complement
2	instanceof	b instanceof a	true	tests class membership
3	*	5 * 6	30	multiplication
3	/	10 / 5	2	division
3	%	9 % 5	4	modulus

Precedence Level	Operator	Example Usage	Example Result	Description
4	+	5 + 6	11	addition
4	-	6 - 5	1	subtraction
5	<<	5 << 1	10	left shift
5	>>	-6 >> 1	-3	right shift (keep sign)
5	>>>	-6 >>> 1	125	right shift (zero fill)
6	<	5 < 6	true	less than
6	>	5 > 6	false	greater than
6	<=	5 <= 6	true	less than/equal
6	>=	5 >= 6	false	greater than/equal
7	==	5 == 6	false	is equal to
7	!=	5 != 6	true	is not equal to
8	&	5 & 3	1	bitwise AND
9	^	5 ^ 3	6	bitwise XOR
10	|	5 | 3	7	bitwise OR
11	&&	true && true	true	Boolean AND
12	||	true || true	true	Boolean OR
13	? :	true?5:6	5	conditional expression
14	=	x = 5	5	assignment
14	op=	x += 5	x+5	binary op assignment

Table 5-1 List of arithmetic/Boolean operators in Java (values are bytes)

Several operators are worth special note. The `?:` operator is a conditional expression that, according to the Boolean evaluation before the question mark, returns the first expression for true and the second (past the colon) for false. This could also be accomplished by

```
if (before_question_mark) return first;
 else return second;
```

The `?:` operator is borrowed from C/C++. It provides a quick and clean method to do conditional assignments.

The `instanceof` operator applies to classes, subclasses, and their objects. As in the example, it could test whether object **b** is an instance of class **a** or one of its subclasses (in the example it's assumed it is).

Operations on Integers

To no great surprise, standard operations such as addition, subtraction, multiplication, and division all work on integers as expected. Remember that unless one or more of the values/variables in the expression is defined to be `long`, the result will always be `int`—never `short` or `byte`. It is also possible with integer arithmetic to cause a runtime arithmetic exception by attempting to divide by zero. Remember, this is only with integer arithmetic; an exception will not be thrown with floating point arithmetic.

As in C/C++, the `++` and `--` operators perform an increment or decrement by one respectively, and also as in C/C++ it depends where they are placed in order to predict their effect on an expression.

```
int x,y;

x = 5;
y = ++x * 2;            // after this statement, x == 6 and y == 12

x = 5;
y = x++ * 2;            // after this statement, x == 6 and y == 10
```

A preceding `++` (or `--`) that performs the increment before the variable is used within the expression and a succeeding `++` that performs the increment after the variable is used within the expression.

The tilde (~) is used for a bitwise complement operation. Figure 5-3 shows an example: convert the number to base 2, change all the ones to zeros and zeros to ones, and convert it back to base 10 (the figure uses an intermediate conversion to base 16 for clarity). The sign bit (the most significant bit) is destined to change, which inevitably changes the sign of the base 10 number. This operation along with the bitwise AND, OR, XOR, and shifts are direct descendants from C/C++.

The `>>>` operator differs from the `>>` operator in that it does not give the sign bit any special consideration when right shifting (i.e., it also gets zero filled without regard). That is the reason the `>>>` example above changes from a negative small number to a large positive number.

Operations on Floating Points

Again, all standard operations such as addition, subtraction, etc., work on floating points. Surprisingly, even the modulus division operator (a historically integer operator) also works on floating point values. Bitwise operations do not work on floating point values, although you could perform a cast of the value to `int` before attempting to apply the operator.

Operations on Booleans

Operations legal on Boolean values include all bitwise operators, all Boolean bit operators, and Boolean negation. Any relation involving greater than, is equal to, etc., will yield a Boolean result even though the operands around the operator are of some other type.

The two types of ANDs and ORs will perform identically, except that the Boolean forms (i.e., **&&** and **||**) will perform short circuiting upon the evaluation. Given the Boolean expression

```
x = 5;
boovar = ((x > 3) || (x < 9));   // is x>3 or x<9??
```

it is evident this statement as a whole is true. However, since the expression has **||** (as opposed to **|**), the runtime would be smart enough to realize that since the left side is true and this is an OR operation, then "true OR anything" is always true. In other words, since the left side is true, there is no reason to evaluate the right-hand side for an OR—it will short-circuit the evaluation. The single bar operator and single ampersand operator are bitwise operators and would evaluate the entire expression (i.e., both sides) without regard to possible shortcuts. This short circuiting also applies to ANDs (the **&&** operator) where the left side is found to be false—"false AND anything" is always false.

FIGURE 5-3

BASE:	10	16	2	Operator	2	16	10
bitwise negation	95	5F	01011111	~	10100000	A0	−96
bitwise AND	5	5	00000101	&	00000001	1	1
	3	3	00000011				
bitwise OR	5	5	00000101	|	00000111	7	7
	3	3	00000011				
bitwise XOR	5	5	00000101	^	00000110	6	6
	3	3	00000011				
left shift	5	5	00000101	<<1	00001010	A	10
right shift >>	−6	FA	11111010	>>1	11111101	FD	−3
right shift >>>	−6	FA	11111010	>>>1	01111101	7D	125

Bit twiddling operators

Expressions and Precedence

This section covers Java's behavior regarding mixing and matching data types within expressions. Some outcomes may surprise even experienced coders. The section also plays some tricky expression games and introduces using Java's `Math` class.

What's an Expression

The word *expression* is used quite liberally throughout this text. This word applies to any legal combination of variables, values, and operators. All of the following are legal Java expressions:

```
x * 2
99
32 + 32 + y + (12 ^ z)
```

Even though 99 is only a single value, it is still considered an expression. This definition enters the depths of Java's underlying grammar definition and what it considers to be an expression. The third expression contains a tedious addition of two 32 values. This odd programming practice still qualifies as a legally formed expression.

Using Variables

Take heed of the precedence ordering outlined in Table 5-1. Most of this ordering is quite standard—i.e., multiply and divide ahead of add and subtract, equal precedence levels run left to right.

Variable Names

Legal variable names in Java are similar to those in most programming languages. Java allows some extra leniency with its implementation of the Unicode character set. All identifiers (variable names, class names, etc.) must start with a character not indicated as a digit in the Unicode standard. What's that? Well, just what you would think, pretty much any letter in an alphabet in Unicode (i.e., using A-Z is just fine). This also includes other symbols, including dollar sign and underscore, which you'll see used in this book.

Subsequent characters of identifiers may be letters or any number from 0-9. This is largely a superset of possible identifier names in other programming languages. Most often you will find yourself using descriptive words for your identifiers to make your code readable (we hope).

Instance Variables

Using the information you've gathered about data types and expressions, let's pull the standalone program code from Chapter 4 and write a slightly more complex program. Recall the skeleton for writing standalone programs:

```
public class MyStandAlone {

  public static void main (String args[]) {

   // code
   }
}
```

As before, the class is called **MyStandAlone** and has only one method, **main**. Since the goal here is to use some data types, you'll need to define some variables. There are two usual places to define variables in the above code; typically variable declarations for a given block are placed immediately after the opening curly brace (**{**). Assume you want to begin by defining two integer variables named **days** and **temporary**. Actually, **temporary** is only being added to facilitate the following discussion. This can be done as follows:

```
public class MyStandAlone {

  static int days=365; // declare 'days' and init to 365
  int temporary;

  public static void main (String args[]) {

    // code
    }
}
```

The two variables **days** and **temporary** are defined outside the confines of any method declaration. Because of this, they are known as *instance* variables. In general, instance variables are available to all methods within the class and are automatically initialized when an object is created. In other words, they don't belong to any specific method; they belong to the object or class. Each nonstatic (like **temporary**) instance variable exists for each object of this class type for the lifetime of the object (the **static** modifier in front of the **days** variable tends to cloud this happy setting; it is explained below). Granted, the above example only has one method (cherish these days of simplicity), but most classes will have many methods. Instance variables represent the data (i.e., state) specific to the class.

Local Variables

Now, say you need another variable called **work**, also of type **int**. This time you will use a *local* variable—i.e., local to some method. Adding it to the code:

```
public class MyStandAlone {

static int days=365;

  public static void main (String args[]) {

    int work;
```

continued on next page

continued from previous page

```
    // code
    }
}
```

Just as an instance variable belongs to an object/class, a local variable (i.e., **work**) belongs to the **main** method. No other methods know that **work** exists, and they certainly cannot access it. The **work** variable is local to **main**. Since the **work** variable is a local variable, it will not be initialized for you (instance variables are automatically initialized, local variables are not); you must do this yourself.

It only exists as long as the method is executing—in this case the point is somewhat moot, since the **main** procedure must be the start and end of any standalone program—i.e., it will exist the entire time the program is running. Most methods repeatedly get called, run, and terminate, continuously creating and destroying their local variables. You cannot assume that a variable is the same way you left it from method call to method call. Once a method terminates, all its local variables are forever lost.

Completing the Code

Adding more statements:

```
public class MyStandAlone {

  static int days = 365;

  public static void main (String args[]) throws java.io.IOException {

      int work;

      work = System.in.read() - '0';
      work = PlusLeaps(work) + work * days;
      System.out.print("That is " + work + " days!");
  }

/* PlusLeaps method */
static int PlusLeaps(int years) {
    int work;

    work = years / 4;
    return work;
  }
}
```

A lot has been added to this code. First, an entirely new method has been added to the **MyStandAlone** class called **PlusLeaps**. This method divides the parameter it is passed by four and returns the result. Since this is entirely integer math, if **years** is not divisible by four, the fraction will be lost.

Notice that both the **main** method and the **PlusLeaps** method have a variable **work**. These two variables are positively different animals. The two methods have absolutely no knowledge of the other's **work** variable. The **work** variables are local to their respective methods. On the other hand, the `days` variable is quite visible within both methods, since it is a variable local to the class (not any particular method).

The `PlusLeaps` method is defined as type `int`. This tells the compiler to expect the method to return a value of this type. In fact, the compiler will then enforce the claim and dispense an error if it sees no `int` value is being returned. In the above case the method returns its `work` variable. This definition of the method's type works with contemporary object-oriented ideals of a more transparent distinction between methods and data.

The three lines within `main` perform straightforward functions:

```
work = System.in.read() - '0';
```

reads in a value from the keyboard (i.e., user enters 0-9). Since the `read` method reads in a character, the code must subtract the value of character zero to return the input to zero to nine (instead of some Unicode value for a character zero to nine). Know that this method of reading keyboard input is quite compact but also quite limited. There are definitive ways to read varied types of keyboard input, but these require many more concepts than are being introduced at the moment. For now, entering one simple digit will be enough for this example.

```
work = PlusLeaps(work) + work * days;
```

This statement calculates the days in that many years (not exactly a precise calculation, but it should suffice for this purpose). The `PlusLeaps` call returns a value for that portion of the equation. According to the precedence rules, you know that `work * days` will occur first, the result of that will be added to `PlusLeaps(work)`, and the result of that will be put back into `work`. The `work` variable does not actually get changed until the entire right-hand side of the equation is evaluated.

```
System.out.print("That is " + work + " days!");
```

This statement prints out the answer. For an input of 7, the output looks like this:

```
That is 2556 days!
```

The print statement uses the plus operator to concatenate strings of characters. The `work` variable is largely a pawn in the operation and is mercilessly treated (or promoted) as a string. Strings will be covered in Chapter 7.

Final Variables

You can also mark a variable as `final`. The declaration looks like this:

```
final float pi = 3.1415F;
```

This modifier tells the compiler this variable will not change. In the above case, `pi` will remain 3.1415 throughout its existence. Obviously, this situation makes `pi` a read-only variable. The usage is evident; your code has no need to ever change the value of `pi`, since it is a mathematical constant. Specifying variables as `final` allows the compiler the ability to perform optimizations concerning that variable. The speed boost from declaring a variable **final** isn't overly dramatic, but if you wish the variable to be constant anyway, it's worth typing the keyword.

Scoping

This should give a feel for the *scope* of variables, i.e., where they are visible. A method's local variables are only visible within that method. Actually, any defined block of code can define its own local variables; a method is just a common block. Instance variables exist in the class definition and are available to all methods in that object. Figure 5-4 illustrates these points and adds one more.

A **static** variable effectively expands the scope of a variable by one bigger step. It is a variable belonging to the class itself (not any individual objects). No object really owns this variable but any can read or write it. This is exceptionally useful to provide a means of communication between objects or for storing data that all objects need to reference.

No matter how many times a class gets instantiated, only one copy of this variable will exist. You may remember that the unchangeable modifiers in front of the **main** function

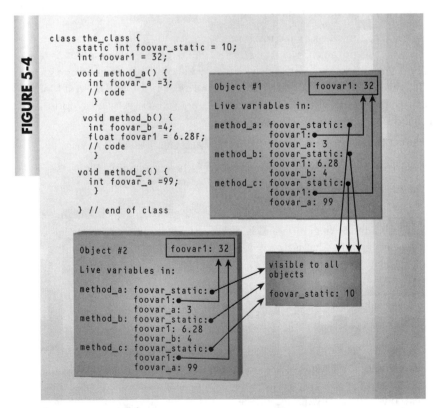

FIGURE 5-4

Scoping variables

also list `static`. The effect is largely the same; there shouldn't be more than one `main` function for any program.

Figure 5-4 also illustrates where a narrow-scoped variable overrides the scope of a wider-scoped variable. The variable `foovar1` is visible within the entire object. However, `method_b` defines its own version of `foovar1` as a `float`. The wider `int` version is not visible within `method_b`. As before with the `work` variable in the `days` program, `method_c` and `method_a` have a commonly named variable. Since these variables are local to the respective methods, there is no conflict.

Mixing and Matching

Figure 5-5 provides a general (and symmetrical) reference chart for how Java returns results of mixed type expressions. This chart should be quite helpful for simple expressions. However, once expressions become more complex, subtle implicit type casts can throw off your results. Consider the following wickedly tailored code segment:

```
float x,y;

x = 3.14159;
y = 10.0;

x = ( (5 > 4) || (8.0/0 < 1) ) ? ((int)x | 3) / 4 * y + 1 : 0;
```

Astute readers will immediately notice that there exists a divide by zero in the relation `(8.0/0 < 1)`. Readers who are even more astute will realize that this will not cause

FIGURE 5-5

	byte	short	int	long	char	float	double
byte	int	int	int	long	int	float	double
short	int	int	int	long	int	float	double
int	int	int	int	long	int	float	double
long	long	long	long	long	long	float	double
char	int	int	int	long	int	float	double
float	float	float	float	float	float	float	double
double	double	double	double	double	double	double	double

Mix and match summary

an arithmetic exception, since **8.0** is listed as a **float**, and there are no exceptions in Java's floating point arithmetic. However, possibly only the astutest readers will realize that none of that matters anyway, since the left-hand side of the Boolean relation **(5>4)** is always true and the OR-ing mechanism used is the **||** operator, which will cause a short circuit; thus, the run will never attempt to evaluate the divide by zero anyway!

The equation on the right of the question mark (which will be returned since the condition on the left was true) is a bit less devious than the Boolean condition but still contains some interesting points. Here is a step-by-step breakdown of how it will be evaluated:

```
((int)x | 3) / 4 * y + 1        // the initial expression
    3     / 4 * y + 1           // x is cast to int and or'd with 3
                                //    i.e. (3 | 3) = 3
        0     * y + 1           // divide 3 by 4 and since they are
                                //    int, answer is truncated to 0
                 0.0  + 1       // 0 * y = 0.0 (y is float so
                                //    answer is float)
                      1.0       // answer is float
```

As you can see, implicit casting can be a nightmare. Java provides (and enforces) the ability to explicitly typecast an expression. This is done by putting the type you wish to cast to in parentheses at the point you wish it to be cast. The following line removes the fractional part of a floating point variable.

```
int t = (int) x;        // x is a float
```

The compiler will be more than happy to tell you when you are required to use an explicit cast.

The Math Class

As with several other languages, Java provides its more complex mathematical functions in an external form. In Java's case they are included in the **java.lang** prebuilt package in the **Math** class. This class includes all the general mathematical functions such as sine, cosine, exponentiation, etc. As with any language, you can still write your own class to implement additional functions that may better suit your type of programming.

Using the Math Class

Usage of the **Math** class is relatively straightforward; it is typically used as follows:

```
x = java.lang.Math.sin(y);
```

This form includes the prefix of the class name followed by the method name. In this case, the variable **y** is a **double** supposedly between zero and two times pi, since all trigonometric functions use radians (not degrees) by default.

In the above case of the sine method, the parameter (i.e., the value you wish to find the sine for) is defined as double. Many methods within the **Math** class are overloaded to accept multiple types. Overloading is an object-oriented tool that basically means using one method name to describe several different methods that process differing types of data. An example of this is the absolute value function.

```
int a;
long b;
float x;
double y;
.
.
.
// a,b,x,y get assigned some values
.
.
.
a = java.lang.Math.abs(a);        // integer abs
b = java.lang.Math.abs(b);        // long abs
x = java.lang.Math.abs(x);        // float abs
y = java.lang.Math.abs(y);        // double y
```

Each call to the **abs** function knows what type of data it is receiving, and because of this it knows which **abs** method it should use. This is important, because at a low level, removing the sign from an **int** type (i.e., taking its absolute value) is quite different from removing it from a **double**. The overloading makes the whole operation painless to the programmer.

Overall, the **Math** class is quite well organized and (as with most things in Java) is largely modeled after C/C++. All standard mathematical functions are there, including a logical set of overloads when applicable.

Random Numbers

A commonly needed function within programming is a random number generator. Java provides a prebuilt generator in the **java.util.Random** class. It also provides a more stripped-down version right inside the **Math** class (guess what, the version in the **Math** class is really just calling the full version in the **java.util.Random** class). The method in the **Math** class is

```
double random();
```

The **Math** class's **random()** function accepts no parameters and provides a pseudo-random number (of type **double**) from 0.0 to 1.0 . Reams of paper have been devoted to technical reports discussing why the number is only *pseudo* random. What it all really boils down to is that computers tend to be creatures that are too precise to actually do something inexact.

In order to have some semblance of spontaneity, random number generators use a seed to, in effect, base their future randomness on. This seed, through some combination of clandestine pagan rituals, influences the random numbers produced by the generator. A common practice is to assign the seed to some permutation of the time of day, which generally produces enough random output to confuse the unwary. This is the default for random number generators in Java.

The following code spits out some randomness:

```
public class MyStandAlone {

 public static void main (String args[]) {

                int day;

                // get random number
                day = (int)(java.lang.Math.random()*365);

                System.out.println("Today is day " + day);
                System.out.println("of this year!!! or is it?");
 }
}
```

The line that actually calls the random number method must perform a cast. It does this since this application is apparently interested in a discrete day of the year. The random method will return a double between 0.0 and 1.0. It is then multiplied by 365 to get a number between 0.0 and 365.0. Finally it is cast down to an integer. The fraction of the day is lost, but since this program is already inaccurate in its claimed results (randomly claiming today's day of the year), there is no need to get precise about it.

The `java.util.Random` class provides you a somewhat better grasp on producing random numbers. It provides specific methods for creating random integers, doubles, floats, etc. If you will be using random numbers a lot, it's probably worthwhile to set up your own random number generator with the `java.util.Random` class (see Appendix) and sorrowfully abandon the simple convenience of the `Math` class's method.

 # Summary

This chapter provided you a fast look at Java's data types and their usage. Hopefully, you see where these concepts can be applied to developing larger-scale applications. Keeping one eye on the specifics outlined in this chapter should propel you into some more significant coding.

The next chapter will assume you're up-to-date on the information in this and the previous chapters. You'll delve into Java's control structures and finally start writing code that performs some serious actions. So get ready—turn on a bright light, find a comfortable chair, and maybe go get yourself a nice cup of hot…coffee.

Questions

1. What data type would you use for variables with the following intended purpose?

    a. Hold the radius of a circle

    b. Hold a person's age

    c. Hold the angle of a turn calculated for a rocket

2. What is the value of **x** after the following code segment?

```
int x;

x = 55;
x = ++x + x++;
x %= 9;
```

3. What is the value of **y** after the following code segment?

```
float y;

y = 3.14159f;
y = y * (50*50);
```

4. What is the value of **b** after the following code segment?

```
boolean b;

b = ( (5<4) || (true) ) && ( ((9 & 1) < 5) & (6 > 1) );
```

5. What is the value of **work** at the time the run reaches the indicated comment?

```
public class watch_comment {

        static int bigvar = 100;
        int a=6,b=99;

        void method_a {

            int work,a = 5;

            a = b * a;
            work = bigvar * a;      // what is 'work' here

            }
        }
```

6. What explicit casts are needed in the following expression? What does **x** equal after this (corrected) code segment?

```
float x=1.0f;

x = (x <= 1.0) ? (1 / 2 * x + 9) - x * 9d : 55 * x;
```

Exercises

1. Write a method to compute the radius and circumference of a circle. Use Java's **Math** class where applicable.

2. Write an expression that decides if a variable is odd or even (use the modulus operator).

3. Rewrite the expression in Exercise 2 using the bitwise AND.

4. Besides the time of day, what is another good method for setting the seed for a random number generator? Write the code using the **java.util.Random** class.

Everything Is Under Control

You will learn about the following in this chapter:

- How to access Java's standard in, out, and error
- How to set up your own I/O streams
- How to use Java's `if` statement
- How to use Java's `switch` statement
- What loop constructs are available in Java
- How to choose the best looping construct for a given purpose
- How to "cheat" on loops with the `break` and `continue` statements

The entire point of programming is seemingly to control the actions of a computer. This chapter examines the constructs available in Java that control the flow of your code, giving you a better handle on what your program is about to do. It will also cover Java's built-in system facilities that allow you to interact with system resources.

It's said that a program spends 90 percent of its time in 10 percent of its code. Of course, either that means that 10 percent of the code is complex stuff the computer really has to think about, or it is code that is iterated over many times (bet on the latter). Iteration and conditional execution are extremely important tools in programming. The foundation presented here will set you well on your way to developing applications far more complex than those you've looked at in previous chapters.

System Interaction

Interacting with your computer is more precarious than it may seem when you program in Java. Again, this stems from the fact that Java will run on many differing machines with endless formulas for accessing their resources. The designers had two interesting problems: one, give every programmer on all platforms the same consistent methods to interact with the system, and two, find a way to write all the machine-specific code to do these operations quickly and efficiently. The designers found good solutions for both. Providing consistent interface to methods is what Java is already all about; the class concept is built to have an object know how to work on itself. So programmers using many different machines can all use the same command built into some system class and each individual machine will know how to do that operation on itself (e.g., time of day, print, etc.)

That part is the front end, i.e., the user's end. What about the back end? Most every type of machine has vastly differing ways of performing even the most simple operations, such as print. There is no question, someone had to write a machine-specific routine to do each of these operations for every machine Java will run on. The fortunate thing for the designers was that much of this functionality had already been created somewhere or another. So the Java designers borrowed this functionality wherever they could. Often, using system C code called as native methods got the job done.

This section focuses on the front end and how Java's predefined streams let you get to a system's input and output devices. That certainly sounds unrestricted, but don't worry, Java's security features are passionately careful about letting you get near the actual computer. So beware, strict rules abound.

Standard Streaming

The `java.lang.System` provides a wide array of prebuilt functionality to access the system your code will be running on. The `System` class contains three standard variables: `err`, `in`, and `out`. These variables are the standard error stream, standard input stream, and standard output stream, respectively. You've seen some of these variables in previous chapters, but a more formal introduction is provided here.

Standard input and output are quite tangible. Usually the standard input is your keyboard and the standard output is your screen. Standard error often performs relatively the same as standard output but is designed to specifically be used for error messages. Since a separate stream is used for errors, you can redirect them (for instance, to an error log) without affecting normal program output.

The Ins

The `System.in` variable provides a system input stream. This provides a standard entry point for programs that require input. The `in` variable has a default relationship to the keyboard but can be changed.

```
c = System.in.read();          // read a char from keyboard
```

This example illustrates how the `System.in` stream is used. Reading only one character at a time might be more useful for reading a binary file than for reading from the keyboard. Java provides additional functionality to read a plethora of different data types from input streams. Unfortunately, the code gets a bit messy and requires several more built-in classes. Let's leave that level of detail for later and for now just focus on the simple wonders of data I/O.

The Outs

The `System.out` variable is basically the converse of the `System.in` variable and provides a default print (output) stream. The `System.out` variable is typically used in printing to the screen. Here is an immediate warning: the `System.out` variable is not glued to the screen and can change where it points (i.e., it can change where it sends its data). For your standalone programs, the default is the screen, but for applets running in HotJava, the default is a disk file named weblog. In other words, anything you plunk into the `System.out` stream while running an applet gets tagged to the bottom of this file and your users will never see it. Here are some examples of printing to this stream.

```
System.out.print("Hi there!");       // print out a string
System.out.println(a + b);           // print out sum of a and b
System.out.println(a + "" + b);      // print out both variables
```

The first statement is a `print` as opposed to a `println`. The `println` causes a new line to be started (i.e., carriage return) after printing the string; a simple `print` does not. The next line prints out the result of the integer expression `a+b`—if `a` equals 10 and `b` equals 20, then the output would be 30. The last line seemingly attempts to add an empty string to `a` and `b`. Actually, its presence forces the compiler to treat `a + "" + b` as a string and not attempt any mathematical addition. The `+` operator here is used as a string concatenation operation. Again, if `a` equals 10 and `b` equals 20, the result this time would be

1020

Most every language seems to come up with its way of printing out combinations of values, variables, and strings. Java does this by connecting everything you want to print with + signs. Of course, one of the elements better be a string, or the plus sign will be used to sum values.

The Errors

The `System.err` variable also acts as a standard Java print stream. The main difference is that `err` is designated for error output (however, it's not beyond abuse). This way a programmer can direct errors wherever is suitable. Figure 6-1 shows a code example of how to redirect `System.err`.

Any of the system variables can be redirected in this manner. What's done here is a file output stream is created (as well as the actual error.log file). The `System.err` stream is then assigned to this new print stream and all subsequent data sent into it get directed into the file.

Your Own Streams

You certainly aren't limited to the three `System` streams. You can create your own with reckless abandon. The redirection example above did this as an intermediate step to redirect

FIGURE 6-1

```
System.out.println("This is to the screen");
System.err.println("This is also to the screen");

FileOutputStream diskfile = new FileOutputStream("error.log");
System.err = new PrintStream(diskfile, true);
System.out.println("This is still to the screen");
System.err.println("This is now to the disk file");
```

System.in	default	→	Keyboard
System.out	default	→	Screen
	default		
System.err	redirection	→	Disk File

Redirection

`System.err`. But the `FileOutputStream` in that example could have been used as a stream in its own right and would have performed just as well (i.e., your new stream isn't limited to `in`, `out`, or `err`; any valid identifier is okay). In other words, you don't need to use the `diskfile` stream as just an indirection to the existing `System.err`.

```
int data = 5;

/* Create the new stream (and disk file) */
FileOutputStream diskfile = new FileOutputStream("myfile.dat");

/* write a byte to the disk file */
diskfile.write(data);
```

The `write` method is another method available for sending data into a stream (the full list of possibilities is in the Appendix). Possibly the most striking element of Java's streams is the absolute number of choices you have as far as different kinds of input and output streams. In actuality, most of the streams are just children or grandchildren of `java.io.InputStream` and `java.io.OutputStream`. This goes for `FileOutputStream` used in the example.

The Appendix lists each of these streams and covers in-depth the most commonly used ones. You'll be most interested in the main input and output parent classes and ones for disk I/O. Java is committed to using these streams as a relatively generic input or output port. Whether data is streaming from a disk, a user, or a network, some flavor of the parent classes `InputStream` and `OutputStream` will be used.

Conditionals

A key ingredient to program control is the ability to conditionally execute sections of code. The statements described in this section of the book are quite explicit about the criteria for conditional code execution. Again, as with most of Java's nuts-and-bolts-level constructs, these statements are extremely close to C/C++'s implementation.

If and/or Else

The `if` statement block allows your program to execute or not execute a block of code directly dependent upon the value of a Boolean expression. Most every program in this book from now on will contain at least one `if` statement. This is not an exaggeration of their usefulness; you can't get much done without them.

How to If

An `if` statement contains a Boolean expression that, if true, allows execution of the `if`'s statement block. It may optionally include an `else` clause that owns a separate statement block that is executed if the Boolean expression proved false. Figure 6-2 shows the `if` statement's flow.

Unlike some languages, C and Java do not have the word "then" as part of the `if` block. In languages with "then", its presence is mainly grammatical and helps to form the statement in English—if `<this is true>` then `<do this>` else `<do that>`. An example of a valid Java `if` command is

```
if (x > 9) {
        x = x - 10;
}
else {
        x++;
}
```

This `if` statement will decrement x by 10 if x is greater than 9. If x is not greater than 9, x is incremented by 1. The Boolean condition `x>9` will return either true or false depending upon the value of x, which then dictates which bolded statement block gets executed.

As a side note, the statement blocks above consist of only a single statement (above in bold). When this is the case, the surrounding curly braces may be removed; Java will then assume that the block is made up of only one statement. This can be done any time a statement block is only one statement.

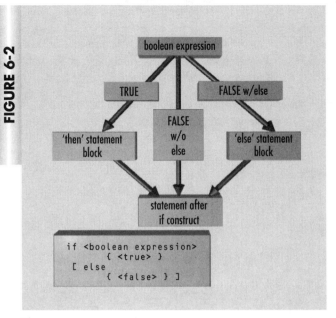

FIGURE 6-2

The `if` statement

```
if (x > 9)
        x = x - 10;            // treated as entire statement block
else
        x++;                   // ditto
```

This practice often cleans up the look of your code and in some compilers even generates slightly fast code, since a compiler considers an explicitly defined block a pretty sacred thing and generates some extra low-level code to handle it.

More If-ing

Let's incorporate the `if` statement into a slightly more complex program.

```
/* Standalone If test */
public class MyStandAlone {

  public static void main (String args[]) {

    char c;

/* Prompt the user and get a response */
    System.out.println("Press any key");
    c = (char)System.in.read();

      if ((c >= '0') && (c <= '9'))     // if A
```

```
        System.out.println("You have entered a number.");
    else
     {

    if ((c >= 'a') && (c <= 'z'))      // if B
        {
        if (c < 'l')                   // if C
                System.out.println("1st half of alphabet");
        else
                System.out.println("2nd half of alphabet");
        }
    else
        System.out.println("I don't recognize that key");

    }
  }
}
```

This program wins for being the nastiest so far. Let's analyze it line by line. It starts out by prompting the user with an informative message, then halts at the `System.in.read` statement until the user presses a key. The key value is assigned to character variable `c`.

The If Block

The `if` block is quite a mess. The first `if` uses the short-circuiting `&&` (i.e., AND) operator to see if the character entered was a numerical digit. If so, it reports that fact and does not execute its `else` counterpart. If the character entered was not a digit, the `else` is executed.

```
if ((c >= '0') && (c <= '9'))      // if A
        System.out.println("You have entered a number.");
else
 {

if ((c >= 'a') && (c <= 'z'))      // if B
        {
        if (c < 'l')                       // if C
                System.out.println("1st half of alphabet");
    else
                System.out.println("2nd half of alphabet");
        }
else
        System.out.println("I don't recognize that key");

    }
```

The first statement after the `else` is labeled `if B` (pertaining to the comment). This `if` also uses the short-circuiting `&&` to determine if the key pressed was between "a" and "z". Assuming that is true, the code immediately reaches `if C` to determine which side of the alphabet the letter resides on. Notice the `else` statement in bold above. This `else` follows two `if` statements. Which `if` owns this `else`? This is a classic ambiguous grammar problem in computer science. Java follows the popular convention of dictating that an **else** belongs to the closest preceding **if** statement. So the bolded else belongs to the **if C**. The indentation of the **else** statement (or any statement for that matter) is immaterial to the compiler.

The final **else** (nonbolded) belongs to the **if B** statement. The outer **if** owns the outer **else**, and the inner **if** owns the inner **else** (seems fair enough).

Just in Case

This section introduces the Java (and yes, effectively the C) **switch** statement. This statement is designed to provide an organized method of executing code associated with a discrete list of possibilities. Figure 6-3 shows its behavior.

Consider the code to print out a word for any vowel entered. You should immediately see how this can be done with **if** statements:

```
if (c == 'a') System.out.println("apple");
 else
if (c == 'e') System.out.println("eggplant");
 else
if (c == 'i') System.out.println("iris");
 else
if (c == 'o') System.out.println("orange");
 else
if (c == 'u') System.out.println("unyon");
 else
System.out.println("That is not a vowel");
```

Undeniably, this method will work correctly, but greater flexibility and organization can be attained by using the **switch** statement. In actuality, you should always be able to use **if** statements for any type of conditional checking, but often you'll find the **switch** statement to be better suited.

```
switch (c) {
        case 'a' : System.out.println("apple");
               break;
        case 'e' : System.out.println("eggplant");
               break;
        case 'i' : System.out.println("iris");
               break;
        case 'o' : System.out.println("orange");
               break;
        case 'u' : System.out.println("unyon");
               break;
        default  : System.out.println("That is not a vowel");
        }
```

As with the above **if** statements, the expression to be tested is the character variable **c**. Its value is compared against the list of possible values. A key point here is that once a **case** statement is matched (say **c == 'o'**), the program not only executes the

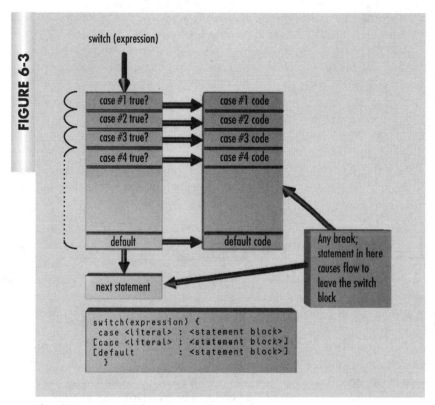

The `switch`/`case` statement

code for that value, but control is actually passed to that point. This is the reason for the **break** statement after each value's code. The **break** statement allows a positive match to execute the assigned code, then leaves the **switch** statement altogether. As soon as a **break** statement is reached, execution continues to the statement after the **switch** block.

If c equaled "o" the code above would print "orange" and exit the **switch** construct. However, if the **break** statement in bold was removed, i.e.,

```
case 'o' : System.out.println("orange");
case 'u' : System.out.println("unyon");
             break;
```

for c equal to "o" the code would now print "orange" followed by "unyon". This **case** statement *fall-through* can be deceptively useful, but it can also cause wonderfully disguised bugs if you forget **break** statements where they're supposed to be.

The **default** statement is optional but acts as a place to put code to be executed if all previous matches prove false. The **case** statements are limited to discrete values; in other words, you cannot specify a range of values. A `case` statement can only contain a single discrete literal (i.e., you can't even use a variable).

If your need satisfies these strict criteria, the `switch` is quite a useful statement. The flexibility of the `switch` allows you another conditional trick: you can assign several values to a section of code.

```
case 's' :
case 't' :
case 'u' : System.out.println("unyon");
              break;
```

Now the values "s", "t", or "u" will all print "unyon". `Switch` statements are a life saver for many situations. `If-else` blocks can get complex and difficult to follow. You quickly learn when and where to use each of these constructs.

 Loop: C Loop

Programs spend most of their time within loops. This shouldn't be any great surprise—how often is it useful for a game to put one dot on the screen or for a banking program to add one number together? Being able to act repeatedly over a set of data is a must in programming. Every usable programming language contains some form of looping, and Java's loop constructs could easily be mistaken for C/C++. Programmers of any popular programming language will undoubtedly immediately see similarities to their language's loop constructs.

Java contains three types of loop constructs, each having a typical purpose. This is not to say you can't force any loop to perform your task; you can. In fact, any of the loop constructs can be coerced to perform exactly like their brethren (possibly requiring the aid of some external statements). However, Java provides three loop constructs, so you typically won't need to do much coercion.

For Looping

Likely the best known and most commonly used loop construct is the `for` loop. The `for` loop is designed primarily as a means of executing the loop body a discrete number of times. In other words, it's usually based upon the desire to do something *x* number of times. The loop is quite well designed for this purpose; it comes with three built-in slots that typically indicate the start, stop, and means to get from one to the other. Figure 6-4 shows the general form and flow of control for the `for` loop.

The first slot contains any set of code that should be performed prior to the loop's actually beginning. This often includes the initialization of a *loop control variable,* i.e., the variable that controls the loop's actions. A typical example for this slot could be `g=1`. Also, it's quite common to use slot 1 to actually declare the loop control variable before initializing it—`int g=1`.

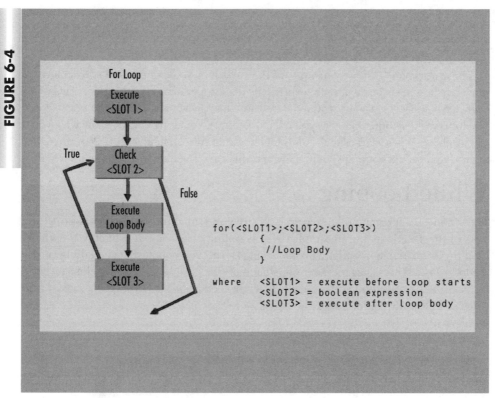

FIGURE 6-4

The `for` loop

The next slot is the *stop* condition for the loop. It is checked prior to each iteration including the first one, and as soon as it evaluates to false, the loop exits. Hence, this slot must contain some type of expression that returns a Boolean result. A typical example (one that would actually cause some looping) for this slot could be `g<10`.

The third slot is performed after each loop iteration and is typically used to modify the loop control variable. Here's an example of a working `for` loop:

```
for (int g=1; g<10; ++g)
  {
    System.out.println("Number: " + g);
  }
```

This loop prints "Number:" followed by the digits 1 to 9. The third slot contains `++g` in order to increment `g` after each iteration so it would eventually reach 10. Look at the following list of `for` loop statements that would perform effectively the same as the above statement.

```
for (int g=1; g<=9; ++g)      // less or equal 9 (i.e. < 10)
for (int g=0; ++g<10; )       // preincrement g
for (int g=1; g<10; g++)      // postincrement g
for (int g=1; g!=10; ++g)     // g is not equal to 10
```

These alternatives show you some of the variations you can use and still achieve the same result. The second example surprisingly does not even use the third slot. This is perfectly legal; in fact, you aren't required to use any slots (which would cause an infinite loop). The loop will perform exactly as you tell it; of course, you don't always know what you're talking about. If you aren't careful, your program could enter an infinite loop. Besides attempting to see how hot your CPU will really get, this isn't a characteristic usage for a loop.

While Looping

The second most common loop form is the `while` loop. This loop lacks the structured slots of the `for` loop, but its simplicity is its selling point. To put it plainly, the `while` loop performs the loop body while *something* is true. As soon as that something is false, the loop ends. This shares the `for` loop's habit of checking the condition before any looping goes on, so if the condition is initially false, the loop body will never get executed. Figure 6-5 shows the `while` loop.

FIGURE 6-5

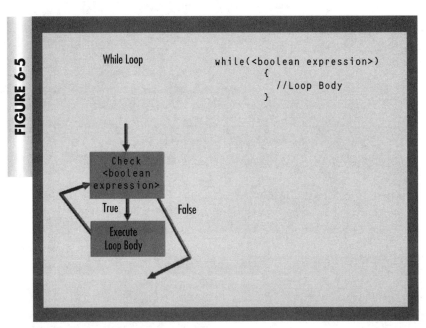

The `while` loop

The `while` loop allows tidy coding of loops that wait for a specific event. Understand that it's quite tangible to think of an event as something like "end-of-file" or "stack empty", but there's no reason it couldn't be some disgustingly long and sordid Boolean expression. As long as it evaluates to true or false, it can be treated as an event and it can be used as the Boolean expression for a `while` loop.

A `for` loop *could* be used for single event termination, but that tends to be overkill. The `for` loop specifically contains slots for initialization and control variable maintenance. A simple "keep going while file not empty" could easily leave slots one and three empty. This practice is not only a bit messy, it could certainly serve to confuse future maintainers/thieves of your code. Here's a simple standalone program using a `while` loop:

```
.
.
.

System.out.println("Hit the 'q' key to quit");

while (System.in.read() != 'q') {
        System.out.println("No! The 'q' key!");
}

System.out.println("Program quitting");
```

This program will wait until the correct key is entered before quitting. Using the `while` loop instead of the `for` loop makes much more intuitive sense. Especially since you can read that statement in English—"while the key entered is not equal to 'q', do the loop body."

Do Looping

The `do` loop in many ways resembles the `while` loop. In fact, the keyword `while` is present within it. As with the `while` loop, its continuation relies on the truth value of some event. What sets the `do` loop apart is that no matter what, the loop will always be executed at least once. This fact can be useful in many situations. Figure 6-6 shows the contrasting flow for the `do` loop.

It is evident from the syntax why the `do` loop executes the loop body in all cases. The check for the truth value on the `<boolean expression>` is not done until the end. This fact is largely what separates the `while` loop from the `do`. Figure 6-7 shows a comparison of all three loops and shows the loop best suited for each hypothetical operation.

All three loops perform the 1 to 1000 iteration with no problem; however, the `for` loop incorporates all aspects the cleanest. The read until end-of-file is oddly constructed with a `for`, and the `do` loop requires the usage of a guarding `if` statement to prevent an attempted read on an empty file. The final "enter passcode" example assumes that a user must enter a valid passcode before passing this point in the code. The `for` and `while` loops require the usage of a pre-read in order to check their condition the first time. The `do`'s ability to allow one unchecked iteration proves useful. The figure shows it is possible to do most anything with any loop; it just may require a little more fudging around.

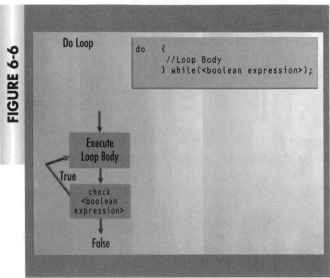

FIGURE 6-6

The do loop

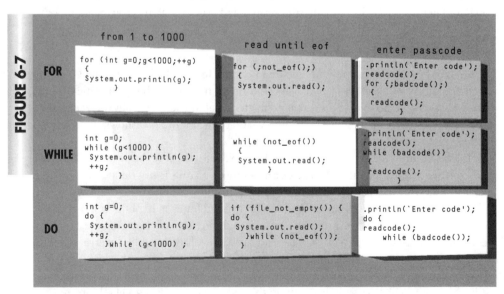

FIGURE 6-7

Comparing loops

Nesting Loops

Complex programs tend to breed complex loops. In fact, quite often you'll see the need to have loops inside of loops—i.e., nested loops. The sample application below prints out a multiplication table. The outer loop starts at one and goes to ten and the inner loop runs from one to whatever the outer loop happens to be for that iteration. The code is

```
for (int g=1;g<=10;++g) {              // outer loop
        for (int h=1;h<=g;++h) {       // inner loop
         System.out.print(g*h + " ");  // inner loop
 }
        System.out.println();          // outer loop
}
```

This code executes the inner loop in its entirety for each time the outer loop iterates. The empty space after the **g*h** expression is just there to ensure pretty spacing between the numbers. Also notice that statement is a **print**, not a **println**, in order to have ten well-formed rows rather than each product having its own line. The final statement **System.out.println**() forces a carriage return for each iteration of **g**.

As you get deeper into using arrays and data manipulation, heavily nested loops will be common in your code.

Checking Out Early

Java provides two main ways to *cheat* on loops. Effectively, the commands discussed here allow you to change the behavior of a loop irrespective of its initial starting and stopping criteria. Many argue usage of these types of commands violates the sacred rules of structured programming and can be a **goto** statement in disguise. (For those unfamiliar with **goto** statements, they are a lawless method to instantly change program flow and are rumored to be devices of evil planted within our society by aliens who are bent on earth's destruction.)

Please Continue

One of Java's loop flow-of-control modifiers is the **continue** statement. When the **continue** statement is reached inside a loop, the loop acts as if it has reached the end of the loop body and proceeds to the next iteration. Here is an example:

```
for (g=0; g<10; ++g) {
  System.out.print("The Number is: ");
  if (g>5) continue;
  System.out.println(g);
}
```

This loop would print out "The Number is: " followed by the value of the **g** variable six times. It will then proceed to print just "The Number is: " string four more times. When the `continue` statement is executed (every iteration when `g>5`), the `println(g)` statement is never reached.

```
The Number is: 0
The Number is: 1
The Number is: 2
The Number is: 3
The Number is: 4
The Number is: 5
The Number is: The Number is: The Number is: The Number is:
```

This method of loop cheating can certainly prove useful. However, if you find yourself using this technique a lot, you should probably rethink how you are designing your loops.

Another interesting point arises in the following situation:

```
for (h=0;h<5;++h) {
 for (g=0; g<10; ++g) {
  System.out.print("The Number is: ");
  if (g>5) continue;
  System.out.println(g);
  }
}
```

This code segment is simply the loop from above nested within an outer `h` loop. Much in the spirit of the dangling-`else` problem discussed earlier, one might now ask "Which of the two loops should the `continue` statement apply to?" This is more of a valid question than it may seem. If the language is already granting programmers the dubious ability to whimsically modify loop flow, given the above example, it makes perfect sense to be able to continue either of the two loops depending upon the application. So how can you specify to which loop the `continue` should apply?

Initially, let it be said that the above code segment will act as you would expect. The `continue` statement applies to the innermost loop. It's basically the same rule the dangling-`else` problem follows, apply to the closest proximity loop. A way to have the `continue` statement apply to the outer loop is through the use of a *label* (doesn't this reek of `goto`).

```
pg:     for (h=0;h<5;++h) {
         for (g=0; g<10; ++g) {
          System.out.print("The Number is: ");
          if (g>5) continue pg;
          System.out.println(g);
          }
        }
```

In Java you may label loops (i.e., give them a name) so that you can identify them to statements such as `continue`. Now the above example has labeled the outer loop `pg` and the `continue` statement is trailed by this label. This specifically tells this `continue` to apply to that loop, hence solving the problem of ambiguous loop continuation.

Break

Java also allows the use of the **break** statement. This statement allows the program to break out of the current loop. This is usually used to exit a loop for some uncommon reason (common loop termination should be within the stop condition) or to allow breaking out of several nested loops. Reworking the example from above:

```
for (g=0; g<10; ++g) {
  System.out.print("The Number is: ");
  if (g>5) break;
  System.out.println(g);
      }
```

The difference here is that the loop only prints the string "The Number is: " and the value of **g** six times. Then the loop exits. This action is a bit more final than the continuation statement and even more of a loop cheat. The output is

```
The Number is: 0
The Number is: 1
The Number is: 2
The Number is: 3
The Number is: 4
The Number is: 5
```

As with **continue** statements, you can also specify labels on **break** statements. The effect is the same; you specify which loop to break out of when there is a possible ambiguity. If you wish to only break out of the innermost loop, then no label is required.

You should also notice the usage of **break** on the **switch** statement discussed earlier. The **break** statement is really not exclusive to loops and applies to blocks of code in general. However, by far the most common uses are found in **switch** and loop blocks.

Summary

Hopefully, by now you've got a good feel for low-level Java programming. If you're relatively new to programming, be confident you have now seen a majority of Java's commands. If you're a C or Pascal guru, you've probably had no trouble looking through Java's constructs. The loops and conditional statements covered here are the backbone of most popular programming languages.

The chapters from here on out start to work more into what makes Java unique. In many respects the following chapters head to the higher levels of how Java code is put together. The next chapter extends Java's data types and looks at Java's interesting way of implementing arrays and strings. As with many things in Java, these relatively straightforward structures got caught in Java's object-oriented wave.

Questions

1. For the following situations, what would be better: an `if-else` block or a `switch` statement?

    a. Assign a grade to a student's percentage, i.e., >90 = A, 80-90 = B, etc.

    b. Decide which variable is larger, `x` or `y`.

    c. Determine if a user's keypress was a number or letter.

    d. From a user's input of an integer where the integer indicates a student number from 1 to 10, print the student's name.

2. Explain the following code:

```
if (a < 5)
  if (a < 3)
      System.out.println(" a is really small");
  else;
else System.out.println(" a might be big");
```

3. Why are these situations bad candidates to use a `switch` statement?

    a. Decide if a variable is between 1 and 100.

    b. Decide if a variable is equal to variables `a`, `b`, or `c`.

    c. Decide if a variable is equal to zero.

4. Rewrite the following statement as concisely as possible:

```
if ( (x > 10) && ( x < 50) )
{ if ( (x !=37) || (x == 5) ) ;
  else if (x == 15)
      System.out.println("Correct.");
}
```

5. What is the value of `x` after the following code segment?

```
x=10;
if (x = 3) x += 4;
```

6. Given the following `for` loop statements, give the range of numbers `g` will visit or label them as looping forever.

    a. for (g=0;g<0;g=g+10)   d. for (g=0; g>0; --g)

    b. for (g=99; g>0; ++g)   e. for (g=10;g!=10;++g)

    c. for (g=0; ; g++)   f. for (g=11;g!=10;++g)

7. Consider the example of the nested loop earlier in this chapter. What does the following code do? (Note that the assignment (h=0) performs two functions—it assigns 0 to h and returns a 0 for use in the "10 +" expression.)

```
public class MyStandAlone {

public static void main (String args[]) {

    for (int g=1,h=1;(h<=10)||(g++<=10+(h=0));++h) {

            System.out.print(g*h + " ");
            if (h==10) System.out.println();
    }
  }
}
```

8. Adding any variables you may need, can you duplicate the functionality of the following statement using only a **while** loop construct?

```
if (x>5) b=b+1;
```

(Hint: yes)

 # Exercises

1. Write a standalone program that will sort three integer variables in ascending order.

2. Write a standalone program to read in ten numbers, sum the input, and output the result.

3. Write a program to give users the choice of which loop construct they wish to run, then have your program execute one of three versions of Exercise 2 according to their choice.

4. Write a program to create a vertically scrolling landscape. The `System.out.println` function will provide the scrolling. You should continuously print out random length rows of "X"s.

Arrays and Strings

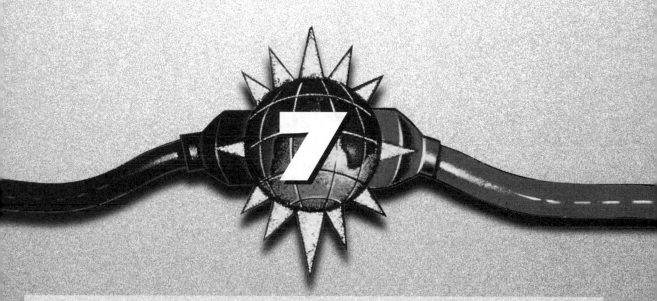

You will learn about the following in this chapter:

- What an array is in Java
- How arrays are related to objects
- How to make arrays of objects
- How to pass arrays as parameters to methods
- How Java handles strings
- When to use the `String` and the `StringBuffer` classes

117

Earlier chapters have covered the entire lot of Java's built-in data types. Although the list is relatively extensive, it's nowhere near enough for real-world use. As your trek through object-oriented programming continues, you'll be creating and manipulating an endless list of new data types. Whether you like it or not, complex programming will require you to expand the basic list that's been handed to you. Java's data types were designed more as a solid foundation than as any attempt at a complete list. The built-in data types will act as the building blocks for you to use to create more complex types.

This chapter looks at two data type structures that are not quite as obvious as the built-in data types. Any experienced programmer will tell you that few programs can be written without arrays and/or strings. Starting in this chapter, you'll notice Java begin to deviate from the programming practices of C and Pascal. You've seen what it borrowed from C; now you'll see what the designers wanted to make better.

Arrays

Arrays are an excellent way to organize large amounts of data in programs. As you'll see, if arrays didn't exist, many trivial applications would be horribly awkward because of the multitude of variable names. Think of the simple operation of storing a value in a variable; now extrapolate the problem to storing a thousand values. This becomes more troublesome. This section covers arrays in general and Java's object-oriented way of implementing and using them.

What's an Array?

Say you would like to write an applet that moves fifty dots in some creative fashion. You will need to store the current position of each dot (its x and y coordinates) so that you can move it with reference to its previous position at each iteration. Consider the silly bit of code below:

```
int ax,bx,cx,dx, ... ,zx,aax,bbx,ccx ... ;
int ay,by,cy,dy, ... ,zy,aay,bby,ccy ... ;


.
. // values are initialized
.

void movedots() {

        ax += movementx();          // movementx() moves the x
        bx += movementx();          //  coordinates
        cx += movementx();


        .
        .
        .


        ay += movementy();          // movementy() moves the y
        by += movementy();          //  coordinates
        cy += movementy();


        .
        .
        .

        }
```

Indeed. Not only would you be forced to declare fifty **x** variables and fifty **y** variables, you would need a hundred statements total to move them. What's worse is that the movement statements all basically do the same thing and seem to be just begging for a loop. Unfortunately, you can't really use a loop, since all the variable names are different—what could you loop through?

The x and y coordinates would best be represented in an *array*. An array is a way of allocating many like-typed variables and accessing them through one *array variable* name. The array variable name is a standard identifier that is augmented with an index value so you can specify which location in the possibly many values you wish to access. Figure 7-1 shows an example.

As you can see from the figure, the actual syntax of specifying an array and its index is the array name followed by a set of brackets with the index enclosed. The index may be a literal value or any legal integer expression. The ability to use an integer expression

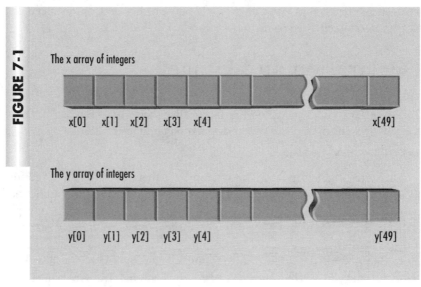

FIGURE 7-1

The x array of integers

x[0] x[1] x[2] x[3] x[4]   x[49]

The y array of integers

y[0] y[1] y[2] y[3] y[4]   y[49]

Array indexing

for the index is largely what makes arrays useful. This can be seen by rewriting the dot-moving code from above:

```
int x[] = new int[50];              // declare the arrays
int y[] = new int[50];

.
. // initialize the arrays
.

void movedots() {

      for (int g=0;g<50;++g) {
        x[g] += movementx();
        y[g] += movementy();
              }
      }
```

This code is worlds apart from the previous version. First, the arrays are declared and then they are initialized. The **movedots** method is much more compact and makes for infinitely better code. The **for** loop runs from 0 to 49 and applies the movement methods to the **x** and **y** array values.

The usefulness of arrays should be plainly obvious. They are invaluable in being able to process large amounts of data. What if the above problem had been 1,000 dots, or 10,000? The version without arrays would have become infeasible (even at 50 it was pretty darn annoying). The version with arrays would only need its declaration statements and loop stop expression changed to the new number of dots.

Declaration and Usage

The declaration of arrays in Java is unlike most other popular languages. This is primarily because Java's arrays are true objects (by now, that should be no surprise). Even its declaration has telltale signs of being an object declaration and instantiation.

```
int x[] = new int[50];
```

An interesting note to non-C programmers is that this array is indexed from `x[0]` to `x[49]`. In other words, from this declaration `x[50]` does not exist, but be comforted that 0 to 49 are still 50 actual elements. Another interesting note especially for C programmers is that in respect for program security, Java makes sure you do not overstep the legal array indices, i.e., it is range checked at run time. Any attempt at accessing the array with an index that is not in the defined range is immediately and harshly dealt with by a runtime error accusing you of being some type of greedy scoundrel. This is a distinct departure from the days of frivolous programming in languages such as C that let you attempt to access any array index with blatant disregard for trivialities such as the actual existence of that indexed element. Java's security controls are too strict to let that sort of thing happen.

An alternate form of array declaration is provided within Java. This method is primarily useful to make declarations of method types arrays look more intuitive. However, it is functionally equivalent to the syntax above. The following two statements are equivalent:

```
int x[] = new int[10];
int[] x = new int[10];
```

As you see, the only difference is the placement of the brackets. This looks slightly awkward for the above variable declaration, but consider the following method declarations:

```
public int inttable()[]
public int[] inttable()
```

Again they are equivalent, but the new form seems more organized. The parentheses immediately followed by the brackets could cause confusion, and the second declaration attempts to alleviate this.

Standard Construction

Possibly the most intriguing aspect that differentiates this declaration from object declarations/instantiations you are used to is that you do not follow the **new** keyword with a method that constructs the array object. Consider the following comparison:

```
Object someobject = new Object();        // Object() constructor
int somearray[] = new int[50];           // int[] isn't a
                                         //  constructor! is it?
```

You know that in the first statement the `new Object()` instantiates an object. If arrays are objects, then where does the instantiation take place? Well, the straight answer is—in the same place, i.e., with the `new` keyword. The only confusion is that arrays provide you an alternative syntax (`new int[50]`) to perform the array object creation. Be assured that this slightly unorthodox look basically fulfills the duties of instantiation and construction. This variation is not of any significant consequence and is mostly just something else you have to remember. It exists this way to create an intuitive (and familiar) way of indexing array elements.

The left side of the previous statement `int x[]` (or `int[] x`) tells the compiler to declare this array variable `x`, which will at some later time point to an array of integers. Well, that later time is quite soon, since the instantiation is also in the declaration (i.e., the right-hand side of the equal sign). The instantiation allocates memory for 50 integers and associates them to the array `x`. You are not required to instantiate the array within the declaration, but you'll find this practice common. For instance, the following two sets of statements produce the same end result:

```
// this form is the same as
int x[] = new int[10];

// this form.
int x[];
x = new int[10];
```

As with all objects, the declaration and instantiation can occur in different statements and at different times. You will see that fact is important for declaring varying sized arrays.

Immediate Initialization

Given an array's ability to hold large amounts of data, it's common for large amounts of data to come from a file or to be calculated. However, sometimes the amount of data isn't so vast and is known before run time. As with normal data types, you can initialize array types at instantiation. In fact, the implementation looks more like an initialization for some already existing structure, but rest assured that the instantiation is there; it's just hiding. The following statements declare, instantiate, and initialize the arrays:

```
int x[] = {1,2,3,4};        // initialize x to 4 int elements
char y[] = {'a','b','c'};    // initialize y to 3 char elements
```

This method is nice when you're able to use it. The size of the array is determined by the compiler from the number of elements within the brackets. This is the de facto standard way to enter relatively small tables of data into static (and typically constant) arrays.

Arrays Are Objects; So What?

The fact that arrays are objects affords them a certain degree of flexibility. Arrays can be any of the built-in types and can also be of another class type. In other words, you can have an array of objects. This is much more freedom than it appears. You now have the ability to create objects full of objects that the compiler views as "just a plain old object" (which it is).

The declaration of arrays as objects also allows you the ability for dynamic memory allocation. This stems from the fact that declaration and instantiation are distinct operations. If your program wants the user to input a certain number of values, but you won't know how many until the user actually runs the program, a dilemma arises. You can just allocate, say, 100 elements to your array and hope the user doesn't want to enter more. On the other hand, if the user only enters 60 elements, then 40 elements of your array are wasted. Sloppy memory management such as this will eventually catch up with you.

The following code handles the situation with a tad more elegance:

```
int thevalues[];            // declaration but no instantiation

x = how_many_values();      // the how_many_values() method will
                            // find out from the user how many
                            // values they wish to enter
thevalues = new int[x];     // instantiate the array with
                            // x elements
```

The instantiation is only made once the number of values is known. This way only the exact amount of memory you will need is allocated.

An array object also has a `length` variable associated with it. This variable always contains the number of elements of a given array. There is no action you need to do to create or maintain the `length` variable. It is inherent in array objects—all you need to do is use it. Any array's length can be determined by tacking `.length` on the end of the name:

```
int a[] = new int[5];

.
.
.

System.out.println(a.length); // prints out "5"
```

In small programs with fixed arrays this information is usually well known. However, as your programs increase in size and complexity, this technique proves useful.

Arrays of Objects

Creating an array of object elements (as opposed to arrays of built-in types which the discussion above focused on) takes one extra step. If you wanted to make an array of objects from a class called `Circle`, you could use the following statement:

```
Circle myarray[] = new Circle[50];
```

After that statement, you have indeed made an array ready to hold `Circle` objects. But consider that there are really two kinds of objects involved in the above statement. The `Circle` objects and the array object. First, think about the array object. With the above statement you have declared and instantiated it. It is an array ready to hold 50 elements of the type `Circle`.

The next thing to consider is the `Circle` objects themselves. Although you have declared a place for 50 `Circle` objects, you have not instantiated any. You must instantiate the `Circle` objects with subsequent code such as

```
for (int g=0;g<49;++g) {

  myarray[g] = new Circle();

}
```

This will loop through the array instantiating a `Circle` object for each element. Don't forget to perform the instantiations for the elements of the array, since without doing so all you have is an array of pointers that are *ready* to point to some objects. This extra step was not required with the arrays of built-in data types seen earlier in this chapter, because built-in data types don't need instantiation. In other words, to bring an integer variable into existence, all you need to do is declare it. To bring an object into existence you need to declare it and instantiate it.

Invisible Pointers

Arrays and memory pointers have often had a close relationship in programming. It is a logical idea that an array name points to some contiguous memory that holds all these values, as in Figure 7-2.

FIGURE 7-2

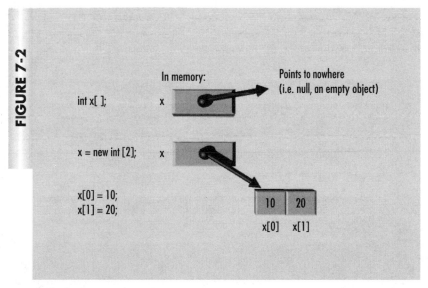

Pointing to an array

Although Java uses pointers to keep track of its arrays, that fact is not for your consumption—never is the programmer allowed to explicitly manipulate a pointer value. This is done for the same reason as bounds checking on arrays, i.e., security. In other words, you can generally have all the memory you want, but Java will manage it for you and never let you even try to see someone else's. To most programmers this is somewhat useful, as Java will carry the burden of finding memory for you and accessing it via the indices you provide. Possibly, some wayward C programmers will find this limiting. In any case, it was a wise security decision on the part of the designers to hide actual memory pointers from the programmers, and it is also assured to weed out a load of errors in seemingly correct C code that people end up porting to Java.

Entering a New Dimension

There is no question as to the usefulness of arrays as outlined above. However, there are cases where adding more dimensions to an array is equally useful. Consider the problem of an array to hold student grades (A through F). There are 10 classes with 100 students in each. Expressing this as a single dimensional array is possible but awkward. Java provides you the ability to have *multidimensional* arrays. For the student example, you would need a two-dimensional array, declared as

```
char student[][] = new char[10][100];
```

This arrangement is represented graphically in Figure 7-3. You can think of a single-dimension array as a row of values, a double-dimension as a grid of values, a triple-dimension array as a cube of values, etc. Very rarely will you find the need to go beyond three or four dimensions.

As in the C language, the underlying representation of a two-dimensional array is actually an array of pointers that point to the data. This information is of less value in Java given its dedication to hiding pointers from the programmer.

Because of Java's firm, albeit hidden, use of pointers to its arrays, tricks concerning otherwise impossible dynamic memory allocation can take place. The following code example does something quite unique:

```
int a[][] = new int[5][];

    .
    .
    .

a[0] = new int[10];
a[1] = new int[3];
a[2] = new int[99];
a[3] = new int[5];
a[4] = new int[10];
```

Because of Java's pointer structure you can instantiate the arrays as having different lengths for each row. This is not to say this can't be done in a language such as C; it can,

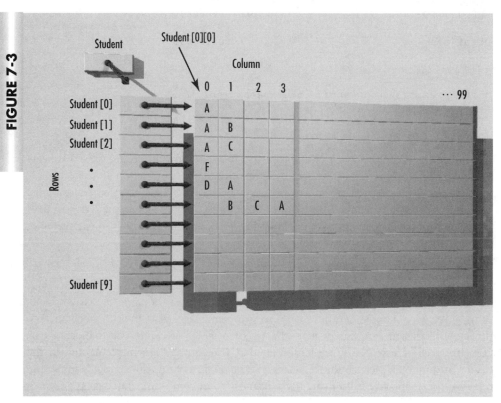

FIGURE 7-3

Dimensioned arrays

but typically it involves the explicit use of pointers, lacking a trifle of the elegance displayed above. Best of all, Java is completely garbage collected, so no matter what mess you make with occluded allocations as above, when you're ready to end the program, just do it. The Java environment will clean up after you.

Postal Arrays

Since arrays are true objects, it's possible to send them as parameters to methods. The following code sends the **a** array to the method, which accepts it as **x**. The **a** array is sent without any brackets, since the compiler already knows it's an array. The **x** array is specified with brackets (empty) to indicate to the compiler this method expects an array. Heed the distinction between a simple type and an array of that type. The identifier **a** is an integer array, but **a[3]** is just an integer.

```
/* the main method */
static public void main(String args[]) {
  int a[] = new int[5];
```

continued on next page

continued from previous page

```
   a[3] = 99;                          // set a[3] to 99

postal(a);                             // call postal

}

/* the postal method (array input parameter) */
static void postal(int x[]) {
  System.out.println(x[3]);            // print x[3]
 }
```

The output is expectedly 99. A fact that seriously affects how arrays are passed is Java's underlying reference to the array. This isn't the normal implementation of arrays in C. It is possible to allocate a pointer to an array in C (and effectively emulate Java's implementation) but a normal C array name is a compile-time label for the bulk of memory and doesn't really exist at runtime. Passing objects in general will be considered further in Chapter 9.

The String Class

Strings are usually thought of as a sequence of characters, i.e., a name, a password, etc. An intuitive way of implementing strings in many languages is as an array of characters. Although the designers may deny it and have scores of high-level methods to hide it, Java's **String** class is essentially implemented that way. Strings are implemented in the **java.lang** prebuilt package, and the class boasts a hard set of rules for its use. Using strings in Java is quite different from using them in most other computing languages.

Don't Hate Me Because I'm Immutable

Well, here goes: According to the language specification, after a string is created in Java, it may *not* change. Pretty much kills the whole idea of a *variable* doesn't it? Well, this implementation surely runs the programmer through a few dance steps in order to perform many simple functions, but this fact allows the compiler to make some assumptions and affords the **String** class some powerful abilities.

Don't get immediately discouraged with Java's strings; the next section covers the **java.lang.StringBuffer** class, which allows for strings that are somewhat more amiable to manipulation but at the cost of more computer time. The quick rule is: If you can get away with just a **String**, do so—if you cannot, use **StringBuffer**.

Implicit Instantiation

Declaration and instantiation of strings is identical to what you've seen from previous sections of this text. But as with arrays, some peculiar things can happen with instantiation. The following two lines are completely legal **String** object declarations and instantiations (i.e., and initializations) and produce the same final result:

```
String myname = new String("Paul Tyma");
String myname = "Paul Tyma";
```

The first is the conventional way and the second is a slightly leaner and meaner version. A more important fact concerning this shorter version is that it is *faster*. The `String` class can instantiate a string simply by seeing a quote-string-quote sequence. This ability is a true instantiation and turns out to be a bit of a Midas touch. In the right context, this sequence always induces a string instantiation. With this information it's evident that the longer version above ends up instantiating the "Paul Tyma" string twice. Once upon sight of the "Paul Tyma" and once again using the formal `new String()` constructor. The formal constructor version is actually instantiating a new version of an existing string. This extra instantiation is wasteful and shouldn't be performed. Stick with the short version for string literal instantiations.

More Constructors

The `String` class implements several other constructors for your instantiating pleasure. You can use an array of characters or an array of bytes to instantiate a string. The character array instantiation is a testament to the `String` class's underlying implementation.

```
char x[] = {'A','B','C'};
String xstring = new String(x);
```

That code should be pretty straightforward; it creates an object named `xstring` that contains "ABC". The designers stress at this point that you should not change the character array anymore. As if the array has caught some dreaded immutability disease from the string. Defying authority, you can change the character array after these statements and in effect, change the unchangeable string. Although this practice may seem to work, it is not an official usage and heaven only knows what havoc you may cause to the underlying representation. This practice also seriously jeopardizes the `String` class's guarantee of immutability to any process that may access it. To sum it up—bad idea.

Scads of Methods

The full list of methods for the `java.lang.String` class is available in the Appendix. Several of the more interesting ones are addressed here. Supporting the notion of the string being unchangeable is a collection of read-only methods. These methods provide you information using strings that make no attempt to make a modification. Below is a code segment illustrating some important string methods. Anyone familiar with strings in any language will see similarities.

```
int i;
boolean b;
String myString = "TallyHo";
```

continued on next page

continued from previous page

```
// case sensitive comparison (b==false)
b = myString.equals("tallyho");

// case insensitive comparison (b==true)
b = myString.equalsIgnoreCase("tallyho");

// finds first occurrence of a character (i==2)
i = myString.indexOf('l');

// finds last occurrence of a character (i==3)
i = myString.lastIndexOf('l');

// finds first occurrence of a string (i==5)
i = myString.indexOf("Ho");

// returns a substring of the original (Santa=="Ho")
String Santa = myString.substring(i);

// modifies and returns the original string concatenated with
// the parameter string (Santa == "HoHoHo")
// Note: this uses StringBuffers to do the work
Santa = Santa.concat(Santa).concat(Santa);
```

The `String` class is not quite as unchangeable as it was intended. Several methods exist that even allow pseudo-modification. It's pseudo because the `String` object is actually converted to a `StringBuffer`, manipulated, and then brought back. This is costly, but seemingly transparent.

The StringBuffer Class

The `java.lang` package also includes a class called `StringBuffer`. This class differs externally from `String` by officially being changeable and providing some usable methods to accomplish this. However, it doesn't include the useful comparison facilities of the `String` class. It differs internally by having the ability to dynamically increase its size if needed. The `StringBuffer` class is not meant to be shared (it can be changed) and thus has many fewer rules governing its use. The class is often used as an intermediary for methods in the `String` class that appear to change a string.

The point should be noted, ignoring performance issues, that `String` objects and `StringBuffer` objects can be converted to each other with relative ease. This usually only involves the class toggling a flag. Somehow, careless switching back and forth seems to be a taboo, but it's done plenty within Java's APIs. In fact, there are clean-cut ways to move from one to the other when you need to.

The need for a comprehensive ability to manipulate strings requires the usage of this class. It does provide many methods that would have to be user written in C or Pascal. This flexibility is the class's strongest asset.

Constructors

The list of constructors for this class is actually more limited than in the `String` class. Overall, that makes sense, since you're pretty free to do whatever you wish with a `StringBuffer` object once it's created—the presence of flashy constructors is unneeded. There are three constructors for the `StringBuffer` class. One creates an object of zero length (i.e., an empty `StringBuffer`), the second creates an object of a specified integer length, and the third creates an object from an input string.

```
StringBuffer x = new StringBuffer();        // empty SB
StringBuffer y = new StringBuffer(4);       // SB size 4
StringBuffer z = new StringBuffer("HI");    // SB size 2
```

The ability to create an empty `StringBuffer` can be more useful than the constructor that creates an empty `String`. Although the `StringBuffer` brags of the ability to dynamically increase its size, this operation is costly. It's quite important to attempt to instantiate your `StringBuffer` objects with a good estimate of the size you think you'll need (even an empty buffer has some room ready and is waiting to receive characters). Of course, you won't always be right, and sometimes you'll need more than you guessed—no problem, the class is there to serve and will allocate the needed memory. It's just best to avoid that situation when possible. The second constructor above is well suited to instantiating a `StringBuffer` of your estimated size.

Possibly as vehemently as the `String` class insists its objects will not change, the `StringBuffer` class insists its objects will. If you use a `StringBuffer` and never change it, you're probably using the wrong class.

Bufferage

Actually, you're already an old hand at `StringBuffer` objects. Java uses them under the covers all over the place. The simple statement

```
System.out.println("The value is: " + 10);
```

uses `StringBuffer` objects to allocate and manipulate those two elements into one `StringBuffer`. The following code example displays some more of its capabilities:

```
int i;
boolean b;
char c;
StringBuffer mySBuffer = new StringBuffer("TallyHo");

// append the parameter string to the StringBuffer
// (mySBuffer=="TallyHoho")
mySBuffer.append("ho");

// returns capacity of the buffer - this number reflects the
// amount of storage currently allocated.
i = mySBuffer.capacity();
```

continued on next page

continued from previous page

```
// returns the char at the specified location (c=='H')
c = mySBuffer.charAt(5);

// inserts a character into the buffer
// (mySBuffer=="Tally Hoho")
mySBuffer.insert(5,' ');

// inserts a String into the buffer
// (mySBuffer=="Tally Ho - ho")
mySBuffer.insert(8," - ");

// returns the character count of the buffer (i==13)
i = mySBuffer.length();

// sets the length of the buffer (mySBuffer=="Tally Ho")
mySBuffer.setLength(8);
```

The `StringBuffer` class's underlying representation is basically the same as the `String` class. Two things largely set it apart: it does not guarantee to the compiler, nor any running processes, that it will remain constant in any way, and if it needs to increase in size on the fly, it has that ability built in.

In the long run, it's best to use the `java.lang.String` class when you can. `StringBuffer` objects have already found their place in Java's APIs as intermediate string manipulation tools. This is likely where you'll find them useful too.

Summary

This chapter was a concise overview of two extremely important Java objects, arrays and strings. It should now be obvious where these structures can be used in your code. As your programs become more graphical, the string classes' importance will shift from printed strings to using them as passed parameters (a common usage in the API classes). Arrays are mandatory in everything from your browser's hotlist to the coordinates of all your enemy's spaceships. For experienced programmers, Java's unique implementation is something to get used to, but it quickly becomes intuitive for all.

The next chapter takes a cold, hard look at methods; their declaration, usage, and features. Then, using arrays from this chapter, you'll build a basic browser applet from start to finish. You really have all the taken-for-granted data types behind you—from here out, all that's left are objects! Of course, that's kind of saying you've conquered the world, but welcome to the universe.

Questions

1. Write a statement to declare and instantiate an array to hold student numbers in different courses at different colleges. There are up to 100 students per class, up to 200 courses per college, and there are 15 colleges.

2. How many total students could be stored in the array from Question 1?

3. The following code segment prints out 10. Why does this work? What is the **b** array after this code?

```
int a[][] = new int[10][10];
int b[];

b = a[3];
a[3][5] = 10;

System.out.println(b[5]);
```

(Hint: See Figure 7-3.)

4. What does the **c** array contain after the following code segment?

```
int g;
char c[] = {'c', 'x', 'a', 'm', 'x', ' ', ' '};

for (g=0;g<c.length;++g)
  if (c[g] == 'x') c[g] = 'e';

for (g--;g>1;--g) c[g] = c[g-1];

c[1] = c[6] = 'r';
```

5. What are the errors in this code segment?

```
int g;
int a[] = int[10];
int[] b = int[11];

for (g=1;g<=10;++g)
   a[g] = b[g] = g;

a = b = new int[50];
for (g=0;g<10;++g) System.out.println(a[g]);
```

6. Consider the following code:

```
int x[] = new int[10];
int y[] = new int[10];

.
. // code that initializes x and y
.

x=y;
```

After this point, **x** and **y** point to the same array. Assume you wanted the original **x** array back. Can you reassign **x** to it? Where is it?

7. Consider Figure 7-3. What would that figure look like for an array of three dimensions?

8. Assuming this statement is legal, what must it be referring to?

```
country[23].region[10].city[2] = "Kosice";
```

 # Exercises

1. Write a program to sort an array of a thousand integers. Use random numbers to initially fill the array.

2. Use your sort routine from Exercise 1 to sort a double-dimension array (i.e., 100 by 100) by column, then by row. You should first sort each row as a separate entity. Then sort the array by using the first element of each row as the sorting criterion. You can use pointer assignments to switch the rows around in the second step. Use random numbers to initially fill the array.

3. Write a method called `delete(int x, String S)` that returns the input string with the xth element removed. Use a conversion to a `StringBuffer` object to accomplish the task.

4. Write a program that prompts the user for a string. Print out whether the string entered was a file name, person's name, street address, or unknown according to the following criteria:

> **file name:** Will be a sequence of characters with no spaces and will have a period somewhere in the middle
>
> **person's name:** Will be two or more sequences of characters separated by a space, no numbers
>
> **street address:** Will be two or more sequences of characters where the first sequence is only numbers
>
> **unknown:** Everything else

Designer Methods

8

You will learn about the following in this chapter:

- The ins and outs of Java's parameter passing
- How to modularize your code
- When to rely on recursive methods
- What a Java constructor is
- The modifiers that affect method behavior
- How to begin programming with threads

Methods are everything. Yes, you read earlier that variables or iteration or conditional execution were everything—but those were all lies just to get you to read the sections more carefully; *this* is the truth. Everything that happens in Java happens in methods. Their design is crucial to the efficiency, correctness, and maintainability of your programs. Object-oriented programming relies on objects being aware of how to perform functions within their context. Sensibly designing your methods will give other programmers the ability to use your classes easily and efficiently.

You've already had an introduction to method usage in earlier chapters; here you'll solidify the concepts and encounter yet more magic. At the end of this chapter you'll create a real-time graphical applet that ties together the concepts you've learned. Even for a simple applet, the code will be much more involved than you have seen so far. Good-bye "Hello World."

More on Methods

You've already seen most of the important constructs in Java. This gives you a good background to take a closer look at methods. Once again, methods define the behavior of your classes. They contain the code that actually gets run in your program. There are many rules for using methods. As with functions in C and Pascal, the general modularization ideas are the same, but methods tend to be more tightly knit into the scheme of class structure. This influences their design and operation. This chapter will present additional concepts about methods and will hopefully give you an idea on how to best use them.

What Goes In...

A method is often defined with a list of input parameters. This list indicates what input values the method needs/wants/yearns for in order to perform its task. Regardless of whether all the parameters will actually be used, a caller must provide the list exactly as the method expects it. As far as the method is concerned, parameters are variable declarations with the added bonus that all these variables are initialized before the method begins.

Parameters are usually thought of as one of the data types described in Chapter 5. That's true much of the time, but keep in mind that this is an object-oriented language, and because of this fact, objects themselves may be passed as parameters. To C or Pascal programmers this is distantly analogous to passing a structure or a record as a parameter. This chapter will later use this idea as it touches upon the thread concept.

Methods in Java are call-by-value. That is, only a value is sent from caller to callee, and the callee method creates a new variable within its scope to hold the value. Any modifications to the variable within the callee method do not affect the value in the outside world. Figure 8-1 illustrates this point.

A simple example could be that of a method that calculates the future value of a principal amount of money.

```
float calc_future (float principal, float interest, int years)
```

FIGURE 8-1

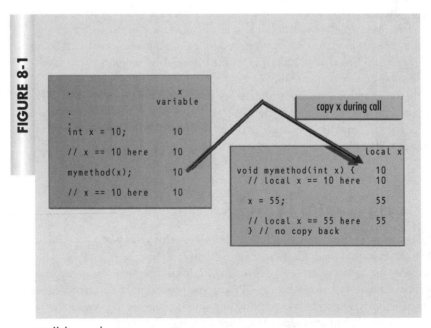

Call-by-value

This method takes as input a **float** variable **principal**, a **float** variable **interest**, and an **int** variable **years**. For the **principal** and **interest** variables, the decision to make these **float** and not **double** is relatively straightforward. Making them all **double** is likely overkill, since money transactions usually round to some hundredths value. Obviously, the **years** variable would have to be floating point if the calculation wishes to consider fractional years, but for simplicity assume that only time periods of whole years are considered.

...Must Come Out

The **calc_future** method also returns a value (it would be kind of useless if it didn't). Returning a value from a method is accomplished with the **return** statement. In general, the **return** statement restores program control back to the caller and can return a value. It is imperative that the value returned be the same type as the method's. If the method is of type **void,** then nothing is returned, and even the use of the **return** statement is optional (the end of the method will act as an implicit return).

Returning a value from a method purports the illusion that the method itself has a type, when in effect, it only has a **return** statement that returns a value of that type.

The **calc_future** method's return type is **float**, since the value will pertain to money (see Figure 8-2). What this tells you is that the last statement executed in that method should

FIGURE 8-2

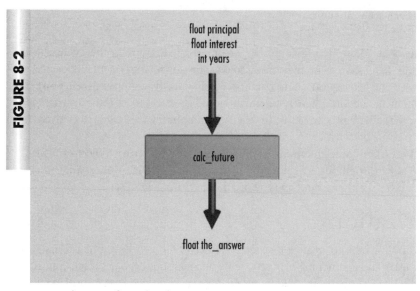

float principal
float interest
int years

calc_future

float the_answer

Ins and outs of methods

be a `return` statement with a floating point expression after it. The `calc_future` method from above may look like this:

```
float calc_future (float principal, float interest, int years)
        {
            float the_answer = principal;

            for (int y=0; y < years; ++y)
                    the_answer += the_answer * interest;

            return the_answer;
        }
```

Wow, rocket science. The `return` statement in this case is at the end of the method. Although this is a typical implementation, it is not a mandatory one. You could have additional `return` statements throughout the method if need be. They can be used much in the spirit of the cheating `break` statement for a fast exit out of a method.

```
float calc_future (float principal, float interest, int years)
            {
        if (principal == 0.0) return 0.0;

        float the_answer = principal;

        for (int y=0; y < years; ++y)
                the_answer += the_answer * interest;

        return the_answer;
    }
```

The statement in bold above bypasses any superfluous calculations in the event the principal is input as zero. There is no real reason to perform any further calculation, since scarcely anyone will pay interest on a zero balance. So, akin to the actions of the `break` statement, no statements beyond the `if` statement would get executed if the principal is zero. Incidentally, the caller has no idea this premature exit from the method has occurred. It will still receive its answer, which in this case is zero.

Continuing the earlier aside, methods are also permitted to return objects to the caller. For the most part, methods are defined quite the same as their counterparts, data elements. They can be of either a built-in type or an object (i.e., class) type.

Modularization

So far, decisions about where to create a method have been relatively easy, but as classes become more complex, the partitioning of functionality into methods becomes more important and more difficult. The question could be posed, given a class's need to perform many functions, how many methods and what kind of methods should be built? In almost every case there is more than one right answer, but also in every case there is more than one wrong answer.

Here are some general rules to follow for method creation:

- If you find multiple methods in your class needing the same piece of code, that code probably warrants its own method.

- If you have a method that is getting too large, breaking it up into smaller methods would improve readability and provide the ability for parts of it to be reused later. Note that what is considered too large a piece of code is a subject of debate; some consider 25 lines a good limit, others simply claim it is too large as soon as it becomes difficult to follow.

- Functionality that is "logically different" should usually be in separate methods. Although you must first draw points in order to draw a line, code to draw points would likely be in another method instead of embedded within the line drawing code.

Calling Yourself

"Hello? Am I there?" A concept that makes theorists and structured programming purists all giddy is called *recursion*. In this context, recursion is defined as the act of a method calling itself. Although this idea seems to be along the lines of throwing another shovelful of manure on the pile to try to cover up the smell, its usefulness in programming can be extraordinary. Recursion often takes what would have been a rather long and drawn-out iterative routine and compacts it down into a tight, well-structured, and pretty darn slow piece of code. The concept is initially a bit daunting, but as you become accustomed to it, using it actually simplifies your code. If you still don't understand recursion, read this paragraph again (and again).

Not to be outdone by every other programming book (with recursion examples) on the planet and likely in the known universe, here is a an example of a factorial method written in Java:

```
long factorial (int value) {
        if (value <= 1) return 1L;
        return value*factorial(value-1);
        }
```

In case anyone has doubted Java's astounding similarity to C so far, this code should convince them. Apart from being valid Java code, it is also perfectly valid C code. There is no question the code is tight and elegant. In fact, the code could even be tighter by removing the **if** statement and rewriting the last **return** statement using the **?:** operator. Examine what the code is doing. Assume it was called with a value of eight. The **if** statement fails since eight is not equal to one, so the code attempts to return eight * **factorial**(seven). But before it may do that, it needs to know what **factorial**(seven) will be, so it calls itself again, this time with a parameter of seven. This dilemma occurs continuously until **factorial** gets called with an input of one. At that point the intercepting **if** statement stops this recursive madness and just returns one. Now the loop unravels and all the previous equations waiting for their `factorial(?)` part to be resolved get their values and return the products of their multiplications one by one until finally the original call returns the final value. Figure 8-3 shows this graphically.

As you see, the trick is that each recursive call passes a different parameter and that there is a safety valve that stopped the recursion and allowed it to unwind. Whereas it may occasionally be useful to have an infinite loop, infinite recursion is guaranteed to add another line to the system crash log file (hopefully through the usage of some well-designed standard error redirection routine).

The iterative version of factorial could be written as

```
long factorial (int value) {
        long work=1L;

        for (long g=2;g<=value;++g)
          work *= g;

        return work;
        }
```

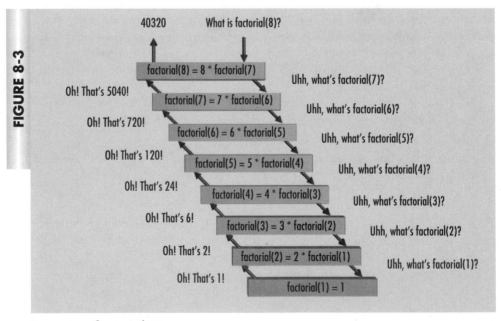

FIGURE 8-3

Recursing factorial(8)

This iterative code example really isn't too difficult. However, as your code becomes more complex, you will definitely see areas where recursion can seriously clean up and tighten your code. A downside to recursion is that the additional processing time of calling many extra functions can be noticeable. The iterative version above (in interpreted Java) runs in approximately three-quarters of the time the recursive method does.

In actuality, if you have code that repeatedly needs factorials, you would be silly to have such a method anyway. Because of factorials' extreme rate of growth, the factorial for 26 will be the first to overflow even a long variable. If you'll really need a lot of factorial calculations, it would be best to precalculate all factorials up to 25 and store them. From then on you can reference them from storage.

Java's Method

The previous discussion could largely apply to functions/methods/procedures of many computer languages. From here on the discussion will focus on aspects that are a bit more Java oriented (although only in a few cases are they Java exclusive). Methods are of course key ingredients in an object-oriented language, and their role there will soon become more apparent.

Constructors

Simply put, *constructors* are methods that primarily perform initialization tasks for an object. They are implicitly called upon the instantiation of a new object for a given class.

Constructing Constructors

There are two distinguishing features that identify a method as a constructor. First, it has no return type. Second, it must be named exactly the same as the class name. Figure 8-4 dissects a declaration and instantiation of a new object for a graphical animation class **Animator**. The declaration of the constructor within the class would be

```
class Animator {

Images images[10];

/* The Animator constructor */
  public Animator () {

      // read in all images

      }

  }
```

FIGURE 8-4

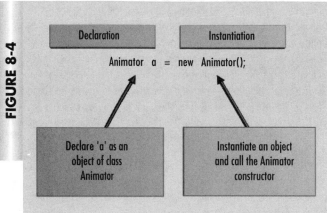

Instantiation and constructor calling

The call of the constructor is not completely implicit. In fact, the call seems to take place right after the **new** keyword. Another key point is that given the **Animator** class and its constructor, which will supposedly read in the images, how does it know (given it could be involved in initializing hundreds of different animations) what disk files hold the images? You'll likely need to pass it a file name (or better yet a file name stub that the code can add an increasing integer to, in order to read all the images, i.e., image1, image2, etc.). This is not a problem—constructors use parameters in the same way as regular methods. Reworking the above code:

```
Animator a = new Animator(the_filestub);

   .
   .
   .

class Animator {

  Images images[10];

/* The Animator Constructor */
  public Animator (String filestub) {

      // read in all images using filestub

      }

   }
```

The purpose of the constructor is to do whatever is necessary to initialize an object. Possibly more precisely, its purpose could be to do as much as it can to set up an object at this early stage.

Call Your Parents

If you define a class without a constructor, Java automatically puts in a default constructor for you. That constructor will take the form

```
/* The default constructor */
yourClass () {
  // call my parent's constructor - i.e. parent()
}
```

All this constructor does is call the parent's class constructor. Since all classes must be the
child of some class (with the notable exception of `java.lang.Object`, which is the parent of all classes), this call is always legal.

In fact, any constructor you create must have as its first action a call to some other constructor. Java uses the class's parent's constructor as the default. You can specify this call
explicitly, or if you don't, Java inserts one for you. The following code illustrates the point:

```
/* the Parent class */
class Parent {

/* Parent's constructor */
  Parent() {
          System.out.println("Parent");
          }
 }

/* The child class */
class Child extends Parent {

/* Child's constructor */
  Child() {
     // involuntary call to Parent's constructor
     System.out.println("Child");
    }
}
```

Since the call to the parent's constructor happens whether you like it or not, the output from instantiating a child object would be

```
Parent
Child
```

Java insists that every constructor must call another constructor as its first action; if you
don't specify one, it uses the parent's default (no parameters) constructor. If you do specify a different constructor to be called (as the first statement of your constructor), you will
have appeased Java and it will not perform the default call to the parent's constructor. Examples
of how to call alternate constructors will be discussed in Chapter 10.

A final note: If the parent did not have a default constructor in the previous code (i.e.,
it had only constructors that required input parameters), then a compiler error would be
generated. This would be because Java blindly inserted a call to the parent's default constructor and didn't find the default constructor in the parent class.

Method Modifiers

Java also provides you with the means to change the abilities or nature of a method through the use of method modifiers. Modifiers are specified before the method name in the declaration (the same place as the method return type). Many of the modifiers listed below have significant ramifications that are covered in other sections of this book. This listing provides a brief overview of each modifier and directs the reader to more information when applicable.

Native

Oddly enough, methods marked as `native` are methods that are not Java methods at all. They are, in fact, methods that have a system-specific implementation. Typically, this translates to calling system-specific C code from within your Java program. The use of native methods largely spoils the brilliant architecture independence that Java holds so dear. This usage should be done sparingly and generally avoided if possible. Chapter 16 covers this topic in depth.

Abstract

Methods defined as abstract have several interesting features. First off, any class that defines a method as `abstract` lists the method declaration followed by a semicolon—i.e., *no* actual method code. The actual implementation of the method occurs in the children of the declaring class. This is bizarre, to say the least. The use of an `abstract` method is to force all subclasses of a class to implement that method. Use of abstract methods (and subsequently classes) is key in the quest for good object-oriented programming. This is discussed further in Chapter 10.

Final

A method marked as `final` indicates that the method may not be overridden by any mischievous subclasses. The method is, as stated, the *final* implementation of this named method within this class hierarchy. This modifier can be used to guarantee a certain method is performed as you intend it to be, i.e., if you insist that all errors in your class go to a file named error.log, you could hardcode this in a final `alloc_error_file` method. Also, declaring a method as final allows the compiler to make some assumptions that typically result in faster code.

Synchronized

`Synchronized` methods are primarily of interest in the context of threads. Threads are covered in Chapter 14.

Public, Private, Protected

These modifiers relate to the *visibility* of a method. This dictates which type of class (i.e., the current one, children, foreign classes) can use or even attempt to use the method. This concept extends into data as well and has deep roots in the entire concept of designing classes. Chapter 9 discusses these modifiers further.

Static

You've already seen the `static` modifier as applied to variables. When a variable is labeled `static`, only one copy exists for all objects within that class. This concept extends to methods in that a `static` method belongs to the class instead of to individual objects.

Creating Applets

With most of Java's low-level constructs and the complex world of method making behind you, it's time to build a representative Java applet. The applet will incorporate many of the concepts illustrated in the preceding chapters and will give a good base to begin designing your own graphical applets.

A Couple of Classes

Since this applet will be doing something having at least a semblance of significance, a class will be defined to encapsulate most of the functionality.

```
class aline {                    // a line class

int x[] = new int[2];            // endpoint x coordinates
int y[] = new int[2];            // endpoint y coordinates

/* The aline constructor */
public aline (int maxval) {

        halfmax = maxval/2;

/* Set the endpoints */
        y[0] = x[0] = (int)(Math.random() * halfmax);
        y[1] = x[1] = -x[0];
        }
}
```

First off, notice this class has no way to run on its own. This is the way most of your classes will look; only one class in your program will be the *runnable* one. All the rest will be the supporting classes, and usually you will need a lot of supporting classes.

The only method present in this class is the `aline` method, which is the constructor. The `aline` constructor has a parameter that indicates the maximum value for both x and y coordinates. Half that value is used in the random statement to create endpoints for the line. Whenever another class creates an instantiation of **aline**, the constructor is automatically called. An instantiation for **aline** could look like this:

```
aline myline = new aline(100);
```

The constructor initializes the class's endpoint arrays to random numbers below or equal to **halfmax**. These variables assumedly will hold the endpoints of a line with respect to some origin. The maximum value is passed to the constructor as a way of confining the line to a given maximum size. Therefore, any class wishing to use this line class need only send a value somewhat smaller than its window size and be confident the line created by the **aline** class will not fall out of its window. Figure 8-5 illustrates the setup.

Now that the constructor is set, another method can be added to manipulate the line.

```
class aline {                          // a line class

        int x[] = new int[2];          // endpoint x coordinates
        int y[] = new int[2];          // endpoint y coordinates

        int rx[] = new int[2];         // rotated endpoint x
        int ry[] = new int[2];         // rotated endpoint y

        int halfmax;

/* The aline constructor */
public aline (int maxval) {

        halfmax = maxval/2;

/* Set the endpoints */
        y[0] = x[0] = (int)(Math.random() * halfmax);
        y[1] = x[1] = -x[0];
        }

/* The rotate method */
public void rotate (int angle) {

        float radangle;

/* Make sure the angle is from 0 to 359 */
        while (angle<0) angle += 360;
        angle = angle%360;

/* Convert from degrees to radians */
        radangle = angle * 0.017453F;   // approximately PI/180

/* Use the magic of sine & cosine to rotate the points */
        for (int g=0;g<2;++g) {
            rx[g] = (int)(Math.sin(radangle) * x[g]) + halfmax;
            ry[g] = (int)(Math.cos(radangle) * y[g]) + halfmax;
            }
        }
}
```

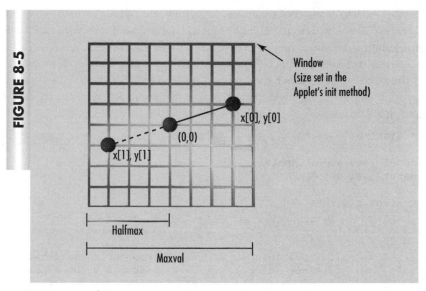

FIGURE 8-5

Window
(size set in the
Applet's init method)

x[0], y[0]

(0,0)

x[1], y[1]

Halfmax

Maxval

An `aline` object construction

The method `rotate` unsurprisingly rotates the line to a specific angle. The angle is initially converted from degrees to radians (the angle measurement units usually used by humans to the units usually used by computers), and then run through the designated math functions. Granted, this class is not too complex, but it's enough of a support class to build the applet.

The Applet

Refresh your memory of the skeleton code for an applet from Chapter 4:

```
import java.applet.Applet;
import java.awt.Graphics;

class MyJavaApp extends Applet {

    public void init()                 // define init method
       {
         // init code
       }

    public void paint(Graphics g)      // define paint method
       {
         // paint code
       }
}
```

Remember that for any applet you need at least two overriding methods: `init` and `paint`. Of course, if you wish to use the `aline` class defined above, there must be a declaration and instantiation somewhere. This will occur in the class definition (i.e., local to the class, not to any particular method). As before, the `init` method will perform its dutiful resize of the window. The `paint` method will be used to call the `rotate` method (with an appropriately changing angle to induce movement) and actually draw the line. Here's the completed code:

```
/* Start of Code */

import java.applet.Applet;
import java.awt.*;

/* aline class */

class aline {                          // a line class

        int x[] = new int[2];          // endpoint x coordinates
        int y[] = new int[2];          // endpoint y coordinates

        int rx[] = new int[2];         // rotated endpoint x
        int ry[] = new int[2];         // rotated endpoint y

        int halfmax;

/* The aline constructor */
public aline (int maxval) {

        halfmax = maxval/2;

/* Set the endpoints */
        y[0] = x[0] = (int)(Math.random() * halfmax);
        y[1] = x[1] = -x[0];
        }

/* The rotate method */
public void rotate (int angle) {

        float radangle;

/* Make sure the angle is from 0 to 359 */
        while (angle<0) angle += 360;
        angle = angle%360;

/* Convert from degrees to radians */
        radangle = angle * 0.017453F;   // approximately PI/180

/* Use the magic of sine & cosine to rotate the points */
        for (int g=0;g<2;++g) {
            rx[g] = (int)(Math.sin(radangle) * x[g]) + halfmax;
            ry[g] = (int)(Math.cos(radangle) * y[g]) + halfmax;
```

```
            }
        }
}


/* MyJavaApp Class */

public class MyJavaApp extends Applet {

        aline myline = new aline(100);
        int angle=0;

        public void init()                    // define init method
          {
          resize(100,100);
          }

        public void paint(Graphics g)         // define paint method
          {
          g.setColor(Color.lightGray);              // set color
          g.drawLine(myline.rx[0],myline.ry[0],     // erase line
                      myline.rx[1],myline.ry[1]);

          myline.rotate(angle);      // rotate the line then
          angle += 8;                // increase the angle
          if (angle>360) angle -= 360;

          g.setColor(Color.black); // set color
          g.drawLine(myline.rx[0],myline.ry[0],  // draw line
                      myline.rx[1],myline.ry[1]);
            }
        }
```

The **paint** method performs three basic operations: it erases the line, moves the line coordinates, and then redraws the line. This will work correctly to move the line, but there is a problem concerning when this method will be called. Because of the nature of an applet, the browser only calls the **paint** method when it needs to. This is initially to bring up the applet, and any time the image may get damaged in the windowing system (these events were outlined in Chapter 4). In other words, the line is not going to spin madly on its own; it will only move when the browser thinks the image may have been damaged and decides to repaint it. For someone expecting a nice twirling line, this will be boring, confusing, and actually rather silly.

Well, making the line spin around on its own is more than the browser is willing to do for you. If the browser decided to give you all its computing time to spin some stupid line, it wouldn't have any left for itself, and it's just not that generous. So what you need to do is have some code that runs independent of the browser. The **init** and **paint** methods were called directly by the browser as part of the browser. You need to *spawn* (i.e., create) a new process that sits beside the browser and moves the line for you. In essence, you are stealing CPU time away from the browser, but if it won't give it freely, you'll be forced to resort to more underhanded means.

An Introduction to Threads

A thread is a popular operating system concept that allows a program to have several copies/parts of itself running simultaneously. Threads are intended to be multiple copies of the same program running with shared data. Java's implementation is one of the few that is built so heavily upon the idea. A program that is currently active may spawn a thread (the fashionable term).

The way to spawn off threads in Java is uniquely well organized. The only real question is how to get the browser to start your thread for you, since the browser is actually the currently active program.

Fortunately, for creating threads in an applet, you can sneak this in when the browser initiates your code. The full course on threads is in Chapter 14, but the concept will be taken far enough here to get that line spinning. A graphical representation of threads is shown in Figure 8-6.

FIGURE 8-6

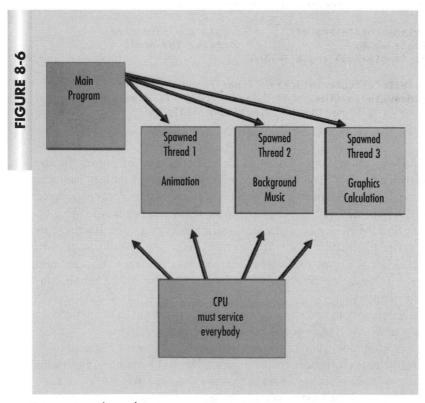

Spawning threads

First off, the browser needs to know what bit of code to spawn off as a thread, when to spawn it off, and it would even be nice to know when to stop it. The starting and stopping are actually easy and stem from two more applet functions judiciously named `start` and `stop`. These methods are invoked as your applet appears and disappears. The `start` method is called when your applet's document is brought to the screen and the `stop` function is called when it leaves—again the actual calling of these functions is done by the browser, you don't need to do it. Here's the applet code again (omitting the `aline` class to save space) with all the thread code implemented.

```
/* MyJavaApp Class */

class MyJavaApp extends Applet implements Runnable {

        aline myline = new aline(100);
        int angle=0;


        Thread mythread=null;

/* Thread methods */

        public void run() {
         while (true) {
             repaint();
             try {
             Thread.sleep(50);
              } catch (java.lang.InterruptedException e) {}
          }
         }


/* Applet Methods */

        public void start() {
         if (mythread == null) {
             mythread = new Thread(this);
             mythread.start();
             }
          }

        public void stop() {
         if (mythread != null) {
             mythread.stop();
             mythread=null;
             }
          }

        public void init()                    // define init method
          {
           resize(100,100);
```

continued on next page

continued from previous page

```
        }

    public void paint(Graphics g)          // define paint method
      {
        g.setColor(Color.lightGray);       // set color
        g.drawLine(myline.rx[0],myline.ry[0],    // erase line
                   myline.rx[1],myline.ry[1]);

        myline.rotate(angle);              // rotate the line then
        angle += 8;                        // increase the angle
        if (angle>360) angle -= 360;

        g.setColor(Color.black);           // set color
        g.drawLine(myline.rx[0],myline.ry[0],    // draw line
                   myline.rx[1],myline.ry[1]);

      }
    }
```

The three new methods are short but necessary. The first thing that was added was the **implements Runnable** on the class statement itself. This is an interface association. Interfaces specify methods that a class must implement. So in order to implement an interface (as in **implements Runnable**), the **MyJavaApp** class must define the methods dictated by the **Runnable** interface. The **Runnable** interface only dictates that the **run** method be defined (often interfaces dictate many methods).

So after all that, what good is it that you are implementing an interface to force yourself to add methods to your class? Well, the goal here is to get your code running in a thread. So somehow the thread needs to know what part of your code it should run. That's where the **run** method comes in. The thread class now knows that you have defined a **run** method because your class implements **Runnable**. Don't get too caught up on interfaces for now (they'll be covered in Chapter 10); just know that any class that implements **Runnable** can be run in a thread.

Next a variable of type **Thread** is declared and initialized to **null**. After **init**, the first method to be called is the **start** method. Once again, because of the class definition this happens automagically. This method checks to see if the thread is already running, and if not, instantiates and **start**s it. It would cause an exception to try to start a running thread.

Once the thread has begun, it heads right for the **run** method and begins to execute it. Notice the **run** method has an infinite loop within it! This is because you are assuming the thread will be stopped by external forces; you don't want it to finish the **run** method and exit on its own. The thread will immediately die (quit running) if its **run** method ends.

Only two statements appear in this infinite loop. The first calls **repaint**. This is another **Applet** method that ends up scheduling a call to the **paint** method. Well, things should be falling into place for you now. The thread was spawned and is stuck in an infinite loop, which is calling **repaint** (i.e., **paint**). The **paint** method is rotating the line—hence the line will now start spinning seemingly on its own.

```
/* Thread methods */

    public void run() {
     while (true) {
         repaint();
         try {
         Thread.sleep(50);
          } catch (java.lang.InterruptedException e) {}
      }
     }
```

The next set of statements in the `run` method put the thread to sleep for a short time. The statement is surrounded by a `try` and `catch` block, which handles a possible exception that the thread could generate. This topic is covered in Chapter 11. Putting threads to sleep is advisable for several reasons. First, in the case of a simple task such as rotating a line, it would actually spin too fast without this statement and would not end up looking like a calmly spinning line. Secondly, the line rotation would eat all the available CPU time, which would degrade performance for other applications/applets trying to use the system. As you begin to use more threads, your prioritization and *yielding* techniques will need to be more sophisticated, but for a simple applet, just knocking the thread out for a little while is sufficient. Figure 8-7 shows a screen shot of the applet.

FIGURE 8-7

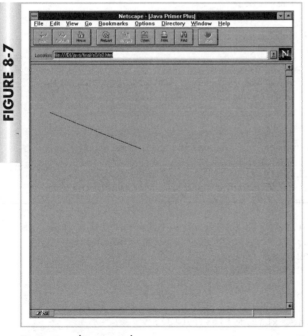

Spinning line applet

So off it will go spinning into oblivion. The thread will eventually be destroyed by the browser at the appropriate time, i.e., when the user has left that page, etc. At that time the **stop** method will be called to stop the thread and tidy up. Try this code for yourself, modifying the thread sleep time and **paint** method. This applet code is a good starting point for many more complex applets.

A Little Mouse Action

You should see the potential of applets even from that simple example. The above applet provides only a slight display of graphics but provides a solid framework for display-only applets. Of course, not all applets are display-only; there will soon be a time when you wish the user to interact with your applet.

Adding user interaction to an applet is relatively easy. The above applet can be given a rudimentary level of control by adding only one method. The **Applet** class contains several methods involving mouse control; this example only uses one but sets a model for using the rest. Here is a stripped version of the above code adding the **mouseDown** method at the end:

```
/* MyJavaApp Class */

public class MyJavaApp extends Applet implements Runnable {

        aline myline = new aline(100);
        int angle=0;
        int anglemod = 8;

        Thread mythread=null;

        .
        .
        .

        public void paint(Graphics g)  // define paint method
          {
            g.setColor(Color.lightGray);        // set color
            g.drawLine(myline.rx[0],myline.ry[0],  // erase line
                    myline.rx[1],myline.ry[1]);

            myline.rotate(angle);             // rotate the line then
            angle += anglemod;                // modify the angle
            if (angle>360) angle -= 360;
            if (angle<360) angle += 360;

            g.setColor(Color.black);      // set color
            g.drawLine(myline.rx[0],myline.ry[0],  // draw line
                    myline.rx[1],myline.ry[1]);

          }
```

```
public boolean mouseDown(Event e,int x, int y) {
        anglemod = -anglemod;
        return true;
        }

   }
```

All added code is in bold. First, the variable `anglemod` is added. This will be used to hold a changing angle modification value (previously it was just the literal 8). Code to handle `anglemod` being positive or negative was added to the `paint` method. Finally, the `mouseDown` method was tacked to the end. This method is called by the browser whenever a mouse button is pressed while the mouse is in the bounds of your applet. The input parameters `x` and `y` will contain the mouse's actual coordinates at the time the button is depressed. This version of `mouseDown` isn't concerned with mouse location, only with the fact that the user clicked the mouse within the applet. As you can see, this causes `anglemod` to change sign, i.e., change the rotational direction of the line.

The `Applet` class provides you overrideable methods for most thinkable mouse occurrences, including button pressed, button released, dragging, etc. Any attempt to model contemporary windowing systems will have you utilizing many of these methods.

Summary

Methods were everything, see? All the executable code you write will be within a method that is within a class that is within a package. As your programs get larger, good design of your methods and classes is not only vital for readability and debugging, but will almost assuredly prove itself useful with the future ability to reuse parts of code you didn't expect to.

It's certainly all coming together now. So far the previous chapters have covered most of the Java language, and even though it may not seem like it, they've only skirted serious object-oriented programming issues. Of course, it's impossible to do anything in Java without implementing at least one class, but the concepts (as you'll see) go much deeper. Java provides you with many more interesting features to work with your objects and classes. If you understand this chapter's applet example, you already have a formidable grasp on low-level programming in Java, but there's plenty more object-oriented stuff to see.

Questions

1. What should be the input parameters and output type for a method that
    a. Fills a rectangle
    b. Calculates what day of the week a date in history fell on
    c. Calculates the angle at the intersection of two lines

2. How could the following parameter list be more efficiently sent?

```
void my_method(int price, int price_plus_10, float tax_rate,
    float tax_on_price)
```

3. Decide what methods you would create for the following sequence of operations need-ed within a class:

```
Draw a horizontal line at 0,0 to 100,0
Draw the string 'Hello' above the line (centered)
Draw a horizontal line at 0,100 to 100,100
Draw the string 'good-bye' below the line (centered)
Draw 100 randomly placed dots between 0,0 and 100,100
```

4. Rewrite the following method recursively:

```
void itmethod (int x) {
    for (int g=x;g>0;--g) {
     for (int h=0;h<g;++h)  {
         System.out.print("X");
         }
       System.out.println();
     }
    }
```

5. What is wrong with the following recursive method? What could you change to fix it?

```
int fibonacci(int inval)      {
    int summ;

    summ = fibonacci(inval-1) + inval;
    }
```

 # Exercises

1. Write a method that calculates how many days a person has lived (the method can demand whatever parameters you feel necessary—birthday might be a good start).

2. Write a recursive method that will list the leaves of a tree in order from leftmost leaf to rightmost. The leaves are embedded within two arrays. The array **left** holds each node's left child, and the array **right** holds each node's right child (a node with no child has a -1 in its left and right array elements). These arrays already contain the struc-ture before they reach your method and you don't need to pass these arrays; they are available in your class. You also know the root of the tree is always array element zero. Print out the array elements corresponding to leaves of the tree. A sample input tree and output of your program follows (your program should handle any given input tree).

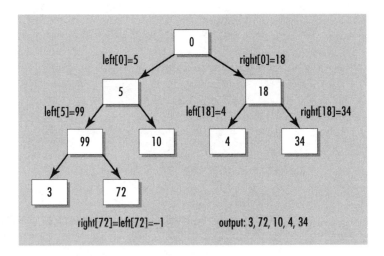

3. Write the above method without using recursion.

4. Modify the applet example so that when the user presses the mouse button, the line will *stick* to the mouse. **Applet** method **mouseDrag** will be useful.

Objects

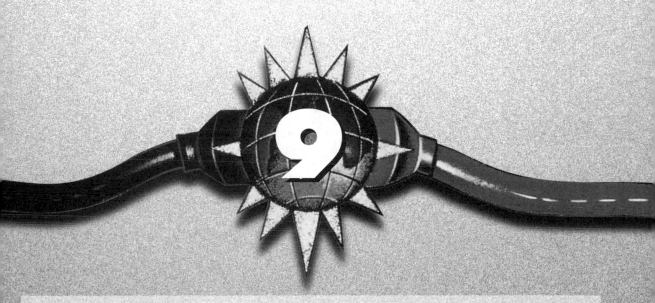

You will learn about the following in this chapter:

- What classes and objects are
- The three steps of object creation
- How to send objects as parameters
- How to utilize Java's object-oriented subclassing and inheritance
- How to override and overload methods
- How and when to use Java's public, private, and protected modifiers

You are now surrounded. It used to be that only in the real world of planes, houses, and puppydogs you were surrounded by objects. You had that safe haven of cyberspace where you could code in functions and unstructured commands. But no more. The objects have won and now infest your code, your computer, and even the Internet. Absolutely nothing can get done in Java without defining classes and making objects. Java and many other contemporary languages purport this ideology as law. C++ does not have the pure object-oriented implementation Java does. C++ dictated you *could* do things with objects, Java says you *will*.

This chapter starts the exploration of how to implement and manipulate classes and objects in Java. You've seen the bare-bones class definitions as incidental parts of preceding code examples; now you get to see how this object-oriented design is really put together. Elegance, utility, and reusability are the words of the day.

Classes and Objects

You're well aware that Java's entire essence is based upon classes and objects. The Java compiler is even written in Java, so not only does it profess that you must program in the object-oriented paradigm, it practices what it preaches. Java allows an amazing array of ways to twist class and object definitions to create useful programs.

Below is a quick review of the object-oriented concepts you've seen earlier. These ideas were brought up incidentally as they were needed throughout the preceding chapters. This section will organize the points for quick reference.

FIGURE 9-1

```
                          class name
                 class AUTO {                    Instance variables
                                                 These variables belong
                    int engine_size;             to the whole class.
                    int tire_size;      }

                    int turn_on_lights() {
                       int brightness;
  Methods:                // code to turn on lights
  i.e. functionality    }
  of your class
                                                 Local variables
                    int start_car() {            These belong
                       // code to start car      to the Declaring
                    }                             method only.

                 }
```

Classifying

Classes

Object-oriented design uses the class concept as a template for the creation of objects. It can be thought of as a feature list of some *thing*. But as with features you'd see with an automobile, this includes not only the actual parts but the methods that get things accomplished—not only the engine, tires, etc., but also how the engine works and how the lights work. Figure 9-1 shows a visual. The following code could be a class for a hard disk:

```
/* A hard disk class */
class Aharddisk {
      int size_of_disk;
      int seek_time;

/* The constructor */
      public Aharddisk(int insize,int inseek) {

            /* Initialize the instance variables */
            size_of_disk = insize;
            seek_time = inseek;
            }

      public void format() {

            // code to format the disk

            }
```

```
public boolean file_existence(String filename) {

    // code to check existence of 'filename'

    }
}
```

This class holds data about the hard disk such as its size and seek time. It also contains the methods about how to act on the hard disk. A familiar notion is that all hard disks have their own size and seek time, and these values can vary greatly from disk to disk. But it's just as true that any hard disk may have its own way of fetching its directory or formatting. Object-oriented programming places the burden of knowing how to do methods upon the object itself—who better knows how to format the hard disk than the hard disk itself?

Objects

An object is an instance of a class. So, given the class defined above, an object is a specific hard disk. There are several stages to creating a class.

Declaration

Declaring an object is similar to declaring a variable. The difference is that after declaring a built-in data type variable (e.g., **int**, **float**, etc.), that variable is ready for use. An object declaration just tells the compiler that at some time you'll be actually creating an object and here's what you'd like to call it. A declaration of the **Aharddisk** class looks like this:

Aharddisk SuperSpin1000;

Since these names were both made up by the programmer, they can sometimes be tough to follow (but perfectly legal). First is the class name, **Aharddisk**, and next is the name of the object, in this case the **SuperSpin1000**. This is really the same format as any other declaration, i.e.:

int x;

The big difference is that **int** is a built-in data type. **Aharddisk** is a type the programmer created. Every time you create a class, in essence, you are creating a new type.

A point to note that will be discussed at length in a moment is that immediately after declaration, the object actually exists. It is just a null object. The variable name **SuperSpin1000** actually owns a memory location that points to nowhere (it will point to an object eventually).

Instantiation

To actually create an object, you need to *instantiate* it. This means you need to tell the computer to create an instance of this object (entailing allocating memory for it and setting some pointers). The **new** command is used for this purpose.

```
SuperSpin1000 = new Aharddisk();
```

The right-hand side instantiates an object of the **Aharddisk** class and calls the class's constructor. It then assigns the pointer to that object to **SuperSpin1000**. The graphical representation is shown in Figure 9-2.

The **SuperSpin1000** reference existed before this instantiation, but it pointed to a null object. Now it points to the new object. This also implies it could point somewhere else later. The relationship between the instantiated object and its assigned name is surprisingly fragile.

Initialization

The final step is initialization of the new object. This usually entails initializing your instance variables. You should make a habit of doing this within the constructor of your class. Java will initialize instance variables for you, but makes a point of not initializing local variables for you (see Figure 9-1). However, that really doesn't matter, since you should be initializing any variables you create anyway. In all fairness, you created them—it's really your job. Do the computing world a favor; initialize your variables. We'll all code better.

Object References

You just saw that immediately upon declaration of an object, the object exists in memory, but it just points to nowhere. This is terribly significant and you should be getting the

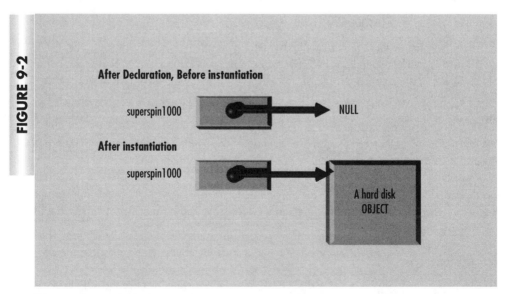

FIGURE 9-2

After Declaration, Before instantiation

superspin1000 →→→→ NULL

After instantiation

superspin1000 →→→→ A hard disk OBJECT

Object instantiation

willies about now. This implementation does not use object names as actual objects, but only as references (i.e., pointers) to objects. What good is all this? Consider the following code:

```
/* The class Purty_worthless */
class Purty_worthless {

  int a = 99;                          // a variable
  public Purty_worthless() {}          // empty constructor

}


/* The class Test */
class Test {

  static public void main(String args[]) {

  purty_worthless OBJ1;                // Object declarations
  purty_worthless OBJ2;

  OBJ1 = new purty_worthless();        // instantiation
  OBJ2 = OBJ1;                         // OBJ2 points to same place
                                       //  as OBJ1

  OBJ1.a = 42;
  System.out.println(OBJ2.a);          // prints out '42'

  }
}
```

The interesting thing about the code is that it sets the **a** variable in object **OBJ1** to 42, which causes the **a** variable in object **OBJ2** to also become 42. Well, not exactly; they are actually the same **a** variable. Since **OBJ2** was set equal to **OBJ1**, it points to the same actual object out in memory space. Figure 9-3 shows the references.

So there really only exists one actual instantiated object with two references pointing to it. Multiple references to the same thing can get confusing, and so can multiple references to the same thing. Hopefully you can see where this can get nasty. In fact, it gets nastier; read on.

Cursed Parameters

The attribute of having a pointer to an object exists for all objects, including arrays. The following code example illustrates this phenomenon over method calls using arrays but applies to objects in general. Again, the code is reworked from Chapter 7.

FIGURE 9-3

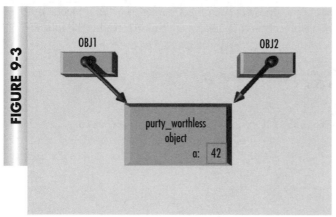

Multiple references

```
        static public void main(String args[]) {

          int a[] = new int[5];

          a[3] = 99;                           // set a[3] to 99
          postal(a);                           // call postal
          System.out.println(a[3]);            // print a[3]
        }

        /* postal method */
static void postal(int x[]) {
          x[3] = 55;                           // set x[3] to 55
        }
```

The interesting point of this program is that the output will be 55. To some degree this doesn't make sense, since you know (from Chapter 8) that all parameters are sent by value. Sending parameters by value loosely translates into "the method only gets a copy of the sent parameters and therefore cannot change the caller's original values." Although this case adds a twist, this fact is still held sternly true. Figure 9-4 shows what's happening.

In essence, only the *pointer* to the array is being passed to the method, not the array itself. Any changes to that array actually happen to the original, because the same array is pointed to in **main** and in **postal**. If the object pointer **x** were changed, that would be where the call-by-value rules would be more clearly seen. Any change to **x** within the **postal** method cannot affect **a**. The call-by-value idea is made clear in the following code:

```
        static public void main(String args[]) {

          int a[] = new int[5];

          a[3] = 99;                           // set a[3] to 99
```

```
    postal(a);                          // call postal
    System.out.println(a[3]);   // print a[3]
}

static void postal(int x[]) {

    x = new int[100];                   // declare a new x
    x[3] = 55;                          // set x[3] to 55
}
```

Now the picture is different. Although the pointer to the **a** array was passed to `postal`, it isn't really used. The **x** array is immediately redefined to a new array of size 100, and that third element is changed. Of course, as soon as the `postal` method ends, this new 100-element array is destroyed. The original **a** array was not changed, so the output of the program is 99. Figure 9-5 shows the new configuration.

Even with Java's strict hands-off pointer usage, knowing how it implements its objects is powerful information. Some wonderful tricks can be played on the compiler (and future readers of your code) with the ability to coerce and redefine object references.

Subclasses

The word "subclass" is a noun, a verb, and likely soon to be an adverb ("He subclassly glanced her way"), but it is surely the basis for extending the given abilities of Java. What this largely boils down to is the ability to extend, enhance, or change the functionality of a class by producing a subclass of it. The term subclass is also known as a *derived* or *child* class. The terms *super* class and *parent* class synonymously refer to the class that was subclassed.

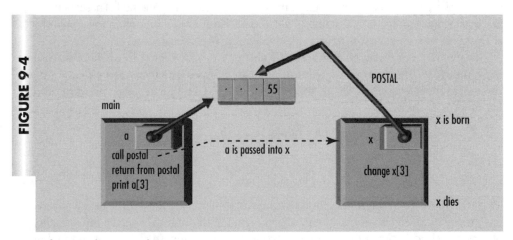

FIGURE 9-4

Referential array changing

FIGURE 9-5

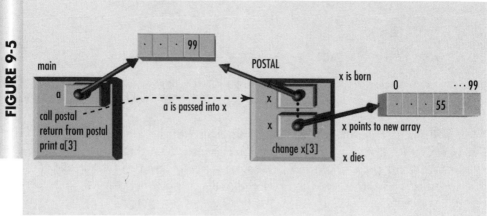

New array

Subclassing for Beginners

Chapter 4 introduced the idea of subclassing, and it will only be quickly reviewed here. A subclass is a class that *inherits* the abilities of the original class. Many classes in Java are designed to always be subclassed. You specify a subclass of another class with the `extends` keyword, such as

```
class Son extends Dad {              // child extends parent
```

As an example, consider the Java prebuilt class `java.applet.Applet`. You have seen this class subclassed several times already in order to create applets. You know that to create an applet you must create at a minimum an `init` and a `paint` method. Those methods are where much of the functionality of your applet resides. If you look in the Appendix at this class you'll notice it is quite extensive. Figure 9-6 gives a visual.

Since you have subclassed `java.applet.Applet`, your applet already knows about these methods. They were inherited from the parent `java.applet.Applet` class. You can access them as needed. The methods in `java.applet.Applet` class perform varying functions, including

- 🌑 isActive()—returns true if the applet is active
- 🌑 play(Audio data location)—plays the given audio sample
- 🌑 showStatus(msg)—displays the status msg

There are many more, but the point is that by virtue of subclassing `Applet`, you already have these methods at your disposal. A good reading through the specific functionality of these methods is advisable before you go off calling them with reckless abandon, but the fact remains that by inheriting functionality from its parents, your little applet class is much more than it seems.

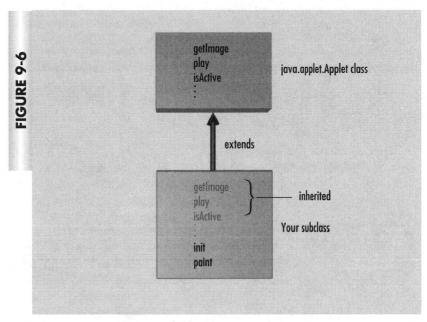

Inheriting methods and data

Object Mom

Here's a nasty realization—*every* class within Java is a subclass of some other class except the class `java.lang.Object`. `Object` is at the top of the entire inheritance tree; i.e., all other classes are children (or grandchildren, etc.) of the class `java.lang.Object`. This is illustrated in Figure 9-7. If you create a class without using the `extends` keyword, that class by default will be the child of the class `java.lang.Object`.

The `Object` class is the highest ancestor of all classes in the Java system. Therefore, all classes inherit the functionality that is within the `Object` class. So as you can see, there truly is no way to escape object-oriented programming in Java; in fact, there is no way to escape subclassing. Every class you define is guaranteed to be a subclass of some other class. If you think about it, this concept is rather appealing. Every class is a mutated version of the class `Object`. All classes have the same ancestry.

Final Classes

The one wrench in this whole hippie ideal of free association and inheritance trees is classes marked as `final`. This modifier can be listed before the word `class` in the class definition. Any class marked as `final` may not be subclassed. The fun stops here.

You read earlier that final variables can't be changed and final methods cannot be overridden; to indicate a class as `final` takes this step one further. A `final` class is a leaf in

FIGURE 9-7

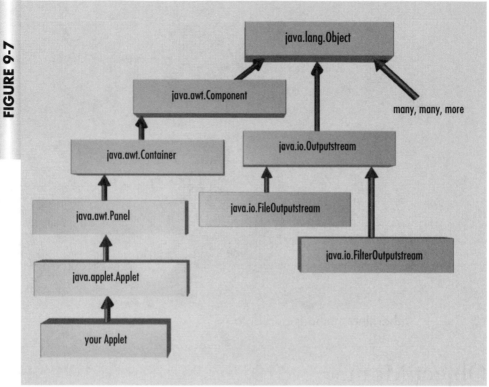

Inheriting methods and data

the inheritance tree—a leaf might not be a final class, but a final class is always a leaf. Many (certainly not all) of Java's prebuilt classes are declared as **final**, preventing you from changing any aspect of how they work.

Annoying Your Methods

This section is devoted to formalizing the concepts of further tormenting your methods. Two main concepts regarding method implementation are covered that expand the notion of methods and their usage.

Overriding

You've already seen a few instances of method overriding in earlier code examples. Overriding allows you to replace some functionality of a parent class with the way you think it should have been done. More precisely, with the way you need it to be done.

Again consider the `java.applet.Applet` class. Before you even get to it, this class already has a method called `init` and a method called `paint`. So when you define these methods in your applet subclass, you are largely telling the compiler that any instantiation of your class (which the browser itself will do) should inherit all of the `java.applet.Applet` class's methods and data except in the case of `init` and `paint`, where it should use your versions instead.

So in addition to the ability for a subclass to add new methods and new functionality, by overriding existing methods it can change existing functionality. If you didn't override the `paint` method in the `Applet` class, things would be a bit boring. Figure 9-8 shows an example of overriding in general.

Your overriding method must have the same name, parameters, and return type as the original. If you declared a method with the same name but differing parameters, then this is not an override—both versions of the method exist; without a perfect match the compiler thinks you want both versions. You also cannot override a method marked as `private`, which is covered in the next section.

FIGURE 9-8

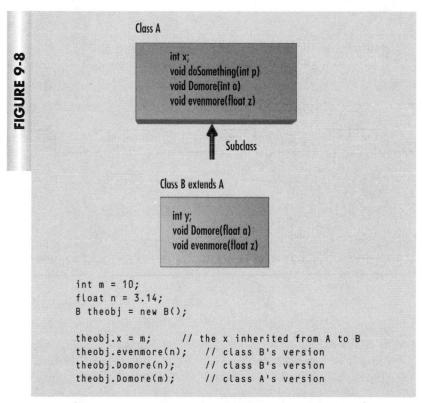

```
Class A

    int x;
    void doSomething(int p)
    void Domore(int a)
    void evenmore(float z)

            ↑ Subclass

Class B extends A

    int y;
    void Domore(float a)
    void evenmore(float z)


int m = 10;
float n = 3.14;
B theobj = new B();

theobj.x = m;        // the x inherited from A to B
theobj.evenmore(n);  // class B's version
theobj.Domore(n);    // class B's version
theobj.Domore(m);    // class A's version
```

Overriding and changing functionality

super and this

There are two variables that exist in every object, **super** and **this**. The **this** variable appropriately is an object reference to the object the program is currently running in. The **super** variable is a reference to the parent class type of the **this** object. Using more one-syllable words, the current object is the **this** variable and its parent class is the **super** variable.

super

In cases where you need to regress to the functionality of the parent class, the **super** variable becomes useful. The **super** variable allows you to be sure you are referencing elements of the parent class and not the current class you are running in. Consider the following two classes:

```
/* The circle class */
class circle {

      int radius;

      public circle(int r) {
              radius = r;  // rudimentary constructor
          }

      public void drawcircle(String today) {
              // code to draw an empty circle
          }
  }

/* The filled circle class, child of circle */
class filled_circle extends circle {

      public filled_circle(int r) {
              super(r);    // call the super's constructor
                           // i.e. circle(r)
          }

      public void drawcircle(String today) {
              if (today == "Thursday") super.drawcircle();
                  else   // code to draw a filled circle
          }
  }
```

Code to actually do the dirty work is not included, as you are more interested in the setup. So the **filled_circle** class is a subclass of the **circle** class. It therefore inherits the **radius** variable and *would* inherit the **draw_circle** method except that it overrides it. The first statement in bold is **super(r)**, which tells the compiler to call the parent class's constructor. This statement satisfies Java's requirement that a constructor's first statement must be a call to another constructor. If that statement were not there, Java would have inserted the statement

```
super();              // call the parent's default constructor
```

which in this case would have caused a compile-time error. Reusing the parent's constructor in this case makes sense, since constructing the values for an empty and a filled circle are likely identical. So, upon instantiation of a filled circle object, i.e.:

```
class foreign {

    filled_circle myCircle = new filled_circle(10);

    .
    .
    .
}
```

control will go to the `filled_circle` constructor, then be passed to the `circle` constructor, and the radius will be set. Of course, the above foreign class does the instantiation but has no idea all this passing of control took place, nor does it care.

The second bolded statement above checks the input variable `today` and compares it to "Thursday". If today is Thursday, then instead of drawing a filled circle, the super's `drawcircle` method gets called. Assumedly, you're not allowed to draw filled circles on Thursdays. The `super` variable is most commonly used when you need to access the parent class's methods from a given subclass.

this

The `this` variable is bit less dazzling. It refers to the current object you are in. Look at a piece of the above code example again:

```
class circle {

    int radius;

    /* constructor */
    public circle(int r) {
        radius = r;
        this.radius =r;
    }

    /* The drawcircle method */
    public void drawcircle(String today) {
        // code to draw an empty circle
    }
}
```

The two bolded statements are functionally identical. They set the radius variable in the context of `this` object. As with many things in Java, you are already a heavy user of the `this` variable and didn't know it. It is implicitly present for any object instance variable reference. Because of its implicit presence, you don't usually include it. Often, the `this` variable is used for an object to send itself to other methods. For a foreign class to send an object of your class is intuitive.

```
MyClass A = new MyClass();

    .
    .
    .

Some_object.some_method(A);
```

But if you wished to do this within a method of `MyClass`, you cannot call the object A—this method code must run for any possible object of that class. So you can use the `this` keyword to send the current object that is running.

```
Some_object.some_method(this);        // send me!
```

You can also use the `this` variable to distinguish between instance and local variables. It provides a means to tell the compiler which variable you're talking about if two variables share the same name.

```
class some_class {

    int x;                      // instance variable 'x'
    public some_class(int x) {  // parameter 'x'
       this.x = x;              // instance = parameter
    }
}
```

If you're fuzzy on when you would actually need these two variables, don't fret. When your coding reaches a point where you do need them, you'll scratch your head once trying to figure out how to accomplish your task and then remember these are at your disposal.

Overloading

Overloading is a common feature in object-oriented programming. Overloading is the ability to have several versions of the same method distinguished only by a differing parameter list. You can then call any version you wish and the compiler has the built-in smarts to know which method you want called. For those C++ programmers out there, note that Java only supports method overloading, not operator overloading.

Perfect Match

The following contrived example exhibits overloading. This example is rather straightforward, given that the methods all perform relatively the same operation. In general, this should be the case for overloaded methods—if one method returns an integer result from a calculation and the other draws a line, these methods should probably have different names. Occasionally, however, certain versions of a method may be used to induce uncharacteristic side effects, such as drawing a line the length of the integer in addition to returning it.

```
/* powers class *
class powers {

        public powers() { };           // null constructor

/* Overloaded power methods */
        public int   power(int x)               { return x*x; }
        public float power(float x)     { return x*x; }
        public int   power(int x,int y) {
                int temp = x;
                while (--y > 0) x *= temp;
                return x;
                }
        public float power(float x,int y) {
                float temp = x;
                while (--y > 0) x *= temp;
                return x;
                }
        }

/* test class */
class test {

    static public void main(String args[]) {

    /* Instantiate a new powers object */
    powers multiplier = new powers();

    /* Call each of the overloaded "versions" */
    System.out.println(multiplier.power(5,3));
    System.out.println(multiplier.power(9));
    System.out.println(multiplier.power(3.1415));
    System.out.println(multiplier.power(1.2,9));

    }
}
```

The `powers` class contains four methods, all named `power`. Each `power` method has an individual list of parameters that distinguishes it for the compiler. The method calls access each method and print the corresponding return values of the given type. If only one parameter is given, then the power function assumes you want the value squared and calls the correct method according to whether you sent an `int` or a `float`. It also returns an `int` or a `float` assuming that you want back what you sent. The order of declaration for the overloaded methods is immaterial. The compiler is much more interested in matching the parameters from your call than worrying about which is declared first.

This ability again gives an air of reusability and robustness to your classes. Many of Java's predefined classes have overloaded methods. A familiar example is the `println` statement; it will happily print strings, integers, floats, etc., without so much as a complaint. The fact is there are several `println` methods that handle each of these special cases. Hopefully, that fact was relatively transparent to you. That's the intent of overloading, allowing the class to handle such details so you have time to worry about more interesting programming pursuits.

A further note is that the return type of a method is not used as a distinguishing factor, only parameter lists. An example displaying the resulting ambiguity follows:

```
float  power (float z) {
double power (float z) {
```

The compiler doesn't use the return type for differentiation and therefore has no way of distinguishing these two methods. If you have two methods with the same name and same parameter lists, you will confuse the compiler. Don't do this; it's bad.

Being Ambiguous

Given the `powers` class above, what happens if you send it a parameter list that doesn't match any of the declared methods? Let's illustrate this by rewriting the above test class:

```
/*  test class */
class test {

    static public void main(String args[]) {

        short s = 3;

        powers multiplier = new powers();

        /* Hmmm, this looks awful short for an int */
        System.out.println(multiplier.power(s));
        }
}
```

Well, you know that the coder of this class seemingly wants the square of the `s` variable. But, `s` is of type `short`, and there are no `power` methods of that type. By all rights Java could spew forth an error and quit. In fact, that's rather the expected response. Instead, in a wild display of unconventionality, Java provides a contingency plan for just such an occurrence.

Java will attempt to find the closest method to the one you are asking to call. Closest means one that has the same number of parameters (i.e., `power` methods had one or two parameters) and has the nearest type (or types) to the one you are sending. However, if you send a data type that does not have an exact method to receive it, and it cannot be safely converted (e.g., converting `double` to `float` is not safe, because this conversion loses data), then the compiler will dispense an error and give up.

Also, if the total conversion cost is equivalent for two possible methods, then Java does poop out and admit defeat. Consider this example:

```
class confusion {

 public confusion() {};

 public void nothing(char x)  {}
 public void nothing(short x) {}

}

    .
    .
    .

confusion total = new confusion();

int x = 99;

total.nothing(x);              // ambiguous
```

The last statement will produce a compile-time error. Java does not know which `confusion` method you want, since `int` is just as close to `char` as it is to `short`. In general, your calls to overloaded methods should be perfect matches. Wide use of this facility should indicate that you are likely not implementing your classes/methods/variables optimally.

Public, Private, and Protected

These keywords are used as modifiers for classes, methods, and variables. They indicate the access level or *visibility* of one of these elements to other classes. In other words, you can declare your variables with specific limitations as to what other classes may access those variables. Correct usage of these modifiers provides a definitive level of data-hiding from unscrupulous foreign classes. In actuality, there are five different types of access specifications in Java (C++ programmers: read closely). In addition to `public`, `private`, and `protected`, there is a combination access level `private protected` and a default access level (i.e., a variable declaration without any of the three keywords `public`, `private`, and `protected`.)

Methods and Variables

Classes do not implement these modifiers as fully as methods and variables do. The following list defines these access modes as they pertain to methods and variables. Note: The definitions use the term "declaring class" to indicate the class that actually declared the variable.

- **Public:** A public method/variable may be accessed by any class in any package.

- **Protected:** A protected method/variable may be accessed within the confines of the declaring class, any subclass of the declaring class, or any class in the same package as the declaring class.

- **Default:** A default method/variable may be accessed within the declaring class and any class in the same package (and subclasses if they are in the same package).

- **Private Protected:** A private protected method/variable may be accessed within the declaring class and any subclass.

- **Private:** A private method/variable may be accessed only within the confines of its class.

As you can see, the modifiers pertain to the accessibility of a given variable or method. This allows the class designer control over who or what can change or even view his or her class's internal variables. Java relies heavily on package membership to decide access. Table 9-1 provides a quick reference.

	Subclass		Nonsubclass	
	Same Package	**Different Package**	**Same Package**	**Different Package**
Public	Yes	Yes	Yes	Yes
Protected	Yes	Yes	Yes	No
Default	Yes	No	Yes	No
Private Protected	Yes	Yes	No	No
Private	No	No	No	No

Table 9-1 Method/variable access

The declaring class isn't included in the table because it always has access to its own variables. As you can see, these five access types all have slightly different rules.

Privacy and Nobody's Business

Private variables really are private. This specification is at the heart of the object-oriented concept *encapsulation*. Encapsulation is the art of making your classes a self-contained unit that provides the desired output but doesn't divulge more of its means than it needs to. The following code example illustrates this concept. We'll define four classes residing in three different packages.

FILE DAD.JAVA

```
/* Start of the "brothers" package */
package brothers;

/* The Dad Class */
     class Dad {

        private boolean sportscar;

        public Dad() {
          sportscar = true;              // Only methods in Dad can
                                         // use sportscar

          }
        }

/* The UncleFrank Class (Dad's brother) */
     class UncleFrank {  /* NOT a subclass of Dad */

        Dad mybro = new Dad();

        public UncleFrank() {
//        mybro.sportscar    = true;      // ERROR! Dad only!
          }
        }
```

FILE SON.JAVA

```
/* Start of the "kids" package */
package kids;

import brothers.Dad;

/* The Son Class */
     class Son extends Dad {

        public Son() {
//        sportscar = true;            // ERROR! Son can't use sportscar
          }
        }
```

FILE NEIGHBOR.JAVA

```
/* Start of the "aliens" package */
package aliens;

import brothers.Dad;
import brothers.UncleFrank;
import kids.Son;
```

continued on next page

continued from previous page

```
/* The nosy_neighbor Class */
      class nosy_neighbor {

        static public void main(String args[]) {

          Dad a_dad = new Dad();
          Son a_son = new Son();

//        a_dad.sportscar = true;  // ERROR! Can't use sportscar
                                     // Note: this translates as the
                                     // neighbor asking the Dad
                                     // for access to the sportscar

          }
        }
```

That seems like a lot of code, but really it is four very basic class definitions and their constructors. All statements that would generate errors are commented out. The modifiers don't kid around. Variables are set to `private` when they are variables that are really nobody else's business. The big argument is that when a foreign class accesses your class (by calling a method or accessing a variable), it only wants a service and/or result. The foreign class doesn't know and really shouldn't care how you got the job done, as long as it's done. This *hiding* allows you to change your class in the future, that is, add features or implement better algorithms; as long as the users of your class get the expected result, they should be happy.

You could also think of this in the context of something like the `java.lang.Math` class (now there's a sneaky rascal). When you call the Math class's `sin` method, you pass it a double precision number and it returns the sine of that number. You don't think for a minute about how it calculated the sine for your number; there's likely some colossal, enigmatic formula involving plus signs and everything that churns out the answer. But do you really care? For most users of the sine method, the inner workings are immaterial—as long as it **works**.

Unfortunately, it is sometimes useful for foreign classes to be able to know the value of some `private` variables. This is a touchy situation. Luckily, it's your class and you have full control over how foreign classes may access your private variables. Of course, the hiding is still in place, and in actuality the foreign class doesn't know it's a private variable, it just wants a value. Small accessor methods often are written for this purpose. For **Dad`s sportscar** variable above:

```
class Dad {

  private boolean sportscar;

  .
  .
  .

  public boolean Dad_uses_sportscar() {
```

```
        return sportscar;
    }

}
```

The `Dad_uses_sportscar` method just returns the value `sportscar`. The thrilling part is that `sportscar` is visible only in `Dad`, but `Dad_uses_sportscar` is visible everywhere (it's public). So this small method allows the outside world access to the `sportscar` variable in a controlled way (i.e., to let the world know Dad uses the sportscar and no one else). The class can dictate how and when others may see private variables. Proper usage of the `private` modifier is a good programming practice and is pretty nifty. What data and methods should be declared private? The broad answer is to make as much data private as possible. In general, your instance variables should be declared private. So should any method that is for use only within the class. No hard and fast rules exist for declaring privacy but, in general, users of your class should only be able to see what they absolutely need to.

Protection and the Family

The `private protected`, `protected`, and default access levels are slightly more lenient than the `private` modifier. They all use subclassing or package membership (or both) as criteria to allow access.

The following code example adds a few new variables to the `Dad` class: a protected `golfclubs` variable, a default `fishingboat` variable, and a "private protected" `familycar` variable. This example focuses on variables, but keep in mind that the same access rules apply to methods. There is a fuzzy line between the distinction of methods and data, and the actions of these modifiers tend to ignore it further.

FILE DAD.JAVA

```
/* Start of the "brothers" package */
package brothers;

/* The Dad Class */
    class Dad {

        private boolean sportscar;
        protected boolean golfclubs;
        boolean fishingboat;                // default
        private protected boolean familycar;

        public Dad() {
          sportscar    = true;              // Dad owns this stuff, he can use
          golfclubs    = true;              // all of it.
          fishingboat  = true;
          familycar    = true;
          }
        }
```

continued on next page

continued from previous page

```
/* The UncleFrank Class (Dad's brother) */
/* This is not a subclass of Dad, but resides in the same package */
        class UncleFrank {

            Dad mybro = new Dad();

            public UncleFrank() {
//              mybro.sportscar    = true;      // ERROR! Dad only!
                mybro.golfclubs    = true;      // OK
                mybro.fishingboat  = true;      // Sure, no problem.
//              mybro.familycar    = true;      // ERROR! Only subclasses access
                }
            }
```

FILE SON.JAVA

```
/* Start of the "kids" package */
package kids;

import brothers.Dad;

/* The Son Class */
/* This is a subclass of Dad, but resides in a foreign package */
        class Son extends Dad {

            public Son() {
//              sportscar    = true;        // ERROR! Son can't use sportscar.
                golfclubs    = true;        // Yeah, fine.
//              fishingboat  = true;        // No, only Dad and Uncle Frank
                familycar    = true;        // OK, but be careful

                }
            }
```

FILE NEIGHBOR.JAVA

```
/* Start of the "aliens" package */
package aliens;

import brothers.Dad;
import brothers.UncleFrank;
import kids.Son;

/* The nosy_neighbor Class */
/* this is not a subclass nor is it in the same package as Dad */
        class nosy_neighbor {

            static public void main(String args[]) {
```

```
              Dad a_dad = new Dad();
              Son a_son = new Son();

//            a_dad.sportscar    = true;      // ERROR! Can't use sportscar.
//            a_dad.golfclubs    = true;      // ERROR! Sorry.
//            a_dad.fishingboat  = true;      // ERROR! Forget it.
//            a_dad.familycar    = true;      // ERROR! No way.

              }
        }
```

As you can see, the rules shine vividly through. Uncle Frank can use everything except the sportscar and the family car (maybe he's a poor driver). The son can use everything but the sportscar and the fishing boat. The neighbor basically can't use anything. These varying levels of access are useful at different times. The Java APIs provide a plethora of examples of where access becomes limited in strange, new ways.

As Public as John Q.

The **public** modifier allows anyone to access the specified element. This can be seen in the example below, using the **lawnmower** variable. Everyone has access to the lawnmower—even the nosy neighbor.

FILE DAD.JAVA

```
/* Start of the "brothers" package */
package brothers;

/* The Dad Class */
      class Dad {
        ...
        public boolean lawnmower;

        public Dad() {
          ...
          lawnmower    = true;      // Dad can use the lawnmower
          }
        }

/* The UncleFrank Class (Dad's brother) */
/* This is not a subclass of Dad, but resides in the same package */
      class UncleFrank {

          mybro.lawnmower    = true;         // Uncle Frank can borrow it
          }
        }


FILE SON.JAVA
/* Start of the "kids" package */
package kids;
```

continued on next page

continued from previous page

```
import brothers.Dad;

/* The Son Class */
/* This is a subclass of Dad, but resides in a foreign package */
      class Son extends Dad {

         public Son() {
           ...
           lawnmower    = true;              // Son can use it (unfortunately)

           }
         }
```

```
FILE NEIGHBOR.JAVA
/* Start of the "aliens" package */
package aliens;

import brothers.Dad;
import brothers.UncleFrank;
import kids.Son;

/* The nosy_neighbor Class */
/* this is not a subclass nor is it in the same package as Dad */
      class nosy_neighbor {

           ...
           a_dad.lawnmower    = true;       // Even the neighbor can access.
           a_son.lawnmower    = true;       // Son says it's OK too.
           }
         }
```

The uses for **public** should be obvious. Without public methods, foreign classes can't do much with your class. Make public what you have to, but keep private what you can.

Access to Classes

Access to classes is much less romantic than the complex configuration of variables/methods and it doesn't warrant such snazzy examples. Primarily, access levels with classes deal with package visibility. Classes are always visible within their own package. But if a class is marked **public**, then that class is visible to other packages as well.

This could be thought of as a higher extension to the internal method paradigm. For example, if you have a graphics package to draw polygons, then you could have a hidden line drawing class (i.e., hidden from other packages) within that package that draws the lines for any of the polygons but is not accessible to external packages. The polygon classes would be declared **public**, but the line class would not.

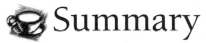 # Summary

This chapter formalized many of the concepts you were already using. The code examples earlier in the book touched on these concepts simply because they had to. There's no way to create a running applet or application without defining a class, subclassing, overriding, etc. Using arrays, late instantiation, and overloading sure don't hurt either. Hopefully now you have a better understanding of what goes on behind the object-scenes and how you can design your classes.

In much of computer science, object-oriented programming has become religion. This religion has induced the birth of languages such as Java. Using this model correctly has great potential and significant ramifications for the future. If you design your classes well, you will find yourself far in the future reusing your same old classes in highly differing applications. Programming with objects in mind strives to eliminate reinventing the wheel. If you wrote a class a year ago, and need something similar today, reusing your old class saves programming time now and gives you the benefit of reusing a tried and true (i.e., tested) class.

The next chapter continues the object-oriented saga and introduces you to some advanced features. These chapters are intended to familiarize you with the language, but as with any language (human or computer), after you see what it looks like, using it is the real way to learn it. The advanced features chapters will guide you as you do just that. They'll focus on specific facets of programming in Java but will hit hard as far as developing complex applications.

 # Questions

1. What is the difference between object declaration and instantiation?

2. Label the following variable uses as being most appropriately private, protected, or public.

   a. A variable holding the amount of free memory left in a memory allocator class

   b. The `System.out` variable

   c. The `illegal_usage` variable in a program monitor class (i.e., which monitors other classes and their behavior)

   d. The name of the URL in a browser application

3. Subclassing affords you many abilities with regard to changing the functionality of the parent class. Usually this is thought of as expanding or changing the parent's abilities; is it possible to restrict them also?

4. Think of some examples of classes that should be marked as `final`.

5. Consider the following code:

```
Some_object A = new Some_object();

 .
 .
 .

A = new Some_object();
```

You should see that the original instantiation actually created an object. After the second instantiation, what happens to the first one?

6. Assume execution enters the code below at the `C` method. What does this code print out?

```
public void A(x[]) {
 x[10] = 50;
 }

public void B(x[][]) {
 for (int g=0;g<10;++g)        A(x[g]);
 }

public void C() {

  int a[][] = new int[20][20];

  B(a);

  for (int g=0;g<20;++g)
   System.out.println(a[g][10]);
 }
```

7. Given the following two classes, label each method in the child class as an "overrider," "overloader," or neither.

```
class parent {

    public parent() { /* code */ }

    public void methodX(int u)   { /* code */ }
    public void methodZ(char p)   { /* code */ }
    private void methodY(float z) { /* code */ }
    }

class child extends parent {

    public child() { super(); }
```

```
public void methodX(int a)   { /* code */ }
public void methodY(float a) { /* code */ }
public int  methodZ(int z)   { /* code */ }
public void methodZ(char o)  { /* code */ }

}
```

 # Exercises

1. Write an integer-array-constructing method that takes an integer as a parameter that indicates how big an array to return. The method should create, populate (with each element being its index, e.g., a[0] = 0, a[1]=1, etc.), and finally return the array.

2. Write an applet that does not override the `init` and/or the `paint` methods of `java.applet.Applet`. What happens?

3. Write a new class with a `printout` (overloaded) method. Use your class as a front end to a slightly prettier way of printing (hiding `System.out.println` from users of your class). Also, your class should correctly print out character variables as characters (e.g., `System.out.println` prints out a character as an unsigned integer, not the actual character). You'll likely need to make good use of the `String` and/or `StringBuffer` classes.

4. Write an applet to allow two players to play tic-tac-toe. You will need to seriously override methods in the `java.applet.Applet` class (including mouse functions).

Object-Oriented Superpowers

10

You will learn about the following in this chapter:

- More about construction and destruction
- How to utilize casting objects in Java
- How Java defines static elements
- How Java's order of execution is defined
- How Java's dynamic object instantiation works
- When to use abstract classes
- When to use interfaces
- How Java's garbage collection facilities take a load off your shoulders

No one knows for certain, but you can be pretty sure Superman approves of object-oriented programming. Why wouldn't he? There is reuse, organization, and a general air of everybody just playing nice together. Okay, he may not be hot on all this information-hiding going on (the big "S" is into everybody sharing), but he likely understands the need for it. Object-oriented programmers sure seem to be the good guys, and Superman always likes the good guys. It's certainly nice to have such a prominent role model supporting the cause.

This chapter heads right into what Superman loves the most. The material will quickly fly past the object-oriented concepts introduced in earlier chapters and use a little X-ray vision to see deeper into Java's advanced features. These features are the sure road to designing bulletproof code.

Nasty Class Notions

There is a plethora of ways to design classes. You already have most of the tools you need to write full programs. The features outlined here will slowly merge with your coding style to streamline and enhance your code.

Construction and Destruction

A good-sized Java program has more construction than the Pennsylvania turnpike in the summertime. It shouldn't be a big surprise; constructors are undeniably convenient. You are given a place that is guaranteed to be called to set up an object before anything else can happen to that object, and it's done somewhat implicitly. Granted, it's not completely implicit, as the constructor name is found in the instantiating statement, but it's almost as if the class thinks you don't know it's calling scads of constructors, and for some reason you willingly play along.

Java's a bit more stingy in the area of destruction. No big deal; it does most everything for you so you have no real need of any serious object-destruction facilities. However, it does afford you some small concessions in case you are one of those compulsively organized programmers and feel the need for some personal tidying before Java goes in and cleans house.

All Kinds of Construction

Remember that constructors are special methods in classes. They have no return type and must have the same name as the class. The previous chapter discussed method overloading. This concept expectedly extends to constructors. In fact, it's quite common to find several versions of constructors for a class. Most often, there is one basic constructor form, but the class designer includes several *convenience* constructors for programmers to use. Usually you can define a default constructor that can be used for the most common constructing case (if that class has such a thing), i.e., it calls another constructor with the most common parameters.

```
class rectangle extends Shape {

  public int width,height;          // rectangle's width & height

  public rectangle(int w, int h) {

      width = w;
      height = h;
  }

  public rectangle() {              // default constructor

      this(10,20);                  // call the first constructor
  }

  public rectangle(int w) {  // one parameter indicates
                             // equal width and height
      this(w,w);                    // call the first constructor
      }
  .
  .
  .
}
```

Assume the default size for a rectangle is 10 by 20. Programmers using this class can instantiate their rectangle with the no-parameters (i.e., default) constructor, which then calls the parametered constructor with the values (10,20). Again, this is merely a convenience constructor for users of your class. Of course, you can also include additional constructors with other parameter lists according to your application.

As was illustrated, the latter two constructors above call the first constructor. Remember that Java requires that the first statement in a constructor be a call to some other constructor, otherwise by default, it calls the parent's default constructor. The latter two constructors do call another constructor and satisfy Java's requirement (they call another constructor in their own class, but this still qualifies). Of course, since the first constructor does not have an explicit call to another constructor, it calls its parent's default constructor (i.e., `Shape`), then performs the assignments.

Not So Senseless Destruction

It would certainly seem logical that where there is construction there would be some type of destruction. The context here is construction of objects where that means handling all the details to initialize a newly created (i.e., newly memory allocated) object. It would follow, then, that there would be a need to take care of all those details when the object is to be destroyed.

Java and C++ both include constructors, but C++ also includes explicit *destructors*. Java doesn't afford you quite such a systematic facility for destroying your objects. As far as cleaning up the memory an object used, Java has extensive garbage collection facilities built in to handle this. So memory is not your worry. The only thing you may want to do is tidy up some occasional external links associated with your object. The classic example is an object that opens disk files. Although the death of your object (as far as memory is concerned) will be handled by the garbage collector, the garbage collector is not smart enough to go off closing files for you. For any actions you wish explicitly performed immediately prior to death of your objects (like closing files), Java provides a magic method called `finalize`. The theory here is of *object finalization*, i.e., giving the object a chance to take care of whatever other business it needs to before it is destroyed. Typically, you won't need to worry about including a `finalize` method, since most of your objects should be sufficiently destroyed by the garbage collector. Only when you know your object will have some unfinished business that the garbage collector doesn't handle is when you resort to `finalize`.

Any class that includes a `void finalize()` method is mildly assured that this method will be called at any of its object's terminations. Note that this is only mildly assured, because there is a certain amount of smoke in front of exactly when and how this method will get called for you. You can explicitly call the `finalize` method, but that's not quite as interesting and doesn't really afford you any capability you didn't already have. The system is supposed to call this method for you, but this depends on several factors, one of which being the asynchronous garbage collector realizing the object is dead.

Several of Java's APIs, which include `java.io.FileInputStream` and `java.io.FileOutputStream`, include a `finalize` method. In line with the disk file example mentioned earlier, these classes use the `finalize` method to close the input/output stream on termination of the object.

Keep in mind that the Java language specification implies an air of caution when using `finalize`. So if you find a use in your code for it, be sure to test it to make sure it's doing what you expect. For the most part, you will know when you are finished with an object, and it behooves you to provide adequate facilities to prepare for its demise. Basically, you should provide explicit methods to clean up any loose ends your object may create.

Casting, Hidden Variables, and Madness

Recall the discussion in Chapter 5 of casting between built-in types in Java. For example, the following code *casts* (i.e., transforms) the integer variable to a floating point to do the assignment:

```
float f;
int i = 10;

f = (float)i;          // the (float) does the cast
                       // f == 10.0
```

Java allows the extension of this concept to casting of objects into different types of classes. This is quite an interesting concept, since classes (and subsequently their objects) can vary greatly. The hitch is that you may only cast up the inheritance tree among classes where one of the classes is a descendant of the other. Mind you, this doesn't have to be as close as a parent-child relationship; any ancestor/descendant relationship will work.

Casting among classes can be surprisingly confusing, so here are a few guidelines to remember:

- Casting among siblings is not allowed.

- Casting, in itself, is not an instantiation—i.e., no new memory is allocated.

- You cannot (trivially) cast a parent to a child. This is because a child basically contains all that the parent did plus more. Since a cast does not add anything to an object (per last bullet), where would this "plus more" come from? A qualifying exception is that if the object is a child casted to a parent, it can be casted back to the child.

To understand casting you need to better understand inheritance. Consider the following two classes:

```
/* Parent Class: Airline Passenger */
class AirlinePassenger {

  public int id = 5551234;              // Passenger phone #
  protected String dietpref = "Chicken";  // meal preference
```

```
    /* Accessor */
    public String whatFood() { return dietpref; }

    public void stowBaggage() {
           System.out.print("Passenger:" + id");
           System.out.println(" Smash into overhead bin");
           }
}

/* Child class: FrequentFlyer is a type of Airline Passenger */
class FrequentFlyer extends AirlinePassenger {

    public int bonusMiles() { /* calc bonus miles */ }

    /* Stow baggage */
    public void stowBaggage() {
           System.out.print("Passenger:" + id);
           System.out.println(" Place into overhead bin");
           }
}
```

The first thing to say is that these classes are tailored for this example; there are no constructors and the instance variables are initialized when they are declared. This is odd but will suffice to make the point.

Assume there is an instantiation of the `FrequentFlyer` class (the child class). You've seen enough "subclassinations" to know what happens, but Figure 10-1 should make it crystal clear just in case. The `FrequentFlyer` class has inherited the instance variable `id`, the instance variable `dietpref`, and a `whatFood` method. It also has its own `bonusMiles` method, and the overrider `stowBaggage` method.

There shouldn't be any surprises there. Any call to the `stowBaggage` method returns "Passenger: 5551234 Place…." The last bullet above addressed the inability to override variables; modifying the `FrequentFlyer` class can illustrate this point.

```
class FrequentFlyer extends AirlinePassenger {

    int id = 435;         // Frequent Flyer ID #

    public int bonusMiles() { /* calc bonus miles */ }

    /* Stow baggage */
    public void stowBaggage() {
           System.out.print("Passenger:" + id);
           System.out.println(" Place into overhead bin");
           }
}
```

All that has been added is an instance variable `id` for the child class. You could assume that frequent flyers are designated by their frequent flyer id number instead of just their phone number like normal passengers. In any case, this variable is purposely named `id` to illustrate the object's underlying representation. Again consider an instantiation of the

FIGURE 10-1

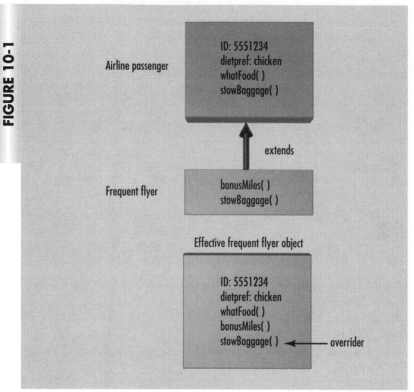

Inheritance revisited

frequent flyer class. It would seem that the frequent flyer class's **id** variable would override the airline passenger's. The real picture of a new **FrequentFlyer** object is shown in Figure 10-2.

The frequent flyer object still inherited its parent's **id** variable. As can be seen from the figure, it has two **id** variables. A call to the **stowBaggage** method will now print "Passenger 435: Place…". In fact, most references to the **id** variable will seem as if they have been overridden. The reason is that the reference to the **id** variable in the **stowBaggage** method has an implicit **this** reference in front of it (this was discussed in Chapter 9). This could be written explicitly and equivalently as

```
public void stowBaggage() {
        System.out.print("Passenger:" + this.id);
        System.out.println(" Place into overhead bin");
        }
```

Since the inherited parent's **id** variable is present within the **FrequentFlyer** object, you can use the **super** variable to get at it.

```
public void stowBaggage() {
        System.out.print("Passenger:" + super.id);
        System.out.println(" Place into overhead bin");
        }
```

This statement would print out "Passenger: 5551234 Place…." The dilemma of hidden inherited variables arises mainly from like-named variables along the inheritance tree (regardless of the number of generations between them). This case should be relatively uncommon, but it was important to point out so you understand the underlying representation of the objects. Besides, every Java class casting code example uses this pitfall to make the point.

The Casting Itself

Because of a lack of the above knowledge, casting code examples tend to confuse most Java programmers the first time they see them. If you have understood the above discussion, you should be well armed for any casting discussion. The code below casts the classes defined

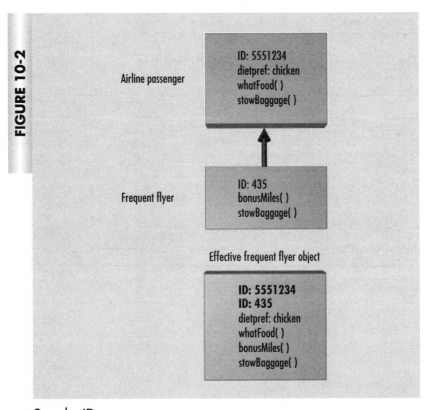

FIGURE 10-2

Sneaky IDs

above. It sets up two object references, Billy and William. Assumedly, Billy is a frequent flyer and William is just a normal airline passenger. Only one object will be instantiated. The object will be an instantiation of the `FrequentFlyer` class (i.e., the child class).

```
/* Parent Class: Airline Passenger */
class AirlinePassenger {

  public int id = 5551234;                    // Passenger phone #
  protected String dietpref = "Chicken";     // meal preference

  public String whatFood() { return dietpref; }
  public void stowBaggage() {
        System.out.print("Passenger:" + id");
        System.out.println(" Smash into overhead bin");
        }
}


/* Child class: FrequentFlyer is a type of Airline Passenger */
class FrequentFlyer extends AirlinePassenger {

  int id = 435;         // Frequent Flyer ID #

  public int bonusMiles() { /* calc bonus miles */ }
  public void stowBaggage() {
        System.out.print("Passenger:" + id);
        System.out.println(" Place into overhead bin");
        }
}


/* ----------------- Runner ---------------------- */
class runner {

  static public void main (String args[]) {

    FrequentFlyer Billy = new FrequentFlyer();
    AirlinePassenger William;                   // no instantiation

    William = (AirlinePassenger)Billy;          // the cast

    System.out.println(Billy.id);
    System.out.println(William.id);

    System.out.println(Billy.whatFood());
    System.out.println(William.whatFood());

    Billy.stowbaggage();
    William.stowbaggage();
    }
}
```

The output of this program is

```
435
5551234
Chicken
Chicken
Passenger 435: Place into overhead bin
Passenger 435: Place into overhead bin
```

Some relatively unexpected things happened throughout that sequence. The number one thing to remember during this discussion is that both `Billy` and `William` are really the same object. The only difference is that `William` is just `Billy` cast into an `AirlinePassenger` (wasn't that a movie?). The first two prints of the `id` variables should be no news, given the previous section and the knowledge that instance variables do not override. Billy printed out the frequent flyer's `id` (435), and William printed out the airline passenger's (5551234). The printout of `dietpref` should also be of no great surprise, since only the parent had a diet preference variable and the child just inherited it. Consider Figure 10-3 for the discussion of the `stowBaggage` method.

Each call to the `stowBaggage` method invoked the frequent flyer's version. This is understandable, since you know methods can be overridden and that's exactly what happens in the case of the `frequentflyer` method. The only question may be why `William` printed out an `id` of 5551234 earlier and now prints out an `id` of 435. Earlier was a direct reference to the variable. Now, `William` merely referenced the child's overridden `stowBaggage` method, which performed the referencing of the `id` variable. Since it was the child's `stowBaggage` method that was called (it doesn't care who calls it), it went on its merry way referencing its variables as it always does, and in this case that meant referencing the child's `id` variable. A bit sticky, but clever nonetheless. C++ programmers should note that all methods in Java are analogous to C++ virtual methods.

FIGURE 10-3

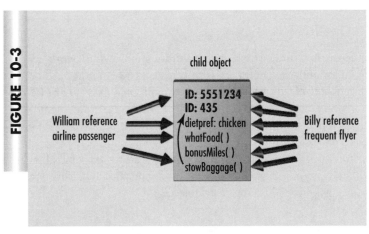

Cast pointing

Note that all this confusion was orchestrated to give you an idea of how objects are laid out. If all instance variables are declared private, then even with casting the parent's attributes will not be visible to the children.

Class casting allows you a great deal of flexibility. It's common to need to subclass a pre-built class to suit your needs. However, you may find out later that yet another facility (e.g., method parameter, etc.) requires an instance of the original class (not some subclass of it). With casting, you can pass off an instance of your subclass as being an instance of its parent. Further concepts in this chapter will make good use of class casting.

Back to Static

Earlier chapters brushed on the usage of static methods and variables; here the discussion will take a harder look at these elements. Static data and methods provide you a way to add to the framework of your class.

Staticism in Context

Assume you are creating a three-dimensional graphics class and you know you will continuously need sine and cosine values for 0—360 degrees. The first optimization you should make is to precalculate all the sines and cosines and store them in an array. That way, future time-critical functions that need a sine or cosine need only look it up in a table instead of having to call the costly mathematical function. Great, so your class could look like this:

```
class threed {

  float sines[]   = new float[360];
  float cosines[] = new float[360];

  .
  .
  .

```

You would then initialize these arrays and be done with it. Although this would work, it's not efficient. Every object you instantiate from this class will create its own sine and cosine arrays and populate them. If you create 100 objects, there will exist 100 `sines[]` arrays, 100 `cosines[]` arrays. Not only have you wasted 100 times too much memory, you have wasted 100 times too much computing power filling the arrays. What's really fusty is that every array contains exactly the same thing.

Converting these arrays to static is obviously the answer. If these arrays are static, then only one copy of them will exist no matter how many objects are instantiated. This one copy belongs to the class itself as opposed to one of its objects.

```
class threed {

  static float sines[]   = new float[360];
  static float cosines[] = new float[360];
```

All objects of this class have access to these arrays. The next question may logically be who will fill these arrays? The sine and cosine calculations must be performed once to fill the array, but if there are a hundred objects of this class, how is it decided who (i.e., which of the 100 objects) does the filling? Typically, none of the objects will fill the array; such duties are taken care of in *static initializer blocks* within the class. Static initializer blocks are blocks of code that exist outside the guarding confines of a method (let the oohs and aahs commence). As with static variables, they belong to the class, not any object. Here's how it could be done:

```
class threed {

  static float sines[]   = new float[360];
  static float cosines[] = new float[360];

  static {
      double gd;
      for (int g=0;g<360;++g) {
        gd = (double)g * 0.01745;
        sines[g]   = (float)Math.sin(gd);
        cosines[g] = (float)Math.cos(gd);
       }
      .
      .
      .
```

This block is not part of any method; it is part of the class and gets executed when the class is loaded. This happens *before* any objects are instantiated. Methods within the **threed** class can access these variables as they would any other instance variable. Methods in foreign classes could also access these variables (if they were defined **public**) by specifying the **threed.sines[]** or **any_object_of_threed.sines[]**. The first syntax makes sense, since these variables belong to the class, not any particular instance of the class. The second syntax allows any object of the **threed** class to also act as a referencer. This is mainly for the convenience of the programmer.

A final note on static variables is that they can be used for more than just lookup tables. Objects can modify them and use them for interobject communication. For example, every object upon its instantiation could increment a **counter** static variable, and assuming you wouldn't otherwise know how many objects were in existence, this counter could keep track. You will see this clearly in Chapter 14, which discusses threads. With threads, many processes/objects can use static variables for communicating with each other.

Methods and Mixing

You can also define methods as static. As with static variables, static methods are methods that belong to the class and not to any one object. You've already seen this with every standalone application in this text. The **main** method of any program must be defined static. Otherwise, if it were possible to create more than one instance of **main** in a class, how then would the environment decide which `main` was the one it should start running?

Although it's usually quite clear (as in the above sines example) when it would be useful to have variables and even methods be static, actually implementing and using them can get frustrating. Overall, this is less of a problem with static variables, but static methods have this annoying tendency of realizing they are one of a kind and get a bit snooty in dealing with those other kinds of instanceable variables and methods. In actuality, the problem often arises when a static method is told to reference a nonstatic variable or method. The same one-to-many problem arises; which one should it choose? Well, as expected, it doesn't choose any and just quits with an error. The following code illustrates some common quandaries:

```java
class testrun {

    int x;                  // instance var
    static int y;           // static instance var

    static public void main (String args[]) {

    y = 10;
    // x = 10;              // ERROR! x isn't static
    // printer(10);         // ERROR! printer isn't static
    }

    void printer(int x) {
      System.out.println(x);
      }
    }
```

The `main` method is well suited for this example since it is a static method. Two statements are commented out because they cause compile-time errors. The reason is that the class `testrun` could feasibly be instantiated many times. When that happens there will be many `x` variables and many copies of the `printer` method. The `main` method has no criteria (and shouldn't have any) to apply in deciding which to use/call. The `y` variable is static, and therefore the `main` method has no trouble using it (there is only one of them, so there is no decision to be made). Figure 10-4 shows the dilemma graphically.

Keep in mind that a static method can instantiate other classes that do not have static methods or variables. This would not be a problem, since that instantiation would have an associating variable name in the `static` method for identification.

```java
class nothing {

    public nothing () {}
    int zz;
    void donothing() {
    System.out.println("nothing");
    }
  }
```

```
class testrun {

static public void main(String args[]) {

        nothing bignothing = new nothing();
        bignothing.zz = 10;
        bignothing.donothing();
        }
 }
```

The variable name for the object above is **bignothing**. As many instances as you want of the **nothing** class could be instantiated as long as you have object names for them. This is no detraction from what you're used to. The place you must be careful is within the class in which you are using static methods. Often you will find yourself making more things static than you intended.

Ordering

The final topic of this section is the implications of static variables and blocks on the order of executed code within a class. As a rule, static initialization blocks and static variable initializations (i.e., included with the declaration) occur at class load time. Wow, this is early! This is guaranteed to be before any objects are created—in order to even think about instantiating an object you must have loaded the class first.

Class Loading

The code from above can be modified to illustrate how the ordering works.

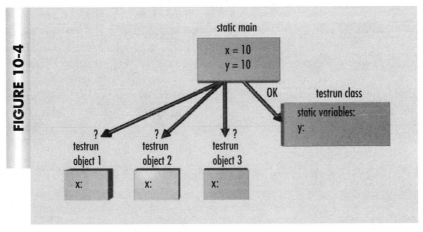

Statics vs. nonstatics

```
class testrun {

      int x = 50;                  // instance var
      static int y = 10;           // static instance var

      static {
        y = 99;
        }

      static public void main (String args[]) {

      y = 10;
      }
  }
```

Before any objects of the **testrun** class exist, the **y** variable will be created as a static variable and initialized to 10. The static initializer will then set it to 99 (silly, but true). The **main** method will not execute until it is called (don't worry, soon). Note that static methods must be called in order to execute, unlike static initialization blocks, which execute simply by virtue of the class being loaded. Once the **testrun** class is actually instantiated, the **x** variable will be created as an instance variable and set to 50. When the **main** method is finally executed, **y** will be set to 10.

Forwardness

Static initializations occur in the order in which they are written at class load time. This is important for resolving apparent forward dependency of variables. The following two sets of variable declarations and initializations result in errors:

```
int x = y * 10;           // y doesn't exist yet!
int y = 5;                // OK, y exists now but too late!

static int a = b * 10;    // b doesn't exist yet!
static int b = 1;         // Again b now exists, but too late!
```

In both cases the first initializer depends upon the second to set its value. This is disallowed for variable initializers for both instance and static variables. The problem with the first two statements is that the instance variable **x** relies on the instance variable **y**, which hasn't been declared yet. The second two statements have an analogous problem; a static variable is relying on an undeclared static variable (i.e., **a** relies on **b**, but at the time **a** is being initialized, **b** hasn't been declared yet). However, consider the following code:

```
int a = b * 10;
static int b = 1;
```

This sequence *is* legal. This is because the static variable **b** was initialized at class load time and the instance variable **a** will not be initialized until the class gets instantiated. Instantiation of objects is assured to be after class load, so the apparent forward dependency is only syntactic, not temporal.

Yet More Supported Diablerie

Java supports several more interesting features that play havoc with the object-oriented model. This section introduces these advanced features and gives examples for their use. It also discusses Java's sophisticated garbage collection facility and all that it does thanklessly for you.

Dynamic Instantiations

Dynamic instantiation of objects is easily the most insidious Java class feature covered so far, and only an introduction to the concept is presented here. It affords you the ability to decide at runtime what class a given object will be an instantiation of.

Which Shape?

For clarification, look at this extremely abbreviated code:

```
class Shape { ... }
class rectangle extends Shape { ... }
class triangle extends Shape { ... }
class circle extends Shape { ... }



     .
     .
     .


Shape MyShape;
```

Now assume that according to some event at runtime (user input, etc.), the **MyShape** object will need to be instantiated as one of the above shape classes (i.e., rectangle, triangle, circle). Since you can't predict which it will be, you can't hardcode it. As an aside, this plays buggers with the compiler, which also can't predict which it will be and can't perform its normal type checking.

Dynamic instantiation allows you to use a string variable as the determinant of which class gets instantiated. A dynamic instantiation for the **MyShape** variable above could be

```
String S = get_shape_type();        // say this returns "rectangle"
     .
     .
     .
Shape MyShape= (Shape)java.lang.Class.forName(S).newInstance();
```

The above statement performs an instantiation of the rectangle class, but its form is quite different from what you're used to. The heart of the dynamic instantiation is the class **java.lang.Class**. Every class running in a Java program has an object of the **java.lang.Class** class associated with it. These objects contain the runtime representations for each class (egad, we're messing with runtime representations of stuff—told you this is insidious).

The above statement uses the static `forName` method within `java.lang.Class` and performs an instantiation of whatever name the string holds. In this example, the string variable `S` could have been removed and the declaration then written as `(Shape)Class.forName("rectangle").newInstance()`, but this isn't exactly too dynamic; why use dynamic instantiation on a hardcoded (i.e., compile-time) declaration?

The compiler generally looks down on dynamic instantiations. The reason is that the `S` variable above could have come from anywhere. The compiler cannot predict the value of `S`. By the time `S` gets to the instantiation statement, it could even be a value that doesn't correspond to any existing classes (if that happens, a runtime error results, and it's none too pretty).

Also, note that the new object is cast to `Shape` and assigned to a `Shape` object variable `MyShape`. Again, this is because at compile time you don't know what type of object it will be, but you know it will be the child of `Shape` (assuming you are in charge of restricting the possible values the string `S` may be). So casting it to the parent is a logical solution.

The Catch

Some important limitations are associated with using dynamically instantiated objects. For instance, your usual flagrant use of varying constructors is stifled. When using this technique, only the default (i.e., no parameter) constructor of the class will get called. This limitation has spurred a pseudo-standard of defining a method named `initialize` within the parent that can do further construction if needed—although it must be explicitly called. A second limitation is that since you have casted this to its parent, you cannot rely on being able to call down into the methods of the child. This is related to the nastiness of casting up an inheritance tree, as discussed earlier in this chapter. This problem can be solved by clever initial setup of the parent but is definitely not intuitive.

All in all this is a precarious technique. For the above contrived example, using standard Java conditional statements could have emulated the same functionality. This would allow the compiler a much better hold on what's going on and would remove the limitations associated with dynamic instantiation. Granted, it would have also increased the code size and hindered your ability to quickly add child class types in the future.

Finding applicable uses for this facility can sometimes be the challenge. The code for the Java environment itself only uses this idea in a select few places. The possibility for implementation of dynamically created classes and their instantiations could insist on this usage, but at least in the beginning, you'll rarely need such things. If you find a place for this, think twice and be sure it's worth the trouble.

Into the Abstract

Java allows you to specify classes and methods as `abstract`. For classes, this signifies that the class itself cannot be instantiated and it *must* be subclassed. Having an abstract class usually means it will have some abstract methods (although it doesn't have to). Abstract methods must be overridden in all child classes of the `abstract` class. Well, if you're the logical type, you've realized that since all abstract classes must be subclassed, and all abstract methods in the `abstract` class must be overridden, then any code written in the parent's `abstract` method will never get executed, since it will always be overridden. Good call. Because of this, `abstract` methods don't have any code—they are simply a one-line declaration of the existence of the `abstract` method. The following is a legal `abstract` class and method definition:

```
abstract class iamabstract {

        public void abstract do_something();
        }
```

In essence, abstract classes allow you to create a protocol (i.e., a set of guidelines) for subclass definitions. Subclasses can implement additional methods and variables as long as all the abstract methods of the parent are also implemented. An abstract method has no method body and cannot be static nor private.

As was said, you cannot instantiate an abstract class. The following is an example abstract class named `Shape`:

```
/* The abstract class Shape - it cannot be instantiated */
abstract class Shape {

    abstract public void drawme();     // abstract method

    public void printmsg() {

            System.out.println("This message comes from a");
            System.out.println("subclass of the abstract class");
            System.out.println("Shape.");
            }


    }

/* class rectangle - it MUST override drawme() */
class rectangle extends Shape {

        int width, height;

        public rectangle(int width,int height) {
                this.width = width;
                this.height = height;
                }

        public void drawme() {     // overrider

                        // code to draw a rectangle

                }
        }
```

As with any subclass of the `Shape` class, the `rectangle` class implements the `drawme` method. This is under the assumption that a triangle's `drawme` method would draw a triangle, a circle's `drawme` method would draw a circle, etc.

Several points to note are that if the `rectangle` class did not override the `drawme` method, it too would become an abstract class—in other words, it didn't follow the rules of overriding the abstract methods of its parent. Hence, it is cursed with being abstract itself. The power of abstracting methods is that a programmer will be assured that any instance of a child of the `Shape` class will have a method that knows how to draw itself regardless of what type of shape that might be. This type of standard-setting becomes quite important in large projects with class hierarchies that continue to expand over time. New child class types can be added, and since they must conform to the abstraction set by the parent, old code will know how to use them immediately. An example displaying the use of abstract classes appears later in this chapter.

Interfaces

Use of subclassing in Java is not only ridiculously useful, it's mandatory. Occasionally, subclassing functionality from a given class is not enough. You will find instances where you may require the functionality of two (or more) different classes. This concept is aptly named *multiple inheritance,* and it is supported in many object-oriented and hybrid languages. In essence, a class may have more than one parent and inherit the functionality from all of its parents. Java does not quite implement this ideal with such crispness.

What They Give You

Consider the following problem, which you've already pondered, worked on, and solved but didn't know it. The applet designed in Chapter 8 spun a line around. By virtue of its being named an "applet," it is implied that it runs within a browser and that it must subclass the `java.applet.Applet` class. That is required if the applet is to inherit the attributes and methods (i.e., `init`, `paint`, etc.) of applets. That isn't too big a deal, since that is exactly what that applet (or any applet) does.

The second consideration is that in that applet you spawned a thread to spin the line. Rightfully, to create your own version of a thread, you should subclass the `Thread` class and override the `Thread` class's `run` method. This is a perfectly legal way to create a thread. Unfortunately, this causes a need for multiple inheritance for applets that wish to spawn threads.

As was explained above, Java does not have true support for multiple inheritance. What Java does have is *interfaces,* as illustrated in Figure 10-5. An interface is something of a workaround for multiple inheritance. To use the word in a sentence, it allows you to interface your classes to other (nonparent) classes. An interface is a specification of how one class may interact with another. For example, consider the electrical socket your toaster is plugged into. The toaster manufacturer assumed that the interface to accessing electricity would be your electrical plug. You could plug the toaster in any acceptable socket, whether

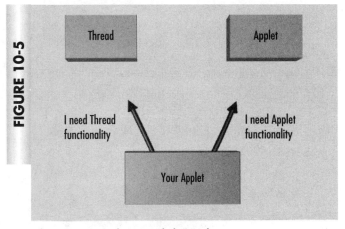

Inheriting applets and threads

it be in an office building, a house, or a restaurant. The power could come from a hydroelectric dam, a nuclear power plant, or a portable generator. The toaster doesn't know or care about all those details, all it cares about is that the socket is designed according to specifications. It will only deal with the socket itself—in other words, that is its designated interface to accessing the functionality of electricity.

It's this definition of an interface that provides the cooperation among very unlike objects. The interface that allows applets to spawn threads is the `java.lang.Runnable` interface. In order to tell the world you are abiding by the specifications of an interface such as `Runnable`, your class declaration specifies that it *implements* `Runnable`.

First some details about creating interfaces. Interfaces are comparable to abstract classes.

- Methods in interfaces do not have method bodies. In appearance, this is similar to defining abstract methods. They may not be static or native.

- Classes that implement the interface must implement the bodies of all its methods. This is, in effect, the common factor for all classes implementing the interface. They all implement common method protocols while spanning multiple inheritance trees.

- Interfaces can be public or private.

- Variables in interfaces are static and final and must be initialized. Variables in interfaces aren't very variable at all in that they are effectively constants.

- Variables in classes may be declared as an interface type. This specifies that the variable can point to any object that implements that interface. Read that again; it's way important.

The Syntax

To have a class implement an interface, it uses the `implements` keyword as did the applet examples.

```
class MyJavaApp extends Applet implements Runnable {
```

The syntax of an interface itself is much like that of a class, with a few significant differences. Shockingly, the keyword `interface` is used in place of the word `class`. Other than that, only method names are listed without bodies.

```
public interface MyInterface {

        void method1(int x);
        void method2(int y);

        }
```

Runnable

To explain the usage of the interfaces, let's examine the `Runnable` interface, since it is a hallmark interface and likely the one you will use the most. As was mentioned, the theoretically proper way to create a thread is to subclass the `java.lang.Thread` class and override the `run` method. When the thread starts, it will execute your overridden `run` method. The `Runnable` interface only specifies one method, which coincidentally happens to be the `run` method. This specifies that all classes that implement this interface must include a `run`. You know that you've already been doing that in applets as a matter of convention. But the real reason you've needed to do it is to appease `Runnable`.

The `Thread` class contains a constructor that allows a parameter of type `Runnable`. This is using the interface as an object type that has the only restriction that the object passed to this constructor must implement `Runnable`.

```
Thread (Runnable target)
```

That's quite nice; it would make sense that since you were unable to subclass `Thread`, you could just send yourself (i.e., your object) to `Thread` and say "spawn this off as a thread." The only snag is that without the benefit of the interface type, what type could you specify as the incoming parameter? An immediate answer may be the `Applet` class type, since you are largely interested in spawning applets with threads. The problem is that you will see threads can be spawned for any class type in standalone programs or applets. There is no way you can restrict the input parameter to an inheritance tree, and since users may define class types at will, there's no way to accommodate all possible object types that want to be threaded.

Using `Runnable` as the input parameter type does two important things. Any class that implements the `Runnable` interface can now send off one of its objects as a legal parameter. This means that any object of any class ever created or that ever will be created, as long as it implements `Runnable`, can be sent to that method (i.e., that method's only input parameter restriction is that the incoming object implement `Runnable`). Secondly, the

`Thread` class doesn't need to know anything more about the incoming object than the fact that it implements `Runnable`. Remember, `Runnable` specifies that all classes implementing *must* contain a `run` method. In essence, that's all the `Thread` class cares about, since that's what it wants to execute inside the created thread. Figure 10-6 shows this lenient acceptance.

This is important and is the beauty of interfaces. The interface is largely a guarantee to all interested classes that implementors of that interface will implement the interface's methods. Interfaces are usually designed so that the included methods are all the information that would be pertinent to external classes. Their use should be clear-cut when you reach a position where you need to inherit functionality from two classes. Encapsulate the functionality in an interface and force the subclasses to implement it.

Using Interfaces and Abstract Classes

You will now build an example to use the concepts of interfaces and abstract classes to firm up the ideas. Assume you are out to design a word processor file viewer. Your biggest challenge is that there are many word processing programs in the world and you want to be able to view a file created by any of them. Obviously, each word processor has its own way

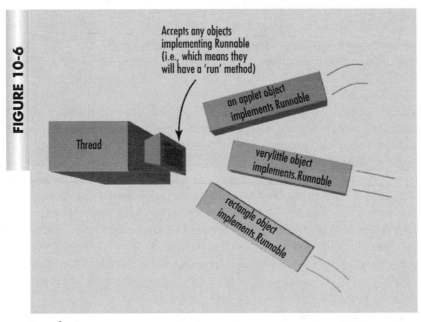

FIGURE 10-6

Accepts any objects implementing Runnable (i.e., which means they will have a 'run' method)

Thread

an applet object implements Runnable

verylittle object implements.Runnable

rectangle object implements.Runnable

Interfacing to Thread

of saving its files—i.e., its own file format. Your task is slightly lessened because you've decided to only create a viewer for these files (you're not trying to make an actual word processor).

Your design is critical. Your first realization is that you know of about four different word processing file formats right now that you wish to include. But you are positive more will come along in the future and you certainly want to add them. Because of the complexities associated with each file format, you will need many specific methods for each type. It's best to give each format its own class. However, although reading the formats is a very personal thing for each type of file, in general, they will all perform the same type of operations, including reading from the disk, displaying on the screen, etc.

Making Something Abstract

Your first step should be to create an abstract class defining what these general operations will be. Assume for now that you will just need two different operations. Your abstract class could be

```
/* Abstract class for word processor files */
abstract class word_processor_file {

/* Non-abstract method for reading binary files */
        public byte[] read_from_disk(String filename) {

                // code to read in disk file and return byte[]

                }

/* Abstract method for displaying format onto the screen */
        abstract public void display_file();

        }
```

The class's first method is `read_from_disk`. This method is not abstract, because you can safely assume that any word processing file can be read in from disk as just a plain binary file. The file is then stored in a byte array and returned to the caller. In other words, reading a file from disk is the same for a Microsoft Word file as it for a WordPerfect file.

The second method is `abstract`. This abstraction dictates that all classes subclassing this class must put the means to display their file onto the screen within this method. Therefore, anyone ever using a child of this class (regardless if that child is for a Microsoft Word file, a WordPerfect file, or any other word processing file) knows that if they call the `display_file` method, the file will be displayed to the screen.

The next step would be to create some subclasses for your abstract class. Infinitely intricate details of deciphering the file formats will be left out—you are only interested in the class setup.

```
class WordPerfect_file extends word_processor_file {

        byte myFile[];
```

```
/* Constructor */
      public WordPerfect_file(String filename) {

         myFile = read_from_disk(filename);

      }


/* Overriding the abstract method */
      public void display_file() {
            // intricate format and screen-displaying details
      }
    }
```

Additional classes like this could be defined for all other formats that you are currently interested in being able to view. The `myFile` array is created in the constructor by calling the parent's `read_from_disk` method. As you can see, because of the standardization developed by the abstract class, users of these classes always know about the `display_file` methods (and any others you may specify) in order to use them. Regardless of whether they are WordPerfect, Microsoft Word, etc., the standardization hides all the details.

Time to Interface

It's now months later. Your word processor viewer has been in the shareware market for a while and registrations are pouring in. You've already added a few more word processor file formats as customers have requested. The additions were straightforward, as you just created more subclasses off your original abstract class. The only problem is that those pesky customers keep requesting features. Their number one request has been the ability to print the documents in addition to just viewing them.

You decide to hunker down and give the people what they want. As you begin your design, you realize that it would be useful to design a print class that in the spirit of object-oriented programming handled all the printer details for you. In addition, it shouldn't be restricted to just printing word processing files; someday you might want to reuse this printing class. You decide to have the class expect just a stream of bytes for printing (Note that the array you have put in your word processing classes is *not* directly suitable, that it still includes all the file formatting—you will need to decode it before sending it to the printer.)

You begin work on your print class. You specify an interface called `byteable` that specifies a `decode_to_bytes` method. Therefore, from now on, any class, whether it contains pictures, word processing files, plain text, etc., can implement this interface and the print class will know how to get the data in its desired byte format. Figure 10-7 shows these relationships.

As you can see from the figure, any class that implements `byteable` may use it to interface to the print class. The print class is designed to accept objects that are `byteable` and know how to access their `decode_to_bytes` methods. The `byteable` interface

FIGURE 10-7

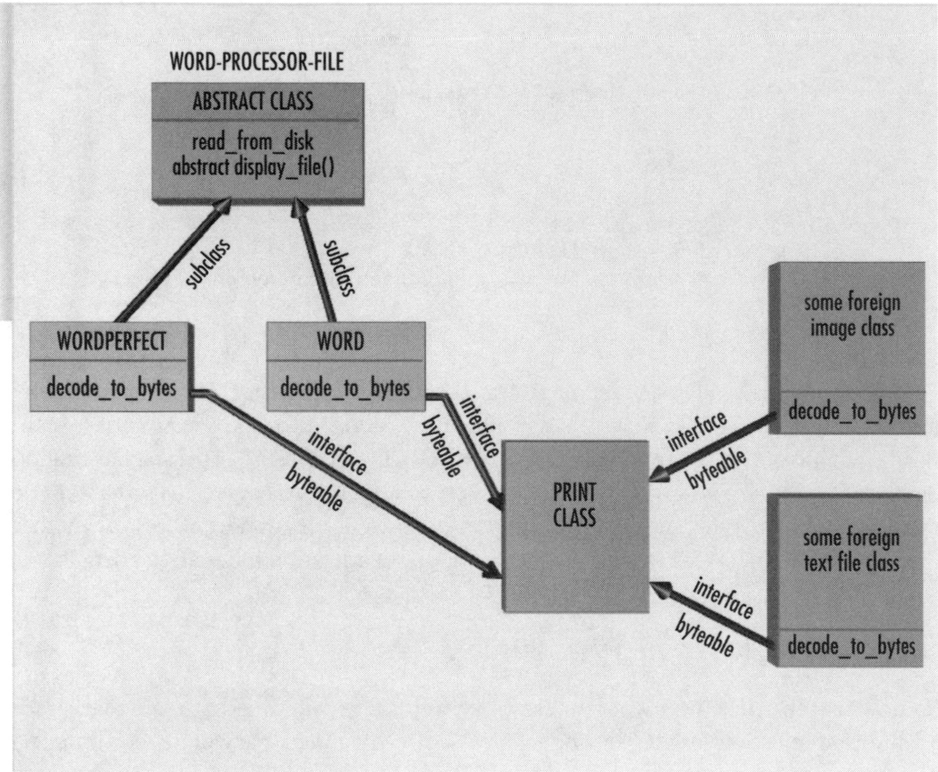

Word processor viewer design

could also be accepted in the future by other appropriate classes, such as serial file transfer class (which would also be happy sending a stream of bytes).

The interface can be defined as

```
interface byteable {

        public byte[] decode_to_bytes();

        }
```

Therefore, classes implementing this interface must only implement one method. Add to the previous code:

```
class WordPerfect_file extends word_processor_file
                                implements byteable {

        byte myFile[];

/* Constructor */
        public WordPerfect_file(String filename) {
```

```
        myFile = read_from_disk(filename);

        }


/* Overriding the abstract method */
      public void display_file() {
            // intricate format and screen-displaying details
        }

/* Satisfy the interface */
      public byte[] decode_to_bytes() {
            // code to decode myFile into a plain stream
            // of text (bytes)
            }
        }
```

The `decode_to_bytes` method will have to be tailored for the specific type of data in the class. The only piece left in this puzzle is how to get the print class to use the interface. In this case, it would be appropriate in its constructor.

```
class print_class {                     // does NOT implement byteable

      byte printMe[];


      public print_class(byteable thing_to_print) {

            printMe = thing_to_print.decode_to_bytes();

        }
        .
        .
        .
```

The constructor receives the `byteable` object (i.e., an object of a class that implements `byteable`) as a parameter and calls its `decode_to_bytes`. The print class has absolutely no inkling of what type of thing it is printing; all it knows is that the incoming object has a `decode_to_bytes` method that will provide the bytes to be printed. New classes implementing `byteable` can be created and still use this print class.

The Garbage Man Cometh

Without Java's premier garbage collection facilities, you would just be a stinky old C programmer. Okay, a stinky old C programmer with some security features and object-oriented superpowers. Oh, and serious internetworking support and more architecture independence than you can shake a `for` loop at. All right, maybe you wouldn't be just a C programmer, but the fact remains that Java's garbage collection facility is clean, fast, and removes a great burden from the programmer.

The designers didn't go to all the trouble of devoting such concerted time into the implementation of Java's garbage collection just to make your life easier (although that was certainly part of it). In reality, it's again all part of their grand security scheme. It's more in keeping with the philosophy that your code will "leave the system as it found it." To allow you to have memory leaks could eventually violate system integrity, and that just wouldn't do.

The garbage collector in Java is a *mark-and-sweep* algorithm. Mark-and-sweep algorithms in general run when needed and check every legal memory reference in the running program to see where it points. Each previously allocated memory chunk that is still being pointed to (i.e., still referenced by an active pointer) is marked on a master list of allocated pieces of memory. When the mark phase is done, the master list is then traversed, removing the marks off of marked pieces and removing unmarked pieces altogether (i.e., declaring them as free memory).

To see Java's garbage collector shine, look at the following code:

```
/* This class is out to cause trouble */
class testrun {

  static int a[];

  static public void main (String args[]) {
      allocer();
      System.gc();
      System.out.println(a[1]);
      }

/* method to create an array then die */
  static void allocer() {
      int x[] = new int[10];
      x[1] = 5;
      a = x;
      }
}
```

After getting called by **main**, the **allocer** method declares an array **x**, assigns one of its elements to 5, points the static instance array **a** to it, then exits. You should see that since **allocer** exited and **x** was a local array to **allocer**, the variable **x** ceased to exist. The memory it pointed to could be thought of as out in space with no ties to reality; that is, of course, except for the **a** variable. This shows the smarts of the garbage collector. Upon returning to **main**, a feeble request is made to the system to initiate the garbage collector. Only in odd, contrived examples for Java programming guides should you ever really have to invoke the garbage collector explicitly. It runs asynchronously in the background when needed—it knows when to run.

The print statement then prints out the correct answer, 5. If the garbage collector did not realize that somebody still pointed at the piece of memory allocated from the instantiation of the **x** array (which was buried deep in a method and is now long gone), it would have cleaned it up and the **a** array would have pointed to free memory space. Pointing to free memory space is a common problem for C/C++ programmers and still provides a consistent method for system lockup. However, you can rest assured; it just cannot happen in Java.

The garbage collector is truly a feature long overdue for modern languages. C/C++ relied solely on the programmer to clean up his or her allocating mess. Inevitably, programmers sometimes forgot to do that, causing memory leaks, dangling pointers, and all sorts of other immoral activities.

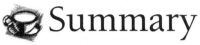

Summary

Java's facilities for class and object manipulation are undeniably vast. In actuality, most of these advanced techniques are present in other languages in one form or another. However, the design of Java was directed to using the best and most secure of the features available. It would seem that the designers did a good job toward that end, as rarely has industry and academia so quickly embraced a new language.

Hopefully, after reading these chapters you've built a solid foundation on Java's low-level coding and its object-oriented principles. You're ready to embark on serious programming endeavors of your own. Subsequent chapters of this book will start focusing on specific, important aspects of Java programming. These topics include debugging, networking, threading, etc. As your knowledge of Java programming has grown, so should have your understanding of its potential. The advanced capabilities of Java do a good job at visibly setting Java apart from other languages. You've seen how it works, now you'll see what it can do.

Questions

1. What are the advantages and disadvantages of having constructors that call other constructors in the same class?

2. Explain why "Passenger 435: place into overhead bin" was printed in both cases in the Billy/William example.

3. What errors exist in the following program?

```
class runner {

        int x = a;
        int y;
        int z = y * 5;
        static int a;

        static { for (int g=0;g<33;++g) a += x; }

        static public void main(String args[]) {

                a = 10;
                z = y;
                }
```

4. The `AirlinePassenger` and `FrequentFlyer` classes were designed in an odd way to prove a point; how could their design be improved?

5. Assume you had a counter class with several child classes. All children were specialized counters from 0 to some number of a different data type (i.e., `int`, `float`, etc.). For this example, why would using dynamic instantiation be limiting?

Exercises

1. Expand the `rectangle` class shown earlier in this chapter. Include additional convenience constructors.

2. Write your own file input routine. Read a disk file and print the contents to the screen. Use a `finalize` method to tidy up.

3. Write an abstract `Shape` class and several subclasses (i.e., rectangle, circle, triangle). Design an applet that randomly picks one of these elements, dynamically instantiates it, and draws the shape on the screen.

4. Redo Exercise 3 using conditional tests to determine which shape to instantiate.

5. Write a program that uses a static long array to hold the factorials up to 20. Allow a user to request a factorial and look it up in the static array.

Exceptions and Debugging

11

You will learn about the following in this chapter:

- What exceptions are
- How to throw system exceptions
- How to define your own exceptions
- How to catch exceptions and handle them
- When you should use exception handling
- How to follow a Java stack trace
- How to debug your code using the JDB debugger

In the good old days of computing, there wasn't all this hubbub about program bugs. The programmers of the day used assembly language and didn't have all the fancy debugging tools available today. There were only three types of program output: correct, incorrect, and system-lockup. Testing programs was a lot like hunting pigeons in a glass factory. Most every shot you'd hear a crash, but the absence of breaking glass didn't necessarily mean that you'd hit a pigeon.

Debugging was done from the back end—you waited for the program to finish, then worked your way back to find where the bug occurred. Well, it's no longer the good old days. Java has taken a state-of-the-art approach to dealing with errors. It goes beyond watching errors happen and allows you to react and recover from even the most insidious violations.

This chapter will provide an overview of Java's exception handling (exceptions are a superset of errors) and its debugging facilities. Given the myriad of debuggers that are popping up and will continue to pop up, this chapter will provide you with a general plan of attack. You should have a better understanding of what pretty debuggers are doing for you and the knowledge to debug without any superenhanced tools. Hopefully the earlier chapters got you quickly on your way to developing Java applications; this one should speed you into squashing any bugs that are holding you up.

Exceptions

Java includes the ability to detect and recover from *exceptions*. An exception is basically a runtime occurrence of something your program wasn't expecting. In most discussions regarding exceptions, such an event is usually an unexpected runtime error. Exceptions and errors have a close relationship in that errors are usually the most common and most interesting type of exception. Fitting the description of an exception, runtime errors are things that your program just didn't know were going to happen.

Defining Exceptions

Runtime errors are not the only types of exceptions. Beyond errors, the definition of exceptions becomes a matter of debate. When you pressed a key, your program was not likely expecting it. Is that an exception? The answer is dependent upon your implementation and what a keypress could mean to your program, but yes, pressing a key could be classified as an exception.

It's important to not get too accustomed to classifying things as exceptions that can be handled by simpler means. Exception handling is not often pretty and can be confusing. Usually the best route is to just naively consider exceptions and errors as one in the same. This innocent view of exceptions will give you a better understanding of when you should be using exception handling techniques to deal with an event and when you should be finding some alternate method.

Who Threw That?

The exception handling paradigm in Java uses the idea that when an exception occurs, that exception is *thrown*. You can think of this as an error-causing Java statement (for example, an arithmetic assignment that causes a divide by zero) that causes an exception and throws it (as if it were a hot potato) to whoever is out there ready to catch it. The statement itself is not designed to deal with errors, so in an act of desperation, it throws the exception in hopes someone at a higher level will know what to do about it. Typically, you are used to the runtime environment catching it, displaying a nasty error message, and terminating the program. With Java exceptions this no longer has to be the case.

Following this paradigm, Java's methods can include the keyword `throws` in method declarations, after the parameter list and before the method body. As in

```
public void myMethod() throws exception_list {
```

This keyword allows for a specification of the exceptions that can occur within the method. In other words, you are admitting that some statement or statements within your method *could* cause a known exception to occur. The compiler insists that all methods with statements that could cause exceptions either handle their exceptions or list them after the `throws` keyword. Handling exceptions will be discussed in depth later, but suffice it to say this basically means that you provide actions for the program to take in case the exception occurs. If you handle the exception, no other methods calling your method will have to worry about it. On the other hand, including it after the `throws` will tell all future callers of your method that your method could generate that exception. Your method isn't handling the exception; it just throws it up to its caller and lets the caller handle it. Since the buck has been passed, callers of your method will need to either handle or list that exception after the **throws** keyword.

For example, assume you wrote a method to read in a file. Attempting to open a nonexistent file would cause a **FileNotFoundException** to be thrown. Many methods in the classes of the **java.io** package declare this as a possibly occurring exception. If you use any of these methods, then you will need to either handle this exception or include that exception after your **throws** keyword. Actually, the only penalty for ignoring possible exceptions is a compiler warning. But in an effort to generate solid code (and warning-free compiles), taking care of possible exceptions is recommended.

Runtime Exceptions

A special type of exception is what the designers of Java have deemed a *runtime* exception. Yes, runtime exceptions happen at runtime, but that's not much of a distinction, because so do normal (i.e., not labeled as runtime) exceptions. What sets runtime exceptions apart is that they can occur almost anywhere. For example, the discussion above was about a file-not-found exception. It's easy for Java to know when that might happen—obviously, only when a file is being searched for. On the other hand, a null pointer exception can happen almost anywhere. Anytime an object is referenced, there is the possibility of generating a null pointer exception. Well, obviously, objects are referenced a lot in Java programs.

The Java designers realized this and the fact that since almost every method could throw a null pointer exception, almost every method would have to declare a null pointer exception after its **throws** keyword. It became kind of redundant. So, they decided to classify certain exceptions as runtime exceptions (children of **java.lang.RuntimeException**). These exceptions don't have to be included in **throws** exception lists.

Also, checking for exceptions is not free in terms of processing time. Runtime exceptions' omnipresence would cause checking for them to cost a great deal of processing time. It just wasn't worth it. So, to wrap it up, any true exception (child of **java.lang.Exception**) must, er…should, be either handled or declared in **throws** anywhere it might occur. Any runtime exception (child of **java.lang.RuntimeException**) doesn't. These sets of exceptions are listed in the Appendix. Don't worry, compiler error messages will alert you when you get them mixed up.

Errors

Java also has what it designates as true errors that may be thrown. Yeah, you were told to consider exceptions and errors as effectively the same thing, and that's true for normal errors. But these errors are thought of as abnormal errors; you'll see what that means momentarily. These errors are **java.lang.Error** class. The good news is you really don't have to worry about them. They exist to start yelling when an abnormal event occurs. Sure, the above discussion on exceptions such as files not being found and the like isn't exactly desirable, but generally that stuff happens in the course of running programs and it's not abnormal. Abnormal here means catastrophic—Java virtual machines crashing, exhausted memory, computer parts flying all over the place, and other bizarre stuff. Anyway, true Java errors are not your concern. Trying to use the exception handling facilities to handle them yourself is possible but generally not a good idea, and it's certainly not recommended. Reproducible errors are probably best to left to the professionals (i.e., get on the Net and e-mail somebody—maybe the Java team?).

 Play Ball!

This section will introduce three new Java keywords: `try`, `throw`, and `catch`. Sure does sound like little league, doesn't it? Notice that here the keyword is `throw`, not the earlier discussed `throws`. These are two separate keywords in Java and perform different, albeit relatively related functions. Java's exception handling paradigm is based on a design by Bjarne Stroustrup, the creator of C++. It extends traditional error handling to a point where the programmer is in control. No longer do errors simply spit out a message and halt the program—unless that's what the programmer wants. The key concept is error recovery.

Suspicion

In order to handle exceptions, you need to know what code you are worried about. This is where the `try` keyword comes in. As if to tell the compiler "I want to try this code out, but things could get ugly." The format is as follows:

```
try {
    a = 0;
    a = 10/a;
    System.out.println("Hey! it worked!");
    }
catch(ArithmeticException e) {
    System.out.println(e.getMessage());
    }
System.out.println("The calculations are complete.");
```

The division by `a` will cause an arithmetic exception, since it is a divide by zero. Arithmetic exceptions are Java runtime exceptions—i.e., they can happen most anywhere. Usually such an error will cause program termination; however, since the exception was thrown within the confines of a `try` block, the `catch` block at the end will be checked for a match. Since you were being the wily programmer you always are, you were prepared for such an eventuality, and there is a specific `catch` statement ready for the exception. In this case, the one and only `catch` statement expects an `ArithmeticException`. When an exception is matched within a `catch` statement's parameter list, the body of the `catch` is then executed. In this case a print statement calls the exception's `getMessage` accessor method and displays "/ by zero". The "Hey! it worked!" would *not* be printed in this case, since execution will exit the `try` block as soon as an exception is thrown. As you will see, this ability to leave a block of code will be exploited in strange, new ways.

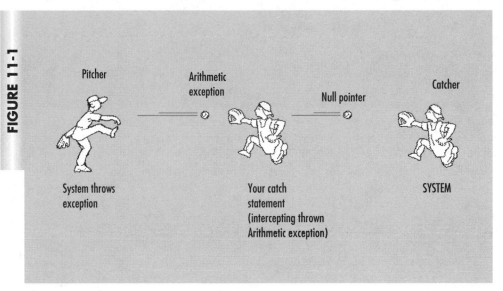

FIGURE 11-1

Pitcher

Arithmetic
exception

Null pointer

Catcher

System throws
exception

Your catch
statement
(intercepting thrown
Arithmetic exception)

SYSTEM

Playing catch

Figure 11-1 shows a depiction of the previous `try-catch` sequence. Arithmetic exceptions are caught because of a `catch` statement with that parameter. But other exceptions (such as a null pointer) would not be. You will need to know what you are intending to catch and plan accordingly. Usually, your list will be small and this will mean a `catch` statement for every type of exception you want to handle.

Incoming

Note that if a divide by zero would occur outside the warm confines of a `try` block (with a matching `catch`) then the arithmetic exception would have been thrown with no one to catch it. Who has to catch it then? The Java runtime environment, that's who—and it's usually none too happy. A horrible error message is displayed, and more importantly, program execution is halted. This was not true for the above example. After catching the exception, it prints "/ by zero", and the code would continue to print "The calculations are complete." This is a distinct advantage with controlling errors; depending on the situation, your code can recover and continue to run.

It is possible to have a `try` statement with several possible `catch` statements. Assuming your coding style is a bit on the aggressive side or a segment of your code uses a lot of exception-prone operations, you can have as many `catch` statements as needed to attempt to quell the fray. The syntax follows:

```
try {
    // exception throwing code
    }
```

continued on next page

continued from previous page

```
catch(Exception1 e) {
    System.out.println("Exception 1");
}
catch(Exception2 e) {
    System.out.println("Exception 2");
}
```

This chain can continue as needed. When an exception is thrown from inside the try block, that exception will be compared to the one listed in the corresponding catch statements. In the above example, if the try block threw an Exception2, then the second catch would nab it and execute its block (printing "Exception 2"). If the exception thrown doesn't match any of the ones listed in catch statements, then the exception is not (and cannot be) handled at this level. So, the exception would be left for someone else to handle—i.e., in a larger-scoped try block or in the throws exception list of the method.

Try's Domain

Once the program execution reaches the try statement, that statement will stay in effect until its block is exited. No matter where the execution within a try block goes (i.e., calls to other methods, calls to API methods, etc.), if an exception occurs, the try block will still have a chance to handle it. For example, the following code illustrates a try block and an exception-causing other method.

```
try {
        other();        // exception will be caught from
                        // this call
        System.out.println("Hey! it worked!");
    }
catch(ArithmeticException e) {
    System.out.println(e.getMessage());
    }
System.out.println("The calculations are complete.");

other();                // exception will not be caught
                        // system will issue an error and
                        // terminate the run
.
.
.

void other() {
        int a;
        a = 0;
        a = 10/a;
        }
```

In the above example the first execution of the other method has its exception caught, and the "/ by zero" message is issued. The program continues and will reach the second call to other. This time it is not contained in a try block, and the system must catch the exception. It will issue an error message and stop the thread.

Projectiles

When a Java built-in exception occurs (arithmetic exceptions, null pointer exceptions, array index out of range, etc.) the system throws it, but it's also possible for you to throw exceptions. Assume you are writing a method that performs some operation upon an object. The object is sent as an input parameter by the caller of your method. As a matter of robustness, you can check to be sure that the object sent is not a null object. Since your method would not likely be able to do much with a null object, you can throw a null pointer exception back at the offending caller.

```
public Object manipulator(Object A) {

  if (A == null)
    throw new NullPointerException();

    .
    .
    .

```

If a null object is sent to this method, it will immediately ricochet a null pointer exception back to the caller. Obviously, it's important to only throw exceptions when the situation warrants it. Throwing exceptions carelessly not only confuses the masses but degrades the importance of exceptions and exception handling.

Throw Your Own

To further this idealistic childhood day out in the backyard playing catch, you aren't limited to throwing the system's defined exceptions. You're quite welcome to create your own exceptions and throw them. You can define a new exception thusly:

```
class DuplicateKeyException extends Exception {
        DuplicateKeyException(String msg) {
        super(msg);
        }
}
```

This is the general form for subclassing the `Exception` class, although it's certainly not the only form. The string `msg` is sent to the `Exception` class's constructor to do whatever it does with those things (generally just prints them at some point). This is really a bare minimum exception definition but is typically an adequate one. The `Exception` class is well defined in that it already holds most of the needed elements.

It's important to remember that exceptions are, in all respects, objects. All exceptions in Java are descendants of the `java.lang.Exception` class (even the `RuntimeException` class subclasses `Exception`). The immediate parent of `java.lang.Exception` is the `java.lang.Throwable` class, and its grandparent is the `java.lang.Object` class. An object must be a descendant of `Throwable` in order for it to be thrown. Here's an example:

```
/* baseball objects can be thrown */
class baseball extends Throwable {
  int speed;
  }


/* The pitcher throws the baseball */
class pitcher {
  public static void main(String args[]) throws baseball {

    throw new baseball();
    }
  }
```

Note that you could feasibly have any class subclass **Throwable** and start flinging its objects around without regard. Obviously, this is not the intent of being able to throw things. You can create some clever, slow, and hard-to-read code by using the throw-catch paradigm in nonstandard ways. It's probably best to leave the game of catch to the exceptions.

Catch All

The decision as to which **catch** block is executed is based upon the type of exception in the **catch**'s parameter list. Direct matches (e.g., an **ArithmeticException** was thrown and there exists a **catch** with an **ArithmeticException** as a parameter) obviously cause that **catch** to be chosen. However, even if the **catch** statement's parameter is a superclass of the thrown object, a match will occur.

```
try {
       .
       .
       .
    }
catch(ArithmeticException e) {       // all Arithmetic
       ...                           // Exceptions will be
                                     // caught
catch(Exception e) {                 // all Exceptions will
       ...                           // be caught
catch(Throwable e) {                 // Everything will be
       ...                           // caught
```

The sequence above goes through sets of possible thrown elements to catch. The first **catch** will catch all thrown arithmetic exceptions. The second will catch any type of exception (e.g., null pointer, array index out of range) except an arithmetic, because that would have been caught in the previous **catch**. The final **catch** will catch any other throwable objects. In fact, the final **catch** is always guaranteed to catch whatever was thrown.

This gives you the ability to catch everything thrown at your code (all exceptions, that is). That's quite an interesting concept—programs that can't end in abnormal termination. Well, don't break out the scotch just yet. You can do this, but it's not smart or overly useful. The best way to handle exceptions is to catch them to thwart expected errors and otherwise to heed their complaints and fix problems in your code. This catch-all implementation of exception handling is extremely powerful, but as with most things, it shouldn't be abused.

Finally

Another ingredient in Java's exception handling is the `finally` keyword. The `finally` keyword signifies that its block should be executed regardless of what happens within the preceding `try` block. In other words, it gives you a place where you can put any code that must be executed in this section regardless of exceptions, returns, etc. An example looks like this:

```
try {
  a = 100/a;

/* If no error, always return at least 10 */
  if (a<10) return 10;

} catch (ArithmeticException e) {
        System.out.println(e.getMessage());
        }

/* This always gets executed */
finally {
        System.out.println("Try is done");
        }

return a;
 }
```

In all cases, the message "Try is done" is printed. The three possibilities, as shown in Figure 11-2, are an arithmetic exception, an early return of 10, or normal passthrough.

Use of the `finally` statement can help clean up situations in which code is suspect of causing exceptions. Don't confuse this with the `finalize` method for object finalization. The `finally` statement is a safe method for cleaning up after your object (often in the form of releasing allocated resources—i.e., files).

When to Use Exception Handling

Java's formal implementation of exception handling is unquestionably a powerful tool. However, always keep in mind that throwing exceptions can be a relatively expensive operation. This is not an attempt to sway you from using exception handling; there are just a few guidelines you should consider when implementing your own exceptions and exception handling routines.

In general, if you encounter a situation that is considered an error but your intent is to deal with it immediately, then going through the trouble of formally defining it as an exception can be wasteful. Consider if you were writing a program to perform the

FIGURE 11-2

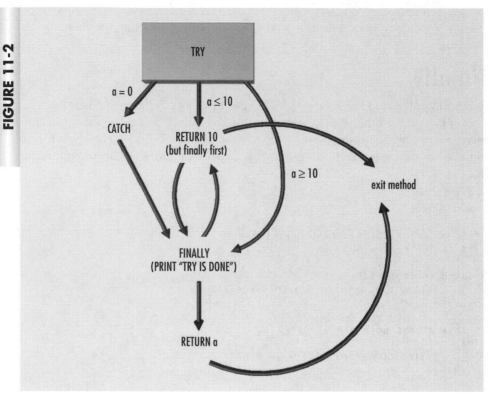

`finally` always gets run

low-level operations for reading from a hard disk. Chances are read errors would be common. Assume the high-level routine that is using your disk reader is a game program trying to read in its "saved game" file. Obviously, the game program is probably not designed with any particular smarts about handling low-level disk errors. Therefore, for such exceptions, having your low-level disk reader throw the game a disk-read exception is probably not the best route.

First of all, disk reads are quite common errors, and many times a retry to the disk (or several retries) will overcome the error. In other words, instead of immediately throwing an exception, the low-level disk program should instead try to solve the error itself first. Obviously, if the disk has died and the "saved game" file is forever lost, then some sort of a report to the high-level game program will be needed (i.e., you can resort to an exception).

The low-level disk routine example raises several points about exception use:

> If the error/exception can best be (or only be) handled by a local routine, then usually a conditional block of code can provide the needed remedy. In other words, if you have a section of code that throws an exception that is

always caught three lines later by the immediately succeeding `catch`, you would probably be better off handling the exception with an `if` statement. The arithmetic exception example earlier in this chapter violated this principle (it did so for simplicity in explaining `try-catch`). For that situation in a real program, it probably would have been better to simply have an `if` statement in front of the division statement to insure there would be no divide by zero. As in

```
/*    try {      */

      if (a != 0) a = 10/a;
        else /* handle the error */

/*      } catch(ArithmeticException e) {}   */
```

- Going hand in hand with the first bullet, the main idea of throwing an exception is to let *users* of your class know there was an exception and that they should handle it. All of Java's file I/O APIs will throw file-not-found exceptions back to you. This is a good idea, since your program will need to know if it is requesting a nonexistent file. After that, only your code knows what to do next, whether that be prompting the user for a new name or displaying a message or just ignoring the whole thing. However, if you are throwing exceptions that you will eventually handle anyway, you may be able to perform the recovery without using elaborate exception mechanisms—i.e., the file I/O APIs might not report to you immediately if they receive a disk-not-ready error. They may retry a few times before giving up.

- If an exception is very common, the performance cost of throwing the exceptions may be significant. For this type of situation it is usually beneficial to design the code to expect common errors and handle them with more grace. For the disk example, usually if you get one bad disk read, most of your retries will fail, too. Your program should be designed to efficiently deal with the retries—throwing a bad-disk-read exception on each retry is wasteful.

This section is in no way trying to dissuade you from defining and using your own exceptions. In many cases, handling Java exceptions is a requirement you'll be forced to live with. Defining exceptions that truly aid in the recovery of unexpected events is quite a useful and powerful tool. However, careless overuse can be costly and can promote poor code.

Debugging

Java spent its childhood in developers' hands at Sun Microsystems. Immediately after Java was made publicly available as an alpha release, programmers swarmed to use it. Two main pieces of the puzzle were already built for them, the compiler and a slick new browser application called HotJava. Unfortunately, there were no definable debugging facilities.

Programmers thrust their hands deep into Java coding and had no great way to find their errors. This was a big gap in Java's overall development environment.

Designers and new users alike were hot on the job. Debugging facilities have now matured for Java programming and are bound to solidify further from third-party software companies. Debugging with these new fancy debuggers should be relative child's play. This part of the chapter will cover a general debugging overview and take a look at Java's first debugger, JDB.

System.out.println("a = " + a);

Print statements are arguably the widest used debugging tools ever. Long before any debuggers existed for Java, C, or any programming language, programmers laced their code with these divulgers of covert activity to find where their programs went haywire. Even with the advanced debuggers coming into the market, sometimes using a quick print statement to follow a variable is still the simplest way to go. Don't be afraid to use them when they're useful and don't be surprised to see them commented out in a lot of new Java code—at least for a while.

Stack Tracing

Second only to a blaring error message, the most evident form of debugging information is available in a stack trace. A typical stack trace could be (in fact, at one point was)

```
java.lang.ArithmeticException: / by zero
        at BinaryTree.searchtree(binarytree.java:50)
        at BinaryTree.addnode(binarytree.java:16)
        at students.main(students.java:9)
```

This trace represents the state of the method call stack when an exception is thrown. The highest level method name `BinaryTree.searchtree` indicates the actual method where the exception occurred and exists in the file binarytree.java. That method was called by `BinaryTree.addnode`, which was called by `students.main`. Using this information, you can immediately decipher where the exception occurred and track down a wayward sequence of calls. Applets often have traces similar to the above, which quickly end up heading into API methods. As your programs become complex, stack traces will get longer and will be filled primarily with your own methods.

You can force your own stack dumps through methods in the `java.lang` classes `Thread` and `Throwable`. The above example was forced with the following code:

```
catch (ArithmeticException e) {
  e.printStackTrace();
  }
```

This allows you to see where a program has been at an exact point, but considering the unattractiveness of the resulting output, this will likely only be done while your code is being tested (random printing of stack traces are proven tools for confusing users).

# JDB

The JDB debugger comes as part of the Java distribution. The designers have been careful to note that this debugger is not meant as an answer to all your debugging needs. It is really just a example of the elements a debugger should have. You'll see it's not particularly friendly, but it does provide you enough functionality to get your debugging endeavors moving (albeit at a slow crawl).

Getting Started

Some distributions of Java include an additional compiler called javac_g. This compiler does not perform all the optimizations that the javac compiler does. Sometimes optimizations can get in the way of pinpointing trouble code, so it's best to use javac_g (if you have it) while testing your code with JDB. If you don't have access to a nonoptimizing compiler, don't worry; you'll still be able to benefit from JDB. For both compilers you should compile using the **–g** option. As in

```
javac_g –g myClass.java
```

The **–g** option instructs the compiler to generate debugging tables that will provide JDB with extra information regarding your classes.

You then can start the debugger followed by the class you wish to load.

```
jdb myClass
```

The debugger will take care of setting up the runtime environment. You can also start the debugger without specifying the class to load and perform the loading later with the appropriately named debugger command **load**.

Starting and Stopping

Let's create an example program to debug.

```
/* Class to store right triangles */
class righttriangle {

  private float height,width,hypot;

    public righttriangle(float h,float w) {

      height = h;
      width = w;
      hypot = (float)Math.sqrt(w*w + h*h);
      }

/* accessor method for hypotenuse */
    public float hypotenuse() {
      return hypot;
```

continued on next page

continued from previous page

```
        }
    }

/* The primary class - debugging will start here */
class debug {

  public static void main (String args[]) {
    righttriangle T = new righttriangle(3F,4F);
    System.out.println(T.hypotenuse());
    }
}
```

After loading the above program (i.e., its compiled version), you can use the debugger's **run** command to begin executing your program. The above program runs without causing any exceptions, so running it will quickly result in the number 5 being printed and the program will terminate. Not too climactic. What you need to do to have the debugger allow you to watch the code execute is to set a breakpoint (a stopping point) within the code. There are two ways to set breakpoints:

```
stop in debug.main
stop at righttriangle:9
```

The first command tells the debugger to set a breakpoint at the **main** method in the **debug** class. Obviously, besides some initialization duties, that is the first place the code will run. The second command sets a breakpoint at line 9 of the code. This is the **height = h;** statement. Now entering the **run** command will result in the following output:

```
> run
run debug
Breakpoint hit: debug.main (debug.main:19)
running...
main[1]
```

The last line is actually your new prompt ready for your next command. It has changed from a greater-than symbol and now specifies the current default thread (with the greater-than sign, there was no default thread). You can also set the default thread (basically a designation to the debugger of which process you are interested in debugging at the moment) by using the **threads** command. The following sequence illustrates how it can be done.

```
> threads
Group system:
1. (java.lang.Thread)0xee300098          clock handler
2. (java.lang.Thread)0xee300290          Idle thread
3. (java.lang.Thread)0xee300308          Async Garbage
4. (java.lang.Thread)0xee300358          Finalizer
5. (java.lang.Thread)0xee300908          Debugger agent
6. (sun.tools.debug.BreakpointHandler)0xee300a60  Breakpoint
Group main:
7. (java.lang.Thread)0xee300048 main suspended
```

```
> thread t@7
main[1]
```

The first command, **threads**, lists all currently running threads. Because of versioning and system thread dependencies, your thread listing may have different threads running. However, your standalone program will be listed as **main**, as in thread number 7. The command is then issued to set the default thread. The designation for the thread is **t@** followed by the thread number, in this case 7. You will need to have your thread of interest (i.e., your **main**) as the default thread in order to retrieve information about it.

Back to your debugging, the code is no longer running at this point and is waiting for your next command. The **list** command will show you a segment of code and the location of the suspended execution.

```
main[1] list
15                  }
16
17         class debug {
18
19     =>          public static void main (String args[]) {
20
21                 righttriangle T = new righttriangle(3F,4F);
22
23                 System.out.println(T.hypotenuse());
main[1]
```

You can continue execution with the **cont** command. This will run until it reaches the other breakpoint you set earlier (ninth line in the **righttriangle** class)

```
main[1] cont
Breakpoint hit: righttriangle.<init> (righttriangle:9)
main[1] list
1    class righttriangle {
2
3        private float height,width,hypot;
4
5     =>   public righttriangle(float h,float w) {
6
7            height = h;
8            width = w;
9            hypot = (float)Math.sqrt(w*w + h*h);
```

You can use the **locals** command to display local variables within the current stack. Other useful commands include **classes** to list the current classes, **catch** to break on the occurrence of exceptions, and **methods class_id** to list a class's methods. The **dump** command displays the instance variables of an object.

```
main[1] dump this
this = (righttriangle)0xee3032d0 {
    private float height = 3
    private float width = 4
    private float hypot = 0
}
```

Remember that you stopped before line 9, so the statement to assign the **hypot** variable has not yet been executed.

Using JDB is definitely an art that hopefully you won't get too good at. Better debuggers should provide you with a more intuitive interface to monitoring code execution. JDB includes a **help** command that lists all legal commands. Experimentation with the various commands should at least put you at a level where you're comfortable knowing how to extract useful information from JDB.

Remote Debugging

A useful feature built into JDB (and hopefully future debuggers) is the ability to debug remotely. This entails running the debugger on one machine and actually running the program to be debugged on another. This type of debugging isolates the debugger from the program being tested. This is useful for testing programs that cause major crashes—the debugger won't get drawn into the crash since it's safely on another machine. It's also useful to separate the debugger to keep it from influencing program behavior.

In order to set up remote debugging, you must run the interpreter on one machine and the debugger on the other. As with the compiler, you should use the **java_g** version of the interpreter to facilitate debugging. You will also need to specify the **-debug** option for the interpreter. Again, if you don't have **java_g**, the normal Java interpreter will also work.

```
java_g -debug myClass
```

The interpreter will then print out a password and begin to listen for a remote debugger. The debugger should be executed specifying the host where you are running the interpreter and the password that was given by the interpreter.

```
jdb -host hostname -password password
```

If all goes well, the debugger and interpreter will make a connection. Typically, you will only use remote debugging when you must. Somehow adding the extra step of network connections always ends up being a nuisance. But when a local debugger becomes affected by a crashing test program, it's the only way to go.

 # Summary

Java's exception and debugging facilities should be a bit clearer now. You should see the great potential available to you in handling exceptions on your terms, not by watching the crash and trying to pick up the pieces. This mode of exception handling is not unique to Java, but it was a wise decision to have it implemented. Don't think that exception handling is only temporary code that lets you find exceptions and then you can remove all traces of trying and catching. The **try** and **catch** statements do have their place in final production code. Classes you develop should conform to standards set by the Java APIs, and if the users of your class deserve a null pointer exception—heck, throw them two.

Debuggers are already out for Java and more are on the way. They only promise more features and higher levels of abstraction from the good-old-days methods of debugging. The industry seems poised to develop debuggers well beyond the capabilities of the humble JDB. That's great and should speed productivity, but it's good to know what happens under the covers with exceptions and bugs within Java programs. In other words, it's great to let the debugger handle the details for you, but it's also good to know what it's doing.

Questions

1. It is perfectly legal to nest **try** blocks. In fact, often the internal block will catch an exception, handle it, and then throw the same exception (to be caught by the external block). Why would you want to do this?

2. If you knew that each of the following statements would throw an exception if executed, what exception would you guess each will throw?

   a. `a[4] = 10;`
   b. `MyObject.printvalues();`
   c. `c = a/b;`

3. Name several possible functions you would likely perform in a **finally** block.

4. Is there any harm in defining a **try** and **catch** block for an exception that you are positive can never be thrown?

Exercises

1. Define a new exception **NoOneIsNamedGeorgeException** that is thrown whenever a string equals "George". Write a code segment that uses your exception.

2. Use the JDB debugger to step through the Billy/William example in Chapter 10. What does the **dump** command display for the two objects? Why?

Java™ vs. C/C++

You will learn about the following in this chapter:

- Constructs shared by Java and C++
- How to compare the keywords in Java and C++
- How Java's garbage collection helps C++ coders
- How Java makes do without C++ pointers

If you have a working knowledge of C or, even better, C++, you should find the transition to writing useful Java code relatively painless. This is not to say that it is an impossible task for those of you who have been coding in the myriad other languages available to today's programmer, it's just that the designers of Java have modeled the language after the popular object-oriented programming language called C++.

C++ is a superset of C, so those of you familiar with C still have a notable advantage when it comes to coding in Java. Java can't really be considered a superset or a subset of C or C++; it's more of a close cousin to C++ and maybe a second cousin to C (that's probably pushing it a little, but you get the point, which is emphasized in Figure 12-1).

Most of your knowledge of the C programming language will still be useful; it will just be necessary to switch to a slightly different programming structure and philosophy. This will also involve learning a few new tricks and dropping some old programming habits that may not translate to the Java paradigm. But you should be confident that your programming skills in C and C++ will get you writing Java applications and applets in a very short time—a few short hours for most, less than that if you are a seasoned object-oriented C++ programmer.

This chapter is aimed at those who already have a working knowledge of C++ or C. The emphasis is on pointing out Java's similarities with these programming languages, reassuring those of you with substantial time investments in C and C++ development that your programming skills are not going to be lost or wasted, and pointing out the pitfalls a transitioning programmer may experience.

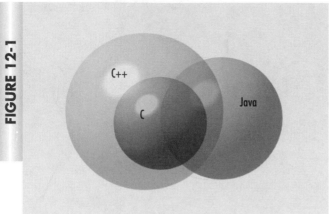

FIGURE 12-1

Overlapping of Java, C, and C++

This chapter will also demonstrate the major differences between Java and C/C++. The intention is to prevent you from getting frustrated over syntactical, structural, and philosophical differences between these languages, and lay the groundwork for new methods and opportunities not available in C and C++.

What's the Same? Similarities of Java, C++, and C

Fortunately, most of the syntax of these three languages is the same on the basic structural level. You have the same methods for branching, the same construct for terminating statements, and the same methods for declaring variables of simple data types. You still use the same methods available for flow control, and a call to a function is still the same, namely a return type, a function name, and a parameter list separated by commas and surrounded by parentheses, as shown in Table 12-1.

C	C++	Java
static int myfunc(int x)	static int myfunc(int x)	static int myfunc(int x)
{...	{...	{...
}	}	}

Table 12-1 Syntactic similarities

There are some differences in where and how these functions may be used, but that will be explained later in this chapter. Note that in Java, a function is generally referred to as a method. To keep things simple, the term "function" in this chapter will be used to label a C function as well as a method within a class description.

Entry and Exit Points

All three languages use a similar method for entering and exiting a program, namely, through calls to `main` and `exit`. In C, the entry point to your program is through a function declared `main` similar to the following:

```
void main(int argc, char *argv[]) { }
```

For a Java application, this is also true, with a slight modification. The entry point for a Java application would look something like this:

```
public static void main(String args[]) { }
```

Java, C, and C++ all use `exit` to terminate execution. The only difference in Java is that you would generally resolve the scope of `exit` by calling the `exit` method of the `System` class with a call similar to this:

```
System.exit(0);
```

There is more on scope resolution later in this chapter.

Other Similarities

You can also rest assured that you still have many of the same data types that are used in C and C++. Namely, Java defines the following types that are the same as, or at least very close to, the data types in C and C++ (shown in Table 12-2). Note that the integer types are the same as most C and C++ implementations, but in Java, the size of these types is machine independent, which is not the case in C or C++. So you don't have to worry about differences across platforms. This topic was discussed in Chapter 5.

TYPE	SIZE
char	16 bits (a char is normally 8 bits in standard C)
short	16 bits
int	32 bits
long	64 bits
float	32 bits (IEEE 754)
double	64 bits (IEEE 754)

Table 12-2 Simple data types

In all three languages, a simple data type is declared in a statement with the type keyword (for example `int`, `char`, `float`, etc.), the variable name, and an optional assignment statement followed by a semicolon. The following declaration statements are valid in all three languages:

```
float f = 1.0;
char c;
int i = 1+50;
static char d = 'x';
```

The one notable difference is where these variables may be declared. In Java, a simple type may only be declared within a class or method (function).

Arrays have many similarities between these languages. They are still declared and indexed in the same fashion, although there are some differences in how they are instanced and limitations on what you can do with an array in Java.

To declare an array of integers in Java, you can use the square brackets after a variable name when declaring it. For example, to declare an array of integers, you would simply type

```
int i[];
```

Likewise, for a two-dimensional array of chars, you would use the statement

```
char c[][];
```

Notice that the size was not specified in the array declaration. This is because an array declaration in Java only tells the compiler "I plan on creating an array instance at some point." The memory for the array is not allocated until you create an instance of an array object or assign an array object to the array that you declared.

To declare and assign memory to an array, you use the keyword **new**. This should ring a familiar bell with the C++ programmer. The **new** keyword tells the compiler to create an object of the type specified and assign it to a variable. To create an array of five integers in Java and create an instance of it, you would use a statement something like this:

```
int c[] = new int[5];
```

Likewise, if you wanted to assign an existing array object to a variable that you have declared, you would use statements such as

```
int c[]; //declare an array of integers
int x[] = new int[5];        //create an instance of an array
                             // of 5 integers and assign it to X
c = x; //assign the array object x to the variable c
```

This leads to the one big difference between arrays in Java and arrays in C. An array in C is simply a pointer to a block in memory; an array in Java *must* be an instance of an array object. In Java, you can use the conventional indexing to address elements in an array, such as `myarray[4]` to address the fifth element of the array (remember, the element with an offset of 4 would be the fifth element if you are including the 0 element). However, in Java you cannot address the fifth element with a statement such as `myarray + 4` as you could in C or C++. This operation is not defined for the array class and would flag a compile-time error.

String Types

Java has two first-class types that are not part of the standard C or C++ implementations: the `String` and `StringBuffer` types.

Rather than being just an array of characters, a string in Java has a type all its own. It can be declared and instantiated in the same manner as any of the other fundamental data types in Java.

The following are all legal statements in Java:

```
String str = new String();
String foo = "Hey, this is a string!";
String bar;
bar = "this is a string";
```

The `String` type is generally meant to be used as a constant once it has been assigned; a second type, called `StringBuffer,` is used when you need to do manipulations on a string. In either case, it's a lot more sane than the C convention of just having a string be a null terminated array of characters.

Differences in Object Code

Another difference between Java and C/C++ is the type of code that is generated. Normally, when you compile a program in C or C++, the code is compiled into a number of object files that are then linked together into a single executable. In Java, this is not the case. When Java is compiled, it creates a separate binary file for each class that is declared in the source code.

So if you have a source file called MyClass.java, and that source file contains source code for the classes `MyClass`, `FooClass`, and `BarClass`, the resulting object files that will be created will be MyClass.class, FooClass.class and BarClass.class. When the main class is called (normally the one containing a `main` method for an application.), it will load dependent classes when they are needed. These classes are not normally linked together as a single executable.

Keywords

Java, C, and C++ all have a set of keywords in common. These keywords are various types such as `int` or `float`, as well as special reserved words such as `while` or `goto`. It's not important to focus on the keywords that are the same throughout, since it is assumed that if you know one language, you are already familiar with these. Table 12-3 is a list of keywords that are used in both languages. Table 12-4 is a list of Java keywords that are unique to Java. Finally, Table 12-5 is a list of keywords that are unique to C++ (i.e., not used in Java).

Common Keywords

The following table is a list of keywords that are common to Java and C++. Since they have similar functionality, no description is given.

break	case	catch	char
class	const	continue	default
do	double	else	float
for	goto	if	int
long	new	private	protected
public	return	short	static
switch	this	throw	try
void	while	false	true

Table 12-3 Common keywords

Java Keywords

The following table is a list of keywords that are unique to Java. In other words, these are keywords and rough descriptions of their functions that are not found in C or C++.

Keyword	Description
abstract	Used when declaring abstract classes and methods.
boolean	Fundamental data type.
byte	Fundamental data type.
byvalue	Reserved, but not currently used in Java.
extends	Used to derive classes.
final	Makes a variable constant, a method unoverridable, and a class un-subclassable.
finally	Called to clean up after an object.
implements	Used to implement an interface.

Keyword	Description
import	Similar to #include. Brings in external compilation units.
instanceof	Checks to see if an object is an instance of some other class. This gives a Boolean result.
interface	A way of defining a common interface among classes.
native	This declares a method to be from an external library that is native to the CPU that the Java interpreter is running on.
null	A constant.
package	This associates a file with a certain package of classes.
super	This is a reference to the superclass of a derived class.
synchronized	Used to synchronize the execution of a method.
throws	Specifies possible exceptions a method may throw.
volatile	Declares that a variable could be changed unpredictably— i.e., compiler implements precautions.

Table 12-4 Java keywords

C++ Keywords

For the purposes of this chapter, it is not really interesting to describe the functions of C++ keywords that are not used in Java, so, the following table is simply a list of these keywords that are not used in Java.

asm	auto	bool	delete
enum	extern	friend	inline
operator	namespace	register	signed
sizeof	struct	using	template
typedef	typeid	union	unsigned
virtual			

Table 12-5 Keywords unique to C++

Public and Private Class Components

In C++, labels are used to mark public and private components of the class. Namely, there are public functions and variables that are available to other classes, and private functions and variables that can only be used by the class itself.

There is a similar notion in Java; however, it is not declared in the same way. In Java, any class, method, or variable can be preceded with a `public`, `private`, or `protected` modifier keyword. A public component is available to anyone. A private component is used only by the class itself, and a protected component can be accessed only by the class and its subclasses.

Table 12-6 demonstrates the conventions in C++ and Java for declaring public and private areas of a class.

C++	Java
``class A {
public:
int x;
void foo() {/* */};
private:
int y;
}```	```class A {
public int x;
public void foo() {/* */};
private int y;
}```

Table 12-6 Public and private parts

Static Parts and Instance Variables

Java supports the notion of static and instance variables and methods. In Java, any method or variable declaration within a class is assumed to be an instance unless it is specifically declared static.

This has the same effect as declaring a static variable in C or in C++. Namely, a static variable is shared among instances of a class, and instance variables have local copies for every instantiation of a class. The following code segment declares two instance variables, one static variable, and a static method.

```
//...
int x; //instance variable
int y; //instance variable
static int z; //static variable
static void DoSomething() {/*   */} //static method
//...
```

In a similar fashion, any class may have a static initializer by using the keyword `static`, followed by a bracket-delimited body. This initializer will be called the first time the class is instantiated. The ability to have static initializer blocks is not found in C++ and is a welcome enhancement to Java. The following class code contains a static initializer:

```
class MyClass {
      static { System.load("lib"); }
      /*    */
}
```

Friends

Sticking with a strict object-oriented philosophy, Java does not have the notion of friend functions. In C++, a friend is a function from a class that has access to the private parts of another class. In Java, private data is kept private, and constructs such as friends are not supported. (Not to say that Java is unfriendly, just that it's trying to keep its private parts out of public scrutiny.)

 # Taking Out the Trash

Don't you hate having to take out the trash? Wouldn't it be nice if the garbage collector just came into your kitchen and emptied the garbage for you? Well, this is another fundamental difference between Java, C, and C++.

In Java, the garbage is collected for you. Whenever you create an instance of an object, memory for that object is allocated and kept as long as it is referenced. But as soon as there are no longer references to that object, the block of memory that was used to store that object is freed by the garbage collector.

The garbage collector is implementation specific, but is normally run as a low-priority thread that uses a simple mark-and-sweep method of garbage collection. The beauty of it is that you, the programmer, don't need to think about it. Just rest assured that any forgotten dangling blocks of memory will be set free if they are no longer necessary.

 # Namespace Resolution

Namespace resolution is not quite the same in Java as it is in C++. In short, the "::" scope operator in C++ is not used in Java. Java uses the notion of packages in order to maintain a large namespace.

A package is essentially a group of like classes. Generally, a company or programmer will create a package of classes that have a common package name to differentiate them from other groups of classes that may have the same names. This way, if you create a class called **DrawCircle**, and someone else creates a class of the same name, there is no name

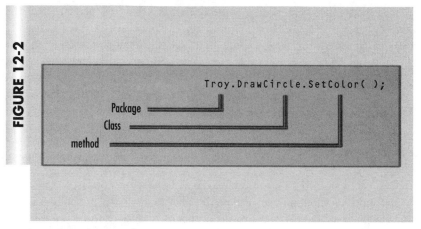

Namespace resolution

conflict as long as you've assigned your class to the `Yourname` package and the other one is assigned to the `JoeCo` package.

The way that Java resolves the scope of a method or class is by using the "." operator. A complete reference to a method may contain a package name followed by a dot, followed by a class name, followed by a dot, and then finally followed by the method name. For example, if you wanted to call a method in the hypothetical `DrawCircle` class mentioned above, and the method name is `SetColor`, you could access this method as shown in Figure 12-2. This clearly distinguishes your `DrawCircle` from the `DrawCircle` that is a member of the `JoeCo` package.

 # Inheritance

Deriving classes from base classes is handled differently in Java than in C++. (This isn't an issue in C, since there really is no notion of classes). First off, Java doesn't allow multiple inheritance. In other words, a derived class can have only one base class. Secondly, the ":" operator is not used to indicate that a class is being derived from another. In C++, a class `B` that extends a class `A` would be written something like this:

```
class A { /*   */}; //declare class A
class B : public A { /*   */}; //class B inherits from A
```

In Java, the keyword `extends` is used to derive class `B` from `A`, as in the following example:

```
class A { /* */} //declare class A
class B extends A {/*   */} //class B inherits from A
```

Notice that semicolons terminate the class declarations in C++. These are omitted in Java.

As mentioned before, multiple inheritance isn't really supported in Java, so a derived class such as

```
class A : public B, public C { /*   */}; //A inherits from B & C
```

isn't allowed in Java. The closest thing Java can do is implement multiple interfaces. This can provide a mechanism for assuring that a class will implement a number of methods, or that any class that implements an interface is guaranteed to have an implementation of the methods of that interface. For example, if you declare an interface that is called `scrollable` and an interface called `clickable`, and you implement these in a class `MyGUI` such as this:

```
class MyGUI implements scrollable, clickable {/*   */}
```

you are essentially promising to support the methods that are declared in `scrollable` and `clickable`. This is not to say, however, that you have to implement them in a specific manner, just that they will be supported. Interfaces are covered in more detail in the sections on Java programming.

Abstract Classes

The notion of abstract classes is slightly different in Java than in C++. An abstract class is one that can't be instantiated on its own, but rather must be subclassed in order to be used. In C++, an abstract class is a class that has one or more pure virtual functions. In other words, virtual functions that are initialized to 0 (zero). In Java, an abstract class must be subclassed and cannot itself be instantiated. It can also specify some or all of its methods as abstract methods. An abstract method is a method that contains no body, and must be overridden in a subclass. Table 12-7 shows examples of a simple abstract class in both C++ and Java.

C++	Java

`class A {`
`  // ...`
`public:`
`  virtual void rotate(int) = 0;`
`};`
	`abstract class A {`
	`//...`
	`abstract void rotate(int);`
	`}`

Table 12-7 An abstract class in C++ and Java

In either case, the method `rotate` cannot be used until it has been implemented in a class derived from class `A`. Which brings up the topic of overloading.

Overloading

There are two types of overloading in C++ and Java: the overloading of methods or functions, and the overloading of operators. Operator overloading isn't really supported in Java, with the few built-in exceptions such as the string concatenation operator. There has been much debate in the Java discussions about supporting operator overloading. Many insist that it is a good thing to have, but the Java development team have as one of their priorities simplicity of the programming language.

One of the major problems with operator overloading is that it gives the programmer the power to easily write code that is difficult to read. Since an operator can work differently in different circumstances, source code can quickly become convoluted. So operator overloading is not a supported programming option in Java.

Method Overloading

Method overloading is supported in Java. In other words, you can use the same method name for many different functions based on the types of the values that are passed to the method. This is a useful programming practice for making sense of data that is treated to achieve a similar end, but that requires different means.

So, if you have a method that draws a circle, called **DrawCircle**, and you want to be able to deal with different types of parameter data, you could overload this method by declaring it a number of times with different parameter sets and whatever operations make sense for those types of data. As an example, let's assume that you want your **DrawCircle** method to accept a **Circle** type, an x,y, and radius in integers, and an x,y, and radius in floats. The following method declarations would deal with calls that contained these different data types:

```
void DrawCircle(Circle c) { /*  */}
void DrawCircle(int x, int y, int r) {/*   */}
void DrawCircle(float x, float y, float r) {/*   */}
```

In this case, a call to **DrawCircle(1.2, 0.3, 0.5);** would call the third overloaded method.

It is also possible to override methods from base classes as long as they are not declared final, or private. The basic rule is that a subclass can override a superclass's methods as long as the method has the same name, same return type, and takes the same parameters.

I/O Streams

It is a common practice for C++ programmers to use the **cin**, **cout**, and **cerr** streams for basic I/O operations. In Java, these streams are present but look and work differently. They are static variables present in the **System** class and are named **System.in**, **System.out**, and **System.err**. Also, Java does not support C++'s << and >> direction operators. Instead, Java utilizes stream methods to get the job done. For example, to print a string to the console, you would use a command similar to the following:

```
System.out.print("This is a" + "single string");
```

Notice that the + operator can be used to concatenate strings in a similar fashion to C++.

The standard in, standard out, and standard error streams are all accessed in a similar fashion. Additional stream manipulation methods can be found in the Appendix.

String Concatenation

As mentioned in the previous section, string concatenation operations are the same in C++ and Java. Namely, a string can be any combination of variables, and literals that are connected by the "+" operator. This is one of the few cases of operator overloading you will find in Java. For example, the following code bit is a valid string, assuming that X, Y, and Z are defined variables:

```
String foo = "This is " + X + Y + Z + " a string";
```

X, Y, and Z would be translated if necessary; i.e., translated from nonstring types to string representations.

Good-Bye Pointers

No more pointers! This may sound a little strange, especially if you've gotten used to passing addresses around and using pointer arithmetic to index array elements. It is common practice in both C and C++ to create a pointer, allocate memory, and assign this memory to the pointer. It is also common to access different parts of this memory by manipulating the address of a pointer, or by indexing a pointer as an array. Also, there are many times when you want to return the address of a variable rather than a copy of the variable. These are all very common practices for the C or C++ programmer. Pointers, in this broad sense, have been completely eliminated from Java. That's not to say that Java itself doesn't use pointers. It would be close to impossible to write a useful language that didn't have some sort of memory indexing, but mainly the programmer's ability to assign an arbitrary address to a variable has been eliminated.

Don't Point, It's Impolite

There are a number of advantages to this seemingly unfair roadblock that make perfect sense if you think about the broader picture. The creators of Java, for various security and related reasons, have disallowed the ability to address arbitrary locations in memory using pointers. This makes it difficult to write malicious or unintentionally damaging applications that might otherwise crash your system, print obscenities, or cause other similar inconveniences. This also helps enforce the object-oriented ideology behind Java, forcing every complex data type to be a class rather than a pointer to a structure or some other complex data type. This also helps keep Java platform neutral. There are no assumptions about how memory is laid out on any specific implementation.

These differences are not simply nuisances but have many advantages. For example, in C, a string is expected to be a pointer to an array of characters, terminated by a null character. You would pass this string to a function by sending the address of the first character, and could get to the component parts of the string either by addressing it as an array of chars or by doing pointer arithmetic to get to the point in the string you are interested in. In Java, there is a string class (`java.Lang.String`). The string class has a number of component methods useful in dealing with strings. The class also prevents you from unintentionally writing off of the edge of the string and into some other bit of memory. (This is a problem you see often in poorly structured C programs).

No Structs and No Unions

You can also say good-bye to structs and unions. In Java, a struct must be a class. Luckily, the format is similar and the component elements of a class are referred to in the same fashion as a struct in the C language. For example, assume the following to be constructs:

C	Java
```struct { int foo; char bar; } My_CStruct;```	```class MyJavaClass { int foo; char bar; }```

To access integer `foo` in the C struct, you would use `My_CStruct.foo.` Likewise, to access the integer `foo` in the Java class, you would use `MyJavaClass.foo`. If you are comparing Java to C++, this also includes references to methods within the class such as `MyJavaClass.do_something()`.

#ifdef JAVA
#define NO_MORE_MACROS
#endif

Well, that pretty much says it. Java has also done away with the standard `#define` macros. Actually, they've done away with the C preprocessor altogether. This is continuing with the "enforced OOP" ideology. Java doesn't use header files or `#define`s when compiling source code. Say good-bye to those huge header files listing function prototypes, typedefs, defines, etc.

This is a little strange for those of us who are accustomed to putting all of our constants in header files, but actually it works out fine. The idea is that an object is instanced with the necessary constants defined. What would normally be a constant that was declared with a #define is now made constant with the keyword **final**. Any data type that is preceded with **final** is not changeable once it is defined. This also helps enforce stronger type checking. For example, assume the following constant is defined in your C program:

```
#define MAX 20
```

There is no way to say that **MAX** is a byte, an int, or some other data type that would accept the value of 20. It would depend on where you used **MAX**. On the other hand, in Java, you know exactly what type a constant is because it is declared as a specific type. For example, if you planned on using **MAX** as an int, the example above would be included in a Java class with a statement like this:

```
final int MAX = 20;
```

Function macros can easily be translated to classes or methods within the classes that would use them. A class, interface, or method can be created just as easily as a macro, and can actually be more useful in certain circumstances defined as a method rather than as a macro.

 Booleans

In Java, there is a true 1 bit Boolean type. The standard convention in C for a Boolean type is to use an integer (ANSI standard C++ does, however, include a type **bool**). If the integer contains a nonzero value, an expression is considered to be true, otherwise, it is false. This leads to constructs such as

```
int x = 10;
while(x--)
   do_something();
```

Unfortunately, this is an error in Java. This will create a compile-time error that states that you cannot convert an integer to a Boolean type. This same code fragment written in a Java method would have to use a Boolean expression rather than simply using the value of the integer directly. This code fragment could be written in Java as

```
int x = 10;
while((x--)>0)
   do_something();
```

In Java, a statement is evaluated with a Boolean value if it is declared as a Boolean type, or uses a comparison operator such as >, <, ==, !=, etc. The following are valid Java statements:

```
boolean done = true;
while(!done)
```

continued on next page

continued from previous page

```
    done = do_something();       // do_something returns a boolean
int x = 5;
char foo[6];
while(x>=0)
    foo[x--] = return_something();
```

It should be obvious now that many of the expressions in Java are also valid expressions in C/C++. The problem is the other way around. A valid statement in C or C++ is not always valid in Java. Most of these minor differences become second nature once you begin writing some Java code. Likewise, it doesn't take long to get used to the Java programming paradigm in the greater sense, it just takes a little time behind the keyboard. Once you start coding, it should all start making sense.

OOPs! Java's Object-Oriented Philosophy

So now you are probably asking yourself, why? Why did the designers of Java decide to give you some of the functionality of C/C++, but then stray down this seemingly limited path? Well, the benefits of the Java structure are manifold. The creators of Java wanted to create a truly object-oriented language that was suited to widely distributed applications. They were also concerned about security issues that arise whenever you talk about distributing applications over a public network. C++ is one of the more popular object-oriented programming languages in use, so it made sense to model Java after this. Some functionality was changed, some was removed, and some was added, so Java can't really be considered a super- or subset of C++. So think of Java as being a secure, OOP-enforced cousin to C++.

Many of the problems programmers have when creating objective code in C++ are eliminated in Java. Forcing the programmer to instance an array class rather than allocating an arbitrary amount of memory in a standard C-style array makes the code much more portable, and easier to recycle further down the line. This also eliminates problems with indexing past the end of an array, hard-to-find memory leaks, and security issues that arise when you allow a programmer to arbitrarily address memory.

Java also facilitates cleaner programming styles. You create packages of classes and interfaces that all tackle related problems. An intelligently designed package can be reused for a variety of different applications. If a class does pretty much what you want but is missing some minor method, you can easily extend the class and/or overload the component parts of it to deal with the present task without having to copy or rewrite any code. What more could you ask?

The other differences between C and Java are trivial to the programmer, but really make the final code much easier to use and extend. For instance, the difference in coding a struct in C and a class in Java is not rocket science. But the fact that Java forces you to use the class structure has the end result of creating easily extensible objects rather than hardcoded structures that either need to be changed, or copied and changed, whenever you want slightly different functionality from two different applications.

One other notable advantage of Java is the ease of multiplatform, or rather, platform neutral development. In Java, all types are machine independent. No longer does the programmer have to worry about the size of an int, the precision of a float, or the byte order of a long. Questions such as "Is that machine big-endian or little-endian?" are no longer of importance. In Java, a Boolean is always 1 bit, an int is always 32 bits, and a char is always 16 bits. Likewise, the byte order never changes, no matter what your target platform is. This makes it much easier for developers who want to share data and applications across nonhomogenous networks of machines. The network application designer no longer has to worry about surrounding integers with **htons()** before sending them over a network. Or with converting them back with **ntohs()**. (**htons()** and **ntohs()** are functions commonly used by network applications programmers for converting byte order to/from host and network formats.)

 Summary

As you can see, with little effort, a seasoned C or C++ programmer can easily switch gears to start writing useful Java code. There are a few new types, a few adjustments in style, a few new constructs, but nothing too difficult. Most C++ programmers will make the Java transition completely painlessly. If you are new to object-oriented programming, the transition may be a little more difficult, but still not exactly a Herculean task.

Questions

1. Which of the following statements are valid Java statements?

    a. ```
        int I[10];
        ```

    b.  ```
        boolean x = false;
        ```

    c. ```
        struct {
            int x;
            int y;
        }
        ```

    d.  ```
        for(int x = 10; x ; x--) do_it();
        ```

2. What is the difference between a class in Java and a struct in C?

3. Where can a method be declared in Java?

4. What is the difference between a Boolean expression in C and one in Java?

5. In C, an array can be referenced by an array variable or a pointer pointing to the array's memory block. Which is closer to Java's underlying implementation?

6. Why is Java a *pure* object-oriented language and C++ is not?

 Exercises

1. Rewrite the following common C functions and data structures in Java.

   a.
   ```c
   struct node {
       char data[10];
       int count;
       struct node *left;
       struct node *right;
   } Tree_Node;
   ```

   b.
   ```c
   int x=10;
       char c[11];
   while(x--) c[x]=x;
   ```

   c.
   ```c
   myfunct(char *instr)
   {
   int n;
       char str[10];
   for(n=0;n<10;n++)
       str[n] = *(instr+n);
   }
   ```

PART III:
Using the Advanced
Capabilities of Java™

Graphics and Sound

You will learn about the following in this chapter:

- How to use the methods in Java's Graphics class
- How to eliminate flicker in your applications
- How to implement an applet/application drawing program
- How to add sound to your Web pages
- How to implement double buffering in Java

You've all seen just how exciting the "server push" can be using the HTML/CGI paradigm. (Just in case you haven't seen this, a server push is a method used by CGI scripts to "push" content to Web browsers, giving the illusion of dynamic documents.) These slide show animations are created by pushing one image over another, each replacing the previous one, image after image painfully clunking into place. Sometimes the updates are snappy, sometimes laborious. The problem with this scheme is that you are dependent on the speed of the network, the speed of the server, and possibly the speed of the user's dialup connection to the Net. There are no mechanisms for controlling timing, or for loading all of the images at once to speed up refresh rates, or at the very least, to try to make them consistent.

Enter Java. Java is the real answer for creating dynamic Web documents. With Java, you have the ability to download data before execution, to control timing, to change patterns based on user input—interactivity that the server-push/client-pull applications couldn't even dream of. You are still subject to the whims of network bandwidth, but you can wait until enough of your content has downloaded before beginning execution, thereby insuring higher quality in your dynamic Web documents.

Although this chapter will show you how to write your own Java graphics and sound applets, you don't have to program a single line of Java code to take advantage of the graphic and sound capabilities of a Java-enabled browser. There are already many precompiled classes that will do inline animations, slide shows, and sonic events. All you need to do is include them in your HTML documents and supply your own images and sound bytes. Take the `ImageLoop` applet, for example. This class is one of the standard Java demos.

FIGURE 13-1

![index.html (Untitled) browser window showing ImageLoop applet with Duke]

ImageLoop applet

It is a simple task to include it in your HTML documents. You can even supply your own images to be used for the animation. The demo version that you are likely to see at the Java Web site contains an animation of Duke waving hello. (Say hello to Duke; he's hanging out in Figure 13-1.)

This chapter will discuss the Applications Program Interface (API) of Java as it relates to graphics and sound. There are a number of primitives for creating graphics objects, as well as image and sound file format data types and methods for retrieving these types of objects. This primer will skip graphics theory and only touch on those key issues that will allow you to write exciting graphics applications. Inline sound will be handled in the same fashion.

Beyond Animation

Java provides a prebuilt applet to perform rudimentary animation. You feed it a sequence of images and it simply displays them, one after the other. Voilà, animation in its purest form. This type of animation is great, but Java provides you with the ability to do many more wondrous things. A comprehensive set of drawing primitives is provided for you as part of Java's graphics class. This includes methods to draw lines, rectangles, circles, etc. In other words, the building blocks for creating magical graphics. All that's needed is your ingenuity.

On top of that, it's only a matter of time before there are even more tools available to the developer who is interested in creating graphics applications in Java. Many companies are creating fast, OpenGL-type 3D graphics libraries that will enable you to move completely out of the 2D realm with relative ease.

The java.awt.Graphics Class

The `java.awt.Graphics` class constructor creates a new object that is a copy of the current *graphics context*. Graphics context means the `java.awt.Graphics` object that is currently being used. This is often the current drawing space within a window, but can also be an offscreen buffer (more on this later in the section on double buffering.)

Most often, the graphics context that you will be dealing with is the `Graphics` object that is passed to the `paint` method in an applet. An instance of the `java.awt.Graphics` class can only be obtained from another graphics element such as an `Image` or a previous instance of a `Graphics` object. To put it another way, you can only get a graphics object from some other already existing graphics object—you can't make one from scratch. Therefore,

```
Graphics g = new Graphics();
```

is invalid. Instead you would use

```
Graphics g = current_context.create();
```

This factory paradigm of object instantiation assumes that the `current_context` object is an existing object of the `java.awt.Graphics` class. In other words, you need some context to base a new `Graphics` object on.

The remainder of this section gives names, parameters, and brief descriptions of the methods that will be used in this chapter for manipulating `Graphics` objects. These methods provide basic drawing functions, as well as the ability to perform clipping and scaling. These methods all work in the context of the given graphics object you specify. For example, if `G1` and `G2` represent two distinct drawing areas on a screen, specifying `G1.drawRect` would ultimately produce a rectangle in the `G1` drawing area.

public abstract void clearRect(int x, int y, int w, int h) The `clearRect` method will clear a rectangle within the given coordinates. It will fill the rectangle with the current background color. The parameters x and y are the origin of the rectangle in pixels of the `Graphics` object. The width and height of the rectangle are specified in the w and h parameters.

public abstract void clipRect(int x, int y, int w, int h) The `clipRect` method sets a clipping region within a graphics context. Any calls to paint or draw on a region outside of this rectangle will be ignored. This method is useful when trying to avoid flickering caused by redrawing an entire graphics context when only a small region changes. The rectangle that limits the drawing area is generally referred to as a clipping region, or clipping area.

public abstract Rectangle getClipRect() This will return the bounding box of the current clipping area.

public abstract void copyArea(int x, int y, int w, int h, int dx, int dy)
This method copies an area from one part of a graphics context to another. The origin, width, and height parameters (x, y, w, h) are copied to the destination origin (dx, dy).

public abstract Graphics create() This method will create a new graphics object that is a duplicate of the current graphics object. If create is called with parameters, namely integers representing x, y, w, and h as in previous examples, the new graphics object will be a duplicate of the subregion of the current object as defined by the parameters.

public abstract void dispose() This will dispose of and dereference the current graphics object. This is useful when freeing up memory for offscreen buffers that are no longer needed.

public abstract Color getColor() This will return the current drawing color.

public abstract void setColor(Color c) This will set the drawing color.

public void draw3DRect(int x, int y, int w, int h, boolean raised)
This method is probably not what you think it is. It does not draw a cube. It draws a rectangle that appears to be raised in the same fashion as those "3D" buttons in many interfaces. The "raised" parameter specifies whether this rectangle should be drawn raised. This is useful for designing your own buttons; the raised parameter could be toggled to represent a button that is selected or not. The Boolean parameter could be toggled between true and false to achieve this effect. This is demonstrated in Figure 13-2.

public void drawArc(int x, int y, int w, int h, int start, int end)
This method will draw an arc within the bounding box specified with x, y, w, and h. The start of the angle is specified in degrees with the start parameter. As would be expected, zero degrees would be directly right of the origin. The end of the arc is also specified in degrees but is relative to the starting point.

public void fillArc(int x, int y, int w, int h, int start, int end) This acts the same as drawArc, but fills the arc in with the current drawing color. Figure 13-3 shows an arc and a filled arc drawn next to each other.

public void drawBytes(byte bytes[], int offset, int len, int x, int y)
This will draw a string of bytes given the specified byte array, offset into the array, length of the subarray to print, and an x and y position to start drawing at. This works similarly to drawString and drawChars, which all use the current color and font of the graphics object they are working from.

public void drawChars(char chars[], int offset, int len, int x, int y)
Draws the specified subarray of characters at the given x and y coordinates.

FIGURE 13-2

Raised and unraised `3DRect`

FIGURE 13-3

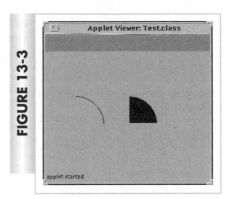

Arc and filled arc

public void drawString(String str, int x, int y) Draws the string specified at the given x and y coordinates. This will use the currently selected font.

public abstract boolean drawImage(Image img, int x, int y, ImageObserver io) This will load and draw an image at the given x and y coordinates. The `ImageObserver` will be notified once the image is complete if it has not been loaded yet.

public abstract boolean drawImage(Image img, int x, int y, int width, int height, ImageObserver io) This works the same as `drawImage(Image, int, int, ImageObserver)`, with one exception. A width and height parameter is passed that defines a bounding rectangle. The image will be scaled to fit the rectangle. Figure 13-4 is an example of an image being drawn with the `drawImage` method. In this

FIGURE 13-4

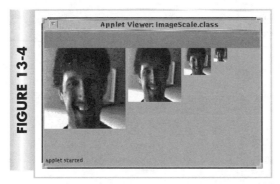

`drawImage` normal, and scaled down

figure, the first image is not scaled, but subsequent images are scaled down using the width and height parameters of the `drawImage` method.

public abstract void drawLine(int x, int y, int x2, int y2) This will draw a line from the given x, y to the given x2, y2.

public abstract void drawOval(int x, int y, int width, int height)
This will draw an oval within the specified rectangle.

public abstract void fillOval(int x, int y, int width, int height)
This is the same as `drawOval`, except the oval will be filled with the current drawing color. Figure 13-5 shows an oval and a filled oval drawn next to each other for comparison.

public abstract void drawPolygon(int x[], int y[], int nvertices)
This will draw a polygon by connecting the vertices specified in x and y. It is assumed that there are `nvertices` number of points in the x and y arrays being passed. The last vertex will be connected to the first to complete the polygon.

public abstract void drawPolygon(Polygon p) This draws the given `Polygon` object. Basically, the `Polygon` class has the same form as the parameters for the previous `drawPolygon` method. The only difference is that here they are encapsulated in their own class.

public abstract void fillPolygon(int x[], int y[], int nvertices) and public abstract void fillPolygon(Polygon p) These work the same as `drawPolygon` but fill the polygon with the current drawing color. See Figure 13-6 for an example of a polygon and the same polygon filled in.

public void drawRect(int x, int y, int width, int height) This draws the rectangle specified with x, y, `height` and `width`.

FIGURE 13-5

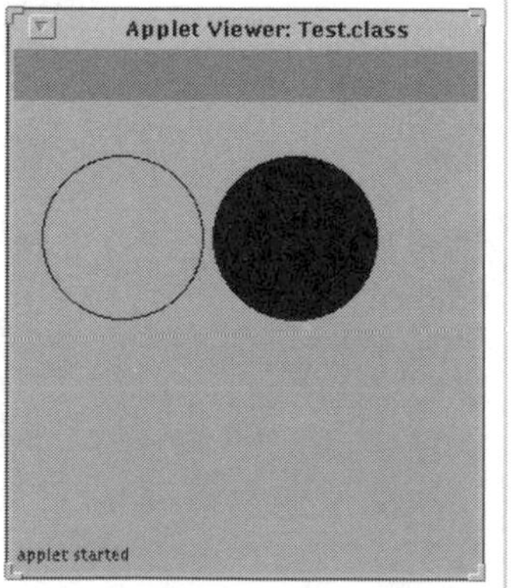

drawOval and fillOval

FIGURE 13-6

drawPolygon and
fillPolygon

FIGURE 13-7

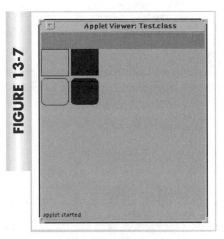

`drawRect`, `fillRect`,
`drawRoundRect`, and
`fillRoundRect`

public abstract void fillRect(int x, int y, int width, int height) This is the same as `drawRect`, but the rectangle is filled with the current drawing color.

public abstract void drawRoundRect(int x, int y, int width, int height, int arcWidth, int arcHeight) This will draw a rectangle with rounded corners. The `arcWidth` is the diameter of the arc, and `arcHeight` is the radius.

public abstract void fillRoundRect(int x, int y, int width, int height, int arcWidth, int arcHeight) This works the same as `drawRoundRect` but fills the rectangle in with the current drawing color. See Figure 13-7 for an example of a rectangle and the same rectangle filled in.

public abstract Font getFont() This will return the current font used for printing characters.

public abstract void setFont (Font f) This will set the current font.

public abstract void scale (float x, float y) This will scale the current graphics context. All operations on this context will be affected after a `scale` method call.

public abstract void setPaintMode() Will set the paint mode to the default settings. This will cause all paint operations to overwrite the destination in the graphics context using the current painting color set with `setColor`;.

public abstract void setXORMode(Color c) This will change the painting mode to alternate between the current painting color and the color passed in the `Color` argument.

public abstract void translate(int x, int y) Resets the origin of the graphics context. The x and y parameters become the new origin for subsequent operations.

For more details on the APIs, check the Appendix. These brief method descriptions are the basics of creating graphics objects in applets, and will be used in the examples of this chapter.

Subclassing java.applet.Applet

In general, calls to methods of a `java.awt.Graphic` object will occur in a `paint` method within your applet or application.

Every user-created applet is essentially a subclass of the `java.applet.Applet` class. The `Applet` class takes care of most of the generic functionality of an applet, and you must extend it to create your own methods for doing what you want. One important thing to note when creating applets with graphical content is that you must override the `paint` method if you want to be able to draw anything to the screen.

The Skeleton

You saw in Chapter 8 the basic skeleton of building an applet. The following will just recap that explanation. Keep in mind that not every applet will have every piece described below— it all depends upon what you're out to do. But if you are out to write an applet that continuously moves some graphics on a screen (like the rotating line of Chapter 8), then the discussion below is right on target.

Here's the applet skeleton with miniexplanations for each method.

```
/* Declare the applet extending java.applet.Applet */
/* and usually implementing Runnable */
class MyJavaApp extends Applet implements Runnable {

/* if this applet is to be threaded, define a thread */
/* variable */
Thread mythread=null;

/* Thread methods */

/* The run method is the thread's main */
   public void run() {
   while (true) {

/* repaint refreshes the applet (calls paint and more) */
   repaint();
```

```
      }
        }


/* Applet Methods */

/* What to do when the applet appears */
   public void start() {
      // start threads, etc.
}

/* What to do when the applet disappears */
   public void stop() {
       // stop threads, etc.
          }


/* Initial stuff for the applet */
   public void init() { resize(100,100); }

/* Do the needed painting */
   public void paint(Graphics g) {
       // Move graphics, paint, etc.
   }

/* Break a bad habit (see next section) */
   public void update(Graphics g) {
      paint(g);
   }
}
```

Well, there it is again. That skeleton is what you will find in most of the applets in existence today. Chances are there will be a significant number of extra support classes, etc., but this code is the heart of it all.

Breaking Update's Clear Screen Habit

When a browser runs an applet and is ready to draw it, the **update** method is called. By default, **update** clears the drawing area, and then calls the **paint** method. It is often useful to override the **update** method in order to modify its "clear the screen first" behavior. In general, you never call **paint** directly. Instead you call the **repaint** method. This basically adds a request to call **update** (which subsequently calls **paint**) to the event queue.

So for most applets with rapidly changing graphics, you'll include an **update** over-rider that looks like this:

```
/* Override update to remove "clear screen" */
public void update(Graphics g) {
  // update "would have" cleared the screen here
  paint(g);
  }
```

This certainly looks useless, but it's not. What you are doing is removing the default **update** method's habit of erasing the screen before calling **paint**.

The Graphics Context You Get

When the **paint** method is called, it is passed a reference to the current graphics context. This is used to modify your images, or to create subcontexts or new **Graphics** objects from. Here is a sample of a **paint** method in an applet:

```
public void paint(Graphics g) {
  g.drawString("Java Primer Plus!",10,10);
  }
```

This method would paint "Java Primer Plus!" on the current graphics context starting at the point (10,10). The easiest way to call your **paint** method after making changes to your graphics elements is to call **repaint**. Normally, if you have data that affects the screen being updated regularly, you can have a thread call **repaint** periodically to make sure that your changes make it to the screen.

 # Picking Up the Pen

Given that Java runs on a plethora of different machines with likely scads of different windowing systems, a tad of standardization is needed in Java to allow it to operate reliably on any screen. As previously said, this chapter won't attempt to teach you computer graphics as a science; instead, it's designed to show you how to adapt common graphics techniques to the Java environment. Here, you'll build some examples that use Java's capabilities and illustrate some techniques to design efficient graphics applications.

Flicker-Free Graphics

One of the most common problems with graphics-intensive Java applets is screen flicker. Flicker can be caused by slow updates, and by redrawing more than you need to. There are a few easy solutions for dealing with these problems. The first is to use double buffering, and the second is to override the **update** method, having it only repaint the regions of the applet that require it.

Double Buffering

Double buffering works by drawing to an offscreen buffer, rather than directly to the current display. This prevents screen updates in the middle of calculating and drawing your screen image. Once you are finished modifying the offscreen image, you copy the entire image to the current display. This technique is particularly useful in animation sequences.

The following two code samples are applets that draw a bouncing picture. The first example draws straight to the screen, and the second implements double buffering. If you run the two side by side, the benefits of double buffering will be obvious.

```java
/* Single buffering example */
import java.awt.*;

public class SingleBuff extends java.applet.Applet implements Runnable {

    /* Variables to hold the dimensions of the applet */
    protected int XRES,YRES;

    /* Width, height, and grid spacing */
    protected int w=100,h=100,gw=10;

    /* X, Y, and previous Y positions */
    protected int x,y=1,oldy=1;

    Thread MyThread;    // main thread for repaints
    /* lx..lw are for concentric circles */
    public int lx,ly,lh,lw;

    public Rectangle AppBorder;

    /* The applet init method */
    public void init() {
      AppBorder = bounds();    // get current applet
      XRES = AppBorder.width;
      YRES = AppBorder.height;
      x = XRES/2-w/2;          // center the image
      }

    /* The paint method */
    public void paint(Graphics g) {

        g.setColor(Color.lightGray);   // background color
        g.fillRect(x,oldy,w+1,h+1);    // cover up last box drawn
        oldy=y;             // remember y for the next coverup

        /* draw background pattern */
        for(int gc=0;gc<XRES;gc+=gw) {
          g.setColor(Color.gray);           // color of gridlines
          g.drawLine(gc,0,gc,YRES);         // draw vertical lines
          g.drawLine(0,gc,XRES,gc);         // draw horizontal lines
          g.setColor(Color.yellow);         // set color to yellow
          g.drawLine(gc,0,0,gc);            // draw diags
          g.setColor(Color.blue);           // set color to blue
          g.drawLine(XRES-gc,0,XRES,gc);    // draw diags
          }

        g.setColor(Color.lightGray);   // background color
        g.fillRect(0,0,100,20);        // clear box for title
        g.setColor(Color.red); // set color to red
        g.drawString("SingleBuffer",0,10);
        g.fillRect(x,y,w,h);           // draw red square
        g.setColor(Color.blue);
```

continued on next page

continued from previous page

```
        int l=0;
            /* Draw circles */
        for (int lh=h;lh>0;l+=4,lh-=8)
                    g.drawOval(x+l,y+l,lh,lh);

    }

/* The thread's run loop */
public void run() {
        int yd = 1;

    while(true) {
            y += yd;
        if (y<=1 || y >= YRES) yd = -yd;

        try {Thread.sleep(5);} catch(InterruptedException e){}
        this.repaint(); //redraw the screen
        }
    }

// ... start, stop, and update aren't listed

}
```

Let's try to digest a bit of that. The first thing to say is that several methods in this applet are not listed, including `start`, `stop`, and `update`. Of course they are present in the actual code, but in this applet (and in most) they take their painfully standard form, so these examples won't waste space relisting them all the time. The `start` and `stop` methods simply handle the thread, and the `update` is there just to avoid the screen clear.

The beginning of the applet just defines some variables to store resolution, coordinate, and dimension data. The `init` method gets the current dimensions of the applet's window, and stores the height and width in the `XRES` and `YRES` variables. The `paint` method is a little more complicated. It figures out where the last object was drawn so that it can tell what area to erase this time around. Then, some lines are drawn in the background, and the floating image is created. The `run` method changes the value of `y` and calls the `repaint` method to create the animation.

When you compile and run the previous example, notice how parts of the image occasionally disappear, and flicker is often unacceptably noticeable. The solution is to do all the drawing to an offscreen buffer—something like a screen that's hidden from view. After that's done, that buffer is copied with all haste, overwriting the visible screen.

The next code example is a subclass of the above single buffer class. It changes functionality as needed so that it draws the image to an offscreen buffer before sending the data to the display.

```
import java.awt.*;

/* Double Buffer subclass */
public class DoubleBuff extends SingleBuff implements Runnable {
    /* double buffering stuff */
```

```java
    Graphics dbuffer;   // Graphics object for offscreen drawing
    Image offscreen;    // Image representing the final screen
                        //   picture

/* overriding init method */
    public void init() {
            AppBorder = bounds();        // get current applet boundary
            XRES = AppBorder.width;
            YRES = AppBorder.height;
            x=XRES/2-w/2; //center the image

            /* Create an image that is the same size */
            /* as the resolution */
            offscreen = createImage(XRES,YRES);

            /* Associate a Graphics object */
            dbuffer = offscreen.getGraphics();
            dbuffer.setColor(Color.lightGray);
            dbuffer.fillRect(0,0,XRES,YRES);  //fill in background
    }

/* The paint method */
    public void paint(Graphics g) {

            /* Basically perform all the same drawing operations */
            /* as Single Buff, except to the dbuffer instead of  */
            /* the viewable graphics context (i.e. g)             */
        dbuffer.setColor(Color.lightGray);
        dbuffer.fillRect(x,oldy,w+1,h+1);
        oldy=y;

        /* draw background pattern */
        for(int gc=0;gc<XRES;gc+=gw) {
          dbuffer.setColor(Color.gray);
          dbuffer.drawLine(gc,0,gc,YRES);
          dbuffer.drawLine(0,gc,XRES,gc);
          dbuffer.setColor(Color.yellow);
          dbuffer.drawLine(gc,0,0,gc);
          dbuffer.setColor(Color.blue);
          dbuffer.drawLine(XRES-gc,0,XRES,gc);
          }

        dbuffer.setColor(Color.lightGray);
        dbuffer.fillRect(0,0,100,20);
        dbuffer.setColor(Color.red);
        dbuffer.drawString("SingleBuffer",0,10);
        dbuffer.fillRect(x,y,w,h);
        dbuffer.setColor(Color.blue);

        int l=0;
        for (int lh=h;lh>0;l+=4,lh-=8)
                dbuffer.drawOval(x+l,y+l,lh,lh);
```

continued on next page

continued from previous page

```
      /* Notice that the only call with the g object  */
      /* is on the following line. All other graphics */
      /* operations happen to the buffer              */

      /* Transfer (blit) the offscreen to the screen  */
    g.drawImage(offscreen,0,0,this);
     }
    }
```

Since `SingleBuff` was subclassed, all the variables and such were inherited. All that was needed was to add the offscreen buffer declarations and operations. This included overriding `init` and `paint`. Running this code you'll notice that the image is much more stable than in the previous example. This is due to the fact that the screen updates can't fall out of sync with your drawing routines. The finished screen is only updated once everything has been drawn. Basically, what is happening in the code that was added is that all calls that were previously made to the graphics object were passed to the `paint` method and were redirected to an offscreen image. The only call to the main graphics object happened at the end of the `paint` method, where the entire offscreen image was drawn at once.

Setting Clipping Regions

Another technique for eliminating applet flicker is to use some sort of region management when updating your display. You do this by setting a clipping area that limits the drawing area to the smallest possible region that needs to be updated. In other words, if the only part of your display that has changed are pixels between (0,0) and (10,15), there is no reason to redraw the entire screen; limit your redraw to the region between (0,0) and (10,15).

The `Graphics.clipRect` method allows you to set the size of your clipping region. It takes four integers as parameters that represent the x and y coordinates, and the width and height of the region (in that order). When you set a clipping region, only the area of the `Graphics` object that lies within that region will be updated. The less that has to be redrawn, the less work your computer has to do to redraw the screen, and the smoother your animations appear.

Going back to the previous example, let's create a clipping region in the `DoubleBuff` class. The following code determines what area of the screen needs to be refreshed, and sets a `clipRect` accordingly.

```
import java.awt.*;

public class ClipRect extends DoubleBuff implements Runnable {

    boolean drewall = false;   // whole screen drawn yet?

    /* The paint method */
    public void paint(Graphics g) {
```

```
  if (!drewall) g.clipRect(0,0,XRES,YRES);
   else
    if (y > oldy) g.clipRect(x,oldy,w+1,y+h);
     else
       g.clipRect(x,y,w+1,oldy+h);
   .
   .  // same drawing primitives
   .
   /* Transfer (blit) the offscreen to the screen  */
   g.drawImage(offscreen,0,0,this);
   drewall = true;
   }

   public void start() {
     drewall = false;
     if (MyThread == null) {
       MyThread = new Thread(this);
       MyThread.start();
     }
   }

 }
```

The main difference between this applet and the `DoubleBuff` applet is the `clipRect` call in the `paint` method. You try to determine if the entire image needs to be redrawn (such as the first time the `paint` method is called, or after the browser window has been resized). You use the `drewall` variable to signal if the entire image needs to be drawn. If this is not the case, you create your clipping area by determining the last coordinates that your image was drawn at and adding that area to the current drawing position. This is your clipping region. All you need to draw is the coverup of the last image, and the new image.

You should notice slightly smoother movement now that less of the screen is being updated. As you can see, just a few relatively painless techniques can greatly increase the quality of your graphics applets.

JavaDraw

Now let's build a more involved applet. It will use many new Java ideas and graphics methods. Wherever possible the following example has been written for clarity above worrying about details. The focus here is on learning to use the API; writing the shrink-wrapped commercial applications can come later.

This example will build a drawing tablet. When run, you can draw lines, circles, rectangles, etc., in several different colors. This applet will be called `JavaDraw`, and the following code bits will be part of a complete applet that will be put together at the end of this section. This example will bring home the straightforward uses for many of the `Graphics` class's methods.

An Empty Canvas

This example will be based upon the `java.awt.Canvas` class. This class is used to abstract a real-world artist's canvas. You know, all that "blank page" and "let your creativity flow" type stuff. Java's version isn't quite so philosophical. The `Canvas` class in Java is primarily a vehicle for you to set up an area for drawing. Of course, as with most classes, only by subclassing can you make it do what you want.

The code listing follows; it's a little broken up so each piece of the class can be explained. The first thing to do is to subclass `java.awt.Canvas` so you can insert your own functionality.

```
/* Creating a Canvas Class */
class MyCanvas extends Canvas {

/* The x,y coordinates, height & width */
   int drawX,drawY,drawH,drawW;
   String mt;

/*  Set these to make the code more readable */
final int _RESET      = 0; //reset drawing field
final int _RECTANGLE  = 1;
final int _FILLEDRECT = 2;
final int _CIRCLE     = 3;
final int _FILLEDCIRC = 4;
final int _LINE       = 5;
final int _TEXT       = 6;

/* current drawing color */
Color drawCol = Color.black;

/* current drawing mode  */
int drawAct = _LINE;
```

These are just the variable initializations. The initial drawing color is specified as black, and the initial drawing shape as a line. The `_SHAPE` convention has been used to create some names for later code readability. In other words, you will be seeing some `switch` statements later that will choose among these shapes. Instead of just having

```
switch (drawAct) {

  case 1:              // draws a rectangle
  .
  .
  .
```

you can use

```
switch (drawAct) {

  case _RECTANGLE:
  .
  .
  .
```

This works toward code readability. The MyCanvas code continues with its paint method.

```
/* The following is the main drawing routine   */
public void paint(Graphics g) {

   g.setColor(Color.lightGray);
   Rectangle r = bounds();

   /* Should we reset the drawing area? */
   if (drawAct == _RESET)
       g.fillRect(0,0,r.width,r.height);
   else {
    g.fillRect(0,0,80,15);
      g.setColor(Color.black);
      g.drawRect(0,0,80,15);
   }

   g.setColor(Color.black);
   g.drawString("JavaDraw",r.width/2-20,15);
   g.drawRect(0,0,r.width-1,r.height-1);
   g.setColor(drawCol);

  /* perform the selected drawing routine */
  switch (drawAct) {

     case _RECTANGLE  : g.drawRect(drawX,drawY,drawW,drawH);
             g.drawString("Rectangle",0,10);
                   break;
     case _FILLEDRECT : g.fillRect(drawX,drawY,drawW,drawH);
             g.drawString("Fill Rectangle",0,10);
                   break;
     case _CIRCLE     : g.drawOval(drawX,drawY,drawW,drawH);
             g.drawString("Circle",0,10);
                   break;
     case _LINE       : g.drawLine(drawX,drawY,drawW,drawH);
             g.drawString("Line",0,10);
                   break;
     case _FILLEDCIRC : g.fillOval(drawX,drawY,drawW,drawH);
             g.drawString("fill Circle",0,10);
                   break;
     case _TEXT       : g.drawString(mt,drawX,drawY);
             g.drawString(mt,0,10);
                   break;
       }
   }
}
```

As with an applet's paint method, this method is in charge of doing the painting. Nothing too magic is involved in the above. The switch statement draws the indicated shape according to the value of the drawAct variable at the given coordinates. You'll notice that nowhere above are the coordinates for the drawAct variable set; don't worry, this comes soon. The class finishes off with

```
/* standard overridden update */
public void update(Graphics g) { paint(g); }

/* set dimensions to zero */
public void redraw() {
  drawX = drawY = drawW = drawH = 0;
  repaint();
}

/* Mouse Handling */
public boolean mouseDown(Event e, int x, int y) {
  drawX=x;
   drawY=y;
   return true;
}

public boolean mouseUp(Event e, int x, int y) {

   if (drawAct == _LINE) {
    drawW=x;
    drawH=y;
    repaint();
    return true;
    }

   /* Not a line, extract the coordinates */
   drawW = java.lang.Math.abs(x - drawX);
   if (x < drawX) drawX = x;

   drawH = java.lang.Math.abs(y - drawY);
   if (y < drawY) drawY = y;

   repaint(); //draw our new object
   return true;
   }
}
```

This is certainly looking an awful lot like a subclass of **Applet** (i.e., it has methods named **paint**, **update**, etc.). Keep in mind that it's not; it's a subclass of **Canvas**. However, both **java.applet.Applet** and **java.awt.Canvas** inherit from **java.awt.Component**. Therefore, many of the methods you've seen in applets (i.e., the mouse methods, the update method, etc.) are present in **java.awt.Component**.

As far as what the above code is doing, it is mainly some administrative details. The **update** is there for usual reasons. In fact, without the override in this application, every time you draw a new object, the previous object will get erased. The mouse methods handle storing coordinates that represent where you indicated to draw objects.

So the class to make the canvas is done. Great. But in and of itself it isn't runnable. It's not an applet or a standalone (i.e., no **main**). The **MyCanvas** class is just a support class for some runnable class. In fact, you'll design more support classes before utilizing them from some runnable program. Also, don't forget that even though this application looks like an applet (because of some of its method names), that is only coincidence, because the `Canvas` class is a sibling (actually, more like an uncle) of the `Applet` class. In other words, they are both descendants of `Component`. This application has not been specifically designed as an applet or a standalone—yet.

Making Widgets

What's a widget? Oh, you know, it's one of those little things that is like about yea-big that has one of those things sticking out of it and it makes that little noise when you push on its one side. Hmm, well maybe a better definition is that it's just a little doodad, or maybe more of a thing-a-ma-bob. Well, how about just saying it's an additional component in a window on your screen. For example, buttons, scroll bars, checkboxes—any little thing that can be stuck on a window and mean something (often, like buttons, it's designed with user interaction in mind). Yeah, that's it.

Well, anyway, whatever they are, you need some. For your drawing application you want users to be able to indicate whether they want to draw a line, rectangle, circle, etc. You can do this by adding some buttons to the top of the drawing area. Whenever one of the buttons is pressed (by a mouse click), then that drawing shape is activated. To do all this magic, you'll create a `MyWidgets` class that subclasses `java.awt.Panel`. A panel is a generic container for graphical elements.

The `MyWidgets` class creates a number of buttons for specifying drawing modes. It also handles button events and, based on the value of the button pressed, passes data up to the `MyCanvas` class that is handling the drawing routines. Here's the start of the class:

```
/* Setup the Widgets */
class MyWidgets extends Panel {

MyCanvas canvas;
TextField mt;

public MyWidgets(MyCanvas canvas) {
    this.canvas = canvas;
    add(mt = new TextField("",10));
    add(new Button("Text"));
    add(new Button("Line"));
    add(new Button("Rect"));
    add(new Button("FillRect"));
    add(new Button("Circle"));
    add(new Button("FillCircle"));
    add(new Button("Reset"));
}
```

The constructor gets passed the applicable canvas, saves this value, and then adds buttons with the names of the legal drawing shapes. The rest of the class handles the events that are issued as a result of the user pressing one of the buttons.

```
/* grab events and look for button events */
public boolean action(Event ev, Object arg) {

    if (ev.target instanceof Button) {

        // Determine which event
        canvas.drawAct = whichact((String)arg);

        if (canvas.drawAct == canvas._TEXT)
          canvas.mt = mt.getText();
        if (canvas.drawAct == canvas._RESET)
                canvas.repaint();

        canvas.redraw();
        return true;
    }
    return false;
}

private int whichact(String T) {

    if (T.equals("Text"))           return canvas._TEXT;
    if (T.equals("Reset"))          return canvas._RESET;
    if (T.equals("Line"))           return canvas._LINE;
    if (T.equals("Rect"))           return canvas._RECTANGLE;
    if (T.equals("FillRect"))       return canvas._FILLEDRECT;
    if (T.equals("Circle"))         return canvas._CIRCLE;
    if (T.equals("FillCircle"))     return canvas._FILLEDCIRC;
return -1;
    }
}
```

The action method is called by the system when an event occurs. What's an event? Well, it's not quite as convoluted as a widget (thank goodness). The Java system defines many different things as events. Often they are asynchronous occurrences pertaining to something the user has done. This includes keypresses, mouse clicks, and the like. Here the focus is on button presses.

According to the button pressed by the user, the `drawAct` variable gets set to the applicable value (remember, `drawAct` will be used in the `MyCanvas paint` method to draw the actual shape). There are specific checks for `_TEXT` and `_RESET`. The `_TEXT` value needs to perform the extra task of fetching the text that the user has entered (it's entered in a small text box in the upper left-hand corner of the application). The `_RESET` should clean the screen.

Colors

You can also add the ability for your users to draw in several colors. Buttons will be used again so that users can click a button for the desired color. Here a `MyColors` class will be created, which will look painfully similar to the `MyWidgets` class. In fact, it's basically the same thing, except its result is to assign the `drawCol` variable instead of the `drawAct` variable.

```
/* MyColors class - setup/maint of color buttons */
class MyColors extends Panel {

MyCanvas canvas; // canvas that calls this

/* Add buttons */
public MyColors (MyCanvas canvas) {
   this.canvas = canvas;
   add(new Button("Blue"));
   add(new Button("Red"));
   add(new Button("Yellow"));
   add(new Button("Black"));
   add(new Button("Green"));
   add(new Button("Gray"));
}

/* Catch the events */
public boolean action(Event ev, Object arg) {
   if(ev.target instanceof Button) {
    String label = (String)arg;

      canvas.drawCol = whichcol((String)arg);

      canvas.redraw();
    return true;
    }
  return false;
}

    /* match the string */
    private Color whichcol(String T) {
        if (T.equals("Blue"))          return Color.blue;
        if (T.equals("Black"))         return Color.black;
        if (T.equals("Yellow"))        return Color.yellow;
        if (T.equals("Red"))           return Color.red;
        if (T.equals("Green"))         return Color.green;
        if (T.equals("Gray"))          return Color.gray;
          return null;
    }
}
```

Besides new names for the buttons and the `drawCol` variable, there is not much new there. All these classes can now be tied together in an application.

Make Me an Applet

You will now use the above classes to create an applet. As has been promised, this applet will give the user a drawing pad where they can create artistic creations beyond their wildest dreams (or at least get as creative as you can with lines, rectangles, and circles). Obviously, if you're going to have an applet, you'll be needing to subclass java.applet.Applet somewhere. No problem. You'll only need one (relatively short) class to put this all together.

```java
import java.awt.*;

public class javadraw extends java.applet.Applet {

MyWidgets WControls;
MyColors ColorControls;
static Rectangle DrawSize;

/* The init of the Applet */
public void init() {
   DrawSize = bounds();
 setLayout(new BorderLayout());

   /* Setup the Canvas */
MyCanvas c = new MyCanvas();

 add("North", WControls = new MyWidgets(c));

   /* Add color buttons to the bottom of the applet */
 add("Center", c);
 add("South", ColorControls = new MyColors(c));
 }

/* Switch stuff on */
public void start() {
  ColorControls.enable();
  WControls.enable();
  }

  /* Switch stuff off */
  public void stop() {
ColorControls.disable();
WControls.disable();
   }
}
```

As promised, JavaDraw subclasses Applet. All the meat is in the init method. The layout is set to a new BorderLayout object. The BorderLayout defines five regions in a "window." These regions are Center, North, South, East, and West. This can be seen in Figure 13-8.

There are other layout schemes available in awt, but this will suffice for these purposes. Next, you define your canvas from the MyCanvas class. The subsequent add statements place the MyWidget buttons at the top and the MyColor buttons at the bottom of the window. Finally, you override the start and stop methods to enable and disable the buttons. Pull this up in a Web browser and the drawing applet will be at your disposal. You can see this in Figure 13-9.

This applet is designed in a relatively generic (i.e., reusable) form. With little additional effort, you can make this a standalone application.

FIGURE 13-8

North

W
e
s
t

Center

E
a
s
t

South

Border layout

FIGURE 13-9

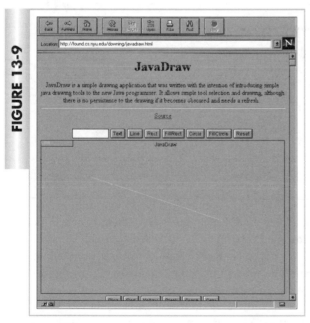

JavaDraw

JavaDraw Standalone

You have to remember that even though you seemingly handled a good portion of the details of creating your windowing environment in the applet example, the browser was present and was providing the underlying framework for the windowing system. To convert this applet to a standalone application, you will need to bear the burden of setting up the window yourself. Your first task will be to change the above `javadraw` class to a subclass of `java.awt.Frame`. The `java.awt.Frame` class is the building block for setting up your own pop-up windows. You'll also rename the class from `javadraw` to `MyFrame`, since you'll need a calling class to set up this frame and you'll want to use the `javadraw` name there.

```java
class MyFrame extends java.awt.Frame {

static Rectangle DrawSize;
MyWidgets WControls;
MyColors ColorControls;

/* The Constructor */
MyFrame() {
   DrawSize = bounds();
setLayout(new BorderLayout());

   /* Setup the Canvas */
   MyCanvas c = new MyCanvas();

   add("North", WControls = new MyWidgets(c));

   /* Add controls to the bottom of the applet */
   add("Center", c);
   add("South", ColorControls = new MyColors(c));
   pack();
   resize(500,200);
   show();
ColorControls.enable();
WControls.enable();

 }
```

The `init` method has also been renamed to be the constructor for the new frame class. Other details include putting in the `pack` method (this adjusts components such as the buttons to their correct size), the `show` method (this makes the frame actually appear), and moving the button enablers into the constructor. The enable methods were moved into the constructor because the `start` and `stop` methods were eliminated (i.e., the browser was calling those, and there is no browser anymore).

Also with that in mind, you don't have a browser around anymore to kill the application when you're done with it. So you need to add an event handler to catch death and destruction events and kill the application. This is done with

```
public boolean handleEvent(Event E) {
  if (E.id == Event.WINDOW_DESTROY)
    System.exit(0);
  return false;
}
```

Those are all the changes you need to make. All the supporting classes (**MyCanvas**, **MyWidgets**, etc.) are okay as is. All that is needed is a small standalone class, again named **JavaDraw**, to start this machine.

```
import java.awt.*;

/* JavaDraw Standalone */
class JavaDraw {
  static public void main(String args[]) {
    MyFrame F = new MyFrame();
  }
}
```

And that's it! The application will look identical to the applet version, of course sans the browser.

You should be able to work with this code to get started on your own windowed applications. Possibly Java's biggest plus (and minus), as far as its windowing applications goes, is its endless possibilities. The **awt** classes involved in creation of windowed applications are many—i.e., getting them all straight can be a chore. So, this is not the only way you could have done this example, but it should give you enough of a base to begin exploring how Java's windowing toolkit works.

The Sound of Java

So, what is the sound of one applet clapping? Or if an applet is running in the forest, and nobody is around, does it make a sound? Your multimedia extravaganzas just aren't going to knock anyone's socks off if all they can hear is the humming of their computer's cooling fan in the background. So, let's take a look at some of the sound capabilities that come built in with the Java standard class libraries.

There are a number of possibilities available to Java developers who want to create sonic events in their projects. Many of these are pretty close to plug-and-play, and are as simple as grabbing a sound file from a URL and playing it.

The following section will discuss the standard sound classes and API.

Audio API

Let's first take a look at the two most interesting API elements that provide audio support to Java applets. The methods listed here are members of the **Applet** class.

public Audioclip getAudioClip(URL url) This method will return a sound file, given the URL to one.

public void play(URL url) This will play the audioclip if found at the given URL. If a sound file is not found at the URL address, no action is taken.

The `AudioClip` interface also contains a few methods that should be inherited by many applets that use audio; these are `loop`, `play`, and `stop`.

Straight from the Box

Probably the simplest way to add sound to your applets is to use the `play` method of the `java.applet.Applet` class. Playing audio in your applets can be as simple as adding the line

```
play(getCodeBase(), "mysound.au");
```

to your applet.

Here is an applet that demonstrates how simple it can be to add audio support to a Java applet. All it does is periodically play a sound clip that it loads from a URL.

```
public class SimpleSound extends Applet {
   final String MySound = "hello.au";

      /* paint - which doesn't do much painting */
      public void paint(Graphics g) {
      g.drawString("Click to play a sound",0,15);
      }

      /* Play the sound when the mouse button is clicked */
      public boolean mouseDown(Event ev, int x, int y) {
             play(getCodeBase(), MySound);
             return true;
      }
}
```

The applet in the previous example grabs a sound file called hello.au. It attempts to download it from the codebase of the applet, namely the URL of the applet. Anytime the `mouseDown` event is captured, the sound is played with the `play` method.

Summary

There are a number of tools available to the Java programmer for creating exciting multimedia content. Many of these are simple plug-and-play utilities such as `getImage` or `play`, and others require a little more thought, such as calculating clipping regions before repainting an applet. This gives a little something to everyone, from the beginner on up to the advanced graphics application programmer.

Be on the lookout for third-party graphics and sound libraries. Many companies are already in the process of creating fast, full-featured 3D graphics libraries for Java applications, as well as VRML support for creating and navigating 3D worlds in Java. We are at the cusp of a very exciting time in the evolution of information technology, and Java gives you the tools you need to keep it exciting.

 # Questions

1. Describe double buffering, and why you would or wouldn't want to use it.

2. How do you redraw only certain parts of a window without affecting the rest?

3. How do you display a GIF image in a `Graphics` object?

4. How is a sound clip loaded and played?

 # Exercises

1. Write an applet that paints a background image and randomly places polygons over that image.

2. Rewrite the previous applet using both double buffering and clipping.

3. Add sound to the previous applet so that a noise is generated every time a new polygon is displayed.

By a Thread

14

You will learn about the following in this chapter:

- What multithreading is
- Why multithreading is useful
- How to create threads in Java
- How to synchronize your threads
- How to set priorities for your threads
- How to make threads play nice and wait for specific events

Actually, you have been using the concept of a thread for a long time. A thread is short for a *thread of control*. For a quick visualization, get a program listing and pound a nail into each statement. Then, tie a thread to the first statement's nail. Now you can traverse through the path that a computer would take when running this code. Every time you need to branch, you just wrap the thread around the branching statement's nail and stream your thread to the new spot. When you finish, the twisty little path your thread has taken represents the thread of control you followed for this code (for a given input). So as you can see, any program you have ever run has followed some thread of control.

To the accolades of programmers everywhere, Java has included support for *multithreading*. Just as it would seem, multithreading is the act of racing several threads through the same program at the same time. The threads can follow different paths through the code if they have been given different input or started in different places. You could imagine that, as with the program listing and nails, stringing several threads simultaneously through the code would quickly become unmanageable; likely your hands would get tangled, you would get peeved, and become generally not nice to be around. Same thing goes for programming multiple threads.

Threads in general, even Java's controlled implementation of them, is a vast topic. This chapter will give you an introduction to the tools Java provides you with to use and control small legions of threads. Threads are quite unpredictable little rascals, and the fact that Java must implement them on a multitude of machines only serves to exacerbate an already tricky situation. The information here will attempt to address how to control threads in all cases, but be ready to expect the unexpected. Prepare to have massive amounts of fun.

What's the Diff?

A popular misconception is that multithreading is the same thing as *multiprocessing*. Nothing could be further from the truth (well, saying multithreading is the same thing as cheese-cake is probably further—but you get the idea). Multiprocessing is an operating system abstraction that allows a computer to seemingly run more than one process (i.e., program) at a time. Always keep in mind that if you are running a single processor machine, your machine really cannot do more than one thing at a time, but through multiprocessing and multithreading (and maybe a bit of smoke and mirrors) it will appear as though all kinds of things are happening simultaneously.

Multithreading, like multiprocessing, also is a way to allow a computer to do more than one thing at a time. However, threads all come from the same program (i.e., same address space); in other words, a program can spawn (create and send off running) threads to run many parts of itself at the same time. Multiprocessing is many *programs* at once, multithreading is *many sections of one program* at once. You've seen this in many applets already; the main thread is the browser, your moving graphics could be another one, your sound could be another, etc.

Figure 14-1 shows a graphical representation of this situation. HotJava is only one application, but several different threads are running within it. Actually, above and beyond the threads you create there are a bunch of threads buzzing along taking care of maintenance activities you aren't even aware of (and you aren't any the worse off for it).

Joining the Circus

For a real-world analogy, think of a three-ring circus. Each ring has a death-defying act going on, but each member of the audience is only watching one act at any moment—

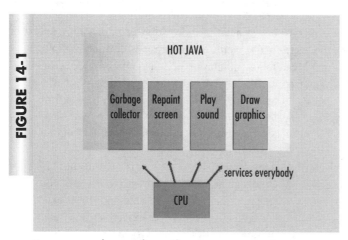

FIGURE 14-1

System and user threads

i.e., the circus is multiprocessing with one show (task) in each ring. You can think of the audience's attention as analogous to the CPU's attention in a computer.

Enter SuperGuy

Okay, then part of a sudden (you were somewhat expecting it), the performers leave the rings, the lights dim, the music builds up, and SuperGuy enters the lone spotlight. SuperGuy then begins to juggle three flaming pomegranates while twirling two plates of flaming ravioli on his head in addition to playing "Oh My Conquistador" on a (likely flaming) guitar with his feet. SuperGuy is multithreading. He is only one act (i.e., one program/process), but he has multiple simultaneous tasks in motion. In truth, the audience is really concentrating on only one of his amazing feats (each of which is analogous to a thread) at any instant.

It should be plain to see that it wouldn't take much of a reach to have threading inside one of the programs that is multiprocessing.

Figure 14-2 shows the circus. SuperGuy is in ring number two doing his flaming extravaganza (he's still multithreading) while Wippy the Magic Duck and Mary and her Wonder

FIGURE 14-2

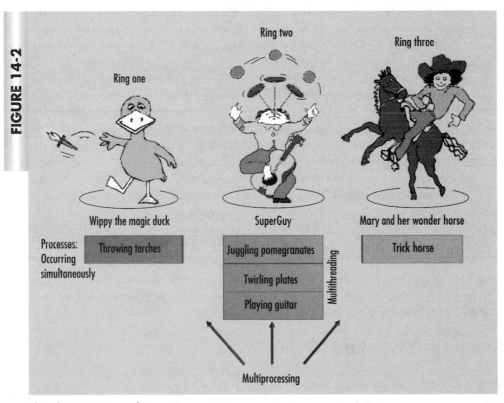

The three-ring multiprocessor

Horses perform in rings one and three, respectively. It's quite common in most (if not all) Java environments that multiprocessing programs can be multithreading, too.

Notice another subtle difference between multithreading and multiprocessing. SuperGuy is obviously well aware of the three feats he's performing; in fact, if the flaming ravioli plates all of a sudden get a bit wobbly and he has to make a daring rescue attempt, he can immediately change the tune on his flaming foot guitar from "Oh My Conquistador" to something a bit more suspenseful. The story is that threads (ravioli plates, guitar, etc.) have shared data and can use this for communication. In contrast, SuperGuy doesn't know about nor does he care about what's going on in rings one and three. As long as Wippy and Mary's Wonder Horses keep out of his way, he is unconcerned with what they do.

Take What You Get

Further differences between multithreading and multiprocessing surface in the deepest, darkest reaches of their conceptual implementations. As was said, multiprocessing is an operating system concept. Therefore, any code you write in C could happily run on a non-multiprocessing operating system such as MS-DOS, happily owning the system and calculating its happy data. Then again, the same program with no modification could run on a multiprocessing operating system such as Windows NT and become a slave to the operating system. It will be time sliced, paged out, and generally coerced into submission subject to the vile interpretation of the multiprocessing scheduler—it only gets as much processing time as the OS sees fit to give it.

Your once super fast C code turns into a veritable sloth, probably because some silly word processing program is hogging the CPU trying to find the correct spelling of the words "Uncle Fudd." The point is, you and your program have no control over this theft of CPU time; you are at its mercy. Same thing at the multiprocessing circus; the individual acts have no control over which act the audience is currently watching (although stepping up their death-defiance factor may increase their portion).

Multithreading really doesn't afford you any more control over how much CPU time you get, but it does provide you the ability to send off pieces of your program as *lightweight processes*. A lightweight process is really just another name for a thread. They don't quite qualify as whole processes, since they are really just pieces of one program. The reason they are termed lightweight is because they will all run within the same address space (i.e., they can share memory) and don't have as much overhead associated with them as actual processes. The advantage is that the operating system can deal with them quickly because of their light overhead. Again, it's quicker for the audience to switch its attention between SuperGuy's different actions than to look to different rings.

Wippy and Wayward Torches

Threads typically don't require any security between each other since they are supposed to be friendly by design. Multiprocessing will let all kinds of different programs run alongside yours, even some that may have stinky attitudes (Wippy the Magic Duck has been known to throw a wayward flaming torch now and then, hitting SuperGuy square). Threads, on the other hand, are all started by you and are from the same program—this makes the idea of thread security somewhat analogous to SuperGuy putting on a helmet in case he *decides* to stop twirling the plates of ravioli and let them come crashing down on his head. If he's worried about getting hurt, he should probably be less concerned about the helmet and devote more time to being sure he doesn't decide to drop the plates in the first place. In other words, multithreading is supposed to be cooperative; no more security is needed than the amount required to protect you from yourself.

Threaded by Design

A final remark distinguishing multiprocessing and multithreading is that multiprocessing is implemented within the operating system. Any program, written in any language, can be unwittingly tossed into a multiprocessing operating system and be subsequently accosted. It's not quite the same for multithreading; it requires support from the operating system as well as the language's specification (enter Java, stage left).

Both of these environments must be designed to support multithreading. Operating system support was the major difficulty with porting Java to Microsoft Windows 3.1. There is no native thread support in that operating system. C and C++, as defined by their language specifications, do not have thread support; however, packages now exist in different environments to implement this feature. This aftermarket implementation is okay, but standardization of the implementation is the needed ingredient (enter Java, stage right).

Few languages in existence have included multithreading within their design with such devotion. This is, to say the least, pretty nifty. As with many of Java's traits, this will standardize the use of threads across a multitude of platforms. Never has the development of multithreaded software been so easy.

In Touch with Your Asexuality

The next question should be, other than for trivial applet animations and sound, why do you need threads? Well, supposedly you don't—C, Pascal, C++, etc., have long survived without asexually spawning off threads to get their work done. The answer is really that multithreading can improve performance and ease programming.

Uncle Fudd Strikes Again

Assume, for example, that your program needs to periodically read from a disk. It goes through a loop reading from the disk, then crunches some mean calculations on the input, and so on. Well, what happens if the next time it goes to read the disk, the disk isn't quite ready? (Probably busy off looking for Uncle Fudd again). What happens is that your program stops. Stops dead; your code needs to read the disk some more before it can do any more calculations, but it can't because of the busy disk—in essence your performance goes to zero. You can see the slowdowns this could cause in the long run, especially if that disk happens to be very busy.

On the other hand, by multithreading you could have two threads, a disk reader thread and a number cruncher thread. The disk reader thread watches a common buffer (common to both threads, that is) to see when it's empty; when that is true, it immediately goes out and tries to read the disk. The number cruncher also watches that buffer, and when it's full (the disk reader filled it), it grabs the data, marks the buffer empty, and starts crunching away.

Given this new scenario, now reconsider the nasty proposition of the disk being unready—the disk reader thread is still thwarted and would have to wait, but the number cruncher can still buzz along doing some heated number crunching (on the data from the previous disk read). Figure 14-3 shows these boys in action.

The hope here is that, given that the number cruncher will need a certain amount of time to do its thing anyway, the disk reader will eventually get dibs on the disk before that time is up. Therefore, the disk holdup didn't slow down your code. A side bonus (gotta love side bonuses) is that the two threads really won't compete much for the CPU. If the disk is unready, the disk reader thread will *block* and end up forfeiting all its CPU time to the cruncher until it has something to do (i.e., the disk frees up). Blocking of a thread means it goes to sleep until it is awoken by some external event. Granted, while the disk reader is reading and the number cruncher is crunching, they are both active and both sharing CPU time. However, this example is quite pretty, since processes that use a lot of CPU (cruncher) and those that use a lot of I/O (reader) don't clash too heavily.

Less Thought, More Code

The second advantage to programming using multiple threads is that some applications are inherently built as two (or more) independent yet complementary functions. Suppose you were developing a piece of software that watched for messages incoming over a network from any of ten different places. Code without threads would probably run through a loop checking each of the ten input lines for data. If a message was found, it could accept the data and process it, then resume its loop. On top of that, you would need to be quite the little caretaker to be sure that messages coming in while the data was being processed did not get lost because no one was listening.

With multithreading you could assign a thread to listen to each of the lines, and if some data came in, it could wake up the data processing routine and go back to listening. You could use the same piece of listening code for each of the ten threads instead of one wildly spinning loop. Adding new input lines in the future would mean you would only need to spawn a new thread. Figure 14-4 shows the conceptual difference.

The code for each listener would be a straightforward method. Admittedly, you have really just moved the loop checking the listeners into the scheduler of the operating

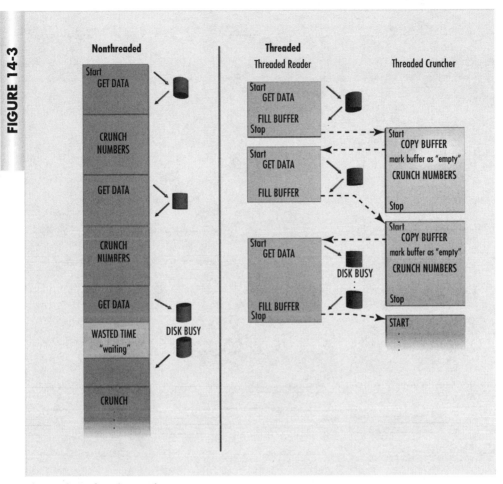

FIGURE 14-3

Threading for throughput

system. However, programming this way will allow you to think of each blob of individual functionality as a unit and structure it as such.

Thread Spawn

Well, you've got the background on threads. How about the foreground? Or, how about the details of starting threads in Java? Pretty much everything to do with threads is encapsulated within the oddly named **java.lang.Thread** class. There are two ways to tap the vast pool of potent functionality—subclassing and interfacing.

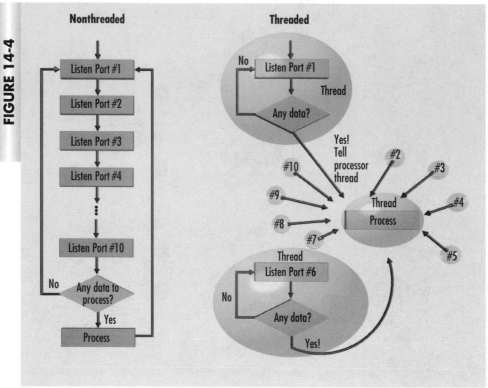

FIGURE 14-4

Listener threads

Subclassing

The most straightforward method is to have your class subclass the `java.lang.Thread` class. How much simpler could it be? Regardless if your class is a background number cruncher or a ping pong ball class, you can subclass the `Thread` class and inherit its threading functionality. The `Thread` class has a `public void run()` method. This method is the magic method that will be called as the main method of the thread.

In order to get any useful work done, you must override the `run` method. Obviously, the `Thread` class's default version of `run` is not particularly useful to you since it doesn't do anything specific to your code. The `run` method is what will be called (by mysterious forces over which you have little control) when an instance of your class is started in its own thread. Of course, your class can still have all kinds of other plump methods that can get called from `run`, but `run` is the entry and exit point. It is somewhat analogous to a `main` method in a standalone application, and just like the `main` method, when `run` ends so does your thread.

This is the reason you will often see an endless loop in the `run` method of an applet. Applets typically are performing some animation or graphics that are meant to continue as long as the viewer can see the applet. In such a case, it's prudent to specify your `run` to loop forever—i.e., keep the thread chugging along with no thoughts of its own about stopping. Once your applet leaves the viewable area, the thread is stopped by external forces (the browser), and the `run` method (and its infinite loop) perish in the fray.

```
/* class trouble - fun with threads */
class trouble extends Thread {

/* The 'p' variable will be shared among the threads */
  static int p;
  int myval;
  boolean flag=true;

/* constructor */
  public trouble (int x) { myval = x; }

/* The infamous run method. This will be the entry and exit */
/*  point of the thread */
  public void run() {
    while (true) { messp(mval); }
    }

/* The 'mess with p' method, called from run() */
  static private void messp(int mval) {
    p = myval;
    p = p + 2;
    System.out.print(p);
    }
  }
```

The above code defines a class `trouble` (the reason for its name will become apparent soon). This class subclasses (as promised) the `Thread` class and inherits its amazing functionality. To create several running threads of this class you could use code like this:

```
.
.
.
trouble A = new trouble(5);
trouble B = new trouble(6);

A.start();
B.start();
.
.
.
```

So from this point on, `A` and `B` go off competing for CPU time, busily printing out sevens and eights—or so it would seem.

Send Me

If you will be writing a lot of Web applets, the interfacing method of thread creation will be your most commonly used technique. Maybe not by choice, but certainly by design. You have seen this in applets already; your applet class must implement the `Runnable` interface. From there you can send your applet to a `java.lang.Thread` object to get it to run. By no means is implementation of the `Runnable` interface limited to applets or applet programming. Basically, you use this interface when you want to thread a class that can't be made a subclass of `Thread`—i.e., you already need to subclass it from some other parent.

This is always the case for all applets, since you must subclass your applet class from the `java.applet.Applet` class. Yet you also need to (or would certainly like to) subclass the `Thread` class so your applet can have its own threads. As you know, this is really a need for multiple inheritance, a big no-no in Java. So you have been provided the `Runnable` interface. This makes for a slightly more complex usage of threads (in concept anyway), but still gets the job done. In the `trouble` class itself, all you need to do is change the class declaration.

```
/* class trouble - fun with threads */
class trouble extends Object implements Runnable  {
```

Usually you will be subclassing a significantly more interesting class than `java.lang.Object`. It was done here just to illustrate using the interface. Everything else about the class is still set up for threading (i.e., the `run` method). A more significant change appears in how you declare and start the threads. The relative equivalent to the subclassing example would be

```
.
.
.

trouble A = new trouble(5);
trouble B = new trouble(6);

Thread Athread = new Thread(A);
Thread Bthread = new Thread(B);

Athread.start();
Bthread.start();
.
.
.
```

You can see the first real difference is that you need to explicitly create some `Thread` objects. Not a shocker; last time the `Thread` objects were the `trouble` objects (children of the `Thread` class). This time the `Thread` objects had to be created explicitly. In order to tell the threads what they should be running, you send the `A` and `B` objects. Pretty tricky, huh?

Of course, the only reason you can send **A** and **B** is because they are **trouble** objects, and **trouble** implemented the **Runnable**. Figure 14-5 compares the previous method of subclassing versus this way of sending the implementing object. The **Thread** class will accept any object from a class that implemented the **Runnable** interface. This is not done by magic; the **Thread** class contains a specific constructor for this purpose.

More Java Thread Stuff

The quick introduction above is really the bulk of the information you need to get some threads buzzing well out of control. Here you'll learn about a few more options at your disposal. Thread away!

Volatile

You may specify a variable as **volatile**. This variable modifier is not directly related to threads but is usually used because of their presence. The name would seem to imply some sort of unsurety or lack of safety in accessing a **volatile** variable. Buzz. Wrong answer. In actuality, it is a specifier that the variable could be changed from uncontrollable sources, and the compiler should take extra steps to be sure that it never makes assumptions about this variable. Of course, to any given thread, all other threads are effectively uncontrollable sources. So, often variables that find themselves being knocked around by

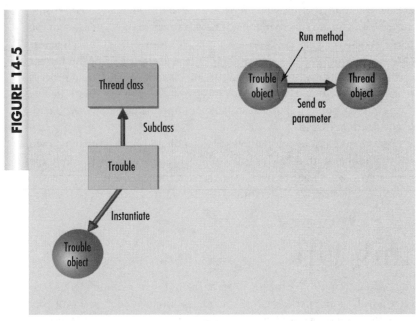

FIGURE 14-5

Comparing subclassing and interfacing

a bunch of threads are best declared as `volatile`. There can be a small performance penalty in using `volatile` variables, but the security you'll receive is often worth the cost.

Stop the Thread, I Wanna Get Off

Above you read how to set up and start a thread. Since all good things must come to an end, the logical question now is how do you stop a thread? With the `stop` method, of course. The actual stopping takes no great thought; just execute the `stop` method on your thread.

However, it's important to be sure the thread you want to stop is actually running, or the system will throw quite an exception. You can do this several ways, including performing a check on the `isAlive` method, which returns a Boolean result as to the state of the thread. Such as:

```
if (mythread.isAlive())
    mythread.stop();
```

Much of the time you will have control enough over your threads to know when they have been started or stopped. Of course, your code is destined to run on machines all over the world with thread implementations that defy comprehension. It's always best to include checks to handle any eventuality.

Daemons

Yes, Virginia, there are such things as *daemons*. When you set a thread as a daemon (using the `setDaemon` method), you are specifying that it now belongs to the system—not the process that spawned it, as is usually the case. Spawning daemons sure sounds like sci-fi, but it is useful to create processes that run even after Java itself exits. The interpreter will exit when all nondaemon threads have ended. In other words, if your main process spawns five user (nondaemon) threads and one daemon thread, it will wait until the five user threads end (of course it could kill them if it becomes impatient) before it will end. It cares not about the daemon thread.

In essence, setting a thread as a daemon allows it to go off and have a life of its own independent of the thread that started it. This is useful for threads you wish to run in the background for extended periods of time. Network game servers, background printing threads, and maybe even garbage collectors could be among the list of threads that would be useful as daemons.

 Synching Up

No sweat. Sending code into multiple threads to have them do your simultaneous bidding sure seems like a walk in the park. Well, if you are a seasoned coder, you probably realize that such powerful techniques must have some limitations (with power comes responsibility). Boy, you got that right. Without question, multithreading does provide you some powerful functionality you didn't have before—unfortunately, it also brings to the surface some maniacal, treacherous, and overall rather academically interesting problems. First and foremost are problems involving synchronization.

Whose Turn Is It?

In your carefree days of purely sequential programming, synchronization problems didn't exist, since the actual structure of your code dictated the order of events. But now, you could feasibly have several eager little threads all trying to access the same resources. Without proper precautions, you have no control over who accesses what resource when. Any thread could steal the CPU from the current one without notice. Here again is the happy little class from above. To illustrate the impending doom:

```
/* class trouble - fun with threads */
class trouble extends Thread {

/* The 'p' variable will be shared among the threads */
   static int p;
   int myval;
   boolean flag=true;

/* constructor */
   public trouble (int x) { myval = x; }

/* The infamous run method. This will be the entry and exit */
/*   point of the thread */
   public void run() {
      while (true) { messp(mval); }
      }

/* The 'mess with p' method, called from run() */
   static private void messp(int myval) {
      p = myval;
      p = p + 2;
      System.out.print(p);
      }
   }
   .
   .
   .
/* Starting the threads */
trouble A = new trouble(5);
trouble B = new trouble(6);

A.start();
B.start();
   .
   .
   .
```

Knowing what you do about the unpredictable behavior of threads, you would expect the output to be something similar to this:

`8878887878777778788877878...`

The two threads compete with each other and end up producing this interesting conglomeration of sevens and eights. Note that your mileage may vary. Since threads do have a severe dependency upon their implementation in the operating system, behavior of threads from system to system can and will be different. It might be better to say that the unpredictable behavior of threads will be even more unpredictable across machines/operating systems. This can wreak havoc on unsuspecting thread programmers. It is often critical that you develop applications that are uniform everywhere (all hail Java's solemn promise of architecture independence). Not to fear, this section will show you methods that help to ensure consistent behavior of threads from operating system to operating system. Using the techniques here will keep you safe in your trek through threadland.

Back to the example, you should be able to count on some permutation of the above string as the expected output. However, now and then, classic synchronization problems dictate that you're bound to see the following anomaly:

`8878887878777798788877878...`

Ack! How did that 9 get in there? You can see from the code above that the two threads have their individual **myval** variables with the **A** object's set to 5 and **B** object's set to 6. So, following through the code you can see that for each thread the **p** variable is set to the respective **myval** variable, then incremented by 2. Therefore, the only possible outputs by the print statement are 7 and 8, right? Well, given the above output, obviously something is not playing by the rules.

From the numbers involved in the code (i.e., 5, 6, 2), the only logical way to get a value of 9 is 5+2+2. But dagnabbit, nowhere does the code add 2 twice. Evil forces must be at work. Figure 14-6 shows how this catastrophe occurs.

As the figure shows, threads can be quite indiscriminate about when they steal control from another thread. In fact, Figure 14-6 shows this stealing at the granularity of Java statements. In reality, control can be stolen within statements. You can see where such blatant disrespect for the sanctity of sequential code could lead to all kinds of immoralities. What's worse is that it could cause erratic, unreproducible errors. Luckily, in their omniscience, the benevolent designers of the Java language smiled heavily upon thread programmers and granted them ever powerful (and hugely sacred) *synchronization* primitives.

Enforcing Critical Sections

The key to thwarting the above inexpedient situation is to secure the *critical section*. A critical section is a section/block of code that contains shared data and produces a result dependent upon which process ran at precisely which instant (for the operating system purists out there this is known as a *race* condition). In other words, it's a section of code you

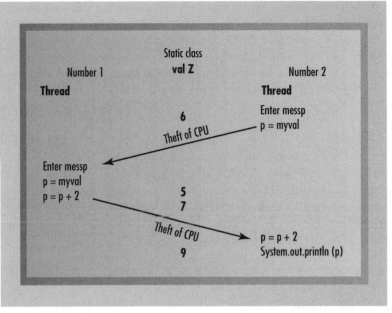

FIGURE 14-6

Out-of-control threads

know you want one thread to run start to finish without any other threads running any of that code.

Common Synchronization

What you need to do is to synchronize the execution of your critical sections. So no matter how many threads want to enter the critical section, you must enforce the rule that only one can be inside that section at a time. Once it leaves, another may enter. Ensuring this level of blessed harmony among conniving threads would be a ghastly proposition if the Java designers weren't well aware of the problem and hadn't provided you specific constructs to work with. All you need to do is to specify the keyword **synchronized** before the method. Consider the code from above:

```
/* The 'mess with p' method, called from run() */
  synchronized static private void messp(int mval) {
    p = myval;
    p = p + 2;
    System.out.print(p);
    }
```

The short story is that the **synchronized** modifier enforces the rule that only one thread may be inside the specified method (**messp** in this case) at a time. To be more precise, what is happening is that a thread entering this method (and seeing the **synchronized** modifier) checks the *lock* for this object. In this context, a lock is just a flag indicating whether or not some thread has locked this object. Every object and every class has its own lock.

If the thread finds that the object has indeed been locked, it does not enter but waits. Several threads may be waiting at the door to the synchronized method before the current thread is done. When the thread inside the method is done, it unlocks the lock and leaves. Finally, one of the threads that is waiting may enter and will set the lock. For the above example, this will guarantee that only one thread will execute within the `messp` method at a time.

You must also remember that each object has only one lock. Therefore, if an object has three synchronized methods, a thread entering any of the methods will set the lock. After that, no thread can enter any of the synchronized methods until the first exits the method it was executing and frees the lock. This is a danger when specifying many methods within classes as synchronized. Deadlock conditions can occur in which two threads each own what the other wants. Since neither can get what it wants, they both continue to hold onto the locks they have, and patiently wait for the ones they don't have—forever.

Static methods that are synchronized use the class's lock, not any particular object's. It's only fair; static methods belong to the class and should hence be using its lock.

Block Synchronization

You are not restricted to synchronization at the granularity of methods. You can bring the synchronization down to the level of a block of statements (or even down to a single statement). Again the whole business depends on obtaining a lock. The `synchronized` keyword also allows you to specify a given object that you wish to obtain a lock on. The `synchronized` keyword defaults to the `this` object (or the current class). Following it with a parameter allows you to specify any legal object.

```
// class guard */
/* trivial class just to illustrate block synchronization */
class guard {
  public int c;
    }



    .
    .
    .

static guard theguard = new guard();

// The 'mess with p' method, called from run()
  static private void messp(int mval) {
    int pvar;

    synchronized (theguard) {
        p = myval;
        p = p + 2;
        theguard.c = pvar = p;
        }
```

```
System.out.print(pvar);
}
```

This code uses the `guard` object as the object whose lock synchronizes the threads. This technique allows you to have several synchronized blocks within a method that has several distinct critical sections. In other words, many threads can still be running inside the same method as long as they are performing tasks that don't conflict with each other. Block level synchronization ensures this.

Peace, Harmony, and Love

Threads are greedy little buggers. You would think that they would be happy just to get the chance to run and express their output. But no, those little scoundrels will cheat, steal, and filch their way to as much CPU time and resources as they can get. So it's your job to keep a tight rein on the situation. Not only must you be sure that threads are respecting each other's feelings, but sometimes you need to play favorites. In many situations, the painful truth is that some threads are just plain more important than others. Consider the browser HotJava; if your little ping pong ball thread gets wily and steals all the CPU away from the browser itself, never again can the browser honor your request to scroll, find a new URL, or anything else. That silly little ping pong ball will be buzzing all over, but the system is effectively hung (in fact, since the browser will not even get enough CPU to redraw the screen, you will not see the ball move).

This section is all about playing nice. First off, on setting your thread's individual priorities, and then about threads working in blissful harmony. It will be a good section; prepare to feel warm all over.

Getting Your Priorities Straight

Java's `Thread` class provides built-in functionality to manipulate the priority of your threads. Although this briskly comes across as a straightforward concept, it gets nutty fast. The familiar notion is that threads with a high priority run first, and threads with low priority run last. Environments like HotJava have a small legion of varied prioritized threads running behind them to handle a collection of duties.

Who Would Want to Be Low?

Running behind the scenes at all times is a *garbage collector* thread. You are well aware of Java's garbage collection facilities, but this thread is the nuts and bolts of where things get done. Also of interest is that this thread is set to a low priority within the scheme of things. So it really only gets to perform its magic when the CPU is seemingly unoccupied. For a garbage collector this is just fine. If that bit of memory you released doesn't get freed just yet, no big loss. The garbage collector will get around to it when it does. Also, if memory were to fill up (because of too much garbage lying around that hasn't been cleaned yet), any process running that requests more memory should block (suspend running) since it can't get the resource it wants, i.e., memory. Of course, if all higher priority threads block, then the lower priority threads will run—namely the garbage collector, which will then come in and clean house.

As you can see from Figure 14-7, the prioritization of threads in HotJava has efficiency in mind. Don't think that low-priority threads do not perform important functions; it's just that there are more important functions that need to occur more frequently. So, having the garbage collector as a low-priority thread makes good sense. If it ran as a high-priority thread, you could count on a squeaky clean memory space and know that the moment you free up some memory, the garbage collector will swoop gallantly in. However, your programs would see a big hit on performance, since the garbage collector would waste a lot of computing power popping in all the time cleaning an already spotless memory space.

Setting Priorities

Expectedly, all the methods and variables for priority manipulation are contained in the `Thread` class. Two methods allow for access:

```
int mypri = mythread.getPriority();

if (mypri < Thread.MAX_PRIORITY)
    mythread.setPriority(mypri+1);
```

The `getPriority` thread returns the thread's priority (boy, there's a shocker). There are three static variables defined to the `Thread` class: `MIN_PRIORITY`, `NORM_PRIOR-ITY`, and `MAX_PRIORITY`. Again, Sun Microsystems took the landmark step of actually naming variables for some semblance of their purpose, so discerning the use of these variables should be relatively easy. But for the benefit of stern FORTRAN programmers who

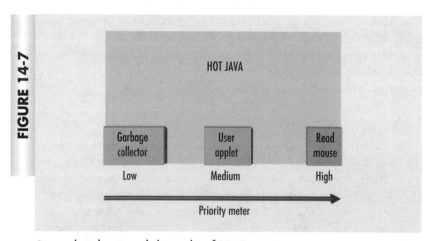

FIGURE 14-7

Some background threads of HotJava

may be confused by this idea (check your shirt pocket; punched cards present? Then, yes, you), a little further discussion.

 `MIN_PRIORITY` and `MAX_PRIORITY` specify the minimum and maximum allowable priorities for threads. Any attempt to set a priority to something outside this range is met with an `IllegalArgumentException`. This is the reason for the `if` statement in the above code. Setting your thread to the `MIN_PRIORITY` will get you something that runs alongside the garbage collector. Setting your thread to the `MAX_PRIORITY` is quite a different and rather dodgy proposition. Typically, your user threads should not venture into such haughty waters. There are threads that you just better not try to outperform. As stated earlier, in HotJava, if a thread were to compete with the resident HotJava thread that updates the screen, the whole happy world would come to a stop.

 The `NORM_PRIORITY` variable is the default priority that is assigned to a thread. The actual thread values are 1 for the min, 10 for the max, and 5 for the norm. You shouldn't really rely on numbers with such specificity. These numbers have been known to change with new releases, and programming with relative priority numbers (as in the above example) provides for more robust code.

What Threads Don't Want You to Know

There are still more facilities available to you to tease your threads. The `synchronized` modifier provides a good method to keep threads playing fair, but sometimes you need a tad more direct control over threads (threads don't want you to read this section). Here, you'll just get an overview of the primary thread control facilities in Java. Following this section, you'll dive headfirst into a multithreading example that will better illustrate their use.

Yield

Let's start out nice. The `yield` method is one of the more productive ways of nixing an overzealous thread. It tells the running thread to stop running and let someone else run if they want to. If nobody is waiting to run, then the thread may continue.

```
/* The infamous run method. This will be the entry and exit */
/*  point of the thread */
  public void run() {
    while (true) {
        messp(myval);
        yield();
        }
}
```

 The code runs as before, but after each execution of `messp`, a `yield` is performed to see if any other threads want access. Of course, it still takes some processing time for the thread to check to see if any others are waiting and to either yield control or continue about its business. The `yield` statement is not involved in synchronization per se. It is only instructing the thread to quit competing for the CPU for a moment to see if anyone else wants to use it.

Suspension

The **suspend** and **resume** methods are included within the **Thread** class to provide a clean way to pause the execution of a thread. While suspended, the thread is in limbo happily doing nothing. Typically these commands are issued from a foreign thread, as in

```
myThread.suspend();
.
.
.
/* at some later time */
myThread.resume();
```

You can think of this as putting the thread to sleep until you give it a wake-up call (the **resume** method). It's possible to have a thread issue a **suspend** on itself, but it would be quite an interesting feat to get a suspended thread to issue a **resume** on itself (that would be kind of like an operating system command turn-power-on).

Wait

The **wait** and **notify** methods are similar to the **suspend** paradigm with three important differences. First, they are methods of the **java.lang.Object** class, not the **java.lang.Thread** class. Second, you can optionally specify a time limit for waiting. Finally, **wait** and its corresponding **notify** may only be present in **synchronized** methods.

Once **wait** is executed, the thread releases any synchronization locks it has and stops. It will not start again until it is notified by some other thread issuing the **notify** method. Notifying is kind of like telling the waiting thread, "Whatever you are waiting for is ready now." Once the thread is notified, it will reacquire the lock and continue.

If many threads are waiting, a **notify** will only notify one of them. To notify them all, you can use the **notifyAll** method. The example ending this chapter will make good use of **wait** and **notify**.

Destroy

Do not pass go. Do not collect two hundred. The **destroy** method is a thread executioner. No letters home, last phone calls, nor any other pansy type stuff—that thread is dead.

This may sound usefully authoritative, but as is common with commands that always work (as opposed to commands that are requests), bad things can happen. The system's reaction to this act of threadicide is unpredictable. Using **destroy** should only be done in extreme circumstances.

Sleep

The **sleep** method is analogous to the above-mentioned **wait** method in that you send the thread a number of milliseconds and instruct it to stop what it is doing and go to sleep for that amount of time. This inherently frees up the CPU for other potential users. A significant difference is that there is not an equivalent **notify** or **resume** for **sleep**. When you specify the time, that's it, the thread will go to sleep for that duration. The **sleep** statement is often specified within the thread's **run** method.

```
/* The infamous run method. This will be the entry and exit */
/*  point of the thread */
  public void run() {
    while (true) {
        messp(myval);
        sleep(50);  // sleep 50 milliseconds
        }
}
```

The **sleep** method can be used much like **yield** in that it will give up the CPU and give others a chance to run. However, unlike **yield**, it will sleep for the specified time period whether anyone is waiting for the CPU or not. The **yield** method is really trying to be nice by checking to see if others need the CPU; on the other hand, **sleep** is unconcerned with other threads and is only worried about putting this thread to sleep—the fact that other threads can now jump in is coincidental.

The **sleep** method is also commonly used as a simple way to slow down a running thread. Be careful with this; attempting to use **sleep** as a timing mechanism for your program is not typically trustworthy. It's kind of like driving on the wrong side of a country road—you'll probably be okay for a while.

Producing and Consuming

This section will design a slightly more complex application using the thread concepts covered. For this example there will be two threads; a Wippy the Magic Duck thread (Wippy shows up in yet another example, reuse! reuse!) and a farmer thread. Wippy's job is to lay eggs, which roll into a tray. The farmer's job is to retrieve the eggs from the tray. So far this sounds suspiciously normal.

Of course, to make this example interesting will require some assumptions. First of all, the tray only has enough capacity to hold ten eggs. Second, since Wippy happens to be a magic duck, she is extremely smart—she knows that the tray can only hold ten eggs and will stop laying if the tray is full. On top of that, now and then both Wippy and the farmer daydream and forget to perform their duties—so sometimes the egg tray fills up and sometimes it empties completely out.

The task at hand is illustrated in Figure 14-8.

Wippy and the Farmer

The code for the Wippy and farmer threads is relatively straightforward. Here's Wippy:

```
/* Wippy the Magic Duck (Producer) */
class Wippy extends Thread {
```

continued on next page

continued from previous page

```
    theTray T;                        // Pointer to the tray

/* Constructor receives the tray reference */
  Wippy(theTray T) { this.T = T; }

/* Wippy's run method */
  public void run() {
    int a=0;

    while (true) {              // lay eggs forever
      try {
        T.layegg(a); // lay an egg (in the tray)
        a = (a+1)%100000;    // increase egg number

      /* daydream a random amount of time */
        sleep((int)(2000*Math.random()));
          } catch (InterruptedException e) {};
      }
    }
}
```

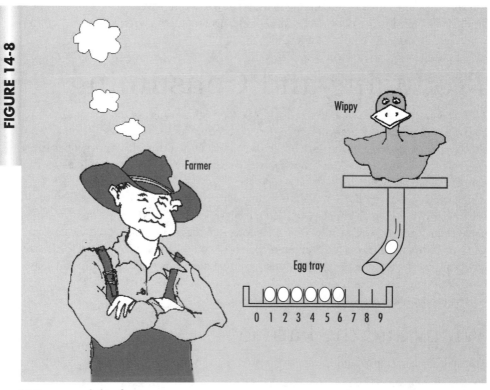

Wippy and the farmer

As you can see, there's not too much there. Wippy's constructor gets a reference to the tray (Wippy and the farmer will obviously need to share the same tray). The **run** method loops forever laying eggs and daydreaming. The daydreaming is accomplished by putting the thread to sleep for a random interval. This daydreaming serves two purposes. One, to prevent both threads from always being ready, this avoids a situation where every time an egg is laid it is immediately taken. That gets boring fast. The second reason is that this allows you to watch the action a little closer. Without sleeping, this code would fly through its print statements and you wouldn't be able to follow what was going on. The farmer class looks painfully similar:

```
/* The Farmer Thread (Consumer) */
 class Farmer extends Thread {

   theTray T;                          // Farmer also needs the tray

/* Constructor */
  Farmer(theTray T) { this.T = T; }

/* Farmer's run method */
    public void run() {
      int a=0;

      while (true) {
        try {
                  a = T.getegg();        // get an egg;

                  /* Daydream */
                  sleep((int)(2000*Math.random())+1000);
                    } catch (InterruptedException e) ;
            }
          }
        }
```

The only real difference here is that the farmer is calling the tray's **getegg** method instead of the **layegg**. This example is actually a flavor of the classic computer science problem called the Producer-Consumer or Bounded-Buffer problem. It applies to many different applications, one of which happens to be eggs.

Life of an Egg Tray

The class describing the egg tray is really where all the synchronization and magic will take place. This class makes good use of synchronized methods to avoid race conditions. The first half (or so) looks like this:

```
/* The tray class (the bounded buffer) */
class theTray {

  static final int traysize = 10;    // constant
  static int count,posW,posF = 0;    // count: # eggs in the tray
```

continued on next page

continued from previous page

```
                                           // posW: Wippy's next slot
                                           // posF: Farmer's next slot

/* the tray array */
  static int tray[] = new int[traysize];

/* the layegg method (called by Wippy) */
  public synchronized void layegg(int x)
                                      throws InterruptedException {

/* Tray is full! Wippy will wait */
    if (count == traysize) {
             System.out.println("Wippy waiting...");
             wait();
             }

/* put in the new egg and increase the counter */
count++;
tray[posW] = x;

/* setup the next position to put an egg */
posW = (posW + 1)%10;
System.out.println("Count: " +count+ " Wippy laid egg #" +x);

/* if tray WAS empty, assume that the farmer is waiting and
   notify him that there is now an egg                         */
if (count == 1) notify();
}
```

The class first sets up some variables. The `count` variable keeps track of how many eggs are currently in the tray. The `posF` and `posW` variables keep track of the next slot in the tray that the farmer will empty and the next slot Wippy will fill, respectively.

The first thing the `layegg` method does is see if there is anyplace to put an egg; if not, Wippy waits. If there is room, the count is increased and the egg is laid (i.e., the array slot is filled). Finally, Wippy checks to see if the `count` variable equals one; if so, then that means the tray was (just prior to the most recent egg) empty. If the tray was empty, then there is a possibility the farmer was waiting, so Wippy does a `notify`. It's important to realize that Wippy doesn't know for sure whether the farmer was actually waiting, but since the tray was empty for some period of time, then it's a likely possibility. So whenever Wippy puts the first egg in an empty tray, the `notify` is done just in case (if it wasn't done and the farmer *was* waiting, the farmer would never know the tray now has an egg to retrieve and would wait forever).

The farmer will call the `tray` class's `getegg` method:

```
/* the getegg method (called by the farmer) */
public synchronized int getegg() throws InterruptedException {
int x;

/* if no eggs to retrieve, then wait */
if (count == 0) {
```

```
            System.out.println("Farmer waiting...");
            wait();
            }

    /* remove the egg */
    count--;
    x = tray[posF];
    posF = (posF+1)%10;
    System.out.println("Count: " +count+ " Farmer got egg #" +x);

    /* if tray has just one empty slot, notify Wippy */
    if (count == traysize-1) notify();
    return x;
    }
}
```

This method is expectedly the converse of the `layegg` method. The farmer will wait if there are no eggs to retrieve. He will also do a **notify** whenever he removes an egg from a full tray. In other words, whenever he realizes Wippy might have been waiting to lay an egg, he does a **notify**. Figure 14-9 shows Wippy and the farmer in their conceptual operations.

Running

Finally, you need a standalone class to put all this together. It's actually rather trivial:

```
    /* Start the action */
    class Duckhouse {

    /* The main method */
      public static void main(String args[]) {

    /* Define the objects */
       theTray B = new theTray();
       Wippy W = new Wippy(B);
       Farmer F = new Farmer(B);

    /* Start the threads */
     W.start();
     F.start();
    }
}
```

You can now compile and run the program. Let's watch the action.

```
    .
    .
    .
Count: 5 Farmer got egg #3
Count: 6 Wippy laid egg #9
Count: 7 Wippy laid egg #10
Count: 8 Wippy laid egg #11
```

continued on next page

continued from previous page

```
Count: 7 Farmer got egg #4
Count: 8 Wippy laid egg #12
Count: 9 Wippy laid egg #13
Count: 8 Farmer got egg #5
Count: 9 Wippy laid egg #14
Count: 10 Wippy laid egg #15
Count: 9 Farmer got egg #6
Count: 10 Wippy laid egg #16
Wippy waiting...
Count: 9 Farmer got egg #7
Count: 10 Wippy laid egg #17
Count: 9 Farmer got egg #8
.
.
.
```

As you can see, the count fluctuates as Wippy puts eggs in and the farmer takes them out. For the above output, it's evident that the farmer seems to be daydreaming more than Wippy (i.e., Wippy is laying eggs more often than the farmer is retrieving them). At one

FIGURE 14-9

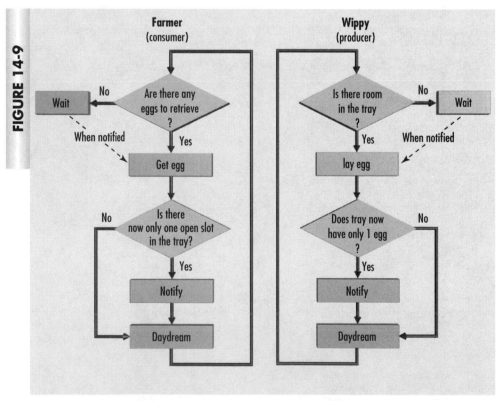

Conceptual Wippy and farmer

point, the tray fills and Wippy must wait. As soon as the farmer removes an egg (number seven in the above case), Wippy immediately lays another.

The usage of the tray class and synchronization primitives were key to preventing race conditions (i.e., securing critical sections). The `wait` and `notify` methods worked well to use as a communication device between the complementary threads.

Summary

Clearly, having a computer do more than one thing at a time is quite a complex situation. This topic has been well studied in academia for many years, and countless texts exist discussing the intricacies. Java's implementation is quick and clean. Liberal use of synchronization and yielding primitives should have you doing most of what you need. If you are the curious type or find yourself doing some advanced work in multithreading, you should consult a solid operating systems text regarding further concepts in this area.

These advanced chapters are showing you just how advanced and how full of features the Java system really is. It goes beyond just a language and a debugger. Solid concepts from many different areas were consciously included to provide this comprehensive development tool. The good news is that there is plenty more to come. The next few chapters discuss yet more features, including Java's built-in support for networking and interfacing to C programs. Is there nothing Java can't do?

Questions

1. What is the difference between *multiprocessing* and *multithreading*? What do you have to do to get your programs multiprocessing? To get them multithreading?

2. Decide on a number of threads for an efficient implementation of the following tasks. What is the purpose of each thread?

    a. A program to decompress an input file and write the result back to disk

    b. The classic arcade game Pong

    c. The classic arcade game Asteroids

3. Is the interfacing method of creating threads only useful when you cannot use the subclassing method?

4. Do blocks of code that only access local variables need synchronization? What about blocks that only access instance and local variables?

5. In the Wippy and farmer example printout, at one point, Wippy was waiting but then started running immediately after the farmer removed just one egg. Could it ever be possible that Wippy will wait for the farmer to remove two (or more) eggs?

6. Give a priority (high, medium, or low) that would probably suit the following threads:

    a. An asteroid in the game Asteroids

    b. The routine to read the player's keyboard commands in a fast action game

    c. A routine to do background printing while the user continues working

    d. A routine to catch input from a slow modem while the user plays a game based on the input data

Exercises

1. Develop an applet that plays the classic arcade game Pong. Allow the computer to play both paddles and use threads for the implementation.

2. Modify the Wippy/farmer program so that if Wippy waits, she will not start up again until the farmer has removed all the eggs.

3. Produce a version of the Wippy/farmer program without using `wait/notify`—use some other thread control concept available in Java.

The Net Works

15

You will learn about the following in this chapter:

- How addressing on the Internet is set up
- How to get your machine out on the Net
- How to design a full-blown client/server application
- How to develop a protocol to suit your needs
- How to read URL pages from Java applications

It seems that cyberspace has many faces. It has both a forbidding and a tempting aspect at the same time. Within its boundaries there have been stories of viruses, worms, and wily hackers. Countless unknowns wait for the unsuspecting Net surfer. However, putting all beasties aside, it undeniably must be a fascinating place. After all, everybody seems to want to get there (although not everybody is sure why). It can provide access to unbelievable amounts of information scattered across the world. It can give you stock updates, chat rooms, and even let you play games with people in other countries. Certainly it sounds neat, but it also sounds like fiction.

As a network programmer, you will need to shift your viewpoint just a bit. You can no longer view the Net in the same way the Net-peasants (i.e., users) do. You must change your thoughts from what you can get from a network to what you can do with a network. Don't worry, your choices are just as vast. The network gives you the ability to link computers across the world. Great new opportunities await the clever person. This is truly the artsy section of the book—and there has never been such a need for creativity.

The Setup of the Net

If you have visited more than a few Web, FTP, or Gopher sites in your time, you know that trying to learn all aspects of the Internet is quite an arduous task. It's kind of like feeding a raccoon so it will leave. You have seemingly conquered the immediate situation, but chances are more raccoons are on the way. Luckily, this discussion does not deal with the whole Internet. Only enough of it to get you going in Java. There are many good books dedicated to exposing the internals of the Internet. If you find yourself needing a more comprehensive approach, you can consult the Waite Group's *Internet How-To* for the wider picture.

Addressing

Every machine on the Internet has an address. This address comes as a 32-bit IP address with delimiting periods. Usually, a symbolic name is associated with this address. You are probably more familiar with accessing machines by their symbolic name, such as kuzlo.cat.syr.edu, instead of 128.230.32.33. Either way is generally okay, but it helps to realize that these two forms exist.

The `java.net.InetAddress` class provides for the creation of Internet address objects. In addition to allowing for a repository to set up your addresses, the class takes care of some organizational details for you. To define an Internet address for your code, you define an `InetAddress` object.

```
InetAddress myadr = InetAddress.getByName("kuzlo.cat.syr.edu");
```

Being the experienced Java programmer you are, this instantiation looks slightly odd in that it is not created via an explicit constructor. In actuality, the `getByName` method is a static method within the `InetAddress` class (hence your ability to call it with the class reference and not that of an object reference). This static method will perform a call to the `InetAddress` constructor for you. This type of static method is known as a "factory method" or "virtual constructor."

Once you have successfully created your `InetAddress` object (i.e., you didn't receive an unknown host exception), you can use the object as a construction parameter for the other primary classes in the `java.net` package. Let it be said that in many cases you can bypass using the `InetAddress` class; however, if your networking gets complex (and will it ever) this level of organization is helpful.

Ports

Consider that machines hooked to the Internet typically offer many possible services. These include WWW, FTP, and Telnet, just to name a few. There are processes (servers) responsible for each of these services all ready and waiting on a target machine to serve incoming users. Since there is this multitude of options, how does a user's application (i.e., their WWW browser or FTP client) know how to talk to the correct waiting server? The answer comes from the knowledge that each of the servers listed above has its own designated *port*. A port is an operating system abstraction that effectively acts as a gate to the outside world. It is obviously vital that a user's program connect to the port it was expecting. Try to connect an unassuming application to the wrong port (and subsequently wrong type of server), and next thing you know there will be dancing, dogs and cats playing together, and eventually full-fledged anarchy! Or at least some nasty network errors. Applications are created with the knowledge of the standard *port number* that their servers are supposed to be listening to. A port is a 16-bit integer as specified by the TCP (i.e., Internet) protocol.

So when your happy Web browser goes off to ogle some strange Web site, the first place it looks to connect is the predefined Web server port number. Such common applications are usually given their standard port number by the system administrator, and you can see a few examples in Figure 15-1. Now that you will be creating network applications, you will often need to decide on a port number that your users will know to come to. If you are an all-powerful system administrator, you can choose any unused port. If you are a lowly programmer, you can use any unused port from 1024 on up. Understanding the ins and outs of ports (hmm, an incidental pun) is beyond the scope of introducing the networking facilities of Java. All you need to know is that you will need to specify one if you plan to develop any applications that will be listening to a network for outside callers. If you are unsure about which to pick, your only restrictions are that it should be above 1024 and currently unused. Not too many in that category are used (if you try to sit on a occupied port, don't worry, the operating system will be happy to tell you), so throw a dart and pick another number; chances are you'll be okay. If not, get out another dart.

Following Protocol

Networks across the world are chock full of all kinds of *protocols*. A protocol across a network is a set of rules and commands that each side agrees upon regarding how communication will take place. (Next time your phone rings, pick up the receiver and say "Good-bye," then hang up. This minor deviation from standard protocol will really make

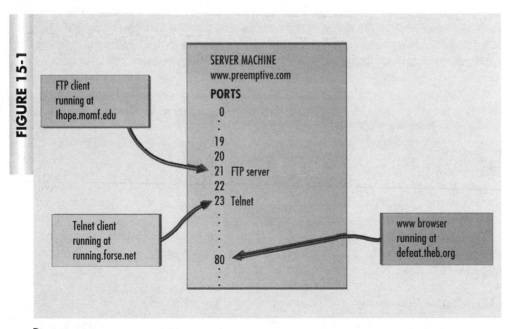

FIGURE 15-1

Ports

people mad. Of course, it could have been someone important, but you won't know; you didn't follow the protocol of asking who it was!) Overall, this sounds like a swell idea—rules and commands are good things. With these agreed-upon standards, protocols can implement compression, security, and other fun stuff that helps facilitate better communication.

Unfortunately, the idea kind of caught on a little too well. There are more protocols flying across the Net than you can spawn a thread at. So, your problem becomes using and accessing the ones you want or need. Not surprisingly, the `java.net` package includes the HTTP protocol for communicating with the World Wide Web. So building applications that need to peruse Web pages is relatively easy, and you'll step through a simple example later. Other protocols can be found in the myriad of class libraries that are available to Java but aren't deemed part of the standard API. This includes Sun Microsystems' sun.net library. The functionality is there if you have these libraries, but since they are not dubbed as a standard part of Java, don't expect every Java programmer to know what they are. As with any environment, as soon as you step away from the sacred standard functions, compatibility and future maintenance issues can enter the equation. In other words, wherever you can, stick to the `java.*` packages and only use add-ons when necessary.

Sockets

Java's low-level communication over networks is done using *sockets*. A socket is an abstraction of an input or output file. In other words, once you hook up your socket to some foreign socket, on a foreign machine (probably in a foreign land), you access it using the standard input and output file I/O operations. The abstraction attempts to (as always) hide the lurid details from the outside world, so in essence, after the connection is set up, you have no idea if the data you are inputting or outputting is connected to a socket, a disk file, or even the keyboard.

Figure 15-2 shows some connections. The communication ports discussed above provide the passthrough point for sockets. It is possible to have many socket connections through one port.

Stream Sockets

A stream socket is also known as a *connected* socket. This is an intuitive way of thinking about a socket connection. The user application connects to the server application, and the connection stays intact throughout their communication. Each can send streams of bytes to and fro with no regard as to rules governing how many bytes are being sent or in what direction (as long as the two ends are in agreement over the protocol). The example below will use this type of socket connection.

Datagram Sockets

A datagram socket is also allowed in Java. This type of communication is known as *connectionless*. Kind of an odd concept that two machines can communicate across a network

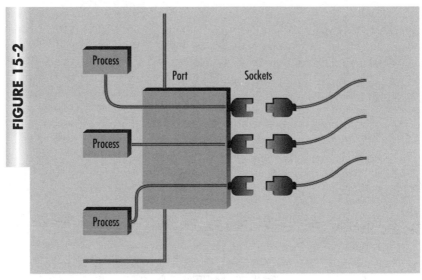

FIGURE 15-2

Sockets

without actually connecting. In essence, for a machine to send data to its intended receiver over this type of communication, it bundles its data into nice little chunks (i.e., packets) and puts the address of the receiver onto each one. The sender also tacks on a sequence number to each packet to be sure the receiver will know the ordering of them as they come in. It then mercilessly dumps these packets onto the Internet and lets the Net handle the routing. The packets will eventually all end up at the destination, but often at different times and out of order. The receiver then uses the sequence numbers and reconstructs the original message.

To specify this type of socket, several `Socket` class constructors have a Boolean parameter to indicate stream or datagram. Make this value false (i.e., not stream), and you will have a datagram socket.

Clients and Servers

It would seem the whole programming world is heading toward this mystical client/server technology. It's not a big wonder; it is a powerful and sensible paradigm. This section will introduce you to how this model works and step you through designing a client/server application.

A Definition

Let's start with a simple definition of a client/server relationship. The *client* is a process running on some machine that, via some form of communication, is exchanging data with

FIGURE 15-3

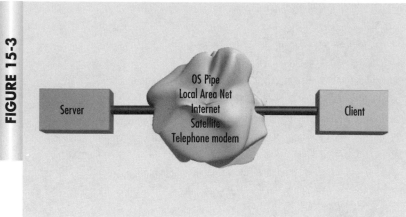

A client and a server

a *server*. The server, of course, is also a process running on some machine. As indicated by the names client and server, the server usually has something the client wants. But as you will see, it can often work both ways. The details are wide open, as shown in Figure 15-3; the client and server could feasibly exist on the same machine or on machines across the world. They could be communicating via operating system pipes or satellite transmission.

Overall, the vast number of possibilities regarding the details of client/server communication are somewhat immaterial. As described in the introduction, hopefully these types of details are largely hidden from the world. The focus here is on discussing the general client/server model as it pertains to any permutation of configurations. You can also assume a typical relationship of only one server that communicates with many possible clients.

An Old Hand

If you are at all familiar with the Web, you are an old hand at being a client. Whenever you bring up your WWW browser and type in a site address, your browser is a client requesting information (i.e., the Web page) from the Web server at that site. If for any reason that site's Web server is down, you will get nothing (and we've all been there).

Figure 15-4 shows that as you are pulling in a page, so may be many other clients. In this type of environment, communication is primarily from server to client. You typically pull down many Web pages, and only rarely do you send something to the server (e.g., a search string or—more dangerously—a credit card number).

A Server in the Making

For this client/server application, let's start by designing the server. Often the server is not as complex or pretty as the client. This is through no fault of its own, it's just because

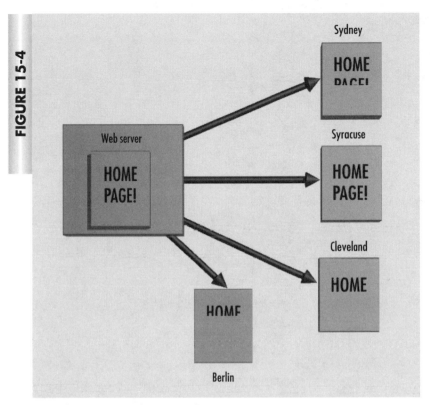

FIGURE 15-4

A Web server and many clients

usually the client is used by the customer (the Web surfer, the game player, etc.) so things need to be flashy. Usually servers don't rely on graphical components and just hum along in the background pumping out the data. It is also quite common for a server program to run as a daemon process, happily listening to a port waiting to link up some sockets.

ServerSocket

The `java.net.ServerSocket` is the class that provides the needed functionality. A common server model works as in Figure 15-5.

This is the model the example here will use, as it is relatively robust at handling several clients. The general idea is that the listener process (i.e., the main program) spawns threads to service a client as needed. This way the main routine can go back to listening in case anyone else may be calling. You could perform the server's function without using threads, but given their flexibility and Java's solid implementation of threads, their use is quite tempting.

The skeleton of the server code is

FIGURE 15-5

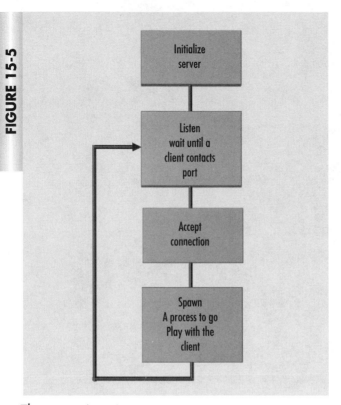

The server's actions

```
/* Network Server Class */
public class Nets {

/* Define variables (static since this is a standalone) */
 static Socket theSocket;
 static ServerThread client[] = new ServerThread[10];
 static ServerSocket SS;

/* Start the main method */
public static void main(String args[]) throws IOException {
/* Iterator variable to find open thread number */
  int g;

  System.out.println("Server coming up....");

/* Start the Server listening to port 1237 */
  SS = new ServerSocket(1237);

  while (true) {
```

```
/* Wait at this statement until a Client tries to connect */
    theSocket = SS.accept();

/* Find an open thread reference (if any) */
    for (g=0;g<10;++g)
        if ((client[g] == null) || (!client[g].isAlive()))
            break;

/* At this point g is the index to an open thread in the    */
/* array or it's equal to 10 if no more clients             */
/* are allowed - i.e. server is 'full'                      */
    if (g<10) {
            client[g] = new ServerThread(theSocket,g);
            client[g].start();
            }
      else System.out.println("Server full, Reject connection");
    }
  }
}
```

One of the first things to notice about the above code is that the threads are controlled by an array that has a size of 10. This indicates there can only be ten clients connected to the server at any time. You'll need lots of testing and a little sweat to figure out a number suitable for your application. The problem is that with too many clients, performance can degrade to beyond usability for any/all clients. Obviously, letting a few clients do something is better than letting a lot of clients do nothing.

The instantiation of the **ServerSocket** occurs in the following statement:

```
SS = new ServerSocket(1237);
```

It uses a hardcoded port assignment of 1237. Again, your mileage may vary. As was said, you can use ports over 1024 for any shameless deed. However, if you are using a multi-user system, there is no guarantee that some other Java-ite (or worse) isn't hogging a given port. If an exception comes sailing your way when your code attempts to instantiate the **ServerSocket**, try barking up another port.

The Magic Loop

The code then enters its wondrous infinite loop as depicted in Figure 15-5. First mission: listen. Actually, the server socket has already been doing that, but you haven't told it yet that you are interested in what it's listening to. That is done with the statement

```
theSocket = SS.accept();
```

The **accept** method blocks execution of the program until some congruous client comes a-calling. The **accept** method returns a reference to the **java.net.Socket** class. After some checking as to which thread isn't busy, the code spawns a thread (sending the socket as a parameter) and gets back to listening. The **Socket** class (as opposed to the **ServerSocket** class) is more than just a listener. It is built to actually perform the communications. Instances of `Socket` will exist on both the server and client side. In fact, there will be a one-to-one correspondence for communication.

One high-level idea that may have gotten lost in all this detail is what data or function does this server provide? Well, the interesting point about that is that this code is quite suitable for most simple server implementations. It really doesn't do any protocol stuff; all it has done is listen and spawn—in other words, the client calls and all this server does is answer the phone and hand it to somebody else (the spawned thread). Wow, let the reuse ooze forth. Figure 15-6 shows how this all fits together. Such a generic class could be used many times.

For clarity, the port and the number of possible clients was hardcoded. This was bad. For a truly generic class, these parameters should get shuffled in. Also, the `ServerThread`

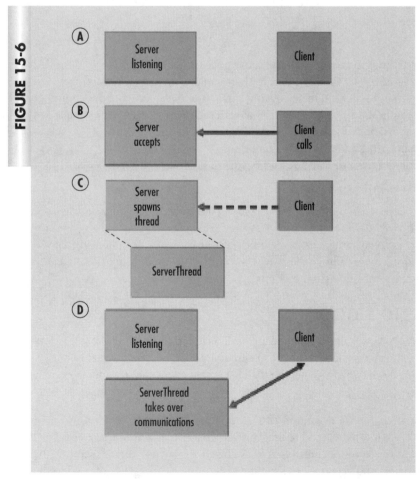

FIGURE 15-6

The server, `ServerThread`, and client

class (defined in a moment) would likely be defined as abstract so users of this server class could define how their protocol should run. Okay, enough of this basking in the healing powers of reuse—on with the client and servering.

The Task at Hand

Before going further, let's get a bit more specific. The task here is to develop a simple application that ends up being representative of a lot of different client/server applications. In this example, each client owns a piece of data and wishes all other clients to know what that data is. So every client wishes to broadcast its data to every other client. The server acts as a liaison for the clients, since no one (besides the server) knows how many or which clients are logged in. Although the server acts as the focal point, it really is just an accessory. It doesn't do anything with the data it has received besides send it on. This can be seen in Figure 15-7.

The server will receive the data from each client and then rebroadcast all the pieces it knows about to all logged in clients. This application could be used in a networked game

FIGURE 15-7

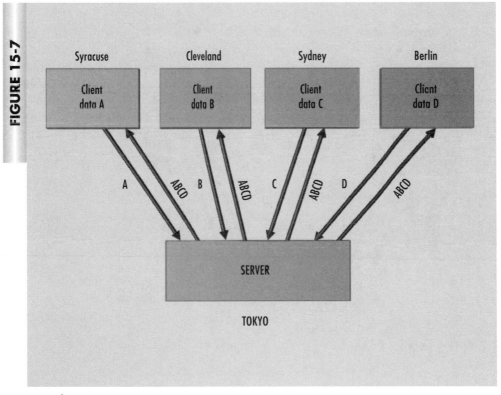

Broadcasting

that needs to transmit the coordinates of every player to every machine. That way, players could run around inside the same cyberworld and find each other.

In order to nonchalantly bypass all the impressive details associated with creating an entire cyberworld, the focus here will be more on networking and less on pizzazz. A simple substitute that still illustrates the concept is a drawing surface on which you can draw with your mouse. In addition, as you draw, each coordinate at which you draw will be sent to the server for redistribution. Therefore, anything you draw will be seen by all other clients currently logged on—and of course, you will see anything that they are drawing. This application will still contain the networking details while keeping the graphical details (see Chapter 13) to a minimum. Figure 15-8 shows the concept.

In this task there is something of a trade-off between performance and accuracy. A perfect model as far as accuracy goes would have the server wait until it has received the data from every client and then perform the broadcasts back to the clients. However, there's a caveat that ruins this happy-go-lucky idea, and it has to do with networks—they can't be trusted.

FIGURE 15-8

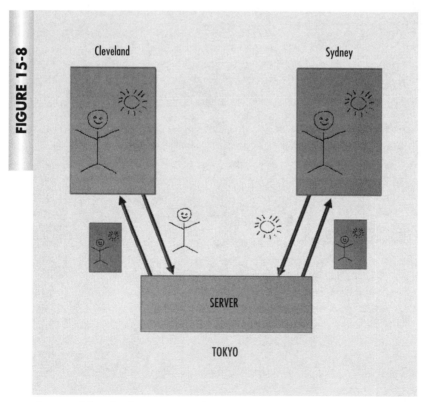

The worldwide drawing pad

Never Trust Your Network

As amazing as the Internet is, it's painfully erratic. You cannot trust that your clients will all send in their data in a timely manner. Sure, the clients may dutifully chug away at spitting out their current coordinates, but if one client is in Australia and the server is in New York, transmission will be slow and error prone through no fault of client or server. If the server were to wait for each client, your game would certainly have its lapses in the action. A more robust method is for the server threads to just spill what they know as fast as they can. This will induce an abundance of network traffic and occasionally be wrong, but for an application as fast and forgiving as a drawing pad (or game), it should be adequate.

My Protocol

Defined here is one of the simplest protocols you will ever see. Figure 15-9 shows the main picture.

The client will start by sending its current location. The server will then respond by sending all the coordinates of all the clients it knows about. The next question is this: how does each know when it's their turn to speak? For the server, it's easy. The client will send its current location, which consists of two bytes. When the server receives those two bytes, it knows it can now transmit.

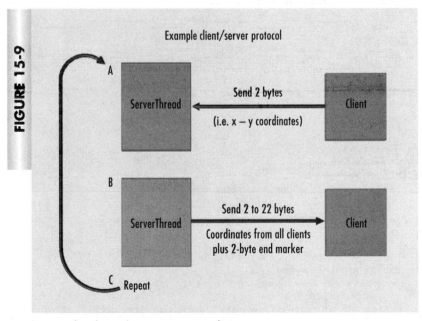

Example client/server protocol

The client must be a tad more careful. Since there can be anywhere from one to ten clients, each client doesn't know how many bytes are coming in. To solve this, the protocol dictates that the server will tack on (–1,–1) as the last coordinate marking the end of its transmission. When the client receives the end marker, it knows it can transmit its new coordinates again.

The ServerThread Class

This class is what will be spawned as a thread by the server. It is in charge of communicating with exactly one client for the life of the connection. Therefore, all the protocol smarts have to be built into it. Also, since it will be a thread, it will be constructed to subclass the `java.lang.Thread` class and conform to the method names that go with it (as outlined in Chapter 14).

Construction

Let's start with the class's instance variables and its constructor.

```
/* ServerThread class - instances of this class get spawned */
/*  as threads to individually handle each client           */
public class ServerThread extends Thread {

/* This array will be used as a repository for each instance */
/* of this class to put its location.                        */
static Point All[] = new java.awt.Point[10];

static {
    for (int j=0;j<10;++j)
     All[j] = new Point(0,0);
    }

/* Instance variables to hold thread specific information */
int myall;
Socket mySocket;
DataInputStream datain;
DataOutputStream dataout;

/* Define the Constructor */
public ServerThread(Socket m,int me) throws IOException {

   mySocket = m;
   myall = me;

/* Define the input and output streams for the socket */
  datain = new DataInputStream(new
         BufferedInputStream(mySocket.getInputStream()));
  dataout = new DataOutputStream(new
             BufferedOutputStream(mySocket.getOutputStream()));

  }
}
```

The most interesting variable is the static array `All` (above in bold). Each `ServerThread` object is passed (as a constructor parameter) an index into this array. Since it is a static array, each thread can access it to see the other threads' data.

Besides some mundane instance variable assignments, the constructor opens the streams for input and output from the socket. After this point, the streams are indistinguishable from streams that aim at files or the keyboard or whatever. Subsequent code no longer needs to know anything about sockets or other mischievous network tomfoolery. It just needs to use the streams (which happen to be attached to sockets).

Making a Run

Since this is an object meant to be run in a thread, it needs a `run` method. It looks like this:

```
/* ServerThread's run method */
public void run() {

try {

/* The busy loop */
  while (talk()) yield();

  mySocket.close();
  } catch (IOException E);

/* Clean out the array entry */
synchronized(All) All[myall].move(0,0);
}
```

The `run` method is short and sweet, because most of the work is done in the `talk` method embedded in the `run` method's `while` loop. Immediately notice the `yield` statement used to insure the other `ServerThread` objects will get their shot at the CPU. Also, since the `All` array is a static array, you know (from Chapter 14's discussion on threading and critical sections) that it is a shared resource. Therefore, when you modify it you throw a lock on the array to keep access exclusive.

The `talk` method is where all the magic networking happens and in effect where the meat of the protocol is defined—at least for the server side of things.

```
/* ServerThread's talk method */
private boolean talk() throws IOException {
  int x,y,g;

/* read in the X and Y coordinates from the client */
  x = datain.read();
  y = datain.read();

/* A -1 indicates the client is terminating the connection */
  if (x == -1) return false;
```

continued on next page

continued from previous page

```
/* Synchronize the block to keep All secure */
synchronized(All) {

/* Move the All array to the new coordinates  */
/* (ignore x=0 & y=0)                         */
  if ((x != 0) || (y != 0))
    All[myall].move(x,y);

/* loop through the All array and send out to the stream */
/* all the active elements                               */
  for (g=0;g<10;++g) {
    if ((All[g].x != 0) || (All[g].y != 0)) {
            dataout.write(All[g].x);
            dataout.write(All[g].y);
            }
    }
    }

/* Write out and end marker and flush the stream */
    dataout.write(-1);
    dataout.write(-1);
    dataout.flush();

  return true;
  }
```

This method follows a two-step process. It reads in the coordinates from the client and sends out all active elements from the static array in exchange. It is vital that the client also keep to this simple but strict protocol.

To get a better idea of what is happening with this **All** array, refer to Figure 15-10. Each active **ServerThread** object is reading and writing in what is ideally a synchronized manner.

Note that the level of synchronization in the above code is debatable. The synchronization primitive could have been put directly on the **talk** method; however; this could cause unnecessary blocking for the initial coordinate reads (which have nothing immediately to do with the **All** array). The current synchronization level is placed at the array object level. You could also lower it to the array element level (i.e., **synchronized** (All[myall])). However, at some point there becomes a trade-off between the cost of obtaining and releasing object locks compared to the amount of unnecessary blocking. Again, testing different cases for your application is usually the best route.

Don't Forget to Flush

Battles have been lost, cities have fallen, and messages by the truckload have been posted to the Internet all because someone forgot to flush. Forgetting this command is an abundant source of hard-to-find errors in network code. The **talk** method above performs a **flush** after sending the **All** array. All that discussion of totally transparent streams pointing to sockets, files, or keyboards tends to quiver a bit at this idea. Writing to a socket is more

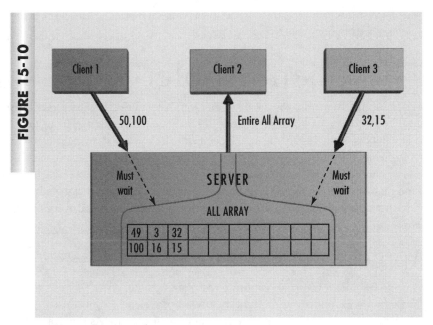

Updating the ALL array

interactive than writing to something like a disk. When you write a byte to disk, you just assume it happened and go on your merry way. However, in this world plagued by buffers and oversmart operating systems, that byte might hang out a while in memory before actually going to the disk. Given the different environments Java will be frolicking in, exactly when the byte goes to disk is a crapshoot. Usually, you don't care as long as it eventually does go. Unfortunately for sockets, this lackadaisical *someday* attitude can be a disaster.

When you send a byte out a socket, you expect it to get to the client with all speed. After all, the client is sitting there waiting for that data and isn't about to go any further without it. So you need to be sure your data goes when you think it goes. The bottom line is to use the `flush` command to insure the data gets pushed out the port. You could do this after sending every byte (but that's a little paranoid). The `ServerThread` sends out the whole array, then follows it up with a `flush`.

Other Types of Sending

By virtue of need, this example has only dealt with sending bytes. But remember that the sockets are attached to streams and streams are pretty versatile (if not demanding) little things. Many methods exist to send a plethora of different types through streams, including strings. You can find the full list of methods in the Appendix. If you have ever done any significant reading or writing off disk, you will find that the parsing aspects of organizing your data coming out of a stream quickly becomes a nuisance. This annoyance will often have you settling for lowly byte transmission.

The Client Applet

Well, it would seem from the above discussion that a perfectly good server is up and running. It's busily humming along waiting for its first client to chance by its port. The client code will be designed as an applet to facilitate the little world drawing pad you are attempting to create. Of course, networking can be done in standalone programs as well as applets. In fact, standalone programs make things a bit easier, since you don't have to contend with some possibly restrictive security rules of a browser. Browser designers have to be careful with security for networked applets. Designing a usable applet that tries to stick its nose across the Net can raise some bright red flags in some browsers.

Applet Initialization

As was said, client code can get quite tedious to create, given that it is the piece of the puzzle that will run right in front of the user's nose. Hence, it must usually include scads of bells and whistles to appease today's demanding users. As a proof of this concept, consider the strides the Web browsers have made from their initial releases. Nowadays, they slice, dice, and pretty much spoon feed you the Web pages all in full color, whereas the unfashionable Web servers usually just print "server up" and go hide in the background.

This example will try to keep the frills to a minimum in order to better relay the networking concepts involved. Here's the start of the client applet:

```
/* Network Client class */
public class Netc extends Applet implements Runnable {

Socket sock;                        // Socket to connect to Server
DataInputStream datain;             // Socket input stream
DataOutputStream dataout;           // Socket output stream
Thread mythread = null;             // Applet Thread
Point All[] = new Point[10];        // Keep track of other clients
Point pos = new Point(254,254);     // To store new mouse position


/* Applet initialization */
public void init() {

  resize(250,250);

  for (int g=0;g<10;++g)
            All[g] = new Point(-1,-1);
  }
```

Given this is being created as an applet, the class statement contains the needed subclassing and implementing. The `init` method is as boring as it's supposed to be. Besides the dutiful `resize`, the `All` array's elements are instantiated.

In an effort to keep you awake, the obligatory applet `start` and `stop` methods are a bit more scandalous.

```
/* Applet start */
public void start() {

/* Open socket to the server and setup the streams */
  try {

/* Create an InetAddress object to the server machine */
   InetAddress addr = InetAddress.getByName("ihope.momf.edu");

   sock = new Socket(addr,1237); // Create/connect the socket

/* Setup socket input stream */
   datain = new DataInputStream(new
           BufferedInputStream(sock.getInputStream()));

/* Setup socket output stream */
   dataout = new DataOutputStream(new
            BufferedOutputStream(sock.getOutputStream()));

   } catch (IOException E);

/* Start thread */
  if (mythread == null) {
        mythread = new Thread(this);
        mythread.start();
        }
  }


/* Applet stop */
public void stop() {

/* Stop thread */
   if (mythread != null) {
        mythread.stop();
        mythread=null;

 /* additional cleanup (closings) */
   try {
     dataout.close();
     datain.close();
     sock.close();
     } catch (IOException E);
   }
   }
```

These methods are the original thread start and stop mechanisms with the added duties of socket connection and setup. The socket connection in the **start** method looks painfully similar to the socket connection code in the **ServerThread** class presented earlier. In all fairness, it should. These two classes are connecting to each other using the same methodology. The connection between these two is only conceptually a client/server relationship. In other words, they are both just using a socket to hook up (i.e., **ServerThread** is not using the **ServerSocket** class). It is almost as if the network server class played matchmaker and now these two classes are hitching it up on their own terms.

And the Run

The **run** method illustrates the client following a complementary routine to that of the **ServerThread**. It first sends out its position, then reads in its **All** array:

```
/* The Thread's run method */
public void run() {
  int tx,ty,num;

/* The telltale Applet endless loop */
  while (true) {
    try {

/* Send coordinates, then zero out */
        synchronized (pos) {
          dataout.write(pos.x);
          dataout.write(pos.y);
          pos.x = pos.y = 0;
          }
          dataout.flush();
          tx = num = 0;

/* Populate All array with incoming data */
      do {
          tx = datain.read();
          ty = datain.read();
          All[num].move(tx,ty);
          num++;
          } while (tx != 255);

    } catch (IOException e);

/* Perform the applet repaint and yield to other threads */
    repaint();
    mythread.yield();
    }
  }
```

The **pos.x** and **pos.y** variables (which you will see more of below) are set to zero immediately after they are sent. If the loop gets to this point again without their changing, the zeroes will get sent. What this does is tell the server that no change occurred and not to set any values in its static `All` array.

From seeing this code and comparing it to the `ServerThread` above, you can see that the network traffic generated by these methods is serious. Besides yielding for other threads, each client and server (thread) will spew data at each other as fast as they possibly can. The first thing to say about this is that it's not fast enough. Since you are trying to catch every coordinate that a user's mouse happens to pass, you don't have a chance. Human hands move faster than mouse mechanics.

Maybe you should be asking, if the mouse doesn't move, why send the zeroes? Why send anything? Can't I just keep quiet? Well, the only problem with that is that any given client needs to be updated with the new locations of all the other clients (otherwise, you would only get other clients' artwork while you are drawing, not if you are just watching). In order for the server to know it is time to send the updated `All` array, the protocol must be followed. In other words, the client must send some set of coordinates, if not to relay true coordinate positions, then just to indicate to the server that it is now waiting for the `All` array transmission. Without this, the server wouldn't know if the client was being quiet or some nefarious Net delay was holding up the client's message.

This type of communication is analogous to short-wave radio communication. Each side (by protocol) always finishes their message with the word "over." Since only one party can speak at a time, this indicates it's the other guy's turn. A solution to this dilemma is to create two-way communication, such as the modern telephone. In the case of the example, this would mean the creation of a second socket. You can then use one for input and the other for output.

Mouse Games and Other Applet Duties

Several other methods are required for this (and most any) applet. The mouse methods are used to capture the mouse coordinates while a button is depressed.

```
/* Mouse Drag or Down indicate the user is drawing */
public boolean mouseDrag(Event E, int x, int y) {
  synchronized(pos) {
    pos.x = x;          // set the pos values
    pos.y = y;
    }
    return true;
    }


/* Mouse down applet method */
public boolean mouseDown(Event E, int x, int y) {
    mouseDrag(E,x,y);  // mouseDown is just the first
    return true;              // instance of a drag
    }
```

continued on next page

continued from previous page

```
/* Override to prevent erasure of drawing field */
public void update(Graphics G) {
    paint(G);
    }

/* Applet paint method */
public void paint(Graphics G) {
        int g = 0;

        G.setColor(Color.red);
        while (All[g].x != -1) {
          G.drawRect(All[g].x,All[g].y,1,1); // draw All array
          g++;
          }
        }
    }
```

The `mouseDown` is for the initial button press, and the `mouseDrag` handles any sweeping motions. The `mouseDown` is viewed as just an instance of a `mouseDrag`, so one calls the other. The `paint` method goes through and plots each point it finds in the `All` array.

This applet is bound to give you hours and hours of senseless fun drawing to people around the world. You can see an image of several applets running (on the same screen but at remote computers) in Figure 15-11. The framework built by this client/server application could be adapted to transmit player coordinates in a maze game or any other broadcast type application. As was said, the server in this instance is really just a collector and distributor of information.

Given its purpose, this client/server application meets the requirements. However, rarely will you meet a networked application that has such lenient regard as to whether accurate transmissions take place. To put it another way, you don't particularly care if a few dots get lost in the fray while drawing. Most of your drawing is adequately represented on your screen and across the Net; for this application that's good enough. The exercises at the end of this chapter will make some strides toward perfecting the networking abilities of this application. Of course, these strides will cost with respect to the complexity that the entire application (and you) must endure.

Accessing the Web

The built-in `java.net` package includes protocol support for the World Wide Web. Given that many Java applications are bound to go backing and forthing all across the Web, this inclusion was a good idea. This section will provide you with some startup code to show you what you need to get going on designing simple Web programs.

The java.net.URL Class

There are several classes in `java.net` that are involved in performing Web access. However, all roads seem to start at `java.net.URL`. An object of this class is a reference

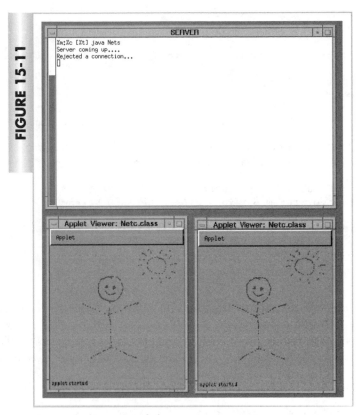

FIGURE 15-11

Several clients and the server

to a location on the Web. Once the object is created, its attributes may not be changed. The common constructor takes the following form:

```
URL myURL = new URL("http://www.preemptive.com");
```

Other constructors are available to specify the parameters differently and/or give a port number.

Also included in the package is the `java.net.URLConnection` class, which is required in order to actually access a page. This class really puts the meat on the bones of the `URL` class. The following example will use it, but keep in mind that the `URL` class relies on it so heavily that it is already well integrated into it, and you could get by with letting `URL` call `URLConnection` as needed.

A Page Reader

Here the `URL` class will be used to develop a simple page reader. Just add a little spice of life, a bunch of pretty graphics, and a lot more features, and this code could be transformed into a fairly rudimentary Web browser.

```
/* URL Page Reader */
public class Urlfun {

 public static void main(String args[]) throws IOException,
                                           MalformedURLException {
 int g;

/* Setup the URL, connection, and input stream */
  URL myURL = new URL("http://www.preemptive.com");

/* Establish connection */
  URLConnection myConn = myURL.openConnection();

/* Establish input stream */
  InputStream datain = myConn.getInputStream();

/* Read in (and print out) each byte */
  while ((g = datain.read()) != -1)
   System.out.write(g);
  }
}
```

Although this is quite a small and rather vanilla piece of code, the function it provides is fairly impressive. All the details of dealing with the HTTP protocol are taken care of for you. The result of the code is to print out the HTML source for the indicated Web page. You could also modify this code to do away with any explicit references to the URLConnection class. This is because the URL class is sophisticated enough to handle all the details if needed (i.e., it will use URLConnection behind the scenes).

```
<title>home page</title>
<hr>
<applet code=amazing.class width=250 height=250>
</applet>
<hr>
```

The above listing is an example run of the URLfun class. As you can see, you have easy access to Web pages within your Java program. Chances are you won't be writing a Web browser (if you are, good luck, there is plenty of strong competition), but given Java's inherent relationship with the Web, applications that can intelligently scan through Web pages are bound to be needed.

Summary

Well, that was the tip of the iceberg. Network programming opens up a new world of opportunity. Fortunately, even in the most complex applications, the bottom line is usually socket use, which you now have an introduction to. If you are interested in advancing your networking skills, many good books exist on network programming. You should easily be able to adapt to the Java paradigm you have seen here.

Just a few more chapters to go, but a ton of functionality still left to cover. You should start to see what was meant by Java's comprehensive list of features. The things covered here are usually set aside as extra features for most programming languages. For Java, that's just not true. All this functionality is part of the package; it is part of Java. This level of integration of tools is what sets Java apart from any other programming environment in use today.

Questions

1. Name an example of an application that would be better with a datagram socket. Besides the example, how about a stream socket?

2. Considering that a Web client can be one of many different browsers designed by different companies, what must they all be doing so that any Web server will respond to them?

3. Both the network client and **ServerThread** classes have an array **ALL**, which performs the same function in each. Why is it static in **ServerThread** and not in network client?

4. As built, the network server class in this chapter ran in a true infinite loop. The only way to stop it was by interrupting the process. What criteria could be defined to allow the process to exit on its own?

5. How would Figure 15-9 change if there were two sockets and two threads for both the client and the server?

6. What dangers would arise if the **ALL** array in the **ServerThread** class was not protected via synchronization? Could this crash the process, or would it just lose a few dots?

Exercises

1. Change the level of synchronization to the array element level in the **ServerThread** code.

2. Redesign the **ServerThread** class to be sure all logged in clients have updated their data before broadcasting the array. Your code should never lose a dot.

3. Modify and use the **URLfun** class to design a Web page searcher that can search several predefined Web pages for a string and report its results.

4. Redesign the **ServerThread** and **Netc** classes to use multiple threads and multiple sockets to reduce network traffic. Note: properly synchronizing everything won't be trivial.

Native Methods: Interfacing to C

You will learn about the following in this chapter:

- How to let your Java program call C code
- How to let C programs access Java data
- How to call Java from C programs
- How to use the javah utility
- How to build a native library

Here's where it all gets ugly. Java in its pure form provides a very elegant and simple way to develop Web applets and standalone applications. Java's designers have given a lot of thought to addressing issues of security and the readability of the source code. The designers also wanted to create a simple, straightforward approach to developing true object-oriented applications. Unfortunately, a bytecode compiled binary is not always the fastest or most efficient executable you can run on a given system. (Not to say that it isn't good; it just doesn't always afford you the performance you may need in certain applications.)

There are times when you may want to take advantage of hardware designed for optimizing certain types of computation, such as geometry transformations for graphics applications, or accessing nonstandard peripherals. For example, you may want to access some special digitizing tablet, or take advantage of a multibutton mouse, or even drive some special data acquisition board needed for your applications. Well, since Java was developed to run on a generic machine architecture, it is unlikely that you will be able to access computer components that one cannot reasonably expect to find on every computer. At least, not using pure Java.

Java allows you to get around this barrier by linking object code that was written and compiled in other languages, such as C, to your Java applications. This means that you will be able to access machine peripherals that would not normally be accessible to a Java program. This also allows you to speed up certain tasks that just aren't fast enough written entirely in Java.

First off, some definitions are in order. A *native method* is a procedure or function that was written in a language other than Java and compiled to be binary compatible with the processor of a specific CPU rather than the Java virtual machine. For example, if you write a series of C functions and compile them to be executed on a Sparc, 486, or other CPU, the object file you create is native to the machine it was compiled for.

A *native library* is a library of native methods that is dynamically loaded and linked to Java objects at runtime. When writing native methods or using libraries of native code, there are a few key issues to keep in mind:

- A Java applet won't run on a machine unless any native calls that it depends on are installed on that machine as a native library. In order for users to be able to run your applet that uses native calls, they must first download your library and install it manually.

- Native libraries are machine/operating system specific. If you compile a library of native methods on a Windows NT machine, this code will not work on a Sparcstation.

- Native methods are no longer objects, but rather methods of objects that are written in Java. This sort of mucks up the eloquence of the pure objectivity of the Java language.

- Security is likely one of the most important issues in running Java and especially in using native methods. Basically, all of the security measures that are enforced in Java disappear once native libraries are introduced. A native method can contain malicious, poorly written, or just plain misbehaving code. A Java interpreter is designed to disallow potentially dangerous access to the client's machine. A method written in C has the same access to the client machine as any standalone application written in C. Therefore, it is a trivial task for someone to write a virus or other damaging piece of software as a native library. This isn't to say "avoid native libraries at all cost"; rather, know where they came from. If you download an intriguing piece of code that depends on native libraries, be sure you know who the author or the organization distributing it is.

This chapter will explain how native methods are called from Java classes. It will discuss methods for accessing Java data structures from C functions as well as passing data from a calling class to a C function. Finally, you'll walk through the techniques necessary to link it all together.

Creating Native Methods

A native method within a Java class isn't much different from a normal Java method. The differences are the keyword **native** that appears before the method declaration, and the absence of a method body after the declaration. The following code bit describes a class that has two Java methods and two native methods:

```
/* Building a class */
public class MyNativeClass {
        private int x;
        private int y;

        static {
            System.loadLibrary("MyNative");
        }

        /* Regular Java accessor methods */
        public int returnx() { return x; }
        public int returny() { return y; }

        /* Define the native methods */
        native void setx(int myx);
        native void sety(int myy);
}
```

In the sample code above, there are two instance variables **x** and **y**. The methods **returnx** and **returny** will return the values of **x** and **y** as expected. These could be accessed from other Java classes using a code bit similar to this:

```
...
MyNativeClass  nativeInstance = new MyNativeClass();
int myx;        //local x
int myy;        //local y

/* Call the native methods with parameters */
nativeInstance.setx(5);
nativeInstance.sety(3);

/* Call java accessor methods */
myx = nativeInstance.returnx();
myy = nativeInstance.returny();
...
```

The above example will call the native methods **setx** and **sety** passing integers as parameters. The native side hasn't been discussed, but let's assume that **setx** and **sety** are implemented in C and have access to the local **x** and **y** instance variables. So you can assume that a call to **nativeInstance.setx(5)** will somehow assign the value 5 to the local variable **x**. Obviously, this is a trivial task to implement in pure Java, but this is just an example of how a native method is declared and used. For a basic diagram outlining the method structure in Java, see Figure 16-1.

Notice the resemblance of the native method declaration to a function prototype in C. It's basically the same thing—it's telling the compiler that another library must be loaded to handle this method call. It also tells the compiler what can be expected as parameters—in this case, integers. A return type must also be declared.

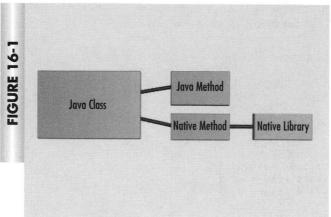

FIGURE 16-1

Method diagram

Loading a Native Library

When you declare a method as being native, you are telling the Java compiler that you plan on dynamically linking to a library that contains the native code for this method before making any calls to this method. In other words, you must specify which library to load before this method can be called. There are no compile-time checks to make sure that these libraries are present or correct. It is up to the developer to make sure that the correct library is loaded.

There are two ways to load a dynamically linked library. Both are declared in the static initializer of a class, and both use methods that can be found in the standard Java class libraries, namely the `System` class. The first method takes an absolute path and file name as its argument. The downside of this is that the machine that is running the code must have the library installed in a well-defined place. This is not always convenient for distributed applications. It does, however, work fine if you are developing applications for in-house use. A native library cannot be used over the Web. It must be manually downloaded and installed before it can be used. This is to prevent a malicious applet from downloading a library and wreaking havoc on your system. The syntax for the load method is

```
System.load(String path_filename);
```

The `System.load` method loads the library specified in its argument. If it is unable to load the library, or if it is unable to resolve any links that are needed by the call, it will throw an exception, and if the exception is not caught, halt execution of the application. Use this method for loading a library only if you are sure the user will have that library installed in a particular directory.

A more reasonable and site-independent way to load a native library is with the `System.loadLibrary(String library)` call. This method will search for the library specified within paths that are listed in environment variables on the users' machines. This gives users the freedom to put the library wherever they want. It allows the client to simply create a path variable that the Java interpreter can use to search for the library (such as the CLASSPATH environment variable in UNIX, or the PATH variable in Windows). A UNIX standard for naming dynamic libraries is to prepend the file name with "lib" and to add the suffix ".so". The `loadLibrary` method uses this same convention, so a call to

```
loadLibrary("foo");
```

would search for a library called libfoo.so. The search path is normally specified on a UNIX machine with the LD_LIBRARY_PATH environment variable. This is a colon-delimited list of directory paths that may contain libraries. To set the LD_LIBRARY_PATH, you would type something like the following statement at the UNIX command prompt:

```
setenv LD_LIBRARY_PATH .:/usr/openwin:/usr/joe/mylibraries
```

This statement would cause the Java interpreter to first search the present directory for libraries to load, then `/usr/openwin`, and finally `/usr/joe/mylibraries`. The technique for specifying a library path is operating system dependent. For example, if you wanted to specify the library path on a Windows NT machine, you would add it to the PATH environment variable using the standard Windows mechanisms for doing that (normally a `set PATH = .` statement.) Also, the native library would be built as a Windows Dynamically Linked Library (DLL) file on the local Windows NT machine.

This should begin to give you an idea of how much more work it is to use native code on multiple platforms. If you are developing straight Java applications, there is no need to worry about compiling for all of the machines you want to support, or how dynamic libraries are implemented on any specific platform.

Implementing Your Native Methods in C

For the purposes of this chapter, native methods will be demonstrated as they would be implemented in C. There are already a number of utilities that make it easy to build wrappers around C functions, and to automatically generate header files that make passing and translating data structures relatively simple. It is also possible to implement your native methods in another language, such as C++ or Pascal, but C is the path of least resistance, and most of the native libraries already out there have been written in C.

Generating Headers and Stubs

Along with the standard Java executables, (java, hotjava, javadoc, etc.) there is a program that will create header files and C files called *stubs*, based on a compiled Java class. These headers and stubs contain function prototypes and `#define`s that can be used to pass information between native methods and the calling Java classes. It is actually very convenient that there is a mechanism for automatically generating these, as they could end up being very tedious to code by hand.

javah

The javah utility comes with the Java Developers Kit. It is used to generate files based on Java classes. This utility takes a number of command-line arguments. In its simplest form javah creates a header file based on a class that contains native methods. It can also be called with a **-stubs** argument to cause it to create the stubs file that will be used by the method. The general command line form of javah is

```
javah [-v] [-stubs] class .
```

The **-v** flag causes javah to execute in verbose mode, **-stubs** causes javah to create the stubs file, and **class** refers to a compiled Java class that contains declarations for native methods. As an example, let's take a look at the earlier class definition for **MyNativeClass**.

```
/* Building a class */
public class MyNativeClass {
        private int x;
        private int y;

        /* Regular Java accessor methods */
        public int returnx() { return x; }
        public int returny() { return y; }

        /* Define the native methods */
        native void setx(int myx);
        native void sety(int myy);
}
```

Compile this class using javac.

```
javac MyNativeClass.java
```

As expected, this will create a file called MyNativeClass.class. Now, to create the header file for the native methods for this class, run javah with the class name as the parameter:

```
javah MyNativeClass
```

This will create a file called MyNativeClass.h. On a Sparcstation running Solaris 2.4, the header file that is generated will look like this:

```
/* DO NOT EDIT THIS FILE - it is machine generated */
#include <native.h>
/* Header for class MyNativeClass */

#ifndef _Included_MyNativeClass
#define _Included_MyNativeClass

typedef struct ClassMyNativeClass {
    long x;
```

```
    long y;
} ClassMyNativeClass;
HandleTo(MyNativeClass);

extern void MyNativeClass_setx(struct HMyNativeClass *,long);
extern void MyNativeClass_sety(struct HMyNativeClass *,long);
#endif
```

This header file should be #included when building your native library. It defines a struct that contains the data of the calling Java class, in this case x and y. It also contains function prototypes for the native methods that you will implement.

The naming convention is as follows: the package name of the class (if you are using packages) followed by the class name followed by the method name. Each element in the name is separated by an underscore. So in the case of the example, a package name wasn't used (just to keep things simple), so the class name was used followed by the method name. The class was **MyNativeClass** and the native methods were **setx** and **sety**; therefore, two functions need to be implemented in C. Namely, **MyNativeClass_setx** and **MyNativeClass_sety**. Just as an example, if **MyNativeClass** was part of the **MyPackage** package, the native methods would subsequently be named **MyPackage_MyNativeClass_setx** and **MyPackage_MyNativeClass_sety** respectively.

The next thing of interest in the function prototypes is the arguments. The first argument passes a pointer to a data structure that represents the calling Java class. The naming convention for this data structure is to use an "H" followed by the class name. In the example, the name **HMyNativeClass** was used to name a data structure that points to the Java class. This data structure is used to give the C function access to data elements in the Java class. The next argument will be passed to the native method when called from the Java side. In the method declaration, a parameter of type **int** was declared. The javah utility translated that to a type **long** for the native implementation. See Table 16-1 for a list of type conversions.

Java Type	Return Type
boolean[ ]	long *
int[ ]	long *
float[ ]	float *
char[ ]	unicode *
short[ ]	long *
ushort[ ]	unsigned short *
double[ ]	float *
Object[ ]	HArrayOfClass *

Table 16-1 Body of return types

When creating the C program, the first argument will be used to get to `MyNativeClass.x` and `MyNativeClass.y`. The integer parameter that the method was called with will be passed as a long integer. For a demonstration of this, take a look at the following C source file:

```
#include "StubPreamble.h"
#include "java_lang_String.h"
#include "MyNativeClass.h"
#include <stdio.h>

void MyNativeClass_setx(struct HMyNativeClass *this, long x)
{
        unhand(this)->x = x; /* dereference the x element of the
                                        calling class and assign it the
                                        value of x */
}


void MyNativeClass_sety(struct HMyNativeClass *this, long y)
{
        unhand(this)->y = y; /* dereference the y element of the
                                        calling class and assign it the
                                        value of y */
}
```

The included files StubPreamble.h and java_lang_String.h are located in the include subdirectory of the Java home directory. These contain macros, typedefs, and constants that are useful in moving data between the C and Java worlds. When you compile this file, you may need to specify the location of this directory in order for your compiler to find the header files. On a UNIX system, assuming that the Java distribution was installed in `/usr/java`, the command to compile this file would be

```
cc -c Native.c -o Native.o -I/usr/java/include
```

These flags tell the compiler to compile the file without linking (`-c`), to create an object file called Native.o (`-o`), and to add /usr/java/include to the search path for header files. (Note that the files have been arbitrarily named `Native.c` and `Native.o`; you may name them whatever makes sense for your application.)

The `unhand` macro dereferences a handle to the Java class data. In the previous example, the class `MyNativeClass` contains two data elements, the integers `x` and `y`. `Unhand` will dereference the `HMyNativeClass` structure, and then the component data elements may be dereferenced with the `->` operator. Thus, `unhand(HMyNativeClass)->x` will point to the `x` instance variable in the `MyNativeClass` class. Any native function will assume that a pointer to a data structure containing the data elements of the calling class will be passed as the first argument. Any arguments that were declared in the native method declaration will follow.

Macros for Dereferencing Data Structures

You have already seen how the **unhand** macro is used to dereference a pointer to the data elements of a Java class. There are a number of other useful C functions for dereferencing pointers to other data types. All of these are defined in the standard Java header files. If you #**include** the files StubPreamble.h and java_lang_String.h as well as any headers that are automatically generated for your classes by javah, you should have access to all of these dereferencing tools.

Just as **unhand** dereferences a handle to a Java class data structure, another useful function is **obj_length** . This function, as you probably guessed from the name, returns the length of an array, given its handle. The value is returned as an integer. The basic structure is

```
int obj_length(HArray *);
```

Another useful macro is **bodyof**. It returns a pointer to the data element of handles to certain data structures. If you pass **bodyof** a handle to a Boolean array, it will return a pointer to the starting offset of the data portion of that array. The basic structure for **bodyof** is

```
Object *bodyof(HArray *);
```

Table 16-1 lists different array types that can be passed to **bodyof** and the corresponding pointer type that is returned. Note that the asterisks in the table represent pointers in C.

Creating Stubs

Once the header file and the C source file have been created, one more file must be generated, compiled, and linked into the native library. The javah utility creates the stub files as well as the header file. To create a stub file for **MyNativeClass**, use the following command:

```
javah -stubs MyNativeClass
```

This will create the following file:

```
/* DO NOT EDIT THIS FILE - it is machine generated */
#include <StubPreamble.h>

/* Stubs for class MyNativeClass */
/* SYMBOL: "MyNativeClass/setx(I)V", Java13_MyNativeClass_setx_stub, */
stack_item *Java13_MyNativeClass_setx_stub(stack_item *_P_,struct execenv *_EE_)
 {
        extern void MyNativeClass_setx(void *,long);
        (void) MyNativeClass_setx(_P_[0].p,((_P_[1].i)));
        return _P_;
}
/* SYMBOL: "MyNativeClass/sety(I)V", Java13_MyNativeClass_sety_stub, */
stack_item *Java13_MyNativeClass_sety_stub(stack_item *_P_,struct execenv *_EE_)
 {
```

continued on next page

continued from previous page

```
    extern void MyNativeClass_sety(void *,long);
    (void) MyNativeClass_sety(_P_[0].p,((_P_[1].i)));
    return _P_;
}
```

Yuck. That's just about ugly. Luckily, the stub file is not something you will usually need to look at. It contains information necessary to execute your native method and to pass the correct parameters. Once this file has been generated, compile it and link it to the source file containing your native method code. This is your native library, so the final file name should be something that makes sense on your system, such as libMyNative.so or whatever is appropriate. On a UNIX system, the command to link these files will be something like

```
ld -G Native.o MyNativeClass.o -o libMyNative.so
```

You would use a similar command in Windows, depending on the linker that you are using. Basically, substitute the `ld` with the name of your linker, and replace the `libMyNative.so` with something like `MyNative.dll`. For example, the command should be something like

```
ld -G Native.o MyNativeClass.o -o MyNative.dll
```

In any case, adjust the previous linker commands to the particular command(s) used on your system for linking object files into libraries.

To recap what you have learned so far:

1. Create a Java source file that contains native method declarations. A native method declaration is similar in form to a C function prototype. Be sure to include a `System.loadLibrary()` call in the static initializer of the class in which the native method is called.

2. Compile the Java source file with the javac compiler.

3. Create a header file with javah.

4. Create a stub file using javah with the `-stubs` flag.

5. Create a C source file containing the functions that correspond to the native methods that you declared in your Java class. Be sure to `#include` `StubPreamble.h` and `java_lang_String.h` as well as the header that you created with javah.

6. Compile the C source files into binary object files using your favorite C compiler (most prefer cc or gcc in UNIX).

7. Link the object files into a library file.

Once the Java class has been built, along with the related library of native code, the class can be imported into a Java application in the same manner as any other Java class. The only difference is that the native methods in this class will only execute properly if the related native libraries are installed on the machine(s) that they are invoked on. So, if you plan on using a class that depends on native methods in a Web-based applet, you must provide the means for your clients to download and install your native libraries on their machines in advance.

Translating Data

When you are passing data from a Java class to a native method, you can't expect the data types to be the same. The sizes and structures of the basic data types in Java are well defined independent of the system that they are running on. This makes porting a nonissue when developing pure Java code. Once native code is introduced, you need to worry about translation of data types and structures. Normally, there will be a translation, such as a Java integer being translated to a long in C. Most of these simple data types are straightforward conversions that can be easily determined by the type that is assigned in the header file generated by javah (See Figure 16-2). Certain data types require extra attention. In the header files

FIGURE 16-2

Java	C argument	C structure
boolean	long	long
int	long	long
float	float	float
char	long	long
short	long	long
ushort	long	long
double	float	float
Object	struct Hjava_lang_Object *	struct Hjava_lang_Object *
boolean[]	long *	long*
int[]	long *	struct HArrayOfLong *
float[]	float *	struct HArrayOfFloat *
char[]	unicode*	struct HArrayOfChar *
short[]	long *	struct HArrayOfLong *
ushort[]	unsigned short *	unsigned short *
double[]	float*	struct HArrayOfFloat*
Object[]	HArrayOfClass	*struct Hjava_lang_object *

Java to C type conversions

that are located in the ~java/include directory, there are a number of functions and macros that can be used to translate a Java string to a C string. The most common is

```
JavaString2CString(char *buf,int len,HJavaString *string)
```

This function takes a pointer to a char array that is of size len (in bytes), and fills it with the converted Java string that is pointed to by the third argument. The resulting C string will be a standard, null-terminated array of bytes. For a complete list of type conversions, see Figure 16-2. This lists the Java type, the C type that would be used when passed as an argument, and the C type that would be used if the type is part of a struct.

Some of the common functions that are available in the java_lang_String.h and related header files are listed in Table 16-2. The table lists the return type, the function name, and the parameter types that it expects. The functionality should be recognizable by the function name, but will be explained in more detail below.

Hjava_lang_String *java_lang_String_float2String(struct Hjava_lang_String *,float);

Hjava_lang_String *java_lang_String_double2String(struct Hjava_lang_String *,double);

char * javaString2CString(Hjava_lang_String *, char * int);

unicode* javaString2Unicode(Hjava_lang_String *, unicode * int);

Table 16-2 Java string conversion functions

These functions should give you the basic conversion tools necessary for translating most data types from Java format to native format. `java_lang_String_float2String` will take a float and translate it into a Java string, `double2String`, `javaString2CString`, and `javaString2Unicode` all work in a similar fashion. To demonstrate a simple string conversion, let's look at the following class declaration:

```
public class StringTest{

  static {
   System.loadLibrary("StringTest"); //load native lib
   }
String foo = "This is a string"; //create a string
public native void printfoo(); //declare a native method
}
```

This is not a very useful class, but is a simple demonstration of passing a string to a C program. Obviously, a function called `StringTest_printfoo` must be created that will print the string that is stored in `foo` to the standard output stream (normally the console). This, of course, could be implemented entirely in Java, but let's take a look at how to access this string in a C function. In the following code, an array of chars is declared that will hold the contents of the string `StringTest.foo`. Then, the array will be printed to standard out.

```
#include "StubPreamble.h"
#include "java_lang_String.h"
#include "StringTest.h" /* created with javah as in the
                                previous example */
#include <stdio.h>
void StringTest_printfoo(HStringTest *this)
{
        char buffer[256]; /* buffer to hold translated string */
        javaString2CString(unhand(this)->foo,
              buffer,sizeof(buffer)); /* unhand is used to dereference
                              the structure to the StringTest class.
                              foo is the instance String that is stored
                              in an instance of this class. */
        printf("The java string contains:  %s",buffer);
}
```

In the C code above, the contents of **MyString.foo** are dereferenced and stored in the local C buffer. If this class was instantiated and the **printfoo** method called, the string

The java string contains: This is a string

would be printed to the standard out stream on the machine executing the application.

Natives Executing Java Methods

It's a little one-sided to assume that you may want to execute native code from Java but that a native application wouldn't want to execute Java methods. Let's take a look at the other side of this. Sometimes it's useful to load and execute class constructors and methods from within your C code. There are a number of functions that are available for finding classes, loading classes, executing class constructors, and executing class methods.

Native methods that call Java methods use a *method signature* to identify the method, its return type, and the types of arguments that it expects. The method signature is made up of package and class names separated by "/" marks, the name of the method, argument types surrounded by parentheses, and a one-letter code that represents the return type of the method (see Table 16-3 for return types.) So, as an example, if you wanted to determine the method signature for a class called **MyString** and a method within this class called **printfoo** that returns void, the method signature would be

MyString/printfoo()V

Likewise, if **MyString** was in the **MyPackage** package, this signature would change to

MyPackage/MyString/printfoo()V

If **printfoo** took two integers as arguments, the signature would change to

`MyPackage/MyString/printfoo(II)V`

Finally, if this same method returned a type **char**, rather than **void**, the signature would be

`MyPackage/MyString/printfoo(II)C`

Type Code	Return Type
I	integer
B	byte
C	char
L	class (the form is Lclassname)
E	enum
F	float
S	unsigned short
Z	boolean
V	void

Table 16-3 Type codes for method signatures

First off, let's take a look at **FindClass**. **FindClass** will find a class with a name passed as a parameter. If **FindClass** is able to resolve the name, the class and all of its superclasses are loaded. Otherwise, a Boolean value is set to false and the class isn't loaded.

```
ClassClass* FindClass(struct execenv *ee, char *name, bool_t resolve);
```

In the prototype for **FindClass**, the first argument is a pointer to an execution environment; if a null pointer is passed, it uses the current environment. The second parameter is a character string containing the name of the class, and finally, the third string is a Boolean set to true if the name can be resolved and false otherwise.

The next interesting function that can be used to call Java components from your C programs is **execute_method**. This function will allow you to call a Java method from C. You pass a pointer to a Java environment (or **NULL** for the current environment), a pointer to an instance of an object, and a character string with the name of the method. Any arguments that will be used by the method follow this string. The method name must be an instance method (there is a separate function for calling static methods), and the name must be a complete method signature as described in Table 16-3. The prototype function for **execute_method** follows:

```
long execute_method(struct execenv *current, void *obj, char *method, .);
```

The routine for calling a static method is similar in form, but a pointer to a class is passed rather than a pointer to an object. The function prototype is

```
long execute_static_method(struct execenv *current, ClassClass *obj,char* method .);
```

The last of the interesting routines for calling Java from your C programs is the `execute_constructor` function. `Execute_constructor` allows you to create a new instance to a Java object. `Execute_constructor` is called with a constructor method signature and returns a pointer to the new object on success. Otherwise, 0 is returned. Arguments to the constructor follow the method signature. The basic form for `execute_constructor` is

```
Hobject *execute_constructor(struct execenv *current, char* methodsig, .);
```

An example call to `execute_constructor` using the method signature from the previous section would be

```
MyObject = execute_constructor('/O', "MyPackage/MyString/printfoo(II)C",3,4);
```

To sum up, there are a number of functions that come with the standard Java Development Kit that allow you to easily call Java class components from within your C programs. These can be used to instantiate classes, call constructors, or just execute class methods. You would use the `execute_method` function for calling a method of a Java class that has been instantiated, `execute_static_method` to call a static method of a Java class, and `execute_constructor` to instantiate a Java class.

Building a Native Library

The best way to learn how to use native libraries is to build one yourself. The following sections will go step by step through creating a package of Java classes that use native methods. Once the classes have been defined, you will see how the C implementations for the native methods are written and how a native library is compiled. The following will assume that you are working on a UNIX system similar to Solaris. Most of it will be the same regardless of the platform, so just change the names of the compiler, linker, and library path as is appropriate for your system.

The package in this example will be called `Native_System`, and will contain classes that have access to some basic UNIX system calls. (Remember that as soon as you start writing native libraries, your code is platform dependent!) Create a directory called Native_System on your system that can be reached through one of the directories specified in your CLASSPATH. (In Windows, this is specified in your PATH variable.) For example, if your CLASSPATH or PATH environment variable contains /mydir/classes (or \mydir\classes in Windows), create the Native_System directory as a subdirectory of /mydir/classes.

```
cd /mydir/classes
mkdir Native_System
```

The first class to create is **Exec**. **Exec** has only one method; it takes a string as its argument, and attempts to run it on the local system. The Java code follows. Place this file in the Native_System directory that you created.

```
/* The package name */
package Native_System;

/* Define the class */
public class Exec {
 static { System.loadLibrary("MyNative"); }

/* run a native method with one arg */
 public native void exec_it(String filename);
}
```

Save this file as Exec.java and compile it with the following command:

```
javac Exec.java
```

Once the class has been compiled, create the header and stub files with the following commands:

```
javah Native_System.Exec
javah -stubs Native_System.Exec
```

Notice that only the class name is used and not the file name. You should now have the two automatically generated files, which follow:

Native_System_Exec.h

```
/* DO NOT EDIT THIS FILE - it is machine generated */
#include <native.h>
/* Header for class Native_System_Exec */

#ifndef _Included_Native_System_Exec
#define _Included_Native_System_Exec

typedef struct ClassNative_System_Exec {
    char PAD; /* ANSI C requires structures to have a least one member */
} ClassNative_System_Exec;
HandleTo(Native_System_Exec);

struct Hjava_lang_String;
extern void Native_System_Exec_exec_it(struct HNative_System_Exec *,struct
Hjava_lang_String *);
#endif
```

Native_System_Exec.c

```
/* DO NOT EDIT THIS FILE - it is machine generated */
#include <StubPreamble.h>
```

```
/* Stubs for class Native_System/Exec */
/* SYMBOL: "Native_System/Exec/exec_it(Ljava/lang/String;)V",
Java18_Native_System_Exec_exec_it_stub, */
stack_item *Java18_Native_System_Exec_exec_it_stub(stack_item *_P_,struct
execenv *_EE_) {
              extern void Native_System_Exec_exec_it(void *,void *);
              (void) Native_System_Exec_exec_it(_P_[0].p,((_P_[1].p)));
              return _P_;
}
```

Notice in the header file, the structure for the **Native_System_Exec** is filled only with a pad character. This is because the class has no static or instance variables, only a method. If there were data elements in the class, they would have been built into this structure. Also notice that the function prototype for the native method is declaring two parameters, a pointer to the class structure, and a pointer to a the Java string that will be passed as a parameter.

The next step is to implement this function in C. The following C source file will take the Java string that is passed, convert it into a C string, and pass that to a **system** call.

exec.c

```
#include "StubPreamble.h"
#include "java_lang_String.h"
#include "Native_System_Exec.h"
#include <stdio.h>
void Native_System_Exec_exec_it(HNative_System_Exec *this, Hjava_lang_String
*filename)
{
       char buffer[256]; /* create a buffer to hold the filename */
       javaString2CString(filename,buffer,sizeof(buffer));
/*convert the string */
       system(buffer); /* execute the system call */
}
```

Compile the C files into object code.

```
cc -c exec.c -o exec.o
cc -c Native_System_Exec.c -o Native_System_Exec.o
```

Link the object code you created into a library.

```
ld -G Native_System_Exec.o exec.o -o libMyNative.so
```

So far, you have created a class with a native method and built the library that resolves the native method call. Now you need to write a small application that uses this code. The following class is a standalone Java application that takes a command-line argument and executes it on the local system.

RunIt.java

```
package Native_System;
import Native_System.Exec;

public class RunIt {
  public static void main (String args[]) {
        Exec.exec_it(args[0]);
  }
}
```

Now the only thing left to do is compile this last class and test it out.

```
javac RunIt.java
java RunIt <command>
```

The command that is specified on the command line should be executed if it is a valid command. In other words, if the command is recognized by the system that the native code is running on, the system will run that command.

Now that you have an idea of how native methods work, the following are a few tidbits of code that can be used directly, or modified for your needs. In the examples, package declarations are not being used just to simplify things slightly, but if you are planning on writing a number of classes, you may want to separate your code into packages of similar utility.

MathClass

The following is basically a template for building a native library of math functions. The intent is to show simple examples that you can then build upon. These methods are not necessarily useful in their current form, but can be customized for your needs.

This example is broken up into the following files:

MathClass.java The java source for the class that declares the native methods

MathClass.c The C stubs file created with javah

MathClass.h The C header file created with javah

mathclass.c The C implementation of the native methods

MathTest.java A simple application that tests the native methods

MathClass.java

```
/* Class using native methods for several Math fctns */
public class MathClass {
```

```
/*load the native library */
 static { System.loadLibrary("mathclass"); }

/* raise b to the eth power */
 static native int IntPower( int b, int e);

/* raise b to the eth power */
  static native float FloatPower(float b, float e);

/* multiply two vectors of length len */
/* store result in target[] */
  static native void VecMult(int[] v1, int[] v2,
                                   int[] target, int len);

/* return the value of Pi */
  static native float Pi();
}
```

MathClass.c

```
/* DO NOT EDIT THIS FILE - it is machine generated */
#include <StubPreamble.h>

/* Stubs for class MathClass */
/* SYMBOL: "MathClass/IntPower(II)I", Java9_MathClass_IntPower_stub, */
stack_item *Java9_MathClass_IntPower_stub(stack_item *_P_,struct execenv *_EE_) {
      extern long MathClass_IntPower(void *,long,long);
      _P_[0].i = MathClass_IntPower(NULL,((_P_[0].i)),((_P_[1].i)));
      return _P_ + 1;
}
/* SYMBOL: "MathClass/FloatPower(FF)F", Java9_MathClass_FloatPower_stub, */
stack_item *Java9_MathClass_FloatPower_stub(stack_item *_P_,struct execenv *_EE_) {
      extern float MathClass_FloatPower(void *,float,float);
      _P_[0].f = MathClass_FloatPower(NULL,((_P_[0].f)),((_P_[1].f)));
      return _P_ + 1;
}
/* SYMBOL: "MathClass/VecMult([I[I[II)V", Java9_MathClass_VecMult_stub, */
stack_item *Java9_MathClass_VecMult_stub(stack_item *_P_,struct execenv *_EE_) {
      extern void MathClass_VecMult(void *,void *,void *,void *,long);
      (void)
MathClass_VecMult(NULL,((_P_[0].p)),((_P_[1].p)),((_P_[2].p)),((_P_[3].i)));
      return _P_;
}
/* SYMBOL: "MathClass/Pi()F", Java9_MathClass_Pi_stub, */
stack_item *Java9_MathClass_Pi_stub(stack_item *_P_,struct execenv *_EE_) {
      extern float MathClass_Pi(void *);
      _P_[0].f = MathClass_Pi(NULL);
      return _P_ + 1;
}
```

MathClass.h

```
/* DO NOT EDIT THIS FILE - it is machine generated */
#include <native.h>
/* Header for class MathClass */

#ifndef _Included_MathClass
#define _Included_MathClass

typedef struct ClassMathClass {
    char PAD; /* ANSI C requires structures to have a least one member */
} ClassMathClass;
HandleTo(MathClass);

extern long MathClass_IntPower(struct HMathClass *,long,long);
extern float MathClass_FloatPower(struct HMathClass *,float,float);
extern void MathClass_VecMult(struct HMathClass *,HArrayOfInt *,HArrayOfInt
*,HArrayOfInt *,long);
extern float MathClass_Pi(struct HMathClass *);
#endif
```

mathclass.c

```
#include "StubPreamble.h"
#include "java_lang_String.h"
#include "MathClass.h"
#include <stdio.h>
#include <math.h>

long MathClass_IntPower(struct HMathClass *this,long b,long p)
{
/* raises b to the power of p and returns the integer answer */

        long base=b; /* store base size */

        if (p==0) return 1;
        if (p==1) return b;
        p--;

        while(p--) /* calculate answer */
          b*=base;

        return b; /* return answer */
}
float MathClass_FloatPower(struct HMathClass *this,float b,
                                    float p)
{
/* raises b to the power of p and returns the float answer */

        long base=b; /* store base size */
```

```
        if (p==0) return 1;
        if (p==1) return b;
        p--;

         while(p--) /*calculate answer */
           b*=base;

         return b; /*return answer */
}
void MathClass_VecMult(struct HMathClass *this,HArrayOfInt *v1,HArrayOfInt *v2,
                    HArrayOfInt *target,long len)
{
/*multiply two vectors of integers, and store them in target*/

        long *vec1; /* pointer to first vector */
        long *vec2; /* pointer to second vector */
        long *tar; /* pointer to target vector */
        long l;  /* used to index vectors */

        /* in the following 3 statements, unhand() dereferences
           the data handles. The body portion refers to the
           actual array within the data structure. */

        vec1 = unhand(v1)->body;
        vec2 = unhand(v2)->body;
        tar = unhand(target)->body;

        /* loop through vectors and multiply */
        tor(l=U;l<=len;l++)
            tar[l]=vec1[l]*vec2[l];
}
float MathClass_Pi(struct HMathClass *this)
{

        /* This is basically a spacer. We leave it up to the reader
           to implement their favorite Pi-calculating
           algorithm. */

        return 3.14159265;
}
```

MathTest.java

```
import MathClass;

        /* Test the native methods in the MathClass class */
        public class MathTest {

        /* The standalone run */
        public static void main(String args[]) {
                int x = 0;   // used to test the IntPower method
```

continued on next page

continued from previous page

```java
        float f = 0; // used to test the FloatPower method
        float p = 0; // used to store Pi
        int v1[] = new int[3]; // a vector
        int v2[] = new int[3]; // another vector
        int t[] =  new int[3]; // the target vector

        /* initialize first 2 vectors */
        v1[0] = 2; v1[1] = 3; v1[2] = 4;
        v2[0] = 2; v2[1] = 2; v2[2] = 4;


        try {
           /* assign 4 to the 2nd to x */
           x = MathClass.IntPower(4,2);

           /* assign 6/2 to the third to f */
           f = MathClass.FloatPower(6/2,3);

           /* assign Pi to p */
           p = MathClass.Pi();

           /* multiply v1 and v2. Store result in t */
           MathClass.VecMult(v1,v2,t,3);
        } catch (UnsatisfiedLinkError e) {

           /* if this exception is thrown, you probably  */
           /* need to either set your PATH, or the        */
           /* LD_LIBRARY_PATH variable to point to your  */
           /* native library                             */

           System.out.println("couldnt find native lib");
           System.exit(1);
        }

        /* print the results */
        System.out.println("IntPower Answer: " + x);
        System.out.println("FloatPower Answer: " + f);
        System.out.println("Pi Answer: " + p);
        System.out.println("VecMult Answer: " + t[0] + ":"
                                          + t[1] + ":" + t[2]);
        }
   }
```

Summary

Creating Java classes that call native methods is a multistep process. You must declare your native methods in a Java class, add a statement to load the appropriate library, generate header and stub files, implement the native code and deal with data translations, and compile and link your native library. For many applications, this is tedious and unnecessary.

It is, however, useful when the full speed of the local processor is needed, or if special system dependent calls are desired.

Native libraries should be used with caution, since they can circumvent the built-in security features of Java.

# Questions

1. At what point is a native library loaded?

2. What argument is always passed to the C side of a native method?

3. How can you access the data elements in a class from a native method?

4. How is a class instantiated from a native method?

# Exercises

1. Write a native method that takes a Java string, reverses it, and puts the modified string back into the calling class.

2. Write a library of native methods that do basic math functions and return the results.

3. Write a native method that returns the contents of the current working directory as a Java string.

Data Structures

17

You will learn about the following in this chapter:

- What kinds of data structures are right for you
- How to use Java's prebuilt Vector class
- How to use Java's prebuilt Hashtable class
- How to build data structure classes from the ground up
- What the Enumeration interface is

Programming is a lot like driving a car. Ask people, "What kind of driver are you?" and a few will say bad, most will say good, and an elite few will say great. But you've been on the road, and you know somebody out there has to be lying. Maybe it's just that some people have too favorable an image of themselves. After all, they get from point a to point b—doesn't everyone get honked at? Why else are there horns?

So, what kind of programmer are you? You've read through all the previous chapters, paid your dues in front of the screen, and consumed enough caffeine to light up a small fishing village—you know Java. That's all well and good, but do you know data structures? Without them, few programmers can get beyond being merely good.

Data structures are ways to store data in an organized fashion. Using the right data structure gives you (or the computer) some convenience or efficiency in using and accessing the data, whether that be easy storage of the elements, easy retrieval, or some combination of those. Sometimes other factors (such as storage space conservation) come into play. The main goal is to use/design a structure that gives you the best performance for your application.

Wily use of the right data structure could win the respect and admiration of your fellow programmers, not to mention possibly speeding your code by orders of magnitude. This chapter addresses several of the most common data structures found in computer programming and how they look in Java. Some of this chapter discusses data structure classes that were prebuilt for you. Beyond that, the chapter will develop classes from the ground up for other classic data structures. So, if you're ready to go and you're sure you are a good driver, here're the keys.

Vectors

The `java.util.Vector` class is supplied as part of the prebuilt API library. The vector is billed as a *growable* array. This is somewhat of an amazing feat—a growable array implies that it can expand from its original size (a well-documented immorality when dealing with arrays, punishable by floggings and runtime errors, among other things). Well, don't get too excited; in actuality the `Vector` class is nothing more than a set of wrapper methods for a normal array—i.e., it is a set of methods that abstract the underlying representation to something more flexible for the user (okay, that statement would probably make a decent definition for object-oriented classes in general). It includes methods to make it appear that you can effortlessly manipulate arrays in ways not previously possible. What is really happening is that it is performing serious amounts of work behind the scenes to bring off its miracles. It's not particularly efficient, but it can make life a little easier.

Using Vectors

The class provides three constructors. The most detailed allows you to specify the initial size (of the array) and capacity increment of the vector. A smart initial size can help minimize the need for the vector to expand (a costly and overall ugly operation). The capacity increment specifies by how much the vector should increase when it must expand. Keep in mind that expansion should be used as an insurance policy, not as an abused feature. The two other constructors allow the class to decide either just the capacity increment or both that and the initial size.

In order to make the `Vector` class widely reusable, it only stores `java.lang.Object`s. This means you can store any object type into it (strings, arrays, user-defined objects, etc.), but you can only get `java.lang.Object` types out of it. So you put in all these wonderfully specifically typed objects, and all you get out are pure objects. So Gilligan, what are you going to do? Right—cast away. You need to cast the object you get from the vector back to what it was when you pushed it on. Take note of the blatant exploitation of the exception to the general inheritance tree casting rule. You are actually casting *down* an inheritance tree, from object to some child. In general, this is a big no-no and often places some sort of extra-limb-growing curse upon the attemptor. However, in this instance you are (or at least should be) casting the object back to what it actually is. Even though it's a cast down the inheritance tree, it's okay, because you are casting it to what it actually is (the Java environment is smart enough to realize this). It's not often you can seemingly shed the rules of object-oriented programming and do something naughty—life is short; revel in the turpitude.

With this, you can see it's quite important to know what you are getting off the vector so you can cast it correctly. For example, assume you have a class `rectangle` and put an instance of that class in a vector.

```
Vector theVector = new Vector();
rectangle A = new rectangle(10,20);

theVector.addElement(A);
```

In order to retrieve this object from the vector you will need to do a cast.

```
A = (rectangle)theVector.lastElement();
```

Figure 17-1 shows this up and down casting business on the inheritance tree. It displays putting objects on to and off of a vector. This is analogous to setting an element of an array and subsequently removing it (by setting the element to some null value).

The vector does not actually hold the objects in it. It is merely a list of references to objects. This allows for some interesting possibilities.

Any Old Object Will Do

Because of the vector's general implementation, there is no restriction to what objects can simultaneously exist on a vector. After all, a vector holds objects of the **java.lang.Object** class, and as you are by now painfully aware, every object in Java is either an object of that class or one of its descendants. Figure 17-2 shows a possible configuration.

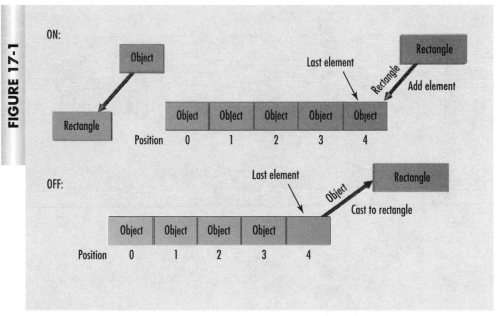

FIGURE 17-1

On to and off of the vector

An array that can hold different types of things opens up new possibilities, but always know what you put in a vector so you know what to expect coming out.

A final note regarding the vector holding `java.lang.Objects`—it is important to remember that Java's built-in data types are not objects. This includes `int`, `float`, `char`, etc. This fact tends to be overlooked when first using this and the subsequent data structures in this chapter (which are also designed for true objects only)—i.e., you cannot use the `Vector` class for straight integers. Of course, you can convert each of your `int` variables to a `java.lang.Integer` object for use on the vector; unfortunately, this gets clunky, and you'll find yourself sending things back and forth faster than a tennis match. If you run across a need for vectoring built-in data types, it would probably be easier and more efficient to create a `Vector` class suited to the built-in data type of your choice.

The Enumeration Interface

The Java prebuilt APIs have defined an interface that allow a data structure class to specify how to step through or enumerate each of the elements on a data structure. It is called the `Enumeration` interface. Considering that many different data structures are and will be implemented, and that each one will have convoluted methods of storing, hiding, and generally teasing data, a standard way to sequentially retrieve data from any of the structures is a welcome feature. The `Vector` class accommodates the `Enumeration` interface so that you may step through the elements of the vector.

FIGURE 17-2

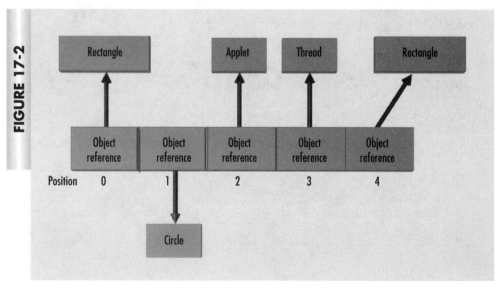

A melting-pot vector

The interface insists on two methods for all its implementors; they are **hasMoreElements** and **nextElement**, both with no input parameters. The **hasMoreElements** returns true if more elements exist within the structure that haven't been enumerated yet (in the current step-through). The **nextElement** method aptly returns the next element in the structure. With these methods there is no way (short of setting up another enumeration) to back up in the sequential step-through.

The **Vector** class provides you with a method called **elements()** that returns an **Enumeration** interface for the vector. It is used as follows:

```
Vector V = new Vector();

.
. // code which populates the Vector V
.

Enumeration E = V.elements();

while (E.hasMoreElements()) {
   processObject(E.nextElement());
   }
```

Supposedly, the **processObject** performs some action upon each of the objects held within the vector. There is no explicit increment, because this must happen implicitly within the **nextElement** method—this interface spreads across many classes; surely they all won't step through their elements the same way. So, the interface relies on the **nextElement** method to continue on its merry trek.

Without using the **Enumeration** interface, you could emulate this functionality by stepping through the index of the vector until you reach the end. However, the **Enumeration** interface is designed to apply across data structures. The built-in **java.lang.Hashtable** class and the **java.lang.Stack** class (which are both discussed later) also use the **Enumeration** interface. It's this level of standardization that makes it powerful. You can think of these types of interfaces as interfaces to you, the programmer. If you know nothing else about a data structure class, you should be able to safely assume that an **elements** method exists to provide you with an **Enumeration** interface, allowing you to step through the elements of any bizarre data structure you encounter.

 Stacks

Stacks are everywhere in computer programs. Operating systems, compilers, and video games all use stacks. A stack is a last-in first-out repository for (in this context) objects. Java's **java.util.Stack** class is a subclass of the aforementioned **java.util.Vector** class and provides you a prebuilt class for your stacking needs. Figure 17-3 shows a visualization of this renowned stack data structure. This structure is probably second only to

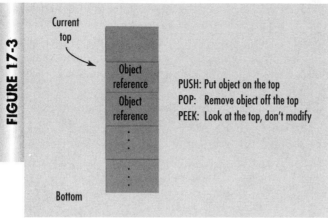

FIGURE 17-3

Current top → Object reference / Object reference ... ... / Bottom

PUSH: Put object on the top
POP: Remove object off the top
PEEK: Look at the top, don't modify

Stacking objects

queues in its permeation of everyday life (getting on a plane you seem to be waiting in a queue, trying to get off you realize it was actually a stack—humph).

The prebuilt **Stack** class in Java is specifically designed to stack objects, since it is a subclass of **Vector**. The vector is well suited to pretend to be a stack. The **Stack** class just uses the **Vector**'s **addElement** method for pushes and the **lastElement** method for pops. This example of class reuse is evident and well done.

The **Stack** class has only one constructor, which takes no parameters. In fact, it only has five methods beyond its constructor, which perform quite mundane stack operations. The following example illustrates using the class.

Checking for Palindromes

Assume you wish to write a palindrome checker program that checks the validity of an input string—i.e., checks that the input string spells the same backwards as forwards. You are not inclined to use arrays, since you have absolutely no idea of the size of the input string (and it would totally ruin the fun of this example). You also know that any character can be input as part of a palindrome except for a dollar sign ($), which indicates the middle of the input string (i.e., where the palindrome starts to reverse). This indicator greatly simplifies the problem, since without it, writing such a program would involve guessing where the middle might be. Often, the guess would be a bad one and the program would return a false conclusion. Vive la différence between computer scientists who would call such an algorithm nondeterministic and computer engineers who would call it wrong.

The following examples display what are and are not valid palindrome strings.

```
abab$baba                    VALID
abab$bab                     INVALID
```

```
123456789$987654321          VALID
123456789$9876543210         INVALID
0$                           INVALID
```

You should be able to see how a stack can be employed to perform this check. The input can be pushed onto the stack initially. When a dollar sign is encountered, the stack can be popped and compared to subsequent input. If every input character from then on matches the popped stack value (i.e., until the stack is empty) then the string is accepted as a palindrome.

You can also implement a space-saving feature, such that any sequences of like characters can be put on the stack as only one object with a counter. Therefore an input like

```
aaaaaaaaaab$baaaaaaaaaa
```

will only occupy two stack positions. The code should still check validity regardless of this compression—i.e., there should be the same number of a's on the left as on the right. Hopefully, this feature will facilitate much larger possible input strings for the check program and allow further manipulation of the stack class.

Here's the code:

```java
import java.util.Stack;

/* inChar class */
class inChar {
        int count = 1;
        char c;

        public inChar(char c) { this.c = c; }        // constructor

        public char          accessc()    { return c; }
        public void          upcount()    { count++; }
        public void          downcount() { count--; }
        public boolean countdone() {
                                return (count==1)?true:false;  }
        }
```

This `inChar` class will be instantiated to create objects that will be pushed onto the stack. It contains variables for the character and a counter. The constructor sets the character and the supporting methods manipulate the counter.

```java
/* the palindrome class */
class palindrome {

  static public void main(String args[]) throws
                                    java.io.IOException {

  char c;
  inChar i;
  boolean accept = true;
  Stack theStack = new Stack();
```

continued on next page

continued from previous page

```
/* read in left side of string */
while ((c = (char)System.in.read()) != '$') {
   if (theStack.empty()) theStack.push(new inChar(c));
    else {
            i = (inChar)theStack.peek();
            if (i.accessc() != c)
               theStack.push(new inChar(c));
            else
              i.upcount();
         }
}
.
.
.
```

The above loop reads in the input until a dollar sign is reached. It first checks to see if the stack is empty in order to avoid an **EmptyStackException**; if it is empty, it pushes the new object on. If it isn't empty, it uses the **peek** method to check the value of the character currently on top of the stack. If it matches the one you wish to **push**, no actual push takes place, and only the counter is incremented—this is the compression discussed earlier. Figure 17-4 shows the state of the stack for a sample input at this point in the code.

The code to validate the palindrome must also consider the compression that was implemented. Now the intrigue begins; to validate the palindrome, each subsequent input should match the top of the stack. Also, the stack should not run out of things to pop too early (i.e., checking for too much input), and when the input is done, the stack should be empty (i.e., checking for not enough input).

```
/* read in right side, pop stack, and compare */
 while ((c = (char)System.in.read()) != '\n') {

    /* quit on stack emptying too quickly */
    if (theStack.empty()) { accept = false;
                                            break;
                                          }
    i = (inChar)theStack.peek();

    /* quit on top of stack mismatch */
    if (i.accessc() != c) { accept = false;
                                      break;
                                     }
    else  if (i.countdone()) theStack.pop();
        else i.downcount();
    }

 /* if stack wasn't completely empty, do not accept */
 if (accept && (!theStack.empty())) accept = false;

 /* output acceptance decision */
 System.out.println();
```

```
 System.out.print("Palindrome");
 if (accept) System.out.println(" Accepted");
  else System.out.println(" Invalid");
 }
}
```

This code finishes the job. The `while` loop will check characters against the top of the stack until a newline character is encountered, unless it detects that the stack has emptied too soon (i.e., the right side was shorter than the left). Finally, a post loop check is done to be sure the stack was emptied completely to exactly match the two sides.

The `Stack` class's methods are relatively self-explanatory, but several points are worth noting. The `peek` method looks at the top of the stack without popping it off. The `pop` and `peek` methods return an object of the `java.lang.Object` class, not of any particular subclass. This is the same story as the `Vector` class, so you will need to be casting what you pop.

The `search` method returns the location of a match between the objects on the stack and the test object. If no match is found, it returns -1. Providing this general framework for stacks within Java was a good decision. The stack is such a underlying concept in programming, standardizing its use will help standardize programming practices in the bigger picture.

Hash Tables

Hash tables are again a core data structure in computer science and are included as a built-in class in the `java.util` package. This section will cover the usage of that class and examine its far-reaching effects into the Java environment. In fact, the hash table paradigm sticks

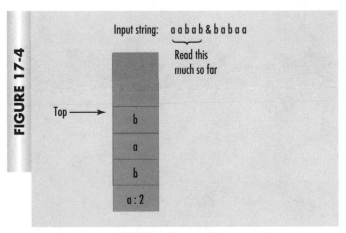

FIGURE 17-4

Input string: a a b a b & b a b a a

Read this much so far

Top →

| b |
| a |
| b |
| a : 2 |

Stack state after left side has been read

its nose throughout the Java environment; even the `java.lang.Object` class includes facilities specifically to accommodate the hashing of objects.

How to Hash

Figure 17-5 shows the setup of a hash table. In essence, a hash table is used to store large numbers of objects where each object is placed into a specific hash table slot according to some categorizing trait. This trait may be specified by the user of the hash table or it may be part of the existing object data. For example, Figure 17-5 uses the first letter of each word to decide which slot to put the word in.

From then on, any search for an object with a given word can start at the slot designated for that word (by its first letter). It should be clear what all the yahoo is about here; with a quick, distinct method of categorizing each piece of data, you need only search the applicable category when you need to find a given object. This adds a tiny bit of overhead to determine the categorizing trait (known as the hashing function) but speeds up the search immensely by reducing the search's possibilities. Such a simple hashing function as Figure 17-5 is not always appropriate, depending upon the size and/or tendencies of the data.

Poorly chosen hash functions can produce unparalleled stinky results. For an immediate example, assume you wished to hash a set of numbers. You could use their first digit, but if there were many thousands of numbers, all ten slots (there are ten slots because there

FIGURE 17-5

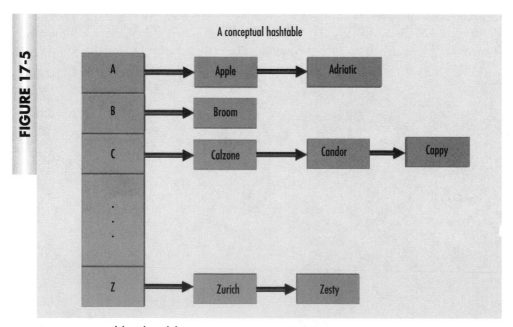

A conceptual hash table

are ten possible first digits) would be quite full, and searching through such mass over-crowding would still be unacceptably slow. To alleviate a bit of the crowd, you could use the first two digits, giving you a hundred slots altogether. This might do the trick unless the values exhibited some bias—e.g., if most were very small, then many upper (high digits) slots would be empty and many lower ones (low digits) crammed full. The point is that a good hash function is often dependent upon the input data and often needs to be specifically tailored to provide best performance.

Java's Hash

Java implements its hash class in the `java.util.Hashtable` class and is a direct descendant of the `java.lang.Object` class. The `java.lang.Object` class includes two methods for interacting with hash tables: `equals` and `hashCode`. It's your job to define these methods within your class to be hashed. The `equals` method tells the hash table how tell if two of your objects are equal. This doesn't sound all that amazing, but different objects have different needs, so you have the option to tailor what equality means. Figure 17-6 shows an example.

The `java.lang.Object` class defines equality as two object references pointing to the same object, whereas the `String` class defines equality as two objects having the same sequence of characters. They can be two separate objects, but if they both contained the sequence of characters "Uncle Fudd," they are equal. Your class should have its own criteria. By default your class will inherit the `java.lang.Object` class's ultrageneric `equals` method, which may be enough for your class, but usually it won't be. Best bet is to override the method for your particular needs.

The `hashCode` method is your way of defining how your object should be classified (i.e., what slot it belongs to). As with `equals`, you can just inherit the `java.lang.Object`

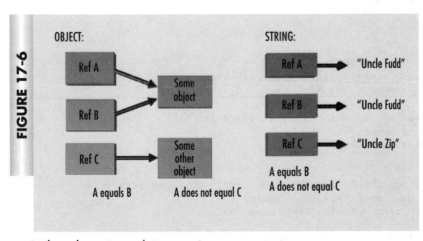

FIGURE 17-6

What does "equals" mean?

class's `hashCode` method, but that's not particularly wise. Tailoring your hash function closer to your data is the key to taking full advantage of the unimaginable powers a hash table can bestow. The `hashCode` function in `java.lang.Object` needs to be general enough for any possible class; tailoring a `hashCode` function for a specific class's needs can provide much better performance. Above, a simple hashing function was defined for words, using their first letter. This basic function is not all bad for small sets of random words. But just as with golf scores, you can always do better.

Are We Hashing Fun Yet?

Let's start an example by defining the class that will be placed on the hash table (i.e., an example class that a user would want to put onto the table). The class will hold some trivial information about a person. With that, you must immediately define what the `hashCode` and `equals` methods will use as their criteria. To realize the example from above, the hash function will be based on the first letter of the person's name. Note that in serious situations, this hash function isn't stupendous for people's names. Above it was said that this function was okay for small sets of random words, and that's true. But not many names start with "Q" (except, of course, for the occasional "Quecilla"). So some hash slots will be relatively full and others relatively empty. For this low-performance example, it will suffice.

Next, the `equals` method can be defined. Again, for this example, no need to get overzealous checking mass amounts of similarity for a match; you will just check the first three letters of the name. The code for the to-be-hashed class is as follows:

```
/* info_about class */
class info_about {

/* personable info */
  String name;
  int age;
  int height;
  int weight;

/* constructor to set the name */
/*  we'll assume other stats get set elsewhere/later */
  public info_about(String S) { name = S; }

/* hashCode method returns the first character */
  public int hashCode() {
    return (int)name.charAt(0);
        }

/* equals methods checks for match on first three characters */
  public boolean equals(Object compare) {
    info_about temp = (info_about)compare;

/* check for first three letter match */
    for (int g=0;g<3;++g) {
```

```
      if (this.name.charAt(g) != temp.name.charAt(g))
            return false;
      }

/* all matched, return true */
  return true;
  }
}
```

The `hashCode` and `equals` methods of this class will be automatically called by the `Hashtable` class when needed. Now, you need another class to create the hash table and start putting in instances of `info_about`.

```
    /* hashing_fun class */
    class hashing_fun {

      static public void main(String args[]) {

    /* create the new hash table */
Hashtable theTable = new Hashtable();
info_about person[] = new info_about[6];

    /* this will be the tester object */
      info_about X = new info_about("Pat");

    /* populate some people */
person[0] = new info_about("Paul Tyma");
person[1] = new info_about("Gabriel Torok");
person[2] = new info_about("Billy Leach");
person[3] = new info_about("Patrick Doughty");
person[4] = new info_about("Troy Downing");
person[5] = new info_about("Yasha Dupa");

/* put the people on the hash table */
  for (int g=0;g<6;++g) {
          theTable.put(person[g],person[g]);
          }

    /* Find X */
      info_about A = (info_about)theTable.get(X);

if (A == null) System.out.println("A is null");
  else System.out.println(A.name);
  }
}
```

The output of running this class is "Patrick Doughty." This is because the **X** object has "Pat" as its name, and that is enough to match to "Patrick Doughty" within the hash table (i.e., same hash code and they satisfy equality). The **put** operation used above uses the same object for the key and the per se object to be hashed. In small examples, this is typical, but extra flexibility can be gained by using the nonkey object for additional, related objects. Figure 17-7 shows the conceptual state of the hash table after all the people are put on.

As you can see, the hash code is basically the decider for which slot an object will go into. Again, the criterion here was the first letter of the name. The `equals` method largely acted as a secondary search criterion for finding the exact name (up to the three characters) within the slot.

Duplicates and Other Details

Note that trouble comes down the pike when two objects are put into the same slot with the same `equals` value. Actually, the hash table class handles it with understanding and compassion; it just overwrites the old instance with the new. Two objects cannot return the same `equals` value in the same slot. You can and are wholeheartedly encouraged to have objects that return the same hash code value. This means slots will have more than one member. (If your hash table has only one member per slot, your hash function is a bit on the wimpy side.) As an alternative way of looking at things, the binary tree class discussed next treats duplicate key entries with much more fervor.

FIGURE 17-7

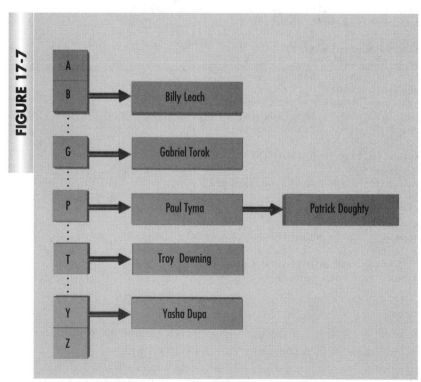

The hash table after modification

As with the `Vector` class, you can use the `Enumeration` interface to provide an organized way to traverse through a hash table. Thank goodness for this token gift of standardization among data structure classes. The code isn't listed here because of its blatant verbatimness to the `Vector`'s rendition.

The best kind of hash table is one with all of its slots full with approximately equal amounts. Well, as long as they're all not too full. In fact, a well-designed hash table needs a bit of experimentation to be sure it will suit your needs. A hash table with all elements in one slot is really just a linked list, and a hash table with only one element per slot is really just an array with a nasty indexing function (even a trivial hashing is usually significantly more complex than an array's normal index lookup). The goal of the hash table is to provide a happy medium between the two.

Binary Search Trees

The previous three data structures were implemented for you as part of Java's prebuilt packages. No muss, no fuss, all you had to do was import and use them. Here a class will be designed from the ground up, making an attempt to follow the conventions set by those prebuilt data structures. To see an implementation from the beginning should give you an insight into the features normally encapsulated (and hidden from you, the mischievous user) within these types of classes.

Early API releases didn't include a binary tree class. This is somewhat surprising, given the binary search tree's importance in computer science and computer programming in general. In any case, it will make for a fine, upstanding young example to see how such a class is built. Very much in the spirit of the prebuilt classes, this class will be based on objects at its nodes. However, given the typical implementation of a binary search, this model will use an additional integer key value (specified by the user of the class) to indicate placement within the tree. This implementation is a bit more mundane than the prebuilt hash tables' somewhat mystical keying method, but keys in binary trees typically carry some significance in and of themselves, whereas hash tables' keys are often just some signature of the actual data used for faster retrieval—i.e., the programmer doesn't always care what the actual hash table key is.

The Structure

Binary trees thoroughly permeate computer science algorithms. Well-balanced trees carry a *log n* worst case lookup time for applications such as searching, Huffman coding, and hidden surface removal. Each node in a binary tree can have zero, one, or two children and at most one parent (only the root has no parent). Figure 17-8 shows a binary search tree and the glory that happens in twos.

Any search for an element of the tree starts at the root. The key being searched for is compared to the root's key; if it's smaller, the search heads left, and if it's larger, the search heads right (if it's equal, the search is done and supreme victory is proclaimed).

For example, a search for the key of 6 will start at the root that has a key of 10. Since 6 is less than 10, the search will head left where it finds 5. Now, the search heads right (since 6 > 5). Following this algorithm, the search encounters 7 and finally finds 6. If it had run out of places to go, the search could have safely assumed that the key was not present on the tree (e.g., key 35 on the tree in Figure 17-8).

The class built here will use keys in the above manner, and in addition will allow the association of an object to each node. In other words, each node will have a simple integer key and an object that is just hitching along for the ride. As with the vector and hash table classes, users of the binary tree class will assumedly be interested in using the binary tree structure as an efficient method of storing objects. These objects of interest will be stored in each node next to the key.

To better abstract the implementation details from users of the class, two classes will be defined for a binary search tree. One is called **BinaryTreeEntry** to hold each node in the binary tree. The second will be called **BinaryTree** and will act as the header to the tree storing the current root node. The organization (once a tree has been built) can be seen in Figure 17-9.

The code for **BinaryTreeEntry** is the simpler of the two; it's really just a data repository for each node.

```
/* BinaryTreeEntry class */
class BinaryTreeEntry {

 Object  node = null;
 int key;
 BinaryTreeEntry  child[] = new BinaryTreeEntry[2]; BinaryTreeEntry  parent = null;

/* null constructor */
 public BinaryTreeEntry() {}
}
```

That was so painless it felt good. The first two instance variables are the **node** and **key**. The **node** is the object associated with this instance (as was said before, the user of this class's object). Notice that the **key** variable is implicitly private; this is super important. If the user of the class accidentally or maliciously changed a node's key value, the integrity of the entire tree would be in jeopardy. Binary trees with poor integrity are not just bad for the user, they're bad for mankind. One wrong key could throw off every search from now on. Only the class itself should be changing the internal key value, nobody else.

Next an array of children is defined. It is widely accepted that binary tree nodes have a left and right child. Furthermore, convention purports the left child has a smaller key and the right child has a larger key than the parent. There is no impending doom to anyone who describes this situation differently, as long as the setup is clear and consistent. In a blatant attempt to conform, this implementation doesn't deviate seriously from this trademark design except that it uses the child array at the code level for the left and right child. This array implementation allows for some sneakier code in specific methods.

The discussion below will sometimes equate `child[0]` to the left child and `child[1]` to the right child to help describe the action.

FIGURE 17-8

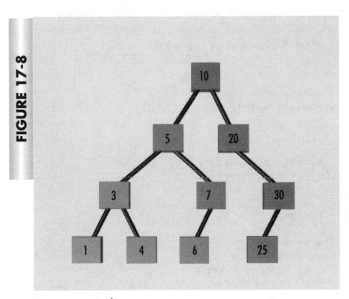

Binary search tree

FIGURE 17-9

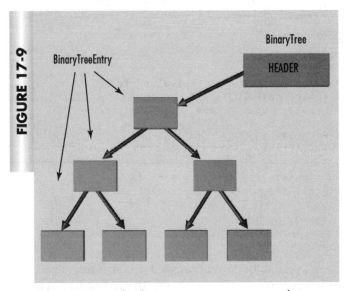

Binary tree with classes `BinaryTree` and `BinaryTreeEntry`

Making Methods

Given that all the meat hidden in this tree is defined within another object, which is pointed to by this class's `node` instance variable, no additional instance variables are needed. Here you are introduced to the relatively mandatory ability to add an element to the tree. This and all methods are in the header class `BinaryTree`.

```
/* BinaryTree Class */
public class BinaryTree {

BinaryTreeEntry root = new BinaryTreeEntry();

public BinaryTree() {}

/* method in Binary Tree class to add nodes */
public void addnode(int k,Object someobject) {

 boolean leftright = true;
 BinaryTreeEntry next,here=null;

/* Is this the first node to be added? */
 if (root.node == null) { root.node = someobject;
                          root.key = k;
                          return;
                          }

/* Traverse the tree according to the key until */
/* a null child is found */
 next = root;
 while (next != null) {
    here = next;
    leftright = (k > here.key);

/* remember the (leftright)?0:1 operation is equivalent to */
/* if (k > here.key) next = here.child[0];              */
/*                   else   next = here.child[1];   */

    next = here.child[(leftright)?0:1];
 }

/* Create the new node and populate its instance vars */
 next = here.child[(leftright)?0:1] = new BinaryTreeEntry();
 next.parent = here;
 next.key = k;
 next.node = someobject;
}
```

The `addnode` method takes the key and the object associated with it as parameters. First off, it checks to see if this is the first element added to this tree. This is done by checking the node of the `this` (implied) object, which is always the root of the tree. If the node is null for the root object, then the tree must be empty. If that's the case, some quick assignments are made and the method returns.

The tree is then traversed starting at the root. It is traversed according to the key (i.e., less than is left, greater than is right). This revelry continues until a null child is encountered, which indicates that this is the spot to place this key/object. To do this you create a new **BinaryTreeEntry** object and set its variables. Note that since a new **BinaryTreeEntry** object is actually instantiated for each node, this structure holds true to the property of binary trees that every subtree is a binary tree by itself; in other words, every node can be thought of as a root for a smaller binary tree.

What to Tree

Remember that the entire reason you are going through all this toil and trouble is to create an abstracted data structure that can be easily used by the most simple-minded user. Well, even simple-minded users probably want to actually put something on the tree— i.e., use the class for real work. So these users will likely come all geared up with the objects they want to tack onto the tree. To actually use the binary tree class you'll need to emulate some type of class that a user might put on the tree. Here's an effort:

```
/* simple_info Class */
class   simple_info {
  int keyval;
  String valname;

  public simple_info(int k,String v) {
          keyval = k;
          valname = v;
          }

/* Accessor methods */
  public void printmyval() {
          System.out.println(valname);
          }

  public int key() { return keyval; }
}
```

This is a relatively scantily clad class. It consists of an **int keyval** instance variable and a **String valname** instance variable and the methods to manipulate them. The **keyval** is there only to initially set the node's key in the binary tree. Once a node is created, **keyval** is copied over to the node's own private key variable. From then on, the node never allows its private key to change. In other words, after you create a node with **keyval** being set as the official key, you can then jump **keyval** through hoops or teach it the hula, but no matter what happens to it, it will have no effect on the now immutable private key of that node.

Using the new class above and the **addnode** method defined earlier, you can build a sample binary search tree. Assume you wish to put a list of students on a binary tree for quick future lookups. Let's reuse the list of people hashed earlier and add a unique student number to each.

Number	Name
29	Paul Tyma
11	Gabriel Torok
78	Billy Leach
77	Patrick Doughty
87	Troy Downing
23	Yasha Dupa

Let's construct a **main** method to instantiate the tree and populate it with these names.

```
/* students Class */
class students {

 static public void main(String args[]) {

  // create a tree, theTree is the root node
  BinaryTree theTree = new BinaryTree();

  // instantiate objects and add them to the tree
  simple_info aname = new simple_info(29,"Paul Tyma");
  theTree.addnode(aname.key(),aname);

  aname = new simple_info(11,"Gabriel Torok");
  theTree.addnode(aname.key(),aname);

   .
   .
   .
```

The above code creates a new binary tree curiously named **theTree**. This object will point to the root of the tree and is the only contact **main** will have with the tree. The **BinaryTree** class abstracts all other operations. Figure 17-10 shows the state of the tree after all names have been added. The root is key 29 because that was the first node added to the tree. All subsequent additions will take into account the state of the tree for their placement.

Adding an object to a binary tree can be a costly operation when compared to adding it to a simple array. After all, all sorts of enigmatic tree traversals have to take place just to find the correct spot to add on an object. However, the cost of lookups later makes up for this disadvantage. Binary search trees are most useful when there are relatively few modifications (additions and deletions) needed for the tree but there are many queries. Binary search trees quickly surpass a linear array search if the number of queries is significant.

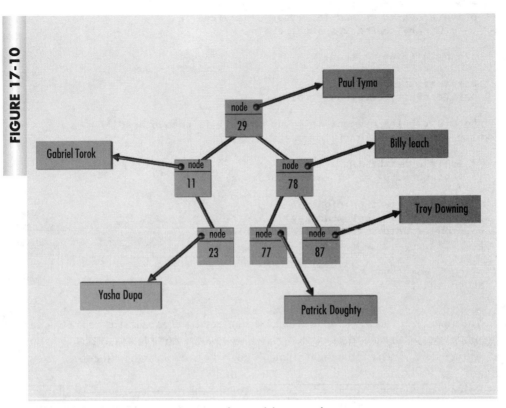

State of the binary search tree after adding nodes

Queries

So, binary trees are great at retrieving data. Unfortunately, this exposes a nasty hole in the current design, namely the lack of any query methods. Okay, no problem. This can be corrected with two methods, one public and one private. The private method will be called by the public method. The reason for this dual implementation isn't just to make things look sneaky; that's only part of it. The other reason is that internal methods (that will be implemented later) will make use of the specially tailored **private** method in order to perform their interesting deeds.

```
/* public search method for class BinaryTree */
public Object searchfor(int k) {

  /* Call the private method, return the Object (or null) */
  BinaryTreeEntry temp = searchtree(k);
  if (temp == null) return null;
  return temp.node;
}
```

continued on next page

continued from previous page

```
/* private search method for class BinaryTree */
private BinaryTreeEntry searchtree(int k) {

 boolean leftright = true;

/* Start at the root */
 BinaryTreeEntry columbus = this;

/* Loop until the element is found or null is encountered */
 while (columbus != null) {

   /* Is it a match? */
   if (columbus.key == k) return columbus;

   /* Decide on left or right */
   leftright = (k > columbus.key);
   columbus = columbus.child[(leftright)?0:1];
   }

/* Target not found */
 return null;
 }
```

The `searchfor` method packages the object for external class calls. The `searchtree` method is where all fate is decided. It declares a temporary variable `columbus` to point at the root. This variable is then sent sailing through the tree to search for the specific key. If it doesn't find it, the method woefully returns null.

On a balanced binary tree, queries using this routine will run in log *n* time—i.e., if there *n* numbers (for example, 512) then at most only log *n* of them will be searched to find the target (for the example, log base 2 of 512 = 9). Not too bad if you consider you could have to search through all *n* (again, all 512) for a linear search. This kind of performance increase is why computer scientists show such zeal for data structures. As with armor-piercing shells, antibiotics, and nine irons, they can do amazing things if used at the right time.

Deletion

The nastiest operation on a binary tree is removal of a node. It's not so much that the little buggers hate to go, it's more that their parent and children are pointing at them, and making them forget requires tact, assertiveness, and a bit of ingenuity. As you know only too well, the ordering of keys in a binary tree is critical. Removal of a node must be done carefully so as to retain the delicate balance already in place. Consider Figure 17-11, which displays three possible removal situations. All deletions are some form of one of these three.

The first one is relatively trivial; since there is only one child (or no children) of the node, the child can be promoted up one level. This applies whether the one child is on the left or on the right.

The second and third handle cases where the node to be deleted is actually the root of some semifull subtree. The prime requisite is that the node to be deleted have both a left

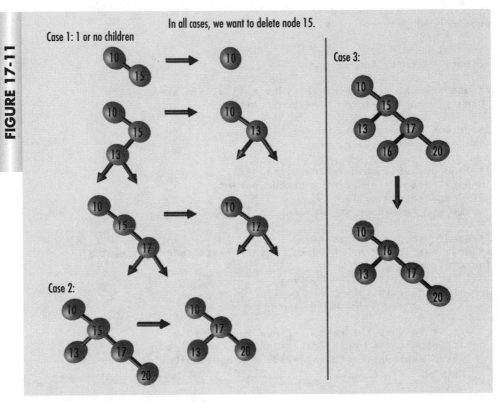

Three possible binary tree deletions

and right child (as node 15 does in the Figure 17-11 for case two and three). Distinguishing between case two and three depends upon the presence of grandchildren.

Case two shows the case where node 17 has no left children; with this information the entire right side can slide up with no danger. The rules of binary trees are guaranteed to still be intact (i.e., 17 is greater than 13 because it was greater than 15).

Case three gets nastier. Since 17 has both its children, you need to find the least node that is to the right of 15 to put in 15's place. Where is that node? Well, follow the first child (17) down its left path as far as you can go. In the figure that's just one hop to 16. So 16 is put in 15's place, again retaining the rules of binary trees (scary, but true).

To implement these cases, a `deleter` method will be defined. The `deleter` method takes special care to modify the root pointed to by the header class when necessary. This is vital, since if the root itself is deleted and the pointer not updated, the entire tree will be lost. The bad news is you will have lost all connection to your tree as it aimlessly floats into oblivion. The good news is the garbage collector knows its way around oblivion pretty well and is bound to find it. The bad news is again that when it does, it will just throw the whole thing away. The moral of the story: never lose your tree.

```
/* public deleter method */
public void deleter(int k) {

 int whichkid = 0;
 BinaryTreeEntry temp;

/* use searchtree to find the victim (i.e. the ex-node) */
 BinaryTreeEntry exnode = searchtree(k);

/* return if nothing to do */
 if (exnode == null) return;

/* find out which kid is the victim */
 BinaryTreeEntry exparent = exnode.parent;
 if (exparent != null)
  whichkid = (exnode == exparent.child[0])?0:1;

/* Handle the easy cases */
/* node has one or no children, attach child to grandparent */
for (int g=0;g<2;++g) {
  if (exnode.child[g] == null) {
    if (exnode.child[1-g] != null)
           exnode.child[1-g].parent = exparent;

   /* if this is the root, set new root */
   if (exparent == null) root = exnode.child[1-g];
    else exparent.child[whichkid] = exnode.child[1-g];
   return;
  }
 }
}
```

The above code handles finding the node to remove (the soon to be ex-node) and checks for the first case. This check is done with a `for` loop that checks for the presence of both children. If only one child exists, then it is promoted to the parent's position. If there is a case where no children exist, a null value is seemingly promoted—in other words, the code assumes that upon finding no first child, there will be a second. So the second is promoted to parent, but since there is no second, it is just a null value, and the promotion is meaningless. Again, C++ers should note that there is no explicit deletion of `exnode`. Just dereferencing it is enough for the garbage collector to come in and take it away.

If the first case is executed and the node to be deleted is the root, then the method returns the new root, which is either null or the root's only child. If the first case is not executed (i.e., the node to be deleted has two children) the following code handles cases two and three.

```
/* Find right child's leftmost child */
temp = exnode.child[1];
while (temp.child[0] != null)
  temp = temp.child[0];
```

```
/* If the right child had some left children remove it from */
/* its location and promote it to root (or subroot) */
 if (temp != exnode.child[1]) {
  deleter(temp.key);
  temp.child[1] = exnode.child[1];
  }

/* The following are involved in the upslide of case two */
/* and the promotion of case three */
 temp.child[0] = exnode.child[0];
 temp.parent   = exparent;

/* replace the root pointer, or the parent's child */
 if (exparent == null) root = temp;
else exparent.child[whichkid] = temp;
return;
}
```

Cases two and three are intertwined in the above code. This is a testament to the fact that case two is something of a special occurrence of case three—namely, when the right child has no left children. This causes more of an upslide of the right side of the subtree instead of a prune and graft, as in a case three. A good deal of extra checking was involved to handle manipulations of the root of the tree. Simple (but unusual) acts such as defining a tree, adding its root, then immediately deleting that root cause a cavalcade of null pointer exceptions if left unchecked. These types of annoying user tendencies (honestly, who defines a tree just to delete it) must be handled. Actually, such silly actions do not typically arise out of purposeful actions of half-wits; more often they happen because another layer of code has abstracted the use of your class, causing occasional aberrations. In any case, a well-designed class should be prepared to handle any eventuality.

No Duplicates

A last consideration in defining this class is the possibility of nodes with duplicate keys. Egad, that is quite a nasty proposition, as searches would never be sure which key was the right one. To insure no duplicates exist in this binary tree, you can throw an exception at any attempt to add a duplicate key. The exception can be defined as

```
class DuplicateKeyException extends java.lang.Exception {
     DuplicateKeyException(String s) {
     super(s);
     }
  }
```

This is a relatively standard way of defining a new exception. The constructor passes the message string onto the **super** class to let it do whatever voodoo it does with message strings. This definition assures a standard exception implementation. Obviously, if you are to throw this exception when a duplicate entry is attempted, the code to do so should be in the **addnode** method. While you're at it, also throw in a check for any malicious person who attempts to put a null object into the tree. The concept of putting a null object into the tree (with a valid key) could be a feasible idea for some applications, but it would be cleaner to enforce having instantiated objects only.

```java
/* method in Binary Tree class to add nodes */
public void addnode(int k,Object someobject) {

 boolean leftright = true;
 BinaryTree next,here=null;

/* Check for null object */
if (someobject == null)
  throw new NullPointerException();

/* Check for duplicate entries */
if (searchtree(k) != null)
  throw new DuplicateKeyException("Key Already Exists");

/* Is this the first node to be added? */
 if (node == null) { node = someobject;
                              key = k;
                              return;
                     }
 .
 .
 .
```

The code is added as the first thing in the method. It uses the `searchtree` method (note that it's not the `searchfor` method) to determine if it can find the element. If it finds it, the exception is thrown.

The Example

Let's continue the students' example to illustrate the additional functionality.

```java
/* class students */
class students {

 static public void main(String args[]) {

  /* create a tree, theTree is the root node */
  BinaryTree theTree = new BinaryTree();

  /* instantiate objects and add them to the tree */
  simple_info aname = new simple_info(29,"Paul Tyma");
  theTree.addnode(aname.key(),aname);

  aname = new simple_info(11,"Gabriel Torok");
  theTree.addnode(aname.key(),aname);

   .
   .
   .
```

```
/* try out the new stuff */
aname = (simple_info)theTree.searchfor(11);
if (aname == null) System.out.println("not found");
 else aname.printmyval();

theTree.deleter(77);
theTree.deleter(29);
}
```

The above **searchfor** would print "Gabriel Torok". Figure 17-12 shows the state of the tree after the above deletions.

This class should prove usable as a general purpose binary search tree implementation. There are undoubtedly many other ways to implement such a class to provide the desired functionality. An immediate thought is to define an interface **Bintreeable** to implement in classes you wish to put on the tree. The interface would guarantee a method that would return the key of that object (and nothing else).

There is also a plethora of additional methods that could provide more functionality to this class. Some would be a great deal of work, some are in the exercises at the end of the chapter, and some are both.

Linked Lists

A linked list is a dynamic structure that is used when you have no idea how many things you'll have to store. It has advantages over a statically defined array and displays a tad more grace than the vector implementation. What it lacks is an ability for random access (the

FIGURE 17-12

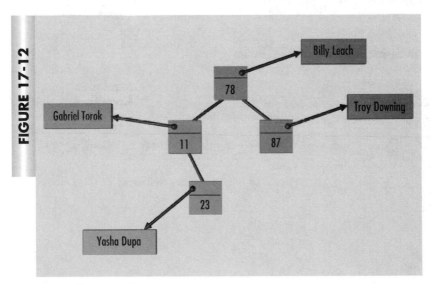

State of the student tree

ability to easily access some specific element). For example, if you wanted the fifth element in an array, you specify `array[4];` in a vector, you would specify `elementAt(5)`. A linked list would need to start at the beginning and traverse past the first four elements to get to the fifth. Figure 17-13 compares the three constructs.

The linked list's advantage stems from its ability to change easily. Assume your set of elements needs to expand; arrays just fail, and vectors need to execute the arduous task of reallocating an underlying array and copying all the current elements to it. A linked list just finds the end of the list and attaches a new element to it. Deletions and insertions are also nightmares for arrays and vectors but are short work for linked lists.

A linked list structure has commonality with the binary tree structure in that there are pointers to other elements of the same kind embedded within each object. With the goal of making this as generic and reusable as possible, a *double-linked* linked list class will be developed. In a double-linked linked list, each element points to its predecessor and its successor. Although this adds more overhead, it allows speedy list traversals in either direction. Figure 17-14 shows the addition of the links.

Setting Up the Class

As with the `BinaryTree` class, two classes will be defined to support a linked list: a `LinkedListEntry` class and a header class (which is what users of your class will use) called `LinkedList`. As you saw from `BinaryTree`, and you didn't see from `Hashtable`

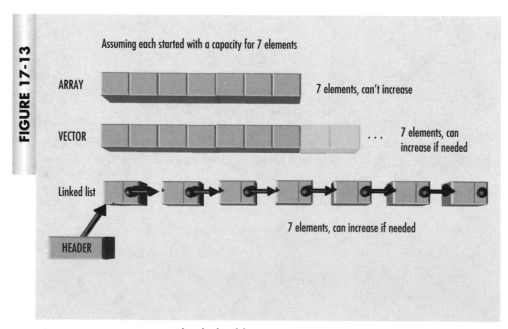

FIGURE 17-13

Assuming each started with a capacity for 7 elements

ARRAY   7 elements, can't increase

VECTOR   ...   7 elements, can increase if needed

Linked list   7 elements, can increase if needed

HEADER

An array, a vector, and a linked list

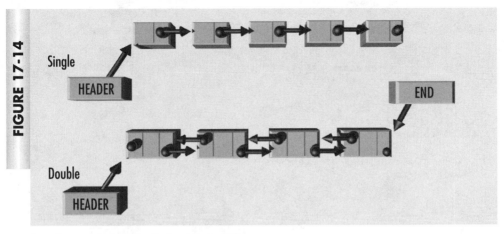

Single- and double-linked linked lists

(but it was really there), these two classes tend to be the standard for defining data structure classes with pointer lists.

The `linkedListEntry` class is the simplest and looks like this:

```
/* The linked-list entry class */
class linkedListEntry {

/* the object held in the list */
 Object  node = null;

/* The pointers to the next and previous links */
 linkedListEntry  next = null;
 linkedListEntry  prev = null;

 linkedListEntry(Object someobject) {
        node = someobject;
    }
}
```

As with the `BinaryTreeEntry` class, this class is mostly just a collection of data for each link. The node points to the object that the user is interested in placing on the linked list, and the `next` and `prev` values are the list connectors.

Appendages

The header class will contain the pointers to the beginning and the end of the list as well as to the methods that do the bulk of the work. You saw in `BinaryTree` that this is a header class because it is really just a front end to the tree, or in this case, the list. The `linkedListEntry` objects go sprawling aimlessly through memory, and you'll never know where they'll pop up next, but you don't care, because you know where the header is. The header always knows where the start of the list is—and if you know where the start of a linked list is, you can always find the rest. It's just a neat little property of linked lists that they tend to be good and linked.

```java
/* The linked-list header class */
public class linkedList {

/* pointers to tbe beginning and end */
linkedListEntry beginning = null;
linkedListEntry end = null;

/* keep track of number of elements */
int numelements;

public linkedList() {}

/* A method to append to the end of the linked-list */
public void append(Object someobject) {

/* Stop any funny business */
if (someobject == null)
        throw new NullPointerException();

/* Create the new entry and increment the total count */
linkedListEntry newelement = new linkedListEntry(someobject);
numelements++;

/* Is this the first element into an empty list? */
if (end == null) { end = newelement;
                beginning = newelement;
                        return;
                        }

/* Attach the new element to the end */
end.next = newelement;
newelement.prev = end;
end = newelement;
}
```

The **append** method is strictly for adding to the end of the list. This operation has proven to be one of the most popular for using linked lists, so giving it its own method allows you to include more specific optimizations. Besides the ever-present checking for null objects and adding an element to an empty list, just tacking another element on the list is the common case.

The operation attaches the new element as the **next** of the current **end** and reassigns the **end**. Overall, by the time it reaches the stage where pointers get madly reassigned, the object to be added already exists. In other words, when the object was created, there were no precautions about placing the object in a convenient spot in memory, as depicted in the pretty Figure 17-14. Fine, this doesn't matter too much, and forsooth, being able to link together massively disorganized bits of memory is what linked lists are all about! Figure

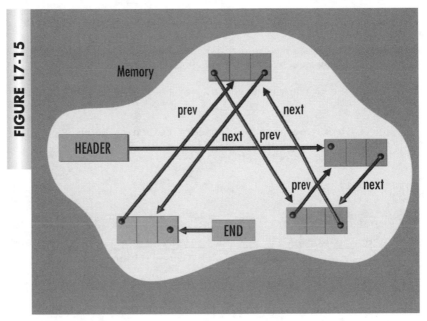

Still linked, but not as pretty

17-15 depicts a more true-to-life scenario for the double-linked linked list in Figure 17-14.

Memory allocation doesn't purposefully try to make things a mess, but it does try to reuse empty spots of memory. Often this results in your linked list bounding about the memory space when following its `next` pointer.

Private Searching

Now a private method `getref` will be defined, which searches for a node within the tree. A successful search returns a reference to the `LinkedListEntry` for that node. This method is private since the external class doesn't know about the `LinkedListEntry` class, and that's just fine—this purports good object-oriented encapsulation. As always, it's best to allow external classes to know as little about a class as possible; you can pretend that all external classes will be written by rude and careless people and are likely chock full of bugs and security improprieties. Design your classes so that they only trust themselves—remember this and you will grow strong.

The `getref` method is used by several other methods to find a reference to an object so it can insert before it, insert after it, or delete it.

```
/* A private method to find a node (object) on the list */
private LinkedListEntry getref(Object someobject) {
```

continued on next page

continued from previous page

```
/* empty list? */
if (beginning == null) return null;

/* Start at the beginning */
linkedListEntry columbus = beginning;

/* Search through until the end, return the reference if it's */
/* found */
do {
    if (columbus.node == someobject) return columbus;
    columbus = columbus.next;
    } while (columbus != null);

return null;
}
```

The loop starts at the beginning and searches through the links. If a match is found, then
columbus is returned. Otherwise, the loop will continue until **columbus** becomes null.
This happens when **columbus** falls off the end of the list…hmmm. There is also no reason the search could not have started at **end** and proceeded through **previous** links.

Insertion: Before and After

The following method **insertAfter** can perform the same functionality as the **append**
method above but with a bit more overhead. The overhead stems from the method's greater
flexibility and overall more studious attitude. It specifically comes from the need for the
method to call **getref** to find out what object the caller wants to use as the **after** object.
Remember, the caller sends in a reference to an object of the type that is to be plunked
on the list, *not* a **linkedListEntry** object. This class truly couldn't give a flying hoot
about what's in the caller's objects. It only cares about linked list stuff (so much more interesting, don't you agree?). Anyway, the method calls **getref** to, in effect, translate the caller's
object reference to a reference to the **linkedListEntry** where that caller's object resides.

```
/* A method to insert after a specified object */
public void insertAfter(Object afterobject,Object someobject) {

if ((someobject == null) || (afterobject == null))
        throw new NullPointerException();

/* Find the node (object) the caller is referring to */
linkedListEntry afterentry = getref(afterobject);

/* If that object isn't on the list throw an exception */
if (afterentry == null)
        throw new NullPointerException();

/* All checks pass, get ready to insert the entry */
numelements++;
linkedListEntry newelement = new linkedListEntry(someobject);
```

```
/* Update links */
newelement.next = afterentry.next;
newelement.prev = afterentry;

/* special care for the 'end' */
if (afterentry == end) end = newelement;
else afterentry.next.prev = newelement;

afterentry.next = newelement;
}
```

The beginning of the method goes through to find the entry and check to make sure everything is okay (nothing is null). The magic happens in adding the links. Figure 17-16 shows the new connections. Reorganizing these connections can be more complex than making a plane reservation. You must be careful about setting your pointers exactly; even a minor mistake and you could see more wrongful pointing than you do at a congressional hearing.

For completeness, the class also includes an `insertBefore` method, which works conversely to the `insertAfter`. Of course, `insertBefore` must take special care when inserting before the `beginning` of the list.

```
/* A method to insert before a specified object */
public void insertBefore(Object beforobject,Object someobject){

if ((someobject == null) || (beforobject == null))
         throw new NullPointerException();

linkedListEntry beforeentry = getref(beforobject);

if (beforeentry == null)
         throw new NullPointerException();

/* All checks pass, get ready to insert the entry */
numelements++;
linkedListEntry newelement = new linkedListEntry(someobject);

/* Update links */
newelement.next = beforeentry;
newelement.prev = beforeentry.prev;

if (beforeentry == beginning) beginning = newelement;
else beforeentry.prev.next = newelement;

beforeentry.prev = newelement;
}
```

Deletion

The final list-modifying operation to implement is deletion. Deletion is as conceptually simple as rerouting the pointers around the to-be-deleted object and letting the garbage

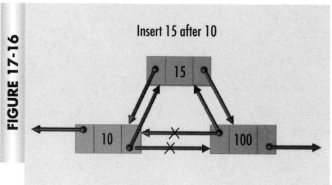

FIGURE 17-16

Insert 15 after 10

`insertAfter`

collector clean up the orphaned object. Of course, "conceptually simple" is never quite "practically simple." The only real nuisance turns out to be handling the deletion of the `beginning` or `end` objects.

```
/* A method to delete a specified object */
public void delete(Object someobject) {

if (someobject == null)
        throw new NullPointerException();

linkedListEntry delentry = getref(someobject);

if (delentry == null)
        throw new NullPointerException();

/* decrement the number of elements, no turning back now */
numelements--;

/* point the element behind to the one ahead of me */
/* as long as I'm not at the beginning */
if (delentry != beginning) delentry.prev.next = delentry.next;
else beginning = delentry.next;

/* point the element ahead of me as long as I'm not */
/* at the end */
if (delentry != end) delentry.next.prev = delentry.prev;
else end = delentry.prev;
}
```

There really isn't any voodoo here. As usual, apart from checking for the odd case, this is just pointer juggling. The object to be removed has the previous object point to its next, and its next object point to its previous. It just removes itself from the chain. Then, as does death with its scythe, the garbage collector with its list of orphaned objects will come and toast the object completely.

Accessors

Several other methods are required to make a complete linked list class. Most notable are methods for finding the **next** object, **previous** object, testing for object existence on the list, and even returning the number of objects on the list. These are implemented as trivial accessor methods and are left as exercises for the reader.

Wanton Desires of Enumeration

To continue an attempt at following convention, accessibility of this (and all standard) data structures should be available through the **Enumeration** interface. You've seen the **Enumeration** interface previously for Java's built-in data structures; now you'll see how it's implemented for your home-grown linked list. This isn't some divine data structuring law; it's just that the creators of the APIs included this interface for this purpose and within all their prebuilt structures. It sure would be neighborly of you (and a solid step toward standardization) to include this where applicable.

To provide this feature, you must create a new class that implements the interface. The header class needs an **elements** method (the seemingly unofficial standard) that returns an **Enumeration** interface for this class.

```
import java.lang.Enumeration;

public synchronized Enumeration elements() {
        return new linkedListEnumerator(this);
        }
```

All this does is instantiate the class (which is defined below) with a reference to the current object as a parameter. This method allows users of the class to follow the standard usage of the **Enumeration** interface to step through the elements of the data structure. The linked list structure is quite amicable to discrete, sequential access, and this shows itself in the simplicity of the **linkedListEnumerator** class.

```
/* A class to enumerate through a linked-list */
/*  This should only be used by the 'elements' method of the */
/*  linked-list class. */
class linkedListEnumerator implements Enumeration {

linkedListEntry position;

/* Constructor, start at the beginning */
linkedListEnumerator(linkedList L) {
        position = L.beginning;
        }

/* Return true if there's more to go */
public boolean hasMoreElements() {
        return (position != null ) ? true : false;
        }
```

continued on next page

continued from previous page

```
/* Position for next time and return current node */
public Object nextElement() {
        if (position == null)
           throw new NoSuchElementException();
        linkedListEntry retpos = position;
        position = position.next;

        return retpos.node;
        }
}
```

The code to take advantage of the enumeration is basically identical to the description in the **Vector** section above; in fact, loops to utilize the enumeration of any data structure should all be the same. A loop governed by the **hasMoreElements** method repeatedly returns **nextElement**. That fact is the obvious strength of using the **Enumeration** interface. Any user of a data structure should always be able to count on using that loop to step through a data structure. This trails back to the wonderful world of interfaces; if users know nothing else about a data structure class, they should know how to step through the elements of a data structure class.

Linked Lists and Vectors

The linked list class closely resembles Java's **Vector** class, and rightly so. In effect, they perform the same functionality. The real difference is their underlying implementation. The vector is a growable array, and the linked list is a truly dynamically allocated structure. Both are capable of holding a set of objects (in sequential order) that can increase in number without significant worry on the part of the class user.

Their real difference stems from what they each are good at. Vectors are better at indexing specifically numbered elements—e.g., the fifth or the twentieth element. However, vectors provide poorer performance when forced to insert an element or increase their capacity. Overall, if your data is more of the type that is static in the structure but your program requires many queries to it, the **Vector** class is better. On the other hand, if your data changes a lot, with many insertions, deletions, and expansions, a linked list is likely more suitable. In the end, both classes provide enough abstraction to hide how things work and provide you the functionality you need. It's kind of like whether you should shoot an M16 or a Howitzer; it really depends upon your target. If performance (or resulting destruction) is not the greatest concern, the choice is less definitive.

 Summary

Well, computer science types should be just basking in their glory by now. This chapter covered several of the heavily used data structures in common programming. Don't think that's it; there are plenty of other data structures that could be implemented into their own classes, and Java's object-oriented organization encapsulates them with buckets of grace and elegance. The binary tree and linked list classes are two examples of building data structure classes from the ground up. These two classes can provide general utility in a staggering number of different situations. The entire idea of the abstraction of this functionality, with the precarious details safely stowed in the class definition, is the hallmark of encapsulation and hopefully reusability.

Classic data structures are fertile ground for developing useful classes right away. The details of worrying about what amazing things a user could throw at you just adds spice to the challenge. Such generic classes usually include several great spots for flinging exceptions back at mischievous users.

Questions

1. Which would be best for the following types of data? An array, vector, or linked list?

    a. 100 integers to be sorted

    b. Input of the lines of a text file

    c. The elements of a slot in a hash table

    d. Elements input from a user that you want to sort inside the structure as they are input

2. You know that the enumeration of a data structure starts at the beginning and then sequentially steps through the elements. An interesting idea is that you receive program control after each object is fetched by the **Enumeration** interface's methods. What danger is there that you might manipulate the structure at this time?

3. Could you stack a set of stacks?

4. If you knew you had 1,000 objects to work with, what criteria would you use to decide whether to store them in an array, vector, hash table, or binary tree?

5. What else could the binary tree class have done (besides throwing an exception) when a user attempted to add a duplicate entry?

6. In the binary tree class (or in the linked list class for that matter), a header class was used to indicate the start of the tree. Couldn't you have just defined a static variable **root** inside the **BinaryTreeEntry** class specifying which entry was the root? Why does this implementation limit the usage of the class?

7. If Java had some type of name aliasing, could you fool unwary class users by calling the **Vector** class a **LinkedList** class? Could anyone tell the difference (short of peeking at the code)?

# Exercises

1. Binary trees lose their performance edge when unbalanced. For example, the tree on the left is poorly designed and would be better off if structured as the one on the right.

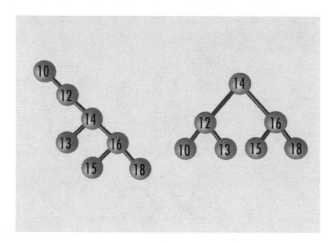

   Create a method that will balance a binary tree.

2. Add a class to utilize the `Enumeration` interface within the binary tree class. It may be easiest to allocate a vector in the elements method and recurse through the tree storing the elements in the vector. From then on, `nextElement` can pilfer the vector's enumeration implementation.

3. Add the methods

   ```
   Object next(Object someobject)
   Object previous(Object someobject)
   ```

   to the linked list class. These methods are really just accessor methods to follow the private links.

4. Design your own `Stack` class specially built for integers (not objects) only.

5. Add the methods

   ```
   Object parent(Object someobject)
   Object leftchild(Object someobject)
   Object rightchild(Object someobject)
   Object successor(Object someobject)
   Object predecessor(Object someobject)
   ```

to the binary tree class. The first three are accessor methods for the objects. The `successor` method should find the node in the tree with the next higher key than the input object, regardless of its position. The `predecessor` should do the converse.

The Future

You will learn about the following in this chapter:

- What Java's potential is
- What tools you can expect in the future for Java development
- Advanced object-oriented programming ideas
- How Java fits into the distributed computing paradigm
- Where you should go from here

What a ride that was. If you read all the previous chapters you should have a solid foundation for programming in Java. As you are now painfully aware, Java has a vast amount of information associated with it. The good news is that you have seen a whole lot of it, including the heart of what Java is all about. The better news is: there's more.

If you think about it, learning Java is definitely a tall order. It combines solid object-oriented programming techniques with internetworking, multithreading, and all kinds of other amazing things. This chapter does not tell you that you've learned everything there is to know about Java. It is more of a guide to tell you where you should go from here. Java is going to move quickly into mainstream computing, and since you have decided to come along for the ride, it might be nice to know the destination.

The Potential

Java's potential is staggering. It is relatively equivalent to C++'s potential when it made its debut. Java is everything C++ is, but it's much better prepared for the distributed computing world of today. In other words, C++ came out to address the computing concerns of the '80s, and Java is here for the '90s and beyond (yeah, it's a bit late). The computing world is a much different place than it was ten years ago, and the demands are much higher. Java was designed to fit the bill.

Don't Get Hung Up on Applets

Here is a little secret. Java is a full-fledged programming language that can do anything C, C++, or Pascal can do. Okay, anyone who has been one notch above sound asleep while reading the previous chapters should have figured that out already.

There is also no question that applets for the World Wide Web are cool, impressive, sexy, and generally nifty. In fact, you can count on seeing applets for as long as the Web is around (which should be a good while, until the next amazing thing comes along). But never forget Java's ability for general programming. Just as Java is the only language for applets, it is better suited for certain applications than many other languages. Sure, you can write a 3D action game in COBOL (shudder), or write a monthly revenue report in C++. Be our guest. But usually languages are suited for general realms of applications, and it's a good bet that 3D action games don't fit into COBOL's realm at all (phew).

Where is Java's realm? Well, to be fair, it should be said that COBOL definitely spits out field delimited reports probably better than any other general purpose language. Java is a bit more in ranks with C and C++. In fact, it should work right up there with those big guys for any suitable application. However, if you find your application requires architecture independence, multithreading, or internetworking—convince the boss to go Java.

What Can't Java Do?

Er, nothing. Well, it can't drive a car. Oh, wait, given the right hardware and a bit of ingenuity—yes it can. Well, it can't skeet shoot. Oops. Wrong again. Ahh, because of its secure design, it can't corrupt system memory! So! If you need a program that corrupts system memory, the C language is a better choice.

Actually, the biggest reason not to use Java instead of C or C++ is because of retraining people or rewriting code. There is no question that learning Java will take some notable amount of time (at least the amount of time to read this book). That is assumedly valuable company time. Also, piles of C and C++ code already exist. Systems currently written in those languages might not be inclined to be redone just for the sake of supporting a new language. These reasons are valid and can't be overlooked. However, for future projects, what should be considered is the advantages Java provides.

Things to Count On

As Java's popularity grows, so will tools and applications developed with and for Java. When Java was first released, no one argued that you didn't have enough tools to get started programming in Java, but that was about it. No bells, no whistles, and certainly nothing with a GUI (graphical user interface).

Programming Environments

Technology has spoiled us. From airplanes to televisions, amazing things of the past are now commonplace. Of course, programming has kept up with the times. Java's initial implementation was a bare-bones compiler. Use the editor of your choice to make your text file Java code and go back to the command prompt for the compile. For many programmers this brought back fond memories of the old days of programming. It was even fun to go back to this rudimentary way of roughing it through your code—it was fun, that is, for about eight minutes. After that, all the reasons for modern programming environments began to shine plainly through.

It won't be long before there are scads of choices as to the programming environments available for Java. The C and C++ languages already enjoy this level of pretty programming. Multicolored text, graphical interfaces, etc., are all available for C/C++ and will soon be for Java. Beyond the beauty comes a lot of functionality, including one-keypress compiling and no-guessing error location. In Java's case, you will also see the ability to test applets inside your programming environment. Expect a wide choice of Java-integrated environments/compilers available in the future.

Debuggers

Integrated with the interactive programming environments described above will hopefully be a good set of debugging tools. In fact, Java's design is so nicely complete that its initial release without debugging facilities was painfully noticeable. Again, mostly because the world had been spoiled by the excellent debuggers available for most other languages. But never fear, with Java's success will come companies ready to supply you with new and better tools. Pretty-boy debuggers should be close to the front of the line.

Applications

As much as solid development tools are necessary to lure programmers to a language, so is solid industry application development to forming full market acceptance for that language. Unfortunately, many great languages have died because they had no way to pierce through the armor shell of industry, which resists having to retrain its professionals to use a new language. Fortunately, Java has a gimmick. Of course, that gimmick is its marriage to the Web. Programmers for fun and business will be dabbling into programming applets. This will keep Java fresh in people's minds and will snowball its exposure.

The whole plan is to get Java into mainstream application development. This seems to be just a matter of time, and with a name like Java, you can expect a vast pool of product names playing off it. Products with names like Creamer, Half-and-Half, Sugar, Stirrer, etc., are bound to pop up and annoy consumers.

Objects Come Alive

The object-oriented concepts introduced here are only the foundation. The entire ideal behind object-oriented programming is to increase the level of abstraction until programming is seemingly this thing you do while sitting in a yoga position pondering the meaning of it all. What does this mean to you? Mainly that you have a lot of books to read.

The freshness and purity of Java make it the perfect starting place for so many good ideas to come to life. Your curiosity should now lead you to read some texts on advanced object-oriented techniques. Some of these have been brushed on in this book, but there are many that have not been.

Divine Reuse

When the C++ prophets started preaching this language back in the '80s, their sermon was *reuse*. This is, of course, the ability to reuse code you've written before, thus saving countless people-hours reinventing wheels. The unbelievers argued loudly and claimed that code in any language can already be reused. The C++ prophets made flailing hand gestures in disagreement and professed that their language had *encapsulation,* and that made reuse a reality. In other words, their enigmatic classes of things encapsulated all the functionality inside. This made for an entity that could be interfaced from anywhere and it would always act the same. Moreover, since it was an entity on its own, to reuse it was as simple as picking it up from one program and placing it in another. Reuse of non-object-oriented programs usually required a bit of code from here and there and inevitably some changes.

Well, the story continues. The unbelievers couldn't rebut this argument much. It seemed too concrete and their woe ran deep. Many of them converted just to see this reuse in action. Others regressed into denial, purporting the wonderfulness of their procedural and less-than-procedural languages, and continued to develop and enhance them regardless of the so-called superiority of object-orientation (hence the amazing survival of BASIC).

As the masses created their stack and hash table classes and reused them, they saw that this was good and they rejoiced heartily. In fact, they found themselves using their stack and hash table classes in situations where they really weren't needed, but the lure of reuse was too great; they started to need to reuse. Unfortunately, rebels began to rattle the equilibrium. The rebels were those among them that realized that the only classes that were being reused were stacks and hash tables. Wasn't this grand scheme of reuse supposed to work for more classes?

The elders had a meeting. It was true. Reuse had seemingly been overrated. What the elders decided was that the people were not using C++ as a means for reuse but were just sitting back hoping C++ would somehow magically make all code reusable. The problem was, the classes were not designed with reuse in mind. The elders devised a plan. They wrote papers. Gave talks. Preached on mountain tops. All to no avail; reuse needed to come from the heart, the people needed to build it into their design, but the people were distraught with the difficulty of C++.

Enter Java. Java was purely object-oriented, and moreover, for those coming from the occluded hills of C++, it was easy to learn. It seemed to have the ingredients for good reuse. But even though the tools had been improved, reuse still needed to be in the design. Relatively generic classes were to attempt to be as reusable as possible by adhering to the following guidelines:

- Put in checks for all possible errors; assume the most malicious user in the world is bent upon sending your class evil incarnate. Never should your class crash because of unexpected input or actions on the part of the user.

- Keep things at the object level. Just as in the cases of the stack and hash table, if you allow your structures to manipulate objects (you can force the user to cast them) then future, yet-to-be-created objects can be ruthlessly shoved into your class—i.e., your class is ready to be reused for wild and unknown purposes.

- Design standard interfaces that will help users reuse other related classes. A simple example would be to always have your graphical objects use a d r a w method to draw themselves. It will give the user an immediate sense of familiarity to classes they've never seen or have forgotten about.

Things look good in the land of reuse. They have a new language and the masses are happily converting over. Hopefully, with their new code in hand, their designs will be unimaginably reusable.

Advanced Object Manipulations

If you are serious about taking full advantage of the abstraction object-oriented programming offers you, you still have a lot of work to do. Many excellent texts in this field exist and provide information on utilizing object-orientation to its fullest. Many of these advanced techniques help enhance object-oriented programming's already sound structure. Some of the shiny new concepts deal with

- Remote objects—Objects here, objects there, objects everywhere! Remote objects allow for your code on one machine to seamlessly access objects across a network. The whole operation is transparent to the running code.

- Object composition—Many schools of thought are swaying away from class inheritance and moving to object composition. Java's ticket to this methodology is its interfaces. Composition relies heavily on knowing how to interface to everybody. If every given type of object had the same method of interfacing, wouldn't the world be a wonderful place?

- Design patterns—This topic is so hot, you better break out a cold one. A basic view of design patterns is a study of higher level organizations of class designs. This doesn't deal so much with how specific classes are put together as it does with going one level higher to look at the problem itself and decide how classes and their interactions should be designed to facilitate a solution.

Don't be too intimidated by these advanced techniques; if your coding is straightforward and your projects stay small, you can get along without their benefits for a while. Of course, that is what theorists told programmers a few years ago about object-oriented programming. It would seem the only difference between theorists and practitioners is about five years.

Where Is Java Headed?

Considering you are at this point in this text, you probably don't need to be convinced that Java was, is, and will be a good idea. But, as with any good idea, expect competition. It is quite safe to say that browsing the World Wide Web will be an interactive experience from here on out. No more will Web pages be static little bits of lifeless data. The interaction will come from a collection of different Web enhancements, only one of which happens to be Java. Will Java survive this onslaught of competing technologies? All indications seem to say yes.

Just Thinking of the Web

Several types of technology exist that provide extra utility to your Web experience. Some of these, such as the Virtual Reality Modeling Language and inevitable enhanced versions of HTML, are not in direct competition with Java. These types of Web enhancements are designed with specific purposes in mind. They are good at what they do but cannot compete with such a general purpose solution as Java.

It should be noted, though, that in the realm of general purpose languages for Web enhancement, Java already has competition. Kaleida Labs' Scriptx language is at least in the same ballpark. It is only a matter of time before many more such competitors surface. Look back at Java for a minute and you should see why it should prevail. Its design was well thought out and satisfyingly complete. Just to catch up, new languages would need to provide the security, architecture independence, and multithreading capabilities Java has now. You've been told these were good ideas; you weren't told they were easy to put together.

Another important factor in favor of Java is its significant industry backing. Java was created by Sun Microsystems, and Sun is not exactly a fly-by-night outfit. Other major Internet players immediately embraced the Java language, including the World Wide Web's early standard-setter, Netscape Communications Corporation. Products and languages often become popular and stay popular just because they came out first and provided functionality never seen before. Usually, once they are the standard, they hold that spot even if something noticeably better comes along. In the case of Java, it is quickly setting the standard, and as far as something noticeably better coming along—good luck.

Never Forget Standalone

Most of the early Java-ites strongly profess Java's Web abilities as insignificant compared to its prowess as a viable programming language for normal applications and system programming. It does not take a lot of research to begin to share their views. The Web is a great place to start, but it is really just the springboard for the great Java vs. C++ fight of the twenty-first century.

In many ways, Java outsteps C++. It is easier to learn and has more potent functionality built in. On top of that, consider an organization that wants to create a new financial application, a new distributed games server, and enhanced Web pages. Their first thoughts (by habit) may be C++ for the first two and Java for the latter. Java is the choice for the latter since that application is beyond the capabilities of C++. Taking the thought process one step further, why train programmers in both C++ and Java, since Java can also do the above tasks? Using Java for all three tasks saves training time and money and increases the chances of being able to reuse code among the tasks. In general, Java is the way to go, but keep in mind that at least for the short run, Java is primarily interpreted and won't be able to compete with C++ for performance. With time, Java's performance will improve (especially with the advent of just-in-time compilers) and will make Java the logical choice for many applications.

In addition to this, go back to the WWW for a moment. Who is active in making their own Web pages today? Or, what group of people quickly become HTML experts? Although the answer could be broad, it would be hard to argue that university students don't definitely qualify as the answer for both questions. This is not because of some mass educational effort on the part of colleges to teach the Web. The Web is fun, and college students are learning for themselves. The logical conclusion is that as the Web shifts to Java, more and more students will be learning it as a by-product of their education. Prospective employers can begin recruiting Java programmers right out of school. This argument is not to somehow say students will know Java and won't know C++. Of course, schools will teach C++ for a long time. But it does say that finding knowledgeable Java programmers will become less and less of a significant problem.

Distributed Computing and Beyond

As the age of computing progressed, some really smart people had some really smart ideas (actually that had been going on for a while). They realized that if a computer with one CPU was fast, wouldn't a computer with two be twice as fast? Or how about a hundred? Or a thousand? Well, enter the age of parallel computers.

A bunch of other smart people who knew more about networking than hooking up CPUs thought, if one PC was fast, wouldn't two communicating over a network and sharing the work be twice as fast? These were the distributed computing folks. These two groups realized they were at least in principle competing with each other, so they made snide comments about each other and generally boasted about why their way was better. The parallel folks built single computers with many CPUs. The distributed folks connected every machine they could find onto a network and designed software to know how to distribute the work.

Digging Trenches

As time went on, both groups realized something. They had both relied on the fact that if one element (CPU or workstation) was a certain speed, working in unison with many other elements should correspondingly multiply that speed. In other words, if one element could do a task in 100 seconds, couldn't 100 elements do it in 1 second? It was right about here they had a bad break. It seems this logic runs along the lines of if one man can dig a hole in 60 seconds, can 60 men dig it in 1 second? Things don't exactly pan out. The unbelievable speed gains were not quite so unbelievable.

So, since this problem affected the parallel folks and the distributed folks, they all had a meeting. What they came up with were a few ways to still get their speed up. Maybe not a one-for-one speedup, but something to justify all their time and effort. Since these were really smart people, they realized that maybe 60 men digging a hole was a bad idea, but maybe 3 could do it and still get a good speedup. Then, what of cases where the men were out to dig a trench? The 60 men could stand next to each other and they could actually get their full speed up then. So the story goes that some problems just weren't nicely suited for parallel or distributed computing (hole digging problems). But that was okay, some were (trench digging problems). Everybody decided to focus on trenches, not holes, and left the meeting.

Nice Cars with Air Conditioning

Work went on. The whole of the university community was out digging trenches. After some time, everybody realized that they should try to sell their ideas to industry. Mainly because industry is where the money is, and if industry buys your ideas, you become famous and usually get a nice car with air conditioning. So, both the parallel folks and the distributed folks went to pitch their ideas to industry.

Industry listened. Industry liked. Everybody explained that mainly they were out to solve the trench-digging problems of the world, not the hole-digging ones. Industry understood and had many trench-digging problems they needed solved. Finally, after all the salesmanship and trench presentations were done, industry asked the pending question, "How much?" The parallel folks explained their new super parallel computer would only cost a few million. With a broad and knowing smile, the distributed folks explained that the industry would need no new computers. Industry already owned hundreds of workstations connected to networks. The hardware was all there. Well, guess which way industry went.

Making Distributed Computing Work

So the distributed folks were sitting pretty. They worked furiously on their ideas, making distributed things a reality. Unfortunately, they found no tools for their task. This was no surprise; no one had ever done all this before. So they made their own tools, mostly in C or C++. Things began to really fly. The ideas caught on, the distributed folks all got famous and got cars with air conditioning. In fact, so many people implemented so many different distributed computing ideas that standardization was nowhere to be found. Another problem was that implementing such a system was not easy.

Java's design has distributed computing in mind. Developing distributed applications has never been easier or more straightforward. For a plainly simple example, a server can exist somewhere that divides a (trench) problem into many different pieces. Computers over the network come in via straight Internet or WWW and offer their services to help solve the problem. The server assigns a reasonable-sized portion of the problem to the incoming system. Once it has the result, it sends it back and the server issues more work. This is a simple setup, but it could work. Java's design of architecture independence, security, and networking facilities make it a perfect target for the distributed folks to come in and finally design some standard ways to compute distributedly.

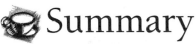

Summary

Please do not exit until the ride has come to a complete stop. You should see how important Java will be in the near future. Your knowledge of Java and its idiosyncrasies is a solid line on your resume. The industry is already embracing Java, and the trend seems to only be increasing. The rest of the book is devoted to providing a reference for Java's API libraries. That is no small feat, considering the scope of what Java provides. You will find yourself referring to the Appendix again and again as you trek into deeper and more complex Java waters.

After conquering this book, you have seen the main pieces of Java and how they come together. Hopefully, you have already been out developing mind-boggling applets and applications. Keep going. Java's flexibility and power are sure to open many new doors for ambitious coders. Just when you think all the cool stuff in the world has already been thought of, developed, or discovered—think again.

Appendix: Java™ APIs

This appendix covers some of the methods used to access the Java APIs (Applications Program Interfaces). Many actions that a Java program may perform are accomplished by invoking an API method. Drawing graphics objects, outputting files, creating sockets, playing audio—all of these and more are handled by the APIs and are included in Java's prebuilt packages. If you have previously programmed with Microsoft Windows, none of this should come as a surprise.

In Microsoft Windows these API procedures are located in files called DLLs (Dynamic Link Libraries). However, in Java, all APIs are implemented as classes and interfaces that are contained in packages. This appendix will cover the Java packages, because they contain the fundamental classes that all Java interpreters will understand.

Overview of Java Packages

The Java packages give the programmer a set of fundamental routines frequently required in everyday programming. They currently consist of eight names: `applet`, `awt`, `awt.image`, `awt.peer`, `io`, `lang`, `net`, and `util`. The `applet` package is used to bring your Web pages alive with animation and sound. The `awt` (abstract windows toolkit) package provides functionality similar to some of the Microsoft Windows APIs. It contains graphical user interface tools such as buttons, frames, scroll bars, etc. The `awt.image` package contains classes to filter and crop images. The `awt.peer` package is one you will not need to deal with directly; it contains the native implementation classes of the `awt` components. The `io` (input/output) package gives easy file and printer access. The `lang` package provides operations on primitive data types and strings, as well as math functions, thread creation, etc. The `net` package provides a means to easily connect networked computers together. The `util` package offers various utilities such as hash tables, stacks, and vectors.

First, a class inheritance diagram for each package will be shown. These class diagrams are very useful for understanding the relationships among classes. Remember that a subclass contains all the methods in its class as well as the methods of its superclasses. Also, because the `Object` class is the parent of all Java classes, every class can access or override its methods.

Next, a more detailed listing of the classes within each package, except `peer`, is shown. `Awt.peer` was omitted because you will not need to deal with it directly. When you create an instance of an `awt` component such as a `Button`, a `peer` component is also created for it. On a Microsoft Windows platform, this is a `WindowsButtonPeer`, and on X-Windows a `MotifButtonPeer`. In other words, it is not necessary to know which system you are running on (as long as Java runs on it); you are simply creating and using a `Button`. Lastly, a listing of the errors and exceptions within the Java classes is provided.

Conventions

The following format is used in this appendix. The use of brackets ([]) denotes contents that are optional. The classes are listed alphabetically within their package, except for some supplemental classes listed separately at the end of the `awt.image`, `io`, and `lang` packages. Interfaces within the package are listed first and designated by (Interface) following the name.

java.package.classname

Description	Brief description about this class or interface. Keywords such as **abstract** will be bolded.
Parent Class	This class's parent class.
[See Also]	A list of other relevant classes or methods.
[Implements]	Any interfaces this class implements.

CONSTRUCTORS

Constructor(type param1 [, type param2] …)

> This lists all constructors of this class and their descriptions. Remember that parameters in brackets are optional. In other words, foo(int color [, int size]) means you can use either foo(int color) or foo(int color, int size).

VARIABLES

variable name

> [final | protected | static…] type:
>
> This lists public and protected variables in this class and their descriptions. All variables are assumed public unless they are marked protected.

METHODS

method name

> [abstract | final | static | synchronized…] type method name(type param1)
>
> This lists the available methods in this class and their descriptions. Note that methods inherited from a superclass that are not specifically overridden are omitted. Methods may be marked abstract, final, static, or synchronized. As with constructors, parameters in brackets are optional.

Class Diagram Conventions

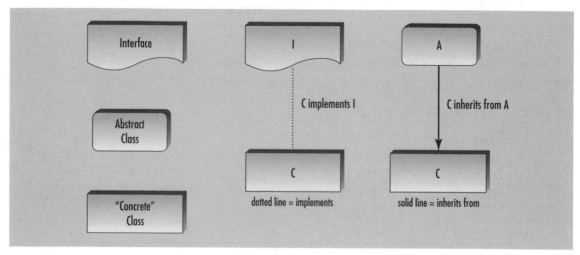

Java Packages Class Diagrams

applet

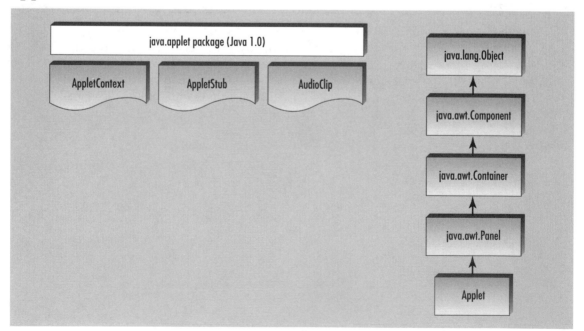

awt

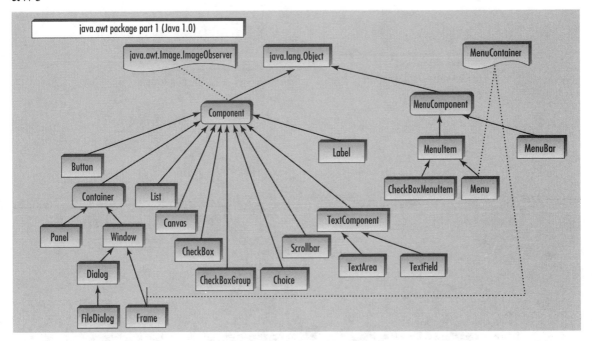

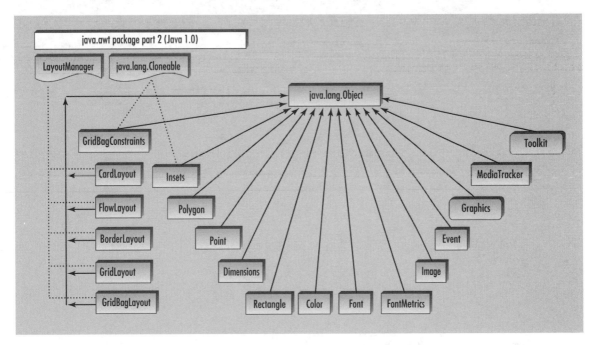

awt.image

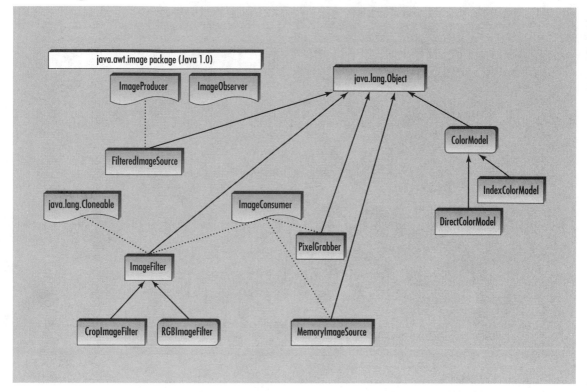

awt.peer

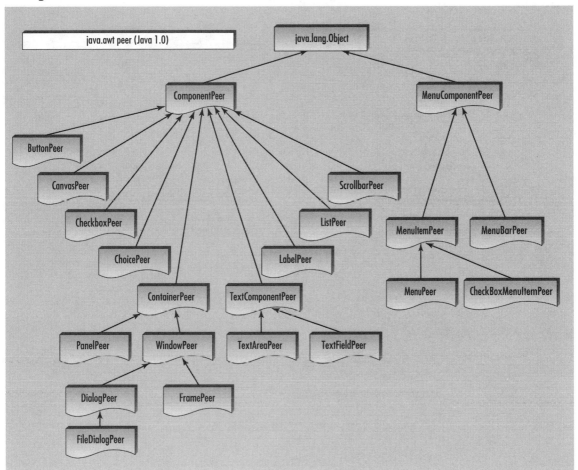

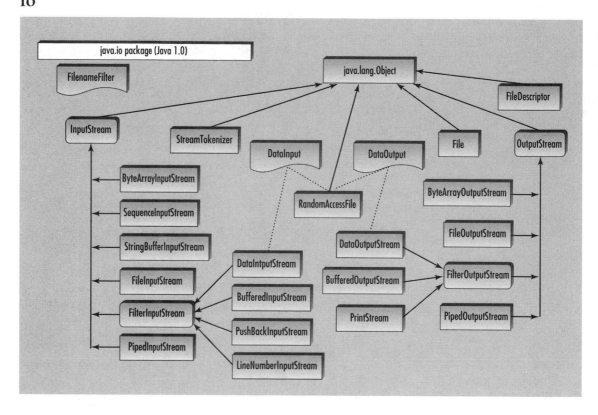

lang

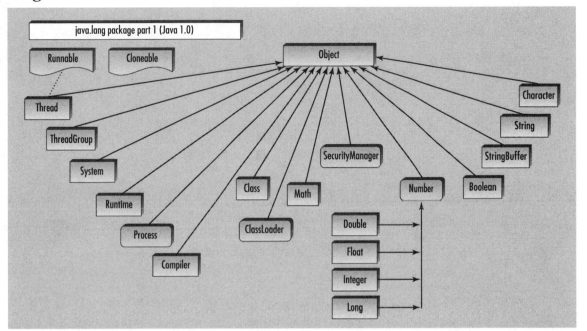

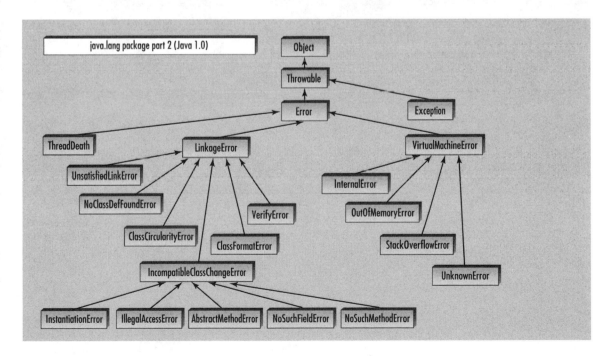

net

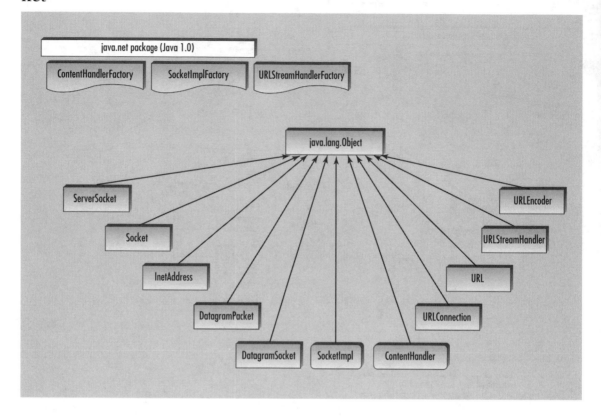

util

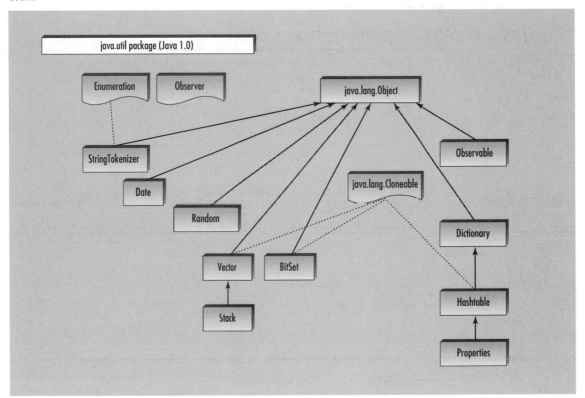

APPLET

java.applet.AppletContext (Interface)

Description	Applets use this interface to retrieve information about their environment (e.g., the browser or viewer running it).
Parent Class	Object
See Also	Applet, AppletStub.getAppletContext()

METHODS

getApplet   abstract Applet getApplet(String name)

Returns an Applet given its *name* or null if not found.

getApplets   abstract Enumeration getApplets()

Returns an enumeration of the accessible Applets in this context.

getAudioClip   abstract AudioClip getAudioClip(URL url)

Returns an audio clip given a *url* or null if not found.

getImage   abstract Image getImage(URL url)

Returns an Image given a *url* or null if not found.

showDocument   abstract void showDocument(URL url)

Shows the document given a *url*.

showDocument   public abstract void showDocument(URL url, String target)

Displays the document at the specified *url* in the *target* window. The target string may contain: _self, _parent, _top, _blank or <other string>. Where _self is the current frame, _parent is the parent frame, _top is the top-most frame, _blank is a new unnamed top level window and <other string> is a new unnamed top level window named <other string>. This may be ignored by the AppletContext.

showStatus   abstract void showStatus(String message)

Shows the specified *message* in the Applet's context.

java.applet.AppletStub (Interface)

Description	This interface can be used to develop an applet viewer. It will not ordinarily be needed by applet programmers.
Parent Class	Object
See Also	Applet, Applet.setStub()

METHODS

appletResize	void appletResize(int width, int height)
	Called when the Applet wants to resize itself to the specified *width* and *height*.
getAppletContext	abstract getAppletContext getAppletContext()
	Returns a handle to this Applet's context.
getCodeBase	abstract URL getCodeBase()
	Returns the base URL.
getDocumentBase	abstract URL getDocumentBase()
	Returns the URL of the document.
getParameter	abstract String getParameter(String name)
	Returns the parameter of the Applet given its *name*.
isActive	abstract boolean isActive()
	Returns true if the Applet is active.

java.applet.AudioClip (Interface)

Description	This interface can be used to implement audio.
Parent Class	Object
See Also	Applet, AppletContext.getAudioClip()

METHODS

loop	abstract void loop()
	Continuously plays the audio clip.
play	void play()
	Plays the audio clip once.
stop	void stop()
	Stops playing the audio clip.

java.applet.Applet

Description	This is the base class for all applets. It contains various methods that help you get images, play audio, and perform other applet manipulations.
Parent Class	Panel
See Also	AppletContext

CONSTRUCTORS

Applet()   Creates an applet.

VARIABLES

None

METHODS

destroy   void destroy()

Destroys this Applet and cleans up any resources it may have held.

getAppletContext   AppletContext getAppletContext()

Returns a handle to this Applet's context. This lets the Applet get information from its environment (usually the browser or viewer).

getAppletInfo   String getAppletInfo()

Returns information about the author, version, and copyright of this Applet.

getAudioClip   AudioClip getAudioClip(URL url)

Returns an audio clip given a URL or null if not found.

getAudioClip   AudioClip getAudioClip(URL url, Sting name)

Returns an audio clip given a *url* and a *name* or null if not found.

getCodeBase   URL getCodeBase()

Returns the URL of the Applet itself.

getDocumentBase   URL getDocumentBase()

Returns the URL of the document where the Applet is embedded.

getImage   Image getImage(URL url [, String imageName])

Returns an image given a *url* and optional *imageName*. This method returns immediately with the instantiated Image object. The actual Image data is only loaded when needed.

getParameter   String getParameter(String name)

Returns the value of a parameter of the Applet given its *name*.

getParameterInfo   String[][] getParameterInfo()

Returns an array of Strings describing parameters known to this Applet. Each array element corresponds to a parameter and is a set of three Strings: name, type, and description.

init   void init()

This method is invoked automatically by the Java environment so that you can initialize your applet when it is created.

isActive	boolean isActive()
	Returns true if this applet is active. An applet becomes active just before the start method is invoked.
play	void play(URL url [, String name])
	Plays an audio clip given a *url* and optional *name*. If the audio clip is not found, then nothing will happen.
resize	void resize(Dimension dim)
	Called to notify this Applet to resize itself to the specified dimension *dim*.
resize	void resize(int width, int height)
	Resizes this Applet to the specified *width* and *height*.
setStub	final void setStub(AppletStub stub)
	The Java environment automatically invokes this to set the applet stub. This method is the interface between this applet and the browser.
showStatus	void showStatus(String message)
	Shows the specified *message* in the Applet's context.
start	void start()
	The Java environment automatically invokes this method to start your Applet when it's first exposed.
stop	void stop()
	The Java environment automatically invokes this method when the applet is no longer on the screen. This method will always be invoked before destroy() is called.

AWT

java.awt.LayoutManager (Interface)

Description	Defines the interface for classes that lay out containers in Java. Currently, you must use one of these classes to lay out your components.
Parent Class	Object
See Also	BorderLayout, CardLayout, FlowLayout, GridBagLayout, GridLayout

METHODS

addLayoutComponent, layoutContainer, minimumLayoutSize, preferredLayoutSize, removeLayoutComponent
See the Layout classes for examples of implementations of these abstract methods.

java.awt.MenuContainer (Interface)

Description	Defines the interface for classes that have menu-related containers.
Parent Class	Object
See Also	Menu, Menubar

METHODS

getFont, postEvent, remove
See the Menu, Menubar, and MenuComponent classes for examples of implementations of these abstract methods.

java.awt.BorderLayout

Description	This class encapsulates a border layout. It allows you to place components in five different regions—"North" (top), "South" (bottom), "East" (left), "West" (right), and "Center" (the remaining space)—when you add it to a container.
Parent Class	Object
Implements	LayoutManager
See Also	CardLayout, FlowLayout, GridBagLayout, GridLayout

CONSTRUCTORS

BorderLayout([int horzGap, int vertGap])
Creates a new BorderLayout with optional horizontal and vertical gaps: *horzGap* and *vertGap*.

VARIABLES

None

METHODS

addLayoutComponent void addLayoutComponent(String location, Component comp)
Adds the specified component *comp* to the layout at the specified *location* (e.g., "North").

layoutContainer	void layoutContainer(Container target)
	Reshapes the components in the specified container *target* to fit within the dimensions of the BorderLayout object.
minimumLayoutSize	Dimension minimumLayoutSize(Container target)
	Returns the minimum dimensions required to lay out the components in the specified container *target*.
preferredLayoutSize	Dimension preferredLayoutSize(Container target)
	Returns the preferred dimensions of this layout calculated using the components in the specified container *target*.
removeLayoutComponent	void removeLayoutComponent(Component comp)
	Deletes the specified component *comp* from the layout.
toString	String toString()
	Returns a String showing this BorderLayout's values.

java.awt.Button

Description	This class encapsulates a labeled, native, GUI Button. When the user clicks on the Button, the handleEvent() and action() methods (remember Button is a subclass of Component) are automatically called. You may choose where to handle the event.
Parent Class	Component
See Also	Component

CONSTRUCTORS

Button([String label])

Creates a new Button with an optional display *label*.

VARIABLES

None

METHODS

addNotify	synchronized void addNotify()
	Creates a peer for this Button.
getLabel	String getLabel()
	Returns the current label of this Button.
paramString	protected String paramString()
	Returns the parameter String of this Button.
setLabel	void setLabel(String label)
	Sets this Button's label to the specified *label*.

java.awt.Canvas

Description	This class encapsulates a canvas. A canvas is a generic drawing surface you may use. This class is fairly abstract; you must subclass it and override its paint() method to add functionality.
Parent Class	Component

CONSTRUCTORS

None

VARIABLES

None

METHODS

addNotify	synchronized void addNotify()
	Creates a peer for this Canvas.
paint	void paint(Graphics g)
	Override this method to draw on your Canvas.

java.awt.CardLayout

Description	This class encapsulates a layout container manager for cards. A CardLayout is similiar to what Microsoft Windows programmers know as "property sheets" or "tabbed dialogs."
Parent Class	Object
Implements	LayoutManager
See Also	BorderLayout, FlowLayout, GridBagLayout, GridLayout

CONSTRUCTORS

CardLayout([int horzGap, int vertGap])

Creates a new CardLayout with optional horizontal and vertical gaps: *horzGap* and *vertGap*.

VARIABLES

None

METHODS

addLayoutComponent void addLayoutComponent(String name, Component comp)

Adds the component *comp* with an associated *name* to the layout.

first	void first(Container target)
	Exposes the first card of the container *target*.
last	void last(Container target)
	Exposes the last card of the container *target*.
layoutContainer	void layoutContainer(Container target)
	Lays out the specified container *target*.
minimumLayoutSize	Dimension minimumLayoutSize(Container target)
	Returns the minimum size for the container *target*.
next	void next(Container target)
	Exposes the next card of the container *target*.
preferredLayoutSize	Dimension preferredLayoutSize(Container target)
	Returns the preferred dimensions of this layout calculated using the components in the specified container *target*.
previous	void previous(Container target)
	Exposes the previous card of the container *target*.
removeLayoutComponent	void removeLayoutComponent(Component comp)
	Removes the component *comp* from the layout.
show	void show(Container target, String name)
	Exposes the named component in the container *target*.
toString	String toString()
	Returns a String showing this CardLayout's values.

java.awt.CheckBox

Description	This class encapsulates a Checkbox. Checkboxes are ideal for specifying binary choices, such as if the status bar should be shown in an application.
Parent Class	Component
See Also	CheckBoxMenuItem, CheckBoxGroup

CONSTRUCTORS

CheckBox([String label])

> Creates a new Checkbox with the optionally specified *label*. It will not have a Checkbox group, and will be initialized to false.

CheckBox(String label, CheckboxGroup group, boolean state)

> Creates a new Checkbox with the specified *label*,Checkbox *group*, and *state*.

VARIABLES

None

METHODS

addNotify	synchronized void addNotify()	
	Creates a peer for this Checkbox.	
getCheckboxGroup	CheckboxGroup getCheckboxGroup()	
	Returns this Checkbox's group.	
getLabel	String getLabel()	
	Returns the label of this Checkbox.	
getState	boolean getState()	
	Returns the current state of this Checkbox.	
paramString	protected String paramString()	
	Returns the parameter String of this Checkbox.	
setCheckboxGroup	void setCheckboxGroup(CheckboxGroup group)	
	Sets the CheckboxGroup of this Checkbox to the specified *group*.	
setLabel	void setLabel(String label)	
	Assigns *label* to this Checkbox.	
setState	void setState(boolean checked)	
	Sets the state of this Checkbox to *checked*.	

java.awt.CheckBoxGroup

Description	This class encapsulates a CheckboxGroup that can be used to group CheckBoxes together for organizational and functional reasons. Only one Checkbox in a CheckboxGroup may be checked at one time.
Parent Class	Component
See Also	CheckBoxMenuItem, CheckBox

CONSTRUCTORS

CheckBoxGroup()   Creates a new CheckboxGroup.

VARIABLES

None

METHODS

getCurrent
Checkbox getCurrent()
Returns the currently selected Checkbox.

setCurrent
synchronized void setCurrent(Checkbox cb)
Checks the specified Checkbox *cb* and unchecks the currently selected Checkbox.

toString
String toString()
Returns a String indicating the currently checked Checkbox.

java.awt.CheckBoxMenuItem

Description	This class encapsulates a check box that is a choice in a menu. This is used to indicate if a menu option is turned on or off.
Parent Class	MenuItem
See Also	MenuItem, Checkbox

CONSTRUCTORS

CheckBoxMenuItem(String label)
Creates a new CheckBoxMenuItem with the specified *label*.

VARIABLES

None

METHODS

addNotify
synchronized void addNotify()
Creates a peer for this CheckBoxMenuItem.

getState
boolean getState()
Returns the state of this CheckBoxMenuItem.

paramString
protected String paramString()
Returns the parameter String of this CheckBoxMenuItem.

setState
void setState(boolean checked)
Sets the state of this CheckBoxMenuItem to *checked*.

java.awt.Choice

Description	This class encapsulates a Choice. This is a pop-up menu of choices where the current choice is displayed as the title of the menu.
Parent Class	Component

See Also	Component

CONSTRUCTORS

Choice()	Creates a new Choice.

VARIABLES

None

METHODS

addItem	synchronized void addItem(String item)
	Adds *item* to this Choice. Throws NullPointerException if this item equals null.
addNotify	synchronized void addNotify()
	Creates a peer for this Choice.
countItems	int countItems()
	Returns the number of items this Choice contains.
getItem	String getItem(int index)
	Returns the String located at the specified *index* of this Choice.
getSelectedIndex	int getSelectedIndex()
	Returns the index of the currently selected item of this Choice.
getSelectedItem	String getSelectedItem()
	Returns a String representating the current choice.
paramString	protected String paramString()
	Returns the parameter String of this Choice.
select	synchronized void select(int position)
	Selects the item at the specified *position*. Throws IllegalArgumentException if this position is not valid.
select	void select(String item)
	Selects the specified *item*.

java.awt.Color

Description	This **final** class encapsulates RGB colors.
Parent Class	Object

CONSTRUCTORS

Color(int red, int green, int blue)

> Attempts to create a color given the *red*, *green*, and *blue* components. Valid parameter values range from 0 to 255.

Color(float red, float green, float blue)

> Attempts to create a color given the *red*, *green*, and *blue* components. Valid parameter values range from 0 to 1.0.

Color(int rgb)

> Attempts to create a color given the combined *rgb* value. The red component is in bits 16-23, the green in bits 8-15, and the blue in bits 0-7.

Note: The actual color depends on obtaining the closest match for the current color space.

VARIABLES

black, blue, cyan, darkGray, gray, green, lightGray, magenta, orange, pink, red, white, yellow

> Static Color: predefined colors available for your use

METHODS

brighter

> Color brighter()
>
> Returns a Color that is a brighter version of this Color, if possible.

darker

> Color darker()
>
> Returns a Color that is a darker version of this Color, if possible.

equals

> boolean equals(Object obj2)
>
> Returns true if *obj2* is a Color object that is the same color as this Color.

getBlue

> int getBlue()
>
> Returns the blue component of this Color.

getColor

> static Color getColor(String propName[, Color value])
>
> Returns a Color property given its property name *propName*. If *propName* is not valid, then null or the optional Color *value* is returned.

getColor

> static Color getColor(String propName, int value)
>
> Returns a Color property given its property name *propName*. If *propName* is not valid, then the Color of *value* is returned.

getGreen

> int getGreen()
>
> Returns the green component of this Color.

getHSBColor	static Color getHSBColor(float hue, float saturation, float brightness)
	Returns a Color object for corresponding RGB color given the specified *hue*, *saturation*, and *brightness*.
getRGB	int getRGB()
	Returns the RGB value for this Color in the default ColorModel. The red component is in bits 16-23, the green in bits 8-15, and the blue in bits 0-7. The high bits 24-31 are all set.
getRed	int getRed()
	Returns the red component of this Color.
hashCode	int hashCode()
	Returns the hash code of this Color.
HSBtoRGB	static int HSBtoRGB(float hue, float saturation, float brightness)
	Returns the RGB value in the default ColorModel of the color corresponding to the specified *hue*, *saturation*, and *brightness* color components.
RGBtoHSB	static float[] HSBtoRGB(int red, int green, int blue, float[] hsb)
	Returns a floating point array of HSB values that corresponds to the color defined by the specified *red*, *green*, and *blue* components.
toString	String toString()
	Returns the String showing this Color's values.

java.awt.Component

Description	This class encapsulates an Abstract Windows Toolkit component. Tools such as a Button, Checkbox, Label, etc., are subclasses of Component and many methods you will use for these controls are found here.
Parent Class	Object
Implements	ImageObserver
See Also	Container

CONSTRUCTORS

None

VARIABLES

None

METHODS

action	boolean action(Event event, Object action)

Called if an action occurs in this Component with the *event* and *action* that is occurring. If you wish to handle an action, you should override this method. You should return true whenever you have completed processing an action, otherwise return false to notify the default awt handler to execute.

addNotify	void addNotify()

Notifies this Component to create its peer.

bounds	Rectangle bounds()

Returns the current boundary Rectangle of this Component.

checkImage	int checkImage(Image image, [int width, int height,] ImageObserver observer)

Returns the construction status of the specified screen *image* and notifies the *observer*. If *width* and *height* are specified, the image is assumed to be scaled accordingly. Note: This method does not cause the image to load. Use prepareImage() to explicitly load the image.

createImage	Image createImage(ImageProducer imageProducer)

Returns an image created from the specified *imageProducer*.

createImage	Image createImage(int width, int height)

Returns an offscreen drawable image with the specified *width* and *height* to be used for double buffering.

deliverEvent	void deliverEvent(Event event)

Delivers *event* to this Component or one of its child Components.

disable	synchronized void disable()

Disables this Component.

enable	synchronized void enable()

Enables this Component.

enable	void enable(boolean enable)

Enables this Component when *enable* is true; else disables it.

getBackground	Color getBackground()

Returns the current background color.

getColorModel	synchronized ColorModel getColorModel()

Returns the ColorModel used to display this Component on the screen.

getFont	Font getFont()

Returns the font of the Component.

getFontMetrics	FontMetrics getFontMetrics(Font font)

Returns the FontMetrics of the specified *font* for this Component.

getForeground	Color getForeground()
	Returns the current foreground color.
getGraphics	Graphics getGraphics()
	Returns a Graphics context for this Component or null if not on screen.
getParent	Container getParent()
	Returns the parent of this Component.
getPeer	ComponentPeer getPeer()
	Returns the peer of this Component.
getToolkit	Toolkit getToolkit()
	Returns the toolkit of this Component.
gotFocus	void gotFocus()
	Called automatically when this Component receives the input focus.
handleEvent	boolean handleEvent(Event event)
	Called if an event occurs in this Component with the appropriate *event*. If you wish to handle an event (e.g., ACTION_EVENT, MOUSE_DOWN—see Event class for list), you should override this method. You should return true whenever you have completed processing an event, otherwise return false to notify the default awt handler to execute.
hide	synchronized void hide()
	Hides this Component.
imageUpdate	boolean imageUpdate(Image image, int flags, int x, int y, int w, int h)
	Repaints the Component if the image has changed. Returns true if the specified *image* is complete and there are no errors.
inside	synchronized boolean inside(int x, int y)
	Returns true if the specified *x,y* location is within this Component's bounding box.
invalidate	void invalidate()
	Invalidates this Component.
isEnabled	boolean isEnabled()
	Returns true if this Component is enabled.
isShowing	boolean isShowing()
	Returns true if this Component is showing on screen.
isValid	boolean isValid()
	Returns true if this Component does not need to be repainted.
isVisible	boolean isVisible()
	Returns true if this Component is visible.

keyDown	boolean keyDown(Event event, int key)
	Called with an *event* and *key* if a key is pressed.
keyUp	boolean keyUp(Event event, int key)
	Called with an *event* and *key* if a key is released.
layout	void layout()
	Lays out this Component.
list	void list()
	Outputs a listing to a print stream.
list	void list(PrintStream out[, int indentation])
	Outputs a listing to the specified PrintStream *out* starting at the beginning or an optionally specified *indentation*.
locate	Component locate(int x, int y)
	Returns the Component or child Component at the *x,y* location.
location	Point location()
	Returns the current *x,y* location of this Component in the parent's coordinate system.
lostFocus	void lostFocus()
	Called automatically when this Component loses the input focus.
minimumSize	Dimension minimumSize()
	Returns the minimum size of this Component.
mouseDown	boolean mouseDown(Event evt, int x, int y)
	Called when the mouse button is depressed.
mouseDrag	boolean mouseDrag(Event evt, int x, int y)
	Called if the mouse is dragged with the mouse button depressed.
mouseEnter	boolean mouseEnter(Event evt, int x, int y)
	Called when the mouse pointer enters this Component.
mouseExit	boolean mouseExit(Event evt, int x, int y)
	Called when the mouse pointer exits this Component.
mouseMove	boolean mouseMove(Event evt, int x, int y)
	Called if the mouse moves with the mouse button up.
mouseUp	boolean mouseUp(Event evt, int x, int y)
	Called when the mouse button is released.
move	void move(int x, int y)
	Moves this Component to a new location (*x,y*) in the parent's coordinate space.
nextFocus	void nextFocus()
	Changes the focus to the next Component.

paint	void paint(Graphics graphicsWindow)
	Paints this Component in the specified *graphicsWindow*.
paintAll	void paintAll(Graphics graphicsWindow)
	Paints this Component and all its child Components in the specified *graphicsWindow*.
paramString	protected String paramString()
	Returns the parameter String of this Component.
postEvent	void postEvent(Event event)
	Posts an *event* to this Component, resulting in a call to handleEvent.
preferredSize	Dimension preferredSize()
	Returns the preferred size of this Component.
prepareImage	boolean prepareImage(Image image, [int width, int height,] ImageObserver imageObserver)
	Prepares the specified *image* for display on this Component. This creates a thread to asynchronously download the image data notifying the specified *observer* as the image is being prepared. Returns true if the image has already been fully prepared, false otherwise. The *width* and *height* of the desired screen representation may also be specified.
print	void print(Graphics graphicsWindow)
	Prints this Component given the specified *graphicsWindow*.
printAll	void printAll(Graphics graphicsWindow)
	Prints the Component and all its child Components given the specified *graphicsWindow*.
removeNotify	synchronized void removeNotify()
	Notifies this Component to destroy its peer.
repaint	void repaint([long maxTime])
	Repaints the Component by calling update as soon as possible or before the specified *maxTime* in milliseconds.
repaint	void repaint([long maxTime,] int x, int y, int width, int height)
	Repaints the part of this Component within *x,y* and *x+width*, *y+height*. It calls update as soon as possible or before a specified *maxTime* in milliseconds.
requestFocus	void requestFocus()
	Requests the input focus. If successful, gotFocus() is then called.
reshape	synchronized void reshape(int x, int y, int width, int height)
	Reshapes this Component to the specified box: *x,y* and *x+width*, *y+height*.

resize	void resize(int width, int height)
	Changes the size of this Component to the specified *width* and *height*.
resize	void resize(Dimension dim)
	Changes the size of this Component to the specified dimension *dim*.
setBackground	synchronized void setBackground(Color color)
	Sets the background color of this Component to the specified *color*.
setFont	synchronized void setFont(Font font)
	Sets the font of this Component to the specified *font*.
setForeground	synchronized void setForeground(Color color)
	Sets the foreground color of this Component to the specified *color*.
show	synchronized void show()
	Shows this Component.
show	void show(boolean show)
	Shows this Component when *show* is true; else hides it.
size	Dimension size()
	Returns the current dimensions of this Component.
toString	String toString()
	Returns a String showing this Component's values.
update	void update(Graphics g)
	This method is called in response to a repaint invocation. You should assume the background is not cleared.
validate	void validate()
	Validates this Component

java.awt.Container

Description	This **abstract** class encapsulates an Abstract Windows Toolkit container object. Containers usually hold other components within them. For example, a panel container may hold several button and label components.
Parent Class	Component
See Also	Component

CONSTRUCTORS

None

VARIABLES

None

METHODS

add   synchronized Component add(Component comp, int position)

Adds the specified component *comp* to this Container at the specified *position*. A *position* of -1 indicates this component should be inserted at the end.

add   synchronized Component add([String name,] Component comp)

Adds the specified component *comp* to this Container. If a *name* (i.e., "North" for a BorderLayout) is specified it will also be added to the layout manager of this Container.

addNotify   synchronized void addNotify()

Creates a peer for this Container.

countComponents   int countComponents()

Returns the number of Components in this Container.

deliverEvent   void deliverEvent(Event event)

Delivers an *event* to the appropriate Component.

getComponent   synchronized Component getComponent(int n)

Returns the *n*th Component in this Container. Throws an ArrayIndexOutOfBoundsException if less than *n* components are in the Container.

getComponents   synchronized Component[] getComponents()

Returns all of the components in this Container.

getLayout   LayoutManager getLayout()

Returns the layout manager of this Container.

insets   Insets insets()

Returns the insets of this Container.

layout   synchronized void layout()

Performs a layout on this Container.

list   void list(PrintStream out, int indentation)

Outputs a listing, starting at the specified *indentation*, to the specified PrintStream *out*.

locate   Component locate(int x, int y)

Returns the component at the specified *x,y* position.

minimumSize   synchronized Dimension minimumSize()

Returns the minimum size of this Container.

paintComponents	void paintComponents(Graphics graphicsWindow)
	Paints the Components in this Container.
paramString	protected String paramString()
	Returns the parameter String of this Container.
preferredSize	synchronized Dimension preferredSize()
	Returns the preferred size of this Container.
printComponents	void printComponents(Graphics graphicsWindow)
	Prints out all the Components in this Container.
remove	synchronized void remove(Component comp)
	Removes the specified Component *comp* from this Container.
removeAll	synchronized void removeAll()
	Removes all the Components from this Container.
removeNotify	synchronized void removeNotify()
	Notifies this Container to remove its peer.
setLayout	void setLayout(LayoutManager layMgr)
	Sets the layout manager to the specified *layMgr* for this Container (e.g., CardLayout, BorderLayout, FlowLayout, GridBagLayout, GridLayout).
validate	synchronized void validate()
	Validates this Container and all its components.

java.awt.Dialog

Description	This class encapsulates a dialog box. A dialog box is usually a small window displayed to request additional input from the user.
Parent Class	Window
See Also	Window

CONSTRUCTORS

Dialog(Frame parent [,String title], boolean modal)

Creates a new dialog box with no title or the optionally specified *title*. You must also specify its *parent* and whether it is *modal*. When a modal dialog box is showing; it will grab all input from the user. Initially the dialog box is invisible; you must invoke the show() method to see it.

VARIABLES

None

METHODS

addNotify	synchronized void addNotify()
	Creates a peer for this Dialog.
getTitle	String getTitle()
	Returns the title of this Dialog.
isModal	boolean isModal()
	Returns true if this Dialog is modal.
isResizable	boolean isResizable()
	Returns true if you can resize this Dialog.
paramString	protected String paramString()
	Returns the parameter String of this Dialog.
setResizable	void setResizable(boolean resizable)
	Allows the Dialog to be resized if the specified *resizable* flag is true.
setTitle	void setTitle(String title)
	Sets the title for this Dialog to the specified *title*.

java.awt.Dimension

Description	This class encapsulates a width and height dimension.
Parent Class	Object
See Also	Object

CONSTRUCTORS

Dimension([Dimension dim])

Creates a new Dimension with a width and height of 0 or the optionally specified Dimension *dim*.

Dimension(int width, int height)

Creates a new Dimension with the specified *width* and *height*.

VARIABLES

height	int: The height dimension.
width	int: The width dimension.

METHODS

toString	String toString()
	Returns a String showing this Dimension's values.

java.awt.Event

Description	This class encapsulates events from a native GUI platform.
Parent Class	Object
See Also	handleEvent() in Component

CONSTRUCTORS

Event(Object targetComponent, int eventType, Object arg)

> Creates an event with the specified *targetComponent*, *eventType*, and argument *arg*.

Event(Object targetComponent, long timeStamp, int eventType, int x, int y, int key, int modifiers [, Object arg])

> Creates an event with the specified *targetComponent*, *timeStamp*, *eventType*, coordinates *x,y*, keyboard *key*, state of *modifiers*, and optional argument *arg*.

VARIABLES

ACTION_EVENT	final static int: An action event that occurs when you press a button, select a menu, etc.
ALT_MASK	final static int: Alternate modifier constant.
CTRL_MASK	final static int: Control modifier constant.
DOWN	final static int: Down arrow key.
END	final static int: End key.
ESC	final static int: Escape key.
F1 to F12	final static int: Function keys.
GOT_FOCUS	final static int: Got focus event.
HOME	final static int: Home key.
KEY_ACTION	final static int: Key action keyboard event.
KEY_ACTION_RELEASE	final static int: Key action release keyboard event.
KEY_PRESS	final static int: Key press event.
KEY_RELEASE	final static int: Key release event.
LEFT	final static int: Left arrow key.
LIST_DESELECT	final static int: An element on a list was unselected.
LIST_EVENT	final static int: List event.
LIST_SELECT	final static int: An element on a list was selected.
LOAD_FILE	final static int: File loading event.
META_MASK	final static int: Meta modifier constant.
LOST_FOCUS	final static int: Lost focus event.
MOUSE_DOWN	final static int: Mouse down event.
MOUSE_DRAG	final static int: Mouse drag event.
MOUSE_ENTER	final static int: Mouse enter event.

MOUSE_EXIT	final static int: Mouse exit event.
MOUSE_MOVE	final static int: Mouse move event.
MOUSE_UP	final static int: Mouse up event.
PGUP	final static int: Page up key.
PGDN	final static int: Page down key.
RIGHT	final static int: Right arrow key.
SAVE_FILE	final static int: File saving event.
SCROLL_ABSOLUTE	final static int: Absolute scroll event.
SCROLL_LINE_DOWN	final static int: Line down scroll event.
SCROLL_LINE_UP	final static int: Line up scroll event.
SCROLL_PAGE_DOWN	final static int: Page down scroll event.
SCROLL_PAGE_UP	final static int: Page up scroll event.
SHIFT_MASK	final static int: Shift modifier constant.
UP	final static int: Up arrow key.
WINDOW_DEICONIFY	final static int: Deiconify window event.
WINDOW_DESTROY	final static int: Destroy window event.
WINDOW_EXPOSE	final static int: Expose window event.
WINDOW_ICONIFY	final static int: Iconify window event.
WINDOW_MOVED	final static int: Move window event.
arg	Object: An arbitrary argument.
evt	Event: Contains the next event. Useful when putting events into a linked list.
id	int: Contains the type of this event, such as MOUSE_MOVE.
key	int: Contains the key that was pressed on the keyboard.
modifiers	int: Contains the state of the modifier keys. See modifer constants above.
target	Object: Contains the target component.
when	long: Contains the time stamp.
x	int: X coordinate of the event.
y	int: Y coordinate of the event.

METHODS

---

controlDown   boolean controlDown()

Returns true if the control key is down.

metaDown   boolean metaDown()

Returns true if the meta key is down.

paramString   protected String paramString()

Returns the parameter String of this Event.

shiftDown   boolean shiftDown()

Returns true if the shift key is down.

toString	String toString()
	Returns a String showing this Event's values.
translate	void translate(int x, int y)
	Translates an event at specified coordinates *x,y* relative to the given component.

java.awt.FileDialog

Description	This class encapsulates a file selection dialog box. A file selection dialog box is modal and will block the calling thread when shown until the user selects a file.
Parent Class	Dialog
See Also	Dialog, java.io.FileNameFilter

CONSTRUCTORS

FileDialog(Frame parent, String title [, int mode])

Creates a new file dialog box with the specified *title* and *parent*. You may also specify its *mode* (LOAD or SAVE). The default is LOAD. Initially the file dialog box is invisible; you must invoke the show() method to see it.

VARIABLES

LOAD	final static int: The file load variable mode constant.
SAVE	final static int: The file save variable mode constant.

METHODS

addNotify	synchronized void addNotify()
	Creates a peer for this FileDialog.
getDirectory	String getDirectory()
	Returns the directory name of this FileDialog.
getFile	String getFile()
	Returns the file name of this FileDialog.
getFilenameFilter	FilenameFilter getFilenameFilter()
	Returns the filter of this FileDialog.
getMode	int getMode()
	Returns the mode of this FileDialog (LOAD or SAVE).
paramString	protected String paramString()
	Returns the parameter String of this FileDialog.

setDirectory	void setDirectory(String directory)
	Sets the directory of this FileDialog to the specified *directory*.
setFile	void setFile(String file)
	Sets the file for this FileDialog to the specified *file*. Invoke this method before show() in order to set a default.
setFilenameFilter	void setFilenameFilter(FilenameFilter filter)
	Sets the filter for this dialog to the specified *filter*.

java.awt.FlowLayout

Description	This class encapsulates a manager used to lay out components on a panel. It will center and arrange the components from left to right in a row. When that row is full, it will begin a new row.
Parent Class	Object
Implements	LayoutManager
See Also	BorderLayout, CardLayout, GridBagLayout, GridLayout

CONSTRUCTORS

FlowLayout([int alignment])

Creates a new flow layout with a centered alignment or the specified *alignment* (CENTER, LEFT, RIGHT).

FlowLayout(int alignment, int horzGap, int vertGap)

Creates a new flow layout with the specified *alignment* and horizontal and vertical gaps: *horzGap* and *vertGap*.

VARIABLES

CENTER	final static int: Layout components starting from the center.
LEFT	final static int: Layout components from left to right.
RIGHT	final static int: Layout components from right to left.

METHODS

addLayoutComponent void addLayoutComponent(String name, Component comp)

Required to implement LayoutManager, but not used here. You need to operate directly on the *target* Container.

layoutContainer void layoutContainer(Container target)

Reshapes the components in the specified container *target* to fit within the dimensions of the FlowLayout object.

minimumLayoutSize Dimension minimumLayoutSize(Container target)

Returns the minimum dimensions required to lay out the components in the specified container *target*.

preferredLayoutSize Dimension preferredLayoutSize(Container target)

Returns the preferred dimensions of this layout calculated using the components in the specified container *target*.

removeLayoutComponent void removeLayoutComponent(Component comp)

Required to implement LayoutManager, but not used here. You need to operate directly on the *target* Container.

toString String toString()

Returns a String showing this FlowLayout's values.

java.awt.Font

Description   This class encapsulates a font, allowing you to define the name and style (i.e., PLAIN, BOLD, ITALIC) of text to be displayed.

Parent Class   Object

See Also   FontMetrics

CONSTRUCTORS

Font(String name, int style, int pointSize)

Creates a new Font with the given *name*, *style*, and *pointSize*.

VARIABLES

PLAIN   final static int: The plain style constant.The constants may be summed to create mixed styles.

BOLD   final static int: The bold style constant.

ITALIC   final static int: The italicized style constant.

name   protected String: The logical name of this font.

style   protected int: The style of the font that is the sum of *PLAIN*, *BOLD*, or *ITALIC*.

size   protected int: The point size of this font.

METHODS

equals   boolean equals(Object obj2)

Returns true if the specified Font object *obj2*'s size, style and name equals this Font's.

getFamily   String getFamily()

Returns the system specific family name of this font.

getFont   static Font getFont(String propertyName[, Font font])

Returns a Font given a system *propertyName*. Optionally, a default *font* may be specified to be returned if *propertyName* is not found.

getName	String getName()	
	Returns the logical name of this Font.	
getSize	int getSize()	
	Returns the point size of this Font.	
getStyle	int getStyle()	
	Returns the style of this Font.	
hashCode	int hashCode()	
	Returns a hash code for this Font.	
isBold	boolean isBold()	
	Returns true if this Font is bold.	
isItalic	boolean isItalic()	
	Returns true if this Font is italic.	
isPlain	boolean isPlain()	
	Returns true if this Font is plain.	
toString	String toString()	
	Returns a String showing the family, name, style, and size of this Font.	

java.awt.FontMetrics

Description This **abstract** class encapsulates a font metrics Object. Font metrics are useful in determining spacing requirements for a specific font. All methods should be overridden with toolkit specific implementations.

Parent Class Object

See Also Font

CONSTRUCTORS

FontMetrics(Font font)**protected**

Creates a new FontMetrics Object for the specified font.

VARIABLES

font protected Font: The actual Font that this object is measuring.

METHODS

bytesWidth int bytesWidth(byte data[], int offset, int length)

Returns the width of *length* bytes in the specified array of *data[]* starting at *offset* for the Font.

charWidth	int charWidth(int ch)
	Returns the width of the specified character *ch* in the Font.
charWidth	int charWidth(char ch)
	Returns the width of the specified character *ch* in the Font.
charsWidth	int charsWidth(char data[], int offset, int length)
	Returns the width of *length* characters in the specified array of *data[]* starting at *offset* for the Font.
getAscent	int getAscent()
	Returns the Font's ascent (i.e., height above baseline).
getDescent	int getDescent()
	Returns the Font's descent (i.e., height below baseline).
getFont	Font getFont()
	Returns the Font.
getHeight	int getHeight()
	Returns the total height of the Font (i.e., leading + ascent + descent).
getLeading	int getLeading()
	Returns the standard line spacing for the Font. This is the extra space between the ascent of a line and the descent of the line above it.
getMaxAdvance	int getMaxAdvance()
	Returns the maximum advance width for any character in the Font.
getMaxAscent	int getMaxAscent()
	Returns the maximum ascent for all characters in the Font.
getMaxDescent	int getMaxDescent()
	Returns the maximum descent for all characters in the Font.
getWidths	int[] getWidths()
	Returns an array containing the widths of the first 256 characters in the Font.
stringWidth	int stringWidth(String str)
	Returns the width of the specified String *str* in the Font.
toString	String toString()
	Returns a String showing the font, name, ascent, descent, and height of the Font.

java.awt.Frame

Description	This class encapsulates a Frame. A Frame is a top-level window with a title. Besides being a window itself, a Frame can be the

parent for other windows. In a standalone Java program, the first thing you must do to display a Window is create and "show" a Frame. However, applets do not require a Frame because they are contained within a panel of the viewer or browser. In an applet, the browser's top-level window is the Frame. BorderLayout is the default layout for Frames.

Parent Class	Window
See Also	Window
Implements	MenuContainer

CONSTRUCTORS

Frame([String title])

Creates a new frame with no title or the specified *title*. Initially the frame is invisible; you must invoke the show() method to see it.

VARIABLES

CROSSHAIR_CURSOR	final static int:
DEFAULT_CURSOR	final static int:
E_RESIZE_CURSOR	final static int:
HAND_CURSOR	final static int:
MOVE_CURSOR	final static int:
NE_RESIZE_CURSOR	final static int:
NW_RESIZE_CURSOR	final static int:
N_RESIZE_CURSOR	final static int:
SE_RESIZE_CURSOR	final static int:
SW_RESIZE_CURSOR	final static int:
S_RESIZE_CURSOR	final static int:
TEXT_CURSOR	final static int:
WAIT_CURSOR	final static int:
W_RESIZE_CURSOR	final static int:

METHODS

addNotify

synchronized void addNotify()

Creates a peer for this Frame.

dispose

synchronized void dispose()

Disposes of this Frame. You should always call this method when you are done with this Frame to release the resources it uses.

getCursorType

int getCursorType()

Returns the current cursor type.

getIconImage	Image getIconImage()
	Returns the icon image for this Frame.
getMenuBar	MenuBar getMenuBar()
	Returns the menu bar for this Frame.
getTitle	String getTitle()
	Returns the title of this Frame.
isResizable	boolean isResizable()
	Returns true if you can resize this Frame.
paramString	protected String paramString()
	Returns the parameter String of this Frame.
remove	synchronized void remove(MenuComponent menuBar)
	Removes the specified *menuBar* from this Frame.
setCursor	void setCursor(int cursorType)
	Sets the cursor image to one of the predefined variable constants. For example, cursorType may be specified as object.CROSSHAIR_CURSOR.
setIconImage	void setIconImage(Image image)
	Sets the icon of this Frame to *image*. It will be displayed when the Frame is iconized.
setMenuBar	synchronized void setMenuBar(MenuBar menuBar)
	Sets the MenuBar on this Frame to the specified *menuBar*.
setResizable	void setResizable(boolean resizable)
	Allows this frame to be resized if the specified *resizable* flag is set to true.
setTitle	void setTitle(String title)
	Sets the title on this Frame to the specified *title*.

java.awt.Graphics

Description	This **abstract** class is the base class for all graphics contexts using various devices.
Parent Class	Object
See Also	Image, Component

CONSTRUCTORS

| **Graphics()** | **protected** |
| | Creates a new Graphics Object. Graphics Objects cannot directly be created; they must be created from a Component or obtained from another graphics context. |

VARIABLES

None

METHODS

clearRect
abstract void clearRect(int x, int y, int width, int height)

Clears the rectangle specified by *x, y, width,* and *height* by filling it with the current drawing surface's background color.

clipRect
abstract void clipRect(int x, int y, int width, int height)

Clips to the rectangle that is the result of the intersection of the rectangle specified by *x, y, width,* and *height* and the current clipping region.

copyArea
abstract void copyArea(int x, int y, int width, int height, int dx, int dy)

Copies an area of the screen specified by *x, y, width,* and *height* to an offset specified by coordinates *dx, dy.*

create
abstract Graphics create()

Returns a copy of this Graphics Object.

create
Graphics create(int x, int y, int width, int height)

Returns a new Graphics Object with the specified parameters, based on this Graphics object.

dispose
abstract void dispose()

Disposes of this Graphics context.

draw3DRect
void draw3DRect(int x, int y, int width, int height, boolean raised)

Draws the specified highlighted 3D rectangle, which is raised if *raised* is true.

drawArc
abstract void drawArc(int x, int y, int width, int height, int startAngle, int arcAngle)

Draws an arc bounded by the specified rectangle from *startAngle* through *arcAngle.* Negative *arcAngles* are clockwise rotations and a *startAngle* of 0 degrees is located at 3 o'clock.

drawBytes
void drawBytes(byte data[], int offset, int length, int x, int y)

Draws *length* bytes starting at *offset* in *data[].* Bytes are drawn at coordinates *x,y* using the current font and color.

drawChars
void drawChars(char data[], int offset, int length, int x, int y)

Draws *length* characters starting at *offset* in *data[].* Characters are drawn at coordinates *x,y* using the current font and color.

drawImage
abstract boolean drawImage(Image img, int x, int y[, int width, int height], ImageObserver obs)

Draws the specified image *img* at the coordinates *x,y.* If the Image is incomplete, the *observer* is notified later. If *width* and *height* are specified, then the image will be scaled to fit the given rectangle if necessary.

drawImage   abstract boolean drawImage(Image img, int x, int y[, int width, int height], Color bkgColor, ImageObserver observer)

Draws the specified image *img* at the coordinates *x, y* using the given background color *bkgColor*. If the Image is incomplete the *observer* is notified later. If *width* and *height* are specified then the image will be scaled to fit the given rectangle if necessary.

drawLine   abstract void drawLine(int x1, int y1, int x2, int y2)

Draws a line between the coordinates *x1,y1* and *x2,y2*.

drawOval   abstract void drawOval(int x, int y, int width, int height)

Draws an oval inside the rectangle specified by *x, y, width,* and *height* using the current color.

drawPolygon   abstract void drawPolygon(int xPoints[], int yPoints[], int nPoints)

Draws a polygon with *nPoints* number of points defined by an array of *xPoints[]* and *yPoints[]*.

drawPolygon   void drawPolygon(Polygon polygon)

Draws a polygon defined by the specified *polygon*.

drawRect   void drawRect(int x, int y, int width, int height)

Draws the outline of the rectangle specified by *x, y, width,* and *height* using the current color.

drawRoundRect   abstract void drawRoundRect(int x, int y, int width, int height, int arcWidth, int arcHeight)

Draws an outlined rectangle specified by *x, y, width,* and *height* with rounded corners using the current color. *arcWidth* specifies the diameter of the arc and *arcHeight* specifies the radius of the arc.

drawString   abstract void drawString(String str, int x, int y)

Draws the specified String starting at coordinates *x,y* using the current font and color.

fill3DRect   void fill3DRect(int x, int y, int width, int height, boolean raised)

Paints a highlighted 3D rectangle specified by *x, y, width,* and *height* using the current color. The rectangle is raised if *raised* is true.

fillArc   abstract void fillArc(int x, int y, int width, int height, int startAngle, int arcAngle)

Fills an arc using the current color. See drawArc for more information.

fillOval   abstract void fillOval(int x, int y, int width, int height)

Fills an oval inside the rectangle specified by *x, y, width,* and *height* using the current color.

fillPolygon   abstract void fillPolygon(int xPoints[], int yPoints[], int nPoints)

Fills a polygon with the current color. The polygon has *nPoints* number of points defined by an array of *xPoints[]* and *yPoints[]*.

fillPolygon	void fillPolygon(Polygon polygon)
	Fills the specified *polygon* using the current color.
fillRect	abstract void fillRect(int x, int y, int width, int height)
	Fills the rectangle specified by *x, y, width,* and *height* with the current color.
fillRoundRect	abstract void fillRoundRect(int x, int y, int width, int height, int arcWidth, int arcHeight)
	Draws a rounded rectangle specified by *x, y, width,* and *height* filled in with the current color. See drawRoundRect for more information.
finalize	void finalize()
	Disposes of this graphics context when it is no longer referenced.
getClipRect	abstract Rectangle getClipRect()
	Returns the bounding rectangle of the current clipping region.
getColor	abstract Color getColor()
	Returns the current Color.
getFont	abstract Font getFont()
	Returns the current Font.
getFontMetrics	FontMetrics getFontMetrics()
	Returns the current FontMetrics.
getFontMetrics	abstract FontMetrics getFontMetrics(Font font)
	Returns the current FontMetrics for the specified *font.*
setColor	abstract void setColor(Color color)
	Sets the current color to the specified *color.*
setFont	abstract void setFont(Font font)
	Sets the font to the specified *font* for all subsequent text-drawing operations.
setPaintMode	abstract void setPaintMode()
	Sets the paint mode to overwrite the destination with the current color.
setXORMode	abstract void setXORMode(Color color)
	Sets the paint mode to alternate between the current color and the specified *color.*
toString	String toString()
	Returns a String showing information about this Graphics object.
translate	abstract void translate(int x, int y)
	Translates the specified coordinates *x,y* into the origin of the graphics context.

java.awt.GridBagConstraints

Description	This class specifies the constraints on components laid out with the GridBagLayout class. In other words, how the GridBagLayout places a component depends on that component's GridBagConstraints settings.
Parent Class	Object
Implements	Cloneable
See Also	GridBagLayout

CONSTRUCTORS

GridBagConstraints()

> Creates a new GridBagConstraint.

VARIABLES

BOTH	final static int: Resize the component to fill its requested display area.
CENTER	final static int: Place this component in the center.
EAST	final static int: Place this component at the right.
HORIZONTAL	final static int: Resize the component to fill its requested display area horizontally but not vertically.
NONE	final static int: Do not resize the component to fill its requested display area. This is the default.
NORTH	final static int: Place this component at the top.
NORTHEAST	final static int: Place this component at the top right.
NORTHWEST	final static int: Place this component at the top left.
RELATIVE	final static int: Specifies this component's placement as just below (using gridy) or just right of (using gridx) the component last laid.
REMAINDER	final static int: Specifies this component's placement as the last in its row (using gridwidth) or column (using gridheight) of the component last laid.
SOUTH	final static int: Place this component at the bottom.
SOUTHEAST	final static int: Place this component at the bottom right.
SOUTHWEST	final static int: Place this component at the bottom left.
VERTICAL	final static int Resize the component to fill its requested display area vertically but not horizontally.
WEST	final static int: Place this component at the left.
anchor	int: Determines where to place this component (e.g., constraints.anchor = GridBagConstraints.NORTHEAST).
fill	int: Specifies the behavior when the component's display area is larger than the component (e.g., constraints.fill = GridBagConstraints.BOTH).

gridheight	int: Specifies the number of cells in a column for this component.
gridwidth	int: Specifies the number of cells in a row for this component.
gridx	int: Specifies the leftmost edge of the cell on the component where 0 is the leftmost edge of the component.
gridy	int: Specifies the topmost edge of the cell on the component where 0 is the topmost edge of the component.
insets	Insets: Specifies the padding or minimum amount of space between the component and its display area's edge.
ipadx	int: Specifies the amount of internal padding. The minimum width of the component will be its width + ipadx * 2.
ipady	int: Specifies the amount of internal padding. The minimum height of the component will be its height + ipady * 2.
weightx	double: Horizontal weight of components. 0 is the default and causes components to be horizontally grouped in the center. You should specify a weight of 1 or more to prevent this from happening.
weighty	double: Vertical weight of components. 0 is the default and causes components to be vertically grouped in the center. You should specify a weight of 1 or more to prevent this from happening.

METHODS

clone	Object clone()
	Returns a clone of this Object.

awt.GridBagLayout

Description	This class encapsulates a flexible layout, allowing you to lay out components horizontally and vertically without requiring that the components be the same size. Components are laid out on display areas and each display area occupies one or more rectangular cells of a grid. Every component managed by a GridBagLayout is also tied to a GridBagConstraints instance that specifies the layout of the component within its display area. You should customize the GridBagConstraints of the individual components on a GridBagLayout to achieve maximum results from this class.
Parent Class	Object
Implements	LayoutManager
See Also	BorderLayout, CardLayout, FlowLayout, GridLayout

CONSTRUCTORS

GridBagLayout()

Creates a new GridBagLayout.

VARIABLES

MAXGRIDSIZE	protected final static int: The maximum size of the grids.
MINSIZE	protected final static int: The minimum size of the grids.
PREFERREDSIZE	protected final static int: The preferred size of the grids.
comptable	protected Hashtable: The hashtable for the component constraints.
defaultConstraints	protected GridBagConstraints: The default Constraints.

METHODS

addLayoutComponent void addLayoutComponent(String name, Component comp)

Required to implement LayoutManager, but not used here. You need to operate directly on the *target* Container.

adjustForGravity protected void adjustForGravity(GridBagConstraints constraints, Rectangle rectangle)

Adjusts the size of the specified *rectangle* given the padding and geometry of the specified *constraints*.

arrangeGrid protected void arrangeGrid(Container parent)

Lays out the grid for the *parent* container.

dumpConstraints protected void dumpConstraints(GridBagConstraints constraints)

Prints the specified *constraints* (i.e., its weight, box, min, and pad values).

dumpLayoutInfo protected void dumpLayoutInfo(GridBagLayoutInfo info)

Prints the specified layout *info* (i.e., its row, width, column, height, and weight values).

getConstraints GridBagConstraints getConstraints(Component comp)

Returns a copy of the constraints upon the specified component *comp*.

getLayoutDimensions int[][] getLayoutDimensions()

Returns a 2D array of integers containing the layout dimensions.

getLayoutInfo protected GridBagLayoutInfo getLayoutInfo(Container parent, int sizeflag)

Returns the layout information given a *parent* and *sizeflag*.

getLayoutOrigin Point getLayoutOrigin()

Returns a point containing the origin of the layout.

getLayoutWeights double[][] getLayoutWeights()

Returns a 2D array of doubles containing the layout weights.

getMinSize protected Dimension getMinSize(Container parent, int GridBagLayoutInfo info)

Returns the layout dimension given a *parent* and layout *info*.

layoutContainer	void layoutContainer(Container target)
	Reshapes the components in the specified container *target* to fit within the dimensions of the GridBagLayout object.
location	Point location(int x, int y)
	Returns the cell location in this GridBagLayout given *x* and *y* coordinates.
lookupConstraints	protected GridBagConstraints lookupConstraints(Component comp)
	Returns the actual (not copied) constraints for the specified component *comp*.
minimumLayoutSize	Dimension minimumLayoutSize(Container target)
	Returns the minimum dimensions required to lay out the components in the specified container *target*.
preferredLayoutSize	Dimension preferredLayoutSize(Container target)
	Returns the preferred dimensions of this layout calculated using the components in the specified container *target*.
removeLayoutComponent	void removeLayoutComponent(Component comp)
	Required to implement LayoutManager, but not used here. You need to operate directly on the *target* Container.
setConstraints	void setConstraints(Component comp, GridBagConstraints constraints)
	Associates the specified *constraints* to the given component *comp*.
toString	String toString()
	Returns a String showing this GridBagLayout's values.

java.awt.GridLayout

Description	This class encapsulates a layout container manager for grids. This allows you to lay out components in a gridlike manner as opposed to specifying "Center" or "South."
Parent Class	Object
Implements	LayoutManager
See Also	CardLayout, FlowLayout, BorderLayout

CONSTRUCTORS

GridLayout(int rows, int columns [,int horzGap, int vertGap]))

Creates a new GridLayout with the specified number of *rows* and *columns*. You can also specify horizontal and vertical gaps: *horzGap* and *vertGap*. Throws IllegalArgumentException if the rows and colums are not valid.

VARIABLES

None

METHODS

addLayoutComponent void addLayoutComponent(String name, Component comp)

Required to implement LayoutManager, but not used here. You need to operate directly on the *target* Container.

layoutContainer void layoutContainer(Container target)

Reshapes the components in the specified container *target* to fit within the dimensions of the GridLayout object.

minimumLayoutSize Dimension minimumLayoutSize(Container target)

Returns the minimum dimensions required to lay out the components in the specified container *target*.

preferredLayoutSize Dimension preferredLayoutSize(Container target)

Returns the preferred dimensions of this layout calculated using the components in the specified container *target*.

removeLayoutComponent void removeLayoutComponent(Component comp)

Required to implement LayoutManager, but not used here. You need to operate directly on the *target* Container.

toString String toString()

Returns a String showing this GridLayout's values.

java.awt.Image

Description This **abstract** class encapsulates a platform specific image.
Parent Class Object
See Also Graphics

CONSTRUCTORS

None

VARIABLES

UndefinedProperty final static Object: This Object should be returned when a property that is not defined for a particular image is requested.

METHODS

flush abstract void flush()

Flushes all resources used by this Image such as cached pixel data.

getGraphics   abstract Graphics getGraphics()

Returns a Graphics Object to draw into this Image. This only works for offscreen images.

getHeight   abstract int getHeight(ImageObserver observer)

Returns the actual height of this Image. If the Image is currently undefined, it returns -1 and the *observer* is notified later.

getProperty   abstract Object getProperty(String name, ImageObserver observer)

Returns a property of this Image by *name*. If the property is not defined for this Image, it returns the UndefinedProperty Object. If the property is not yet known, it returns null and the *observer* is notified later.

getSource   abstract ImageProducer getSource()

Returns the object that produces the pixels for this Image. This is used by the Image filtering classes.

getWidth   abstract int getWidth(ImageObserver observer)

Returns the actual width of this Image. If the Image is currently undefined, it returns -1 and the *observer* is notified later.

java.awt.Insets

Description	This class encapsulates the insets of a container. It is used by layout managers.
Parent Class	Object
Implements	Cloneable
See Also	Container, LayoutManager

CONSTRUCTORS

Insets(int top, int left, int bottom, int right)

Creates a new inset with the specified *top, left, bottom,* and *right.*

VARIABLES

top	int: The inset from the top.
left	int: The inset from the left.
bottom	int: The inset from the bottom.
right	int: The inset from the right.

METHODS

clone   Object clone()

Returns a clone of this Inset.

toString   String toString()

Returns a String showing the values for this Inset.

java.awt.Label

Description	This class encapsulates a single line of read-only text.
Parent Class	Component
See Also	TextField

CONSTRUCTORS

Label()   Creates a new empty label.

Label(String text [, int alignment])

Creates a new empty label with the specified text and optional *alignment* (LEFT, CENTER, RIGHT). The default alignment is LEFT.

VARIABLES

LEFT	final static int: The left alignment.
CENTER	final static int: The center alignment.
RIGHT	final static int: The right alignment.

METHODS

addNotify   synchronized void addNotify()

Creates a peer for this Label.

getAlignment   int getAlignment()

Returns the current alignment of this Label.

getText   String getText()

Returns the text of this Label.

paramString   protected String paramString()

Returns the parameter String of this Label.

setAlignment   void setAlignment(int alignment)

Sets the alignment to the specified *alignment* for this Label. Throws AWTException if an improper alignment is specifed.

setText   void setText(String text)

Sets the text for this Label to the specified *text*.

java.awt.List

Description	This class encapsulates a scrolling list of selectable text items. The selected item or items will be highlighted. Many of you may already know this as a list box.
Parent Class	Component

CONSTRUCTORS

List([int rows, boolean multipleSelections])

Creates a new empty scrolling list box or one with the optionally specified number of *rows*. The scrolling list will allow *multipleSelections* to be selected when it is true.

VARIABLES

None

METHODS

addItem   synchronized void addItem(String item, int index)

Adds the specified *item* at location *index* of this scrolling List. An index of 0 indicates this item should be placed first on the list.

addNotify   synchronized void addNotify()

Creates a peer for this List.

allowsMultipleSelections boolean allowsMultipleSelections()

Returns true if this List allows for multiple selections.

clear   synchronized void clear()

Clears this List.

countItems   int countItems()

Returns the number of items in this List.

delItem   synchronized void delItem(int index)

Deletes the item located at the specified *index*.

delItems   synchronized void delItems(int start, int end)

Deletes the items located between *start* and *end*.

deselect   synchronized void deselect(int index)

Deselects the item located at the specified *index*.

getItem   String getItem(int index)

Returns the item located at the specified *index*.

getRows   int getRows()

Returns the number of visible lines in this List.

getSelectedIndex   synchronized int getSelectedIndex()

Returns the selected item's index or -1 if no item is selected.

getSelectedIndexes   synchronized int[] getSelectedIndexes()

Returns the selected indexes on this List.

getSelectedItem   synchronized String getSelectedItem()

Returns the selected item on the list or null if there is no item selected.

getSelectedItems   synchronized String[] getSelectedItems()

Returns the selected items on this List.

getVisibleIndex   int getVisibleIndex()

Returns the index of the item last made visible by the method makeVisible.

isSelected   synchronized boolean isSelected(int index)

Returns true if the item at the specified *index* has been selected.

makeVisible   void makeVisible(int index)

Forces the item at the specified *index* to be visible.

minimumSize   Dimension minimumSize(int rows)

Returns the minimum dimensions required for the specified number of *rows*.

minimumSize   Dimension minimumSize()

Returns the minimum dimensions for this List.

paramString   protected String paramString()

Returns the parameter String of this List.

preferredSize   Dimension preferredSize(int rows)

Returns the preferred dimensions required for the specified number of *rows*.

preferredSize   Dimension preferredSize()

Returns the preferred dimensions for this List.

removeNotify   synchronized void removeNotify()

Removes the peer for this List.

replaceItem   synchronized void replaceItem(String newItem, int index)

Replaces the item at location *index* on this scrolling List with *newItem*.

select   synchronized void select(int index)

Selects the item located at the specified *index*.

setMultipleSelections   void setMultipleSelections(boolean multSelect)

If called with *multSelect* as true, then this List will allow multiple selections; otherwise it will not.

java.awt.MediaTracker

Description	This class is used to track the status of media objects. To use the tracker, create an instance of it and invoke its addImage() method for each image you wish to track. Each image should be assigned a unique id number to identify its priority or subset grouping.
Parent Class	Object
See Also	Image

CONSTRUCTORS

MediaTracker(Component comp)

Creates a new MediaTracker that tracks images for the specified component *comp* where the images will eventually be shown.

VARIABLES

ABORTED	final static int: The download of a media was aborted.
COMPLETE	final static int: The download of a media was successfully completed.
ERRORED	final static int: The download of a media encountered an error.
LOADING	final static int: The downloading of a media is in progress.

METHODS

addImage

void addImage(Image image, int id)

Adds the specified *image* and *id* to the tracked list. When shown this image will be full size.

addImage

synchronized void addImage(Image image, int id, int width, int height)

Adds the specified *image* and *id* to the tracked list. When shown this image will have the specified *width* and *height*.

checkAll

synchronized boolean checkAll(boolean load)

Returns true if all images have finished loading, false otherwise. Also, if *load* is specified as true, then it starts loading any image not currently being loaded.

checkID

boolean checkID(int id)

Returns true if all images with the specified *id* have finished loading, false otherwise.

getErrorsAny

synchronized Object[] getErrorsAny()

Returns an array of media Objects that have encountered an error. Returns null if no errors were encountered.

getErrorsID synchronized Object[] getErrorsID(int id)

Returns an array of media Objects with the specified *id* that have encountered an error. Returns null if no errors were encountered.

isErrorAny synchronized boolean isErrorAny()

Returns true if any images had an error while loading, false otherwise.

isErrorID synchronized boolean isErrorID(int id)

Returns true if any images with the specified *id* had an error while loading, false otherwise.

statusAll int statusAll(boolean load)

Returns the boolean OR of all the tracked media statuses. These statuses consist of LOADING, COMPLETE, ERRORED, ABORTED. If *load* is specified as true, the media will be loaded if required.

statusId int statusId(int id, boolean load)

Returns the boolean OR of all tracked images with the specified *id*. These statuses consist of LOADING, COMPLETE, ERRORED, ABORTED. If *load* is specified as true, the media will be loaded if required.

waitForAll synchronized void waitForAll() *

Begins loading all images and waits until they are done or an error occurs. An image is considered complete if an error occurs while loading or displaying it.

waitForID synchronized void waitForID(int id) *

Begins loading all images with the specified *id* and waits until they are done or an error occurs. An image is considered complete if an error occurs loading or displaying it.

waitForID synchronized void waitForID(int id, long time) *

Begins loading all images with the specified *id* and waits until they are done, or until an error occurs, or until the specified *time* in milliseconds has elapsed. An image is considered complete if an error occurs while loading or displaying it.

* Throws InterruptedException if the operation is interrupted.

java.awt.Menu

Description This class encapsulates a top-level label of a menu bar. As an example, File, Edit, View, etc.. might be menus. There is no concept of a resource file in Java, but manually creating menus is fairly easy.

Parent Class	MenuItem
See Also	MenuItem, CheckBoxMenuItem, MenuBar
Implements	MenuContainer

CONSTRUCTORS

Menu(String title[, boolean tearOff] [])

> Creates a new top-level Menu with the specified *title*. If *tearOff* is omitted or specified as false, then the menu will not be able to be torn off. A torn-off menu is one that stays dropped down when you let off the mouse (default in MS Windows). A non-torn-off menu is one where the menu only stays dropped until the mouse button is released (default in X-Windows).

VARIABLES

None

METHODS

add   synchronized MenuItem add(MenuItem item)

> Adds the specified *item* to this Menu.

add   void add(String label)

> Creates a MenuItem with the specified *label* and adds it to this Menu.

addNotify   synchronized void addNotify()

> Creates a peer for this Menu.

addSeparator   void addSeparator()

> Adds a separator line to the Menu at the current position.

countItems   int countItems()

> Returns the current number of elements in this Menu.

getItem   MenuItem getItem(int index)

> Returns the menu item located at the specified *index* of this Menu.

isTearOff   boolean isTearOff()

> Returns true if this Menu may be torn off.

remove   synchronized void remove(int index)

> Deletes the item located at the specified *index* from this Menu.

remove   synchronized void remove(MenuComponent item)

> Deletes the specified *item* from this Menu.

removeNotify	synchronized void removeNotify()
	Removes the peer for this Menu.

java.awt.MenuBar

Description	This class encapsulates the native implementation of a menu bar on the top of a frame. Call the Frame.setMenuBar() method to associate the MenuBar with its Frame.
Parent Class	MenuComponent
See Also	Menu, Frame
Implements	MenuContainer

CONSTRUCTORS

MenuBar()	Creates a new MenuBar.

VARIABLES

None

METHODS

add	synchronized Menu add(Menu menu)
	Adds the specified *menu* to this MenuBar.
addNotify	synchronized void addNotify()
	Creates a peer for this MenuBar.
countMenus	int countMenus()
	Returns the number of menus in this MenuBar.
getHelpMenu	Menu getHelpMenu()
	Returns the help menu on this MenuBar.
getMenu	Menu getMenu(int index)
	Returns the menu at the specified *index*.
remove	synchronized void remove(int index)
	Deletes the menu located at the specified *index* from this MenuBar.
remove	synchronized void remove(MenuComponent menuComp)
	Deletes the specified *menuComp* from this MenuBar.
removeNotify	void removeNotify()
	Removes the peer for this MenuBar.
setHelpMenu	synchronized void setHelpMenu(Menu menu)
	Sets the help menu to the specified *menu*.

java.awt.MenuComponent

Description	This **abstract** class is the superclass of all menu-related components.
Parent Class	Object
See Also	MenuItem, MenuBar

CONSTRUCTORS

None

VARIABLES

None

METHODS

getFont
    Font getFont()

Returns the Font used for this Menu; if nothing is set, then it returns the Font for the parent MenuContainer.

getParent
    MenuContainer getParent()

Returns the parent MenuContainer.

getPeer
    MenuComponentPeer getPeer()

Returns the MenuComponent's peer.

paramString
    protected String paramString()

Returns the String parameter of this MenuComponent.

postEvent
    void postEvent(Event event)

Posts the specified *event* to the parent MenuContainer.

removeNotify
    void removeNotify()

Removes the peer for this MenuComponent.

setFont
    void setFont(Font font)

Sets the Font for this MenuComponent to the specified *font*.

toString
    String toString()

Returns a String showing this MenuComponent's values.

java.awt.MenuItem

Description	This class encapsulates a sublevel "pull-down" label of a particular menu. As an example, if File is a top-level menu, then New, Open, Close, etc., might be menu items underneath it.
Parent Class	MenuComponent
See Also	McnuBar, Menu

CONSTRUCTORS

MenuItem(String label)

        Constructs a menu item with the specified *label*.

VARIABLES

None

METHODS

addNotify	synchronized void addNotify() Creates a peer for this MenuItem.
disable	void disable() Sets this MenuItem to unselectable.
enable	void enable() Sets this MenuItem to selectable.
enable	void enable(boolean enabled) Sets this MenuItem to selectable when *enabled* is true; otherwise disables it.
getLabel	String getLabel() Returns the label for this MenuItem.
isEnabled	boolean isEnabled() Returns true if this MenuItem is enabled.
paramString	String paramString() Returns the String parameter of the MenuItem.
setLabel	void setLabel(String label) Sets this MenuItem's label to the specified *label*.

java.awt.Panel

Description	This class encapsulates a panel. A panel is a generic container for other graphical elements.
Parent Class	Container
See Also	Window, FlowLayout

CONSTRUCTORS

Panel()   Creates a new panel with a FlowLayout.

VARIABLES

None

METHODS

addNotify   synchronized void addNotify()

Creates a peer for this Panel.

java.awt.Point

Description	This class encapsulates a point on a plane.
Parent Class	Object
See Also	Polygon, Rectangle

CONSTRUCTORS

Point(int x,int y)   Constructs a new Point at the specified *x,y* coordinate.

VARIABLES

x   int: The x coordinate of this Point.

y   int: The y coordinate of this Point.

METHODS

equals   boolean equals(Object obj2)

Returns true if this Point and Point *obj2* are at the same location.

hashCode   int hashCode()

Returns the hash code for this Point.

move   void move(int x, int y)

Moves this Point to coordinates *x,y*.

toString   String toString()

Returns a String showing this Point's values.

translate   void translate(int x, int y)

Moves this Point by an offset of *x,y*.

java.awt.Polygon

Description	This class implements a polygon. A polygon is a closed figure composed of three or more straight lines.
Parent Class	Object
See Also	Rectangle, Point

CONSTRUCTORS

Polygon([int xpoints[], int ypoints[], int numPoints])

> Constructs a new empty Polygon or a Polygon with a total number of points *numPoints* whose x and y coordinates are specified in *xpoints[]* and *ypoints[]* respectively.

VARIABLES

npoints	int: The total number of points in this Polygon
xpoints	int[]: The array of x coordinates.
ypoints	int[]: The array of y coordinates.

METHODS

addPoint   void addPoint(int x, int y)

> Appends a point at coordinates *x,y* to this Polygon.

getBoundingBox   Rectangle getBoundingBox()

> Returns a Rectangle bounding the area taken up by this Polygon.

inside   boolean inside(int x, int y)

> Returns true if the points *x* and *y* are inside of this Polygon, false otherwise.

java.awt.Rectangle

Description	This class implements a rectangle.
Parent Class	Object
See Also	Polygon, Point

CONSTRUCTORS

Rectangle([int width, int height])

> Constructs a new rectangle with no dimensions or with the optionally specified *width* and *height* dimensions whose upper left corner is at (0, 0).

Rectangle(int x, int y, int width, int height)

> Constructs a new rectangle with the specified coordinates *x,y* and *width* and *height*.

Rectangle(Point point[, Dimension dimension])

> Constructs a new rectangle with the specified *point* and assumed dimension of 0 or with the specified *dimension*.

Rectangle(Dimension dimension)

>   Constructs a new rectangle at (0,0) with the specified *dimension*.

VARIABLES

height	int: The height of this rectangle.
width	int: The width of this rectangle.
x	int: The upper left x coordinate of this rectangle.
y	int: The upper left y coordinate of this rectangle.

METHODS

add   void add(int x, int y)

>   Adds a point at coordinates *x,y* to this Rectangle. The Rectangle will grow such that it is the smallest possible Rectangle containing the point and the Rectangle.

add   void add(Point point)

>   Adds the specified *point* to this Rectangle. See above.

add   void add(Rectangle rect2)

>   Adds *rect2* to this Rectangle. The resulting Rectangle is the union of this Rectangle and *rect2*.

equals   boolean equals(Object obj2)

>   Returns true if this Rectangle and Rectangle *obj2* have the same dimensions and position.

grow   void grow(int h, int v)

>   Increases the size of this Rectangle horizontally by *h*2* and vertically by *v*2* while keeping the center constant.

hashCode   int hashCode()

>   Returns the hash code for this Rectangle.

inside   boolean inside(int x, int y)

>   Checks to see if the specified point at *x,y* lies inside this Rectangle.

intersection   Rectangle intersection(Rectangle rect2)

>   Returns the intersection of this Rectangle and *rect2*.

intersects   boolean intersects(Rectangle rect2)

>   Returns true if this rectangle and *rect2* intersect.

isEmpty   boolean isEmpty()

>   Returns true if either the width or height of this Rectangle is less than or equal to zero.

move   void move(int x, int y)

>   Moves this Rectangle to coordinates *x,y*.

reshape	void reshape(int x, int y, int width, int height)
	Reshapes this Rectangle to coordinates *x,y* with the specified *width* and *height*.
resize	void resize(int width, int height)
	Resizes this Rectangle to the specified *width* and *height*.
toString	String toString()
	Returns a String showing this Rectangle's values.
translate	void translate(int x, int y)
	Moves this Rectangle by an offset of *x,y*.
union	Rectangle union(Rectangle rect2)
	Returns the union of this Rectangle and *rect2*.

java.awt.ScrollBar

Description	This class implements a native scroll bar. Scroll bars allow a user to enter numerical data with a mouse by dragging a sliding bar or clicking an increase or decrease button at its ends. Their primary use is to scroll through large amounts of data (e.g., word processors, list boxes).
Parent Class	Component

CONSTRUCTORS

Scrollbar([int orientation])

Creates a scroll bar with a vertical orientation or the specified *orientation* (HORIZONTAL or VERTICAL). Throws IllegalArgumentException if an illegal orientation is specified.

Scrollbar(int orientation, int value, int visible, int min, int max)

Creates a scroll bar with the specified *orientation* (HORIZONTAL or VERTICAL), *value*, size of the *visible* portion, and the *max* and *min* values.

VARIABLES

HORIZONTAL	final static int: Used to set the Scrollbar orientation.
VERTICAL	final static int: Used to set the Scrollbar orientation.

METHODS

addNotify	synchronized void addNotify()
	Creates a peer for this Scrollbar.

getLineIncrement	int getLineIncrement()
	Returns the line increment of this Scrollbar.
getMaximum	int getMaximum()
	Returns the maximum value of this Scrollbar.
getMinimum	int getMinimum()
	Returns the minimum value of this Scrollbar.
getOrientation	int getOrientation()
	Returns the orientation of this Scrollbar (HORIZONTAL or VERTICAL).
getPageIncrement	int getPageIncrement()
	Returns the page increment of this Scrollbar.
getValue	int getValue()
	Returns the current value of this Scrollbar.
getVisible	int getVisible()
	Returns the amount of the visible part of the Scrollbar.
paramString	protected String paramString()
	Returns the String parameters for this Scrollbar.
setLineIncrement	void setLineIncrement(int inc)
	Sets the line increment of this Scrollbar to *inc*.
setPageIncrement	void setPageIncrement(int inc)
	Sets the page increment of this Scrollbar to *inc*.
setValue	void setValue(int value)
	Sets the value of this Scrollbar to the specified *value*. If the value is out of range, the value becomes the new max or min.
setValues	void setValues(int value, int visible, int min, int max)
	Sets the *value*, *visible* amount, *min* and *max* values for this Scrollbar.

java.awt.TextArea

Description	This class encapsulates a GUI element that allows you to display and possibly edit multiple line blocks of text.
Parent Class	TextComponent
See Also	TextField

CONSTRUCTORS

TextArea([int columns, int rows])

Creates an empty multiline text area with an optional number of *columns* and *rows*.

TextArea(String text [,int columns, int rows])

> Creates a multiline text area with the specified text and an optional number of *columns* and *rows*.

VARIABLES

None

METHODS

addNotify   synchronized void addNotify()

> Creates a peer for this TextArea.

appendText   void appendText(String text)

> Appends the specified *text* at the end.

getColumns   int getColumns()

> Returns the number of columns in this TextArea.

getRows   int getRows()

> Returns the number of rows in this TextArea.

insertText   void insertText(String text, int position)

> Inserts the specified *text* at the *position* specified.

minimumSize   Dimension minimumSize([int rows, int columns])

> Returns a Dimension with the minimum size of this TextField. Optionally, you may specify the mimimum number of *rows* and *columns*.

paramString   protected String paramString()

> Returns the String of parameters for this TextArea.

preferredSize   Dimension preferredSize([int rows, int columns])

> Returns a Dimension with the preferred size of this TextField. Optionally, you may specify the preferred number of *rows* and *columns*.

replaceText   void replaceText(String newText, int start, int end)

> Replaces the current text from the specified *start* to *end* position with *newText*.

java.awt.TextComponent

Description	This class encapsulates a Component that allows editing of text.
Parent Class	Component
See Also	TextArea, TextField

CONSTRUCTORS

None

VARIABLES

None

METHODS

getSelectedText	String getSelectedText()
	Returns the selected text.
getSelectionEnd	int getSelectionEnd()
	Returns the end position of the selected text.
getSelectionStart	int getSelectionStart()
	Returns the start position of the selected text.
getText	String getText()
	Returns the text contained in this TextComponent.
isEditable	boolean isEditable()
	Returns true if this TextComponent is editable; false if not.
paramString	protected String paramString()
	Returns the String of parameters for this TextComponent.
removeNotify	synchronized void removeNotify()
	Removes the TextComponent's peer.
select	void select(int start, int end)
	Selects the text between the specified *start* and *end* position.
selectAll	void selectAll()
	Selects all the text in this TextComponent.
setEditable	void setEditable(boolean isEditable)
	Sets this TextComponent as editable if *isEditable* is true.
setText	void setText(String text)
	Sets the text in this TextComponent to the specified *text*.

java.awt.TextField

Description	This class encapsulates a single line of editable text.
Parent Class	TextComponent
See Also	TextArea

CONSTRUCTORS

TextField([int columns])

Creates a new TextField, optionally initialized to the specified number of *columns*.

TextField(String initialText[,int columns])

Creates a new TextField with the specified *initialText*, optionally initialized to the specified number of *columns*.

VARIABLES

None

METHODS

addNotify synchronized void addNotify()

Creates a peer for this TextField.

echoCharIsSet boolean echoCharIsSet()

Returns true if the echo character has been set for this TextField.

getColumns int getColumns()

Returns the number of columns in this TextField.

getEchoChar char getEchoChar()

Returns the character used for echoing.

minimumSize Dimension minimumSize([int columns])

Returns a Dimension with the minimum size needed for this TextField. Optionally, the number of *columns* may be specified.

paramString protected String paramString()

Returns the String of parameters for this TextField.

preferredSize Dimension preferredSize([int columns])

Returns a Dimension with the preferred size for this TextField. Optionally, the number of *columns* may be specified.

setEchoCharacter void setEchoCharacter(char ch)

Sets the echo character for this TextField to *ch*.

java.awt.Toolkit

Description This **abstract** class is a factory used to bind the abstract Windows toolkit to a platform specific toolkit implementation.

Parent Class Object

CONSTRUCTORS

None

VARIABLES

None

METHODS

checkImage   abstract int checkImage(Image image, int width, int height, ImageObserver observer)

Returns the construction status of the specifed *image* with *width* and *height* on the default screen.

createButton   protected abstract ButtonPeer createButton(Button target)

Creates a new Button using the specified Peer interface.

createCanvas   protected abstract CanvasPeer createCanvas(Canvas target)

Creates a new Canvas using the specified Peer interface.

createCheckBox   protected abstract CheckboxPeer createCheckBox(Checkbox target)

Creates a new Checkbox using the specified Peer interface.

createCheckBoxMenuItem   protected abstract CheckboxMenuItemPeer createCheckBoxMenuItem (CheckboxMenuItem target)

Creates a new CheckboxMenuItem using the specified Peer interface.

createChoice   protected abstract ChoicePeer createChoice(Choice target)

Creates a new Choice using the specified Peer interface.

createDialog   protected abstract DialogPeer createDialog(Dialog target)

Creates a new Dialog using the specified Peer interface.

createFileDialog   protected abstract FileDialogPeer createFileDialog(FileDialog target)

Creates a new FileDialog using the specified Peer interface.

createFrame   protected abstract FramePeer createFrame(Frame target)

Creates a new Frame using the specified Peer interface.

createImage   abstract Image createImage(ImageProducer producer)

Creates an image with the specified image producer.

createLabel   protected abstract LabelPeer createLabel(Label target)

Creates a new Label using the specified Peer interface.

createList   protected abstract ListPeer createList(List target)

Creates a new List using the specified Peer interface.

createMenu   protected abstract MenuPeer createMenu(Menu target)

Creates a new Menu using the specified Peer interface.

createMenuBar   protected abstract MenuBarPeer createMenuBar(MenuBar target)

Creates a new MenuBar using the specified Peer interface.

createMenuItem	protected abstract MenuItemPeer createMenuItem(MenuItem target)
	Creates a new MenuItem using the specified Peer interface.
createPanel	protected abstract PanelPeer createPanel(Panel target)
	Creates a new Panel using the specified Peer interface.
createScrollbar	protected abstract ScrollbarPeer createScrollbar(Scrollbar target)
	Creates a new Scrollbar using the specified Peer interface.
createTextArea	protected abstract TextAreaPeer createTextArea(TextArea target)
	Creates a new TextArea using the specified Peer interface.
createTextField	protected abstract TextFieldPeer createTextField(TextField target)
	Creates a new TextField using the specified Peer interface.
createWindow	protected abstract WindowPeer createWindow(Window target)
	Creates a new Window using the specified Peer interface.
getColorModel	abstract ColorModel getColorModel()
	Returns the ColorModel of the display.
getDefaultToolkit	static synchronized Toolkit getDefaultToolkit()
	Returns the default toolkit. Throws ClassNotFoundException if the toolkit is not found and InstantiationException if the toolkit could not be instantiated.
getFontList	abstract String[] getFontList()
	Returns a String array containing the names of the available fonts.
getFontMetrics	abstract FontMetrics getFontMetrics(Font font)
	Returns a FontMetrics object of the specified *font*.
getImage	abstract Image getImage(String file)
	Returns an Image obtained from pixel data in the specified *file*.
getImage	abstract Image getImage(URL url)
	Returns an Image obtained from pixel data at the specified *url*.
getScreenResolution	abstract int getScreenResolution()
	Returns the screen resolution in dots per inch.
getScreenSize	abstract Dimension getScreenSize()
	Returns the size of the screen.
prepareImage	abstract int prepareImage(Image image, int width, int height, ImageObserver observer)
	Prepares the specifed *image* with *width* and *height* for rendering on the default screen.
sync	abstract void sync()
	Syncs the graphics state, useful when performing animation.

java.awt.Window

Description	This class encapsulates a general purpose top-level window with no borders or menu bar. Its default layout is BorderLayout.
Parent Class	Container
See Also	Frame

CONSTRUCTORS

Window(Frame parent)

Creates a new modal (blocks all input to other windows when shown) window. Initially the window is invisible; you must invoke its show() method to see it.

VARIABLES

None

METHODS

addNotify   synchronized void addNotify()

Creates a peer for this Window.

dispose   synchronized void dispose()

Destroys this Window.

getToolkit   Toolkit getToolkit()

Returns the toolkit of this Window.

getWarningStatus   final String getWarningStatus()

Returns the security warning status of this Window.

pack   synchronized void pack()

Packs the components of this Window.

show   synchronized void show()

Shows this Window and brings it to the front.

toBack   void toBack()

Moves the Frame behind this Window.

toFront   void toFront()

Brings the Frame in front of this Window.

AWT.IMAGE

java.awt.Image.ImageConsumer (Interface)

Description	This interface is used by ImageProducer to deliver image data to interested objects. In other words, when a consumer is added to an ImageProducer, the producer will deliver the image data using the method calls defined in this interface.
Parent Class	Object
See Also	ImageProducer

VARIABLES

COMPLETESCANLINES final static int: When specified as a hint flag, pixels will be delivered in multiples of complete scanlines.

IMAGEERROR final static int: An error was encountered while producing an image.

RANDOMPIXELORDER final static int: When specified as a hint flag, pixels will be delivered in a random order. In other words, the ImageConsumer will not use any optimizations that depend on the order of pixel delivery. This is the default assumption without a call to the setHints method.

SINGLEFRAME final static int: When specified as a hint flag, the image contains a single static frame. The pixels will be defined in calls to the setPixels methods, after which the imageComplete method will be called with the STATICIMAGEDONE flag, indicating that no more image data will be delivered.

SINGLEFRAMEDONE final static int: One frame of the image is done; however, there are more frames yet to be delivered.

SINGLEPASS final static int: When specified as a hint flag, the pixels will be delivered in a single pass. In other words, each pixel will appear after only one call to any of the setPixels methods. Some formats, such as a progressive JPEG image, define pixels in multiple passes (each more and more refined) and therefore will not work in a single pass.

STATICIMAGEDONE final static int: The image is done; there are no more pixels or frames requiring delivery.

TOPDOWNLEFTRIGHT final static int: When specified as a hint flag, pixels will be delivered in top-down, left-to-right order.

METHODS

imageComplete void imageComplete(int status)

This method is called when the ImageProducer has delivered all of the pixels contained in the source image, or when a single frame of a multiframe animation has finished, or when an error loading or producing the image has occurred. Status will contain STATICIMAGEDONE, SINGLEFRAMEDONE or IMAGEERROR respectively.

setColorModel	void setColorModel(ColorModel model)

Sets the ColorModel object used for the majority of pixels to *model*.

setDimensions	void setDimensions(int width, int height)

Sets the dimensions of the source image to *width* and *height*.

setHints	void setHints(int hintflags)

The ImageProducer is capable of delivering the pixels in any order, but the ImageConsumer may be able to scale or convert the pixels to the destination ColorModel more effectively knowing something about how the pixels will be delivered. This method should be called before any calls to the setPixels method. Predefined *hintflags* bits are: COMPLETESCANLINES, RANDOM-PIXELORDER, SINGLEFRAME, SINGLEPASS *or* TOPDOWN-LEFTRIGHT.

setPixels	void setPixels(int x, int y, int w, int h, ColorModel m, byte pix[], int off, int s)

The pixels of the image are delivered using one or more calls to this method. *x, y, w, h* define the rectangle of source data contained in the pixel array. The ColorModel *m* should be used to convert the pixels to their color and alpha components. The byte pixels *pix*[a,b] are stored in the pixel array at (b * s + a + off) where *s* is the scansize and *off* the offset.

setPixels	void setPixels(int x, int y, int w, int h, ColorModel m, int pixels[], int off, int s)

The pixels of the image are delivered using one or more calls to this method. This works the same as above, only the pixels returned are stored as integers rather than bytes.

setProperties	void setProperties(Hashtable props)

Sets the extensible property list associated with this image.

java.awt.Image.ImageObserver (Interface)

Description	This interface provides an asynchronous callback method that may be used to update objects interested in displaying images. For example, a call to awt.Image.getHeight() will return the Image height if it is available, and if not, a call to imageUpdate() is guaranteed as soon as the height becomes available.
Parent Class	Object
See Also	ImageProducer, awt.Image

VARIABLES

ALLBITS	final static int: A previously drawn static image is now finished and can be redrawn in its final form. The x, y, width, and height arguments of the imageUpdate callback method should not be used.
ERROR	final static int: An image that was tracked asynchronously encountered an error. It will not be drawn.
FRAMEBITS	final static int: The next frame of a previously drawn multiframe image is now available to be drawn. The x, y, width, and height arguments of the imageUpdate callback method should not be used.
HEIGHT	final static int: The base image height is currently in the height argument of the imageUpdate callback method.
PROPERTIES	final static int: The image properties are now available.
SOMEBITS	final static int: Additional pixels needed for drawing a scaled image are ready. The bounding box of the new pixels is contained in the x, y, width, and height arguments of the imageUpdate callback method.
WIDTH	final static int: The base image width is currently in the width argument of the imageUpdate callback method.

METHODS

imageUpdate

boolean imageUpdate(Image img, int infoflags, int x, int y, int width, int height)

This method is called when information about an image previously requested using an asynchronous interface becomes available. The Image being tracked is passed in as *img*. The *infoflags* will contain one or more of the predefined values shown in the variable section. The interpretation of *x, y, width*, and *height* depend on the *infoflags* values. When you implement this method, you should return false if further updates are needed and true if they are not.

java.awt.Image.ImageProducer (Interface)

Description	This interface is used by ImageConsumer to request information about images from objects that build them.
Parent Class	Object
See Also	ImageConsumer

VARIABLES

None

METHODS

addConsumer   void addConsumer(ImageConsumer ic)

This method registers the specified ImageConsumer *ic* with the ImageProducer. It may now access the image data during a reconstruction of the Image.

isConsumer   boolean isConsumer(ImageConsumer ic)

Returns true if the specified ImageConsumer *ic* is currently registered with this ImageProducer as one of its consumers.

removeConsumer   void removeConsumer(ImageConsumer ic)

This method removes the specified ImageConsumer *ic* from the list of consumers currently registered to receive image data.

requestTopDownLeftRightResend   void requestTopDownLeftRightResend(ImageConsumer ic)

This method is used by the specified ImageConsumer *ic* to request the ImageProducer to resend the image data in TOP-DOWNLEFTRIGHT order so that better conversion algorithms, which depend on receiving pixels in order, can be used to produce a higher quality image. The ImageProducer may ignore the request if it is not possible.

startProduction   void startProduction(ImageConsumer ic)

This method registers the specified ImageConsumer *ic* as a consumer and begins an immediate reconstruction of the image data. As soon as possible, the data is delivered to this consumer and other registered consumers.

java.awt.Image.ColorModel

Description   This **abstract** class encapsulates methods that translate from pixel values in an image to the corresponding transparency and color components.

Parent Class   Object

See Also   DirectColorModel, IndexColorModel

CONSTRUCTORS

ColorModel(int bits)

Creates a ColorModel defining a pixel with the specified *bits* of depth.

VARIABLES

pixel_bits   protected int: Number of bits representing a pixel.

METHODS

getAlpha	abstract int getAlpha(int pixel)
	Returns the alpha transparency component for the specified *pixel*.
getBlue	abstract int getBlue(int pixel)
	Returns the blue color component for the specified *pixel*.
getGreen	abstract int getGreen(int pixel)
	Returns the green color component for the specified *pixel*.
getPixelSize	int getPixelSize()
	Returns the number of bits per pixel for this ColorModel.
getRed	abstract int getRed(int pixel)
	Returns the red color component for the specified *pixel*.
getRGB	int getRGB(int pixel)
	Returns the color of the pixel in the default RGB color model.
getRGBdefault	static ColorModel getRGBdefault()
	Returns a ColorModel that describes the default format for integer RGB values. This format consists of (from high byte to low) alpha, red, green, and blue color components in a packed 32-bit integer, i.e, 0xAARRGGBB.

java.awt.Image.CropImageFilter

Description	This class encapsulates a means to crop images by extracting a specified rectangular region from an existing image. It provides a source for the new "cropped" image.
Parent Class	ImageFilter
See Also	FilteredImageSource, ImageFilter

CONSTRUCTORS

CropImageFilter(int x, int y, int width, int height)

Creates a new CropImageFilter that gets a rectangular region from its source image. This region is defined by its top left *x,y* coordinates and its *width* and *height*.

VARIABLES

None

METHODS

setDimensions   void setDimensions(int width, int height)

Sets the dimensions of the source image to *width* and *height*, overriding the source image dimensions.

setPixels   void setPixels(int x, int y, int w, int h, ColorModel model, byte pixels[], int off, int scansize)

Delivers only the byte pixels of this image contained in the region to be obtained. See this method in ImageConsumer for an explanation of its parameters.

setPixels   void setPixels(int x, int y, int w, int h, ColorModel model, int pixels[], int off, int scansize)

Delivers only the integer pixels of this image contained in the region to be obtained. See this method in ImageConsumer for an explanation of its parameters.

setProperties   void setProperties(Hashtable props)

Passes the properties *props* from the source object after adding a property indicating the cropped region.

java.awt.Image.DirectColorModel

Description   This class implements a ColorModel where pixel values themselves contain transparency and color components. It also provides methods for translating between pixel values to transparency and color components for these pixels.

Parent Class   ColorModel

See Also   ColorModel, IndexColorModel

CONSTRUCTORS

DirectColorModel(int bits, int redMask, int greenMask, int blueMask [,alphaMask])

Creates a DirectColorModel with the specified masks indicating which bits represent the red, green, blue, and optional alpha components. If the *alphaMask* is not specified, a fully opaque value of 255 is assumed. All of the mask bits must be contiguous and fit in the specified least significant *bits* of the integer.

VARIABLES

None

METHODS

getAlpha   int getAlpha(int pixel)

Returns the alpha transparency value (0-255) for the specified *pixel*.

getAlphaMask   int getAlphaMask()

Returns the mask showing which bits within the pixel represent the alpha transparency component.

getBlue   int getBlue(int pixel)

Returns the blue color value (0-255) for the specified *pixel*.

getBlueMask   int getBlueMask()

Returns the mask showing which bits within the pixel represent the blue color component.

getGreen   int getGreen(int pixel)

Returns the green color value (0-255) for the specified *pixel*.

getGreenMask   int getGreenMask()

Returns the mask showing which bits within the pixel represent the green color component.

getRed   int getRed(int pixel)

Returns the red color value (0-255) for the specified *pixel*.

getRedMask   int getRedMask()

Returns the mask showing which bits within the pixel represent the red color component.

getRGB   final int getRGB(int pixel)

Returns the RGB color of the specified *pixel* using the default ColorModel.

java.awt.Image.FilteredImageSource

Description   This class encapsulates a means to produce a filtered image given an existing image and a filter.

Parent Class   Object

Implements   ImageProducer

See Also   ImageFilter

CONSTRUCTORS

FilteredImageSource(ImageProducer original, ImageFilter imgFilter)

Creates an ImageProducer object from an *original* ImageProducer and an applied *imgFilter*.

VARIABLES

None

METHODS

addConsumer	synchronized void addConsumer(ImageConsumer ic)
	Adds the specified ImageConsumer *ic* to the list of consumers interested in this image's data.
isConsumer	synchronized boolean isConsumer(ImageConsumer ic)
	Returns true if the specified ImageConsumer *ic* is on the list of consumers currently interested in this image's data.
removeConsumer	synchronized void removeConsumer(ImageConsumer ic)
	Removes the specified ImageConsumer *ic* from the list of consumers interested in this image's data.
requestTopDownLeftRightResend	void requestTopDownLeftRightResend(ImageConsumer ic)
	Requests that the specified ImageConsumer *ic* have the image data delivered again in top-down, left-right order.
startProduction	void startProduction(ImageConsumer ic)
	Adds the specified ImageConsumer *ic* to the list of consumers interested in this image's data. It then begins immediate delivery of the image data through the ImageConsumer interface.

java.awt.Image.ImageFilter

Description	This class encapsulates a means to produce a filtered image given an existing image and a filter. The default implementation is a "null filter," which just passes the data through. You should subclass ImageFilter and override its methods to provide your own filter functionality.
Parent Class	Object
Implements	Cloneable, ImageConsumer
See Also	FilteredImageSource, CropImageFilter, RGBImageFilter

CONSTRUCTORS

None

VARIABLES

consumer	protected ImageConsumer: The consumer of the image data stream that this ImageFilter is filtering. Initialized by getFilterInstance().

METHODS

clone
Object clone()
Returns a clone of this ImageFilter.

getFilterInstance
ImageFilter getFilterInstance(ImageConsumer ic)
Returns a unique instance of ImageFilter that will perform the filtering for the specified ImageConsumer *ic*. The default implementation clones this ImageFilter object.

imageComplete
void imageComplete(int status)
This method is called by the ImageProducer when the ImageProducer is finished with an image. Status will contain STATICIMAGEDONE, SINGLEFRAMEDONE, or IMAGEERROR. It allows you to modify the calling parameters before calling the actual method of the ImageConsumer interface.

resendTopDownLeftRight void resendTopDownLeftRight(ImageProducer ip)
Called when the ImageConsumer requests that the specified ImageProducer *ip* deliver the image data again in top-down, left-right order.

setColorModel
void setColorModel(ColorModel model)
This method allows you to modify the calling parameters before calling the actual method of the ImageConsumer interface. Sets the ColorModel object used for the majority of pixels that will be reported using the setPixels method.

setDimensions
void setDimensions(int width, int height)
This method allows you to modify the calling parameters before calling the actual method of the ImageConsumer interface. The dimensions of the source image are reported using the setDimensions method call.

setHints
void setHints(int hintflags)
This method allows you to modify the calling parameters before calling the actual method of the ImageConsumer interface The ImageProducer can deliver the pixels in any order, but the ImageConsumer may be able to scale or convert the pixels to the destination ColorModel more effectively knowing something about how the pixels will be delivered. This method should be called before any calls to the setPixels method. The bitmask *hintflags* may be specified as COMPLETESCANLINES, RANDOMPIXELORDER, SINGLEFRAME, SINGLEPASS, or TOPDOWNLEFTRIGHT.

setPixels
void setPixels(int x, int y, int w, int h, ColorModel m, byte pix[], int off, int s)
This method allows you to modify the calling parameters before calling the actual method of the ImageConsumer interface. The

pixels of the image are delivered using one or more calls to this method. *x, y, w, h* define the rectangle of source data contained in the pixel array. The ColorModel *m* should be used to convert the pixels to their color and alpha components. The byte pixels *pix*[a,b] are stored in the pixel array at (b * s + a + off) where *s* is the scansize and *off* the offset.

setPixels   void setPixels(int x, int y, int w, int h, ColorModel m, int pixels[], int off, int s)

This works the same as above, only the pixels returned are stored as integers rather than bytes.

setProperties   void setProperties(Hashtable props)

This method allows you to modify the calling parameters before calling the actual method of the ImageConsumer interface. You should pass the properties through after adding a property indicating the stream of filters the Image has been through.

java.awt.Image.IndexColorModel

Description   This class implements a ColorModel where pixel values are indexes into a fixed color table. It also provides methods for translating between pixel values to transparency and color components for these pixels.

Parent Class   ColorModel

See Also   ColorModel, DirectColorModel

CONSTRUCTORS

IndexColorModel(int bits, int size, byte red[], byte green[], byte blue[] [, int trans])

Creates an IndexColorModel given *red[], green[]* and *blue[]* arrays and their *size* (all arrays must be at least as large as *size*). If the index of the transparent pixel *trans* is not specified, a fully opaque value of 255 is assumed. The specified *bits* indicate the number of bits in each pixel.

IndexColorModel(int bits, int size, byte red[], byte green[], byte blue[], byte alpha[])

Creates an IndexColorModel given *red[], green[], blue[],* and *alpha[]* arrays and their *size* (all arrays must be at least as large as *size*). The specified *bits* indicate the number of bits in each pixel.

IndexColorModel(int bits, int size, byte cmap[], int start, int hasalpha [, int trans])

Creates an IndexColorModel given a *cmap[]* array that contains single arrays of packed red, green, blue and optional alpha components (assumed when *hasalpha* is true) arrays and their *size* (all arrays must be at least as large as *size*). The specified *bits* indicate the number of bits in each pixel.

VARIABLES

None

METHODS

getAlpha	int getAlpha(int pixel)
	Returns the alpha transparency value (0-255) for the specified *pixel*.
getAlphas	void getAlphas(byte a[])
	Copies the array of alpha transparency values into the specified array *a[]*.
getBlue	int getBlue(int pixel)
	Returns the blue color value (0-255) for the specified *pixel*.
getBlues	void getBlues(byte b[])
	Copies the array of blue color values into the specified array *b[]*.
getGreen	int getGreen(int pixel)
	Returns the green color value (0-255) for the specified *pixel*.
getGreens	void getGreens(byte g[])
	Copies the array of green color values into the specified array *g[]*.
getMapSize	int getMapSize()
	Returns the size of the color component arrays for this IndexColorModel.
getRed	int getRed(int pixel)
	Returns the red color value (0-255) for the specified *pixel*.
getReds	void getReds(byte r[])
	Copies the array of red color values into the specified array *r[]*.
getRGB	int getRGB(int pixel)
	Returns the color of the specified *pixel* using the default RGB color model.
getTransparentPixel	int getTransparentPixel()
	Returns the index for the transparent pixel in this IndexColorModel or -1 if a transparent pixel does not exist.

java.awt.Image.MemoryImageSource

Description	This class is an ImageProducer that uses an array to produce pixel values for an Image.
Parent Class	Object
Implements	ImageProducer
See Also	Image

CONSTRUCTORS

MemoryImageSource(int width, int height, ColorModel model, byte pixels[], int pixelOffset, int scansize[, Hashtable props])

Given the specified parameters, this creates a MemoryImageSource object that uses an array of bytes to produce data for an Image.

MemoryImageSource(int width, int height, ColorModel model, int pixels[], int pixelOffset, int scansize[, Hashtable props])

Given the specified parameters, this creates a MemoryImageSource object that uses an array of integers to produce data for an Image.

MemoryImageSource(int width, int height, int pixels[], int pixelOffset, int scansize[, Hashtable props])

Given the specified parameters, this creates a MemoryImageSource object that uses an array of integers in the default RGB color model to produce data for an Image.

VARIABLES

None

METHODS

addConsumer   synchronized void addConsumer(ImageConsumer ic)

Adds the specified ImageConsumer *ic* to the list of consumers interested in this image's data.

isConsumer   synchronized boolean isConsumer(ImageConsumer ic)

Returns true if the specified ImageConsumer *ic* is on the list of consumers currently interested in this image's data.

removeConsumer   synchronized void removeConsumer(ImageConsumer ic)

Removes the specified ImageConsumer *ic* from the list of consumers interested in this image's data.

requestTopDownLeftRightResend   void requestTopDownLeftRightResend(ImageConsumer ic)

Requests that the specified ImageConsumer *ic* have the image data delivered again in top-down, left-right order.

startProduction   void startProduction(ImageConsumer ic)

Adds the specified ImageConsumer *ic* to the list of consumers interested in this image's data. It then begins immediate delivery of the image data using the ImageConsumer interface.

java.awt.Image.RGBImageFilter

Description   This **abstract** class encapsulates a means to create an ImageFilter that modifies the pixels of an RGB ColorModel Image.

Parent Class	ImageFilter
See Also	ImageFilter

CONSTRUCTORS

None

VARIABLES

canFilterIndexColorModel protected boolean: If true then the filterRGB() method may apply color filtering directly to the color table entries of an IndexColorModel object instead of to each pixel. This variable should be set to true by subclass constructors if their filterRGB() method does not depend on the specific coordinate of the pixel being filtered.

newmodel   protected ColorModel: Model to replace oldmodel.

oldmodel   protected ColorModel: Model to be replaced by newmodel.

METHODS

filterIndexColorModel IndexColorModel filterIndexColorModel(IndexColorModel icm)

Filters an IndexColorModel *icm* by running each entry in its color tables through the filterRGB function of an RGBImageFilter subclass.

filterRGB   int filterRGB(int x, int y, int rgb)

This is the only method that you must override to provide a useful ImageFilter. This method should convert a single input pixel in the default RGB ColorModel to a single output pixel.

filterRGBPixels   void filterRGBPixels(int x, int y, int w, int h, int pixels[], int off, int scansize)

Filters a buffer of pixels in the default RGB ColorModel by passing them one at a time through the filterRGB method.

setColorModel   void setColorModel(ColorModel model)

For an IndexColorModel with the canFilterIndexColorModel flag set to true, you should substitute a filtered version of the ColorModel here and wherever you see the original ColorModel object in the setPixels methods. Otherwise, you should override the default ColorModel used by the ImageProducer and specify the default RGB ColorModel in its place.

setPixels   void setPixels(int x, int y, int w, int h, ColorModel model, byte pixels[], int off, int scansize)

When the ColorModel object has already been converted, you should simply pass the pixels through with the converted ColorModel. Otherwise, you should convert the buffer of byte pixels to the default RGB ColorModel and pass the converted buffer to the filterRGBPixels method to be converted one at a time.

setPixels   void setPixels(int x, int y, int w, int h, ColorModel model, int pixels[], int off, int scansize)

Same as above, only the pixels returned are stored as integers and not bytes.

substituteColorModel   void substituteColorModel(ColorModel oldcm, ColorModel newcm)

Register ColorModels *oldcm* and *newcm* for substitution. Whenever *oldcm* is seen in a setPixels call, *newcm* is substituted; pixels are passed through untouched.

Other Classes in java.awt.image:

java.awt.image.PixelGrabber

Description	This class encapsulates a means to obtain a subset of pixels of an image from an attached Image or ImageProducer Object.
Parent Class	Object
Implements	ImageConsumer

CONSTRUCTORS

PixelGrabber   (Image image, int x, int y, int width, int height, int pix[], int off, int s)

PixelGrabber   (ImageProducer imgProd, int x, int y, int width, int height, int pix[], int off, int s)

Creates a PixelGrabber to obtain the rectangular area defined by *x, y, width,* and *height* from the *image* and places the pixels into the array *pixel[]* using the default RGB ColorModel. Pix[a,b] are stored in the pixel array at (b-y) * s + (a-x) + off where *s* is the scansize and *off* the offset.

VARIABLES

None

METHODS

boolean **grabPixels**() *	synchronized boolean **grabPixels**(longmillisecs) *
void **imageComplete**(int status)	void **setColorModel**(ColorModel model)
void **setDimensions**(int width, int height)	void **setHints**(int hintflags)
void **setPixels**(int x, int y, int w, int h, ColorModel m, byte pix[], int off, int s)	
void **setPixels**(int x, int y, int w, int h, ColorModel m, int pixels[], int off, int s)	
void **setProperties**(Hashtable props)	synchronized int **status**()

* Throws: InterruptedException if the operation is interrupted.

IO

java.io.DataInput (Interface)

Description	This interface describes a means to read primitive Java data types from a stream in a machine-independent manner.
Parent Class	Object
See Also	DataInputStream

METHODS

readBoolean, readByte, readChar, readDouble, readFloat, readFully, readInt, readLine, readLong, readShort, readUnsignedByte, readUnsignedShort, readUTF, skipBytes

See DataInputStream for an example of an implementation of these abstract methods.

java.io.DataOutput (Interface)

Description	This interface describes a means to write output to a stream in a machine-independent manner.
Parent Class	Object
See Also	DataOutputStream

METHODS

write, writeBoolean, writeByte, writeBytes, writeChar, writeChars, writeDouble, writeFloat, writeInt, writeLong, writeShort, writeUTF

See DataOutputStream for an example of an implementation of these abstract methods.

java.io.FilenameFilter (Interface)

Description	This interface describes a filter for file names.
Parent Class	Object
See Also	File, awt.FileDialog

METHODS

accept	boolean accept(File dirName, String fileName)
	Returns true if a name should be included in the file list given a directory *dirName* and the file *fileName*.

java.io.BufferedInputStream

Description	This stream allows you to read characters without causing a device access for each read. The data is read into a buffer, and subsequent reads obtain the data from the buffer instead of the device, resulting in faster access.
Parent Class	FilterInputStream
See Also	BufferedOutputStream, InputStream

CONSTRUCTORS

BufferedInputStream(InputStream in [, int bufSize])

> Creates a new buffered stream *in* with the default buffer size or with the optional buffer size *bufSize*.

VARIABLES

buf[]	protected byte: The buffer.
count	protected int: Number of bytes in the buffer.
markpos	protected int: Current mark position in the buffer or -1 if there is no current mark.
marklimit	protected int: Maximum read ahead past a mark.
pos	protected int: Current position in the buffer.

METHODS

available   synchronized int available()

> Returns the number of bytes that may be read without blocking.

mark   synchronized void mark(int readlimit) *

> Marks the current position in the input stream. A future call to reset() will reposition the stream to the last marked position so that subsequent reads will read the same bytes again.

markSupported   boolean markSupported()

> Returns true because this stream type supports marks.

read   synchronized int read([byte buf[], int startingByte, int numBytesToRead]) *

> Reads a byte and returns it as an integer, or reads optional *numBytesToRead* beginning with *startingByte* into an array of bytes *buf* and returns the actual number of bytes read. This method will block until some input is available and return -1 when the end of the stream is reached.

reset   synchronized void reset() *

> Repositions the stream to the last marked position. An IOException is thrown if the stream has not been marked or if

the mark has been invalidated. Stream marks are ideal for situations where you need to read ahead a little to see the contents of the stream.

skip   synchronized int skip(int n) *

Skips *n* bytes of input. Returns the actual number of bytes skipped.

* Throws IOException if an I/O error occurs.

java.io.BufferedOutputStream

Description   This stream allows you to write characters to a stream without causing a device access for each write. The data is written into a buffer until the buffer is full or the stream is flushed.

Parent Class   FilterOutputStream

See Also   BufferedInputStream, OutputStream

CONSTRUCTORS

BufferedOutputStream(OutputStream out [, int bufSize])

Creates a buffered stream from an existing OutputStream *out* with the default buffer size or with the optional buffer size *bufSize*.

VARIABLES

buf[]   protected byte: The data buffer.

count   protected int: Number of bytes in the buffer.

METHODS

flush   synchronized void flush() *

Flushes the buffer by forcing any data remaining in the buffer to the stream.

write   synchronized void write(byte b) *

Writes a byte *b* and will block until the byte is actually written.

write   synchronized void write(byte buf[],int startingByte, int numBytesToWrite) *

Writes *numBytesToWrite* beginning with *startingByte* from an array of bytes *buf* to the stream and blocks until the bytes are actually written.

* Throws IOException if an I/O error occurs.

java.io.DataInputStream

Description	This stream allows you to read primitive Java data types from a stream. An example of a primitive data type is an integer or a float.
Parent Class	FilterInputStream
Implements	DataInput
See Also	DataOutputStream

CONSTRUCTORS

DataInputStream(InputStream in)

Creates a data stream from an existing InputStream *in*.

VARIABLES

None

METHODS

read   final int read(byte buf[] [, int startingByte, int numBytesToRead]) *

Reads bytes into an array of bytes *buf* and blocks until some input is available, optionally *numBytesToRead* beginning with *startingByte* may be specified. Returns the actual number of bytes read or -1 when the end of the stream is reached.

readBoolean   final boolean readBoolean() *

Reads a boolean.

readByte   final byte readByte() *

Reads an 8-bit byte integer.

readChar   final char readChar() *

Reads a 16-bit char.

readDouble   final double readDouble() *

Reads a 64-bit double.

readFloat   final float readFloat() *

Reads a 32-bit float.

readFully   final int readFully(byte buf[] [, int startingByte, int numBytesToRead]) *

Functions the same as read(...), but blocks until all bytes are read. Throws EOFException if an EOF is encountered before all the bytes are read.

readInt   final int readInt() *

Reads a 32-bit integer.

readLine	final String readLine() *
	Reads a line terminated by a "\n" or EOF.
readLong	final long readLong() *
	Reads a 64-bit long integer.
readShort	final short readShort() *
	Reads a 16-bit short integer.
readUnsignedByte	final byte readUnsignedByte() *
	Reads an unsigned 8-bit byte integer.
readUnsignedShort	final byte readUnsignedShort() *
	Reads an unsigned 16-bit short integer.
readUTF	final String readUTF() *
	Reads a UTF format String from this stream.
readUTF	final static String readUTF(DataInput in) *
	Reads a UTF format String from the specified input stream *in*.
skipBytes	final int skipBytes(int n) *
	Skips *n* bytes and blocks until all bytes are skipped. Returns the number of bytes actually skipped. *

* Throws IOException if an I/O error occurs.

java.io.DataOutputStream

Description	This stream allows you to write primitive Java data types to a stream. The data may be read back using a DataInputStream.
Parent Class	FilterOutputStream
Implements	DataOutput
See Also	DataInputStream

CONSTRUCTORS

DataOutputStream(OutputStream out)

Creates a new data stream from an existing OutputStream *out*.

VARIABLES

written   protected int: The total number of bytes written thus far.

METHODS

flush	synchronized void flush() *
	Flushes the stream, forcing latent writes to complete.

size	final int size()
	Returns the number of bytes written thus far.
write	synchronized void write(int by) *
	Writes a byte *by* and blocks until it is written.
write	synchronized void write(byte buf[], int startingByte, int numBytesToWrite) *
	Writes *numBytesToWrite* from *buf[]* beginning with *startingByte*. This blocks until all the bytes are actually written.
writeBoolean	final boolean writeBoolean(boolean b) *
	Writes the specified boolean *b*.
writeByte	final byte writeByte(byte by) *
	Writes the specified 8-bit byte integer *by*.
writeBytes	final byte writeBytes(String str) *
	Writes the specified String *str* as a sequence of bytes.
writeChar	final char writeChar(char ch) *
	Writes the specified 16-bit Unicode character *ch*.
writeChars	final char writeChars(String str) *
	Writes the specified String *str* as a sequence of chars.
writeDouble	final double writeDouble(double d) *
	Writes the specified 64-bit double *d*.
writeFloat	final float writeFloat(float f) *
	Writes the specified 32-bit float *f*.
writeInt	final int writeInt(int n) *
	Writes the specified 32-bit integer *n*.
writeLong	final long writeLong(long l) *
	Writes the specified 64-bit long integer *l*.
writeShort	final short writeShort(short sh) *
	Writes the specified 16-bit short integer *sh*.
writeUTF	final String writeUTF(String str) *
	Writes the specified UTF format String *str*.

* Throws IOException if an I/O error occurs.

java.io.File

Description	This class represents a file name in the form specific to the host system. In other words, it should use the file name conventions of the host platform. The file name can be absolute or relative. This class deals with most of the system dependent file name features such as the separator character, root, device name, etc.

Parent Class	Object

CONSTRUCTORS

File(String path)

Creates a File object given a *path*.

File(String path, String fileName)

Creates a File object given a *path* and *fileName*.

File(File directory, String fileName)

Creates a File object given a *directory* File object and *fileName*.

VARIABLES

pathSeparator	final static String: System specific path separator String.
pathSeparatorChar	final static char: System specific path separator character.
separator	final static String: System specific file separator string.
separatorChar	final static char: System specific file separator character.

METHODS

canRead
boolean canRead() *

Returns true if an existing File is readable.

canWrite
boolean canWrite() *

Returns true if an existing File is writable.

delete
boolean delete()

Deletes this File and returns true if successful.

equals
boolean equals(Object obj2)

Returns true if this File and File *obj2* have the same path and name.

exists
boolean exists() *

Returns true if this File exists.

getAbsolutePath
String getAbsolutePath()

Returns the complete path of this File.

getName
String getName()

Returns only the name of this File.

getParent
String getParent()

Returns the name of the parent directory or null if this File is at the root level.

getPath
String getPath()

Returns the path of this File.

hashCode	int hashCode()
	Returns a hash code for this File.
isAbsolute	boolean isAbsolute()
	Returns true if this File name is absolute.
isDirectory	boolean isDirectory() *
	Returns true if this directory File exists.
isFile	boolean isFile() *
	Returns true if this File is normal, i.e., not a directory.
lastModified	long lastModified() *
	Returns last modification time of this File; it is meant to be used to compare modification dates and times and not absolute times.
length	long length() *
	Returns the length of this File.
list	String list([FilenameFilter filter]) *
	Returns an array of all the file names in the directory or optionally returns a filtered array of file names in a directory specified by *filter*.
mkdir	boolean mkdir() *
	Creates a directory. Returns true if successful.
mkdirs	boolean mkdirs() *
	Creates all directories in this path. Returns true if successful.
renameTo	boolean renameTo(File newName)
	Renames this File to the specified *newName*. Returns true if successful.
toString	String toString()
	Returns a String showing this File's path.

* Throws IOException if an I/O error occurs.

java.io.FileDescriptor

Description	This **final** class encapsulates a file descriptor which is a handle to a file.
Parent Class	Object

CONSTRUCTORS

FileDescriptor()	Creates a FileDescriptor

VARIABLES

in	final static FileDescriptor: Handle to standard input.
out	final static FileDescriptor: Handle to standard output.
err	final static FileDescriptor: Handle to standard error.

METHODS

valid
        boolean valid()

Returns true if the file descriptor is valid.

java.io.FileInputStream

Description	This class implements a file input stream and is frequently used to read bytes from a file. When its constructor is called, this class will throw an IOException if the file cannot be opened. You should always catch this exception.
Parent Class	InputStream
See Also	FileOutputStream

CONSTRUCTORS

FileInputStream(String fileName)

Creates an input file given a *fileName* using host platform conventions.

FileInputStream(FileDescriptor fileDescriptor)

Creates an input file given a system specific *fileDescriptor*.

FileInputStream(File fileObject)

Creates an input file given a *fileObject*.

VARIABLES

None

METHODS

available
        int available() *

Returns the total number of available bytes (initially equal to the file size).

close
        void close() *

Closes the input stream and releases all resources tied to this stream.

finalize
:   protected void finalize() *

    Disposes of this input stream when garbage is collected.

getFD
:   final int getFD()

    Returns the file descriptor connected with this stream.

read
:   int read() *

    Reads a byte and will block if no input is available. Returns the byte read in as an integer, or -1 if the end of the stream is reached.

read
:   int read(byte buf[] [, int startingByte, int numBytesToRead]) *

    Reads into an array of bytes *buf* or optionally reads *numBytesToRead* beginning with *startingByte* into this array of bytes *buf*. This method will block until some input is available. It returns the actual number of bytes read or -1 when the end of the stream is reached.

skip
:   long skip(long numBytes) *

    Skips *numBytes* bytes of input. Returns the number of bytes actually skipped.

* Throws IOException if an I/O error occurs.

java.io.FileOutputStream

Description
:   This class implements an output stream that is frequently used to write bytes to a file. When its constructor is called, this class will throw an IOException if the file cannot be opened.

Parent Class
:   OutputStream

See Also
:   FileInputStream

CONSTRUCTORS

FileOutputStream(String fileName)

    Creates an output file given a *fileName* using host platform conventions.

FileOutputStream(FileDescriptor fileDescriptor)

    Creates an output file given a system specific *fileDescriptor*.

FileOutputStream(File fileObject)

    Creates an output file given a *fileObject*.

VARIABLES

None

METHODS

close   synchronized void close() *

Closes the output stream and releases all resources tied to this stream.

finalize   protected void finalize() *

Disposes of this output stream when garbage is collected.

getFD   final int getFD()

Returns the file descriptor connected with this stream.

write   void write(int b) *

Writes a byte and blocks until the byte is actually written.

write   void write(byte buf[] [, int startingByte, int numBytesToWrite]) *

Writes an array of bytes *buf* or optionally writes *numBytesToWrite* from *buf[]* beginning with *startingByte*. This method blocks until the output is actually written.

* Throws IOException if an I/O error occurs.

java.io.PrintStream

Description   This class implements a special output stream containing additional methods for printing. The high byte of a 16-bit character is discarded when printing. If you have ever used "System.out.println("my value =" + value)", then you have already run across a PrintStream object encapsulated inside the System class.

Parent Class   FilterOutputStream

CONSTRUCTORS

PrintStream(OutputStream out [, boolean autoFlush])

Creates a print stream from an existing OutputStream *out* with optional automatic flushing when *autoFlush* is used and set to true. Automatic flushing means that the stream writes its output when a newline character is encountered.

VARIABLES

None

METHODS

checkError   void checkError()

Flushes this PrintStream and returns true if it has ever had an error on the output stream.

close	void close()
	Closes the print stream and releases all resources tied to this stream.
flush	void flush() *
	Flushes the buffer by writing any data remaining in the buffer.
print	synchronized void print(String str)
	Prints the specified String *str*.
print	synchronized void print(char ch[])
	Prints the specified array of characters *ch[]*.
print	void print(boolean b)
	Prints the specified boolean *b*.
print	void print(char ch)
	Prints the specified character *ch*.
print	void print(double d)
	Prints the specified 64-bit double *d*.
print	void print(float f)
	Prints the specified 32-bit float *f*.
print	void print(int n)
	Prints the specified 32-bit integer *n*.
print	void print(long l)
	Prints the specified 64-bit long integer *l*.
print	void print(Object obj)
	Prints the specified Object *obj*.
println	void println()
	Prints a newline.
write	void write(int by) *
	Prints a byte *by* and will block until the byte is actual written.
write	void write(byte buf[], int startingByte, int numBytesToWrite) *
	Prints *numBytesToWrite* beginning with *startingByte* from an array of bytes *buf* and blocks until the output is actually written.

Note: All print methods may be called as "println" if a newline character is desired at the end.

* Throws IOException if an I/O error occurs.

java.io.RandomAccessFile

Description	This class implements a random access file system. It is one of the few classes in the java.io package that is not subclassed from InputStream or OutputStream. Because it does not use a sequen-

tial stream, you can store, search, and retrieve nonlinear data more conveniently. Also, it is the only class that allows you to both read and write to a file.

Parent Class   Object

Implements   DataOutput, DataInput

CONSTRUCTORS

RandomAccessFile(String fileName, String mode) *

> Creates a random access file given a *fileName* using host platform conventions. The *mode* indicates the type of file access: "r" for read-only and "rw" for read-write.

RandomAccessFile(FileDescriptor fileDescriptor) *

> Creates a random access file given a system specific *fileDescriptor.*

RandomAccessFile(File fileObject, String mode) *

> Creates a random access file given a *fileObject.* The *mode* indicates the type of file access: "r" for read-only and "rw" for read-write.

VARIABLES

None

METHODS

close	void close() * Closes the file.
getFD	final FileDescriptor getFD() * Returns the FileDescriptor for this File.
getFilePointer	int getFilePointer() * Returns the current location of the file pointer.
length	long length() * Returns the length of the file.
read	int read() * Reads a byte and blocks if no input is available. Returns the byte read in as an integer, or -1 if the end of the stream is reached.
read	int read(byte buf[] [, int startingByte, int numBytesToRead]) * Reads into an array of bytes *buf* or optionally reads *numBytesToRead* beginning with *startingByte* into this array of bytes *buf*. This method blocks until some input is available. It returns the actual number of bytes read or -1 when the end of the stream is reached.

readBoolean	final boolean readBoolean() *
	Reads a boolean.
readByte	final byte readByte() *
	Reads an 8-bit byte integer.
readChar	final char readChar() *
	Reads 16-bit character.
readDouble	final char readDouble() *
	Reads 64-bit double.
readFully	final int readFully(byte buf[] [, int startingByte, int numBytesToRead]) *
	Functions the same as read(...), but blocks until all bytes are read. Throws EOFException if an EOF is encountered before all the bytes are read.
readInt	final int readInt() *
	Reads 32-bit integer.
readLine	final String readLine() *
	Reads a line terminated by a "\n" or EOF.
readLong	final long readLong() *
	Reads 64-bit long integer
readShort	final short readShort() *
	Reads 16-bit short integer.
readUTF	final String readUTF() *
	Reads a UTF format String.
readUnsignedByte	final byte readUnsignedByte() *
	Reads an unsigned 8-bit byte integer.
readUnsignedShort	final byte readUnsignedShort() *
	Reads an unsigned 16-bit short integer.
seek	void seek(long pos) *
	Moves the file pointer to the specified absolute position *pos*.
skipBytes	void skipBytes(int numBytes) *
	Skip specified *numBytes* number of bytes.
write	void write(int b) *
	Writes a byte and will block until the byte is actually written.
write	void write(byte buf[] [, int startingByte, int numBytesToWrite]) *
	Writes from an array of bytes *buf[]* or optionally writes *numBytesToWrite* from *buf[]* beginning with *startingByte*. This method blocks until the output is actually written.
writeBoolean	final boolean writeBoolean(boolean b) *
	Writes the specified boolean *b*.

writeByte	final byte writeByte(byte by) *
	Writes the specified 8-bit byte integer *by*.
writeBytes	final byte writeBytes(String str) *
	Writes the specified String *str* as a sequence of bytes.
writeChar	final char writeChar(char ch) *
	Writes the specified 16-bit Unicode character *ch*.
writeChars	final char writeChars(String str) *
	Writes the specified String *str* as a sequence of chars.
writeDouble	final double writeDouble(double d) *
	Writes the specified 64-bit double *d*.
writeFloat	final float writeFloat(float f) *
	Writes the specified 32-bit float *f*.
writeInt	final int writeInt(int n) *
	Writes the specified 32-bit integer *n*.
writeLong	final long writeLong(long l) *
	Writes the specified 64-bit long integer *l*.
writeShort	final short writeShort(short sh) *
	Writes the specified 16-bit short integer *sh*.
writeUTF	final String writeUTF(String str) *
	Writes the specified UTF format String *str*.

* Throws IOException if an I/O error occurs.

java.io.StreamTokenizer

| **Description** | This class turns an input stream into a stream of tokens. |
| **Parent Class** | Object |

CONSTRUCTORS

StreamTokenizer(InputStream In)

Creates a stream tokenizer that parses the given InputStream *In*. It recognizes numbers, all the characters of the alphabet, and strings quoted with single and double quotes.

VARIABLES

nval	double: Contents of number token.
sval	String: Contents of word token.
ttype	int: The type of the last token returned. It will contain either one of the TT_* constants below, or a character. For example, if a "-" is found and it is not a valid word character, ttype will contain "-".

TT_EOF	final static int: End of file token.
TT_EOL	final static int: End of line token.
TT_NUMBER	final static int: Number token whose value is in nval.
TT_WORD	final static int: Word token whose value is in sval.

METHODS

commentChar

void commentChar(int remChar)

Specifies that character *remChar* starts a single line comment.

eolIsSignificant

void eolIsSignificant(boolean eolSig)

When *eolSig* is true, end-of-lines are significant (i.e., TT_EOL is returned by nextToken()), otherwise EOL will be treated as whitespace.

lineno

int lineno()

Returns the current line number.

lowerCaseMode

void lowerCaseMode(boolean lowerCase)

Forces all TT_WORD tokens to lowercase when *lowerCase* is true.

nextToken

int nextToken() *

Parses the next token from the input stream. The return value will typically be TT_EOF, TT_EOL, TT_NUMBER, TT_WORD, or a single character (see ttype). Normal StreamTokenizer clients set up syntax tables and then loop calling nextToken to parse successive tokens until TT_EOF is returned.

ordinaryChar

void ordinaryChar(int ordChar)

Specifies that character *ordChar* has no special significance. When encountered by the parser, it returns a ttype equal to the character.

ordinaryChars

void ordinaryChars(int low, int hi)

Specifies that characters between *low* and *hi* have no special significance. When encountered by the parser, they return a ttype equal to their character.

parseNumbers

void parseNumbers()

Specifies that numbers should be parsed. It accepts double precision floating point numbers and returns a ttype of TT_NUMBER and the value in nval.

pushBack

void pushBack()

After this is invoked, nextToken() will return the same token again.

quoteChar

void quoteChar(int qChar)

Specifies that matching pairs of *qChar* delimit String constants. When a string constant is found, ttype will contain the character that delimits it, and sval will contain the body of the string.

resetSyntax	void resetSyntax()
	Resets the syntax table making all characters special.
slashSlashComments	void slashSlashComments(boolean flag)
	Set *flag* to true to recognize C++ style "//" comments.
slashStarComments	void slashStarComments(boolean flag)
	Set *flag* to true to recognize C style "/*" comments.
toString	String toString()
	Returns a String showing the current token's value.
whitespaceChars	void whitespaceChars(int low, int hi)
	Specifies that characters between *low* and *hi* are whitespace characters.
wordChars	void wordChars(int low, int hi)
	Specifies that characters between *low* and *hi* are word characters.

Other Classes in java.io:

java.io.ByteArrayInputStream

Description	This class creates a byte buffer that can be used as an input stream.
Parent Class	InputStream

CONSTRUCTORS

ByteArrayInputStream(byte buf[])
ByteArrayInputStream(byte buf[], int startingByte, int numBytesToRead)

VARIABLES

buf[]	protected byte: The data buffer.
count	protected int: Number of characters to use in this buffer.
pos	protected int: Current position in the buffer.

METHODS

synchronized int **available**()　　　　　　　synchronized int **read**()
synchronized int **read**(byte buf[], int startingByte, int numBytesToRead)
synchronized int **skip**(long nBytesToSkip)　　　　synchronized void **reset**()

java.io.ByteArrayOutputStream

Description	This class creates a byte buffer that can be used as an output stream.
Parent Class	OutputStream

CONSTRUCTORS

ByteArrayOutputStream()
ByteArrayOutputStream(int initialSize)

VARIABLES

buf[]	protected byte: The data buffer.
count	protected int: Number of characters to use in this buffer.

METHODS

synchronized void **reset**()

synchronized byte[] **toByteArray** ()

String **toString**(int hiByte)

synchronized void **write**(int byteToWrite)

synchronized void **write**(byte buff[], int startingByte, int numBytestoWrite)

synchronized void **writeTo**(OutputStream out) *

int **size**()

String **toString**()

java.io.FilterInputStream

Description	This **abstract** class is the basis for enhancing input stream functionality. It allows input stream filters to be chained together.
Parent Class	InputStream

CONSTRUCTORS

FilterInputStream(InputStream in)

VARIABLES

in	protected InputStream: The actual input stream.

METHODS

int **available**() *

void **mark**(int readlimit)

int **read**() *

int **read**(byte buf[], int startingByte, int numBytesToRead) *

int **skip**(long nBytesToSkip) *

void **close**() *

boolean **markSupported**()

int **read**(byte buf[]) *

void **reset**() *

java.io.FilterOutputStream

Description	This **abstract** class is the basis for enhancing output stream functionality. It allows output stream filters to be chained together.
Parent Class	OutputStream

CONSTRUCTORS

FilterOutputStream(OutputStream out)

VARIABLES

out   protected OutputStream: The actual output stream.

METHODS

void **close**() *

void **write**(int byteToWrite) *
void **write**(byte buff[], int startingByte, int numBytesToWrite) *

void **flush**() *
void **write**(byte buf[]) *

java.io.InputStream

Description	This **abstract** class is the basis for all input streams.
Parent Class	Object

CONSTRUCTORS

InputStream()

VARIABLES

None

METHODS

int **available**() *
void **mark**(int readlimit)
abstract int **read**() *
int **read**(byte buf[], int startingByte, int numBytesToRead) *
int **skip**(long nBytesToSkip) *

void **close**() *
boolean **markSupported**()
int **read**(byte buf[]) *
void **reset**() *

java.io.LineNumberInputStream

Description	This class implements an input stream that keeps track of line numbers.
Parent Class	FilterInputStream

CONSTRUCTORS

LineNumberInputStream(InputStream in)

VARIABLES

None

METHODS

int **available**() *   void **getLineNumber**()

void **mark**(int readlimit)

int **read**() *   int **read**(byte buf[]) *

int **read**(byte buf[], int startingByte, int numBytesToRead) *   void **reset**() *

int **setLineNumber**(int newLineNumber) *   int **skip**(long nBytesToSkip) *

java.io.OutputStream

Description   This **abstract** class is the basis for all output streams.

Parent Class   Object

CONSTRUCTORS

OutputStream()

VARIABLES

None

METHODS

void **close**() *   void **flush**() *

abstract void **write**(int byteToWrite) *   void **write**(byte buf[]) *

void **write**(byte buff[], int startingByte, int numBytesToWrite) *

java.io.PipedInputStream

Description   This class implements a piped input stream; for this to be useful,
                      you must connect it to a PipedOutputStream.

Parent Class   InputStream

CONSTRUCTORS

PipedInputStream(PipedOutputStream srcStream)

PipedInputStream()

VARIABLES

None

METHODS

void **connect**(PipedOutputStream srcStream) *   void **close**() *

synchronized int **read**(byte buf[], int startingByte, int numBytesToRead) *

synchronized int **read**() *

java.io.PipedOutputStream

Description	This class implements a piped output stream; for this to be useful, you must connect it to a PipedInputStream.
Parent Class	OutputStream

CONSTRUCTORS

PipedOutputStream(PipedInputStream destStream)

PipedOutputStream()

VARIABLES

None

METHODS

void **connect**(PipedOutputStream srcStream) *   void **close**() *

synchronized void **write**(byte buf[], int startingByte, int numBytesToWrite) *

synchronized void **write**() *

java.io.PushbackInputStream

Description	This class implements an input stream with a 1-byte push back buffer.
Parent Class	FilterInputStream

CONSTRUCTORS

PushbackInputStream(InputStream in)

VARIABLES

pushBack   protected int: Push back character.

METHODS

int **available**() *   boolean **markSupported**() *

int **read**(byte buf[], int startingByte, int numBytesToRead) *   **read**() *

unread(int ch) *

java.io. SequenceInputStream

Description   This class converts a series of input streams into an InputStream.
Parent Class   InputStream

CONSTRUCTORS

SequenceInputStream(Enumeration e)
SequenceInputStream(InputStream in1, InputStream in2)

VARIABLES

None

METHODS

int **close**() *   int **read**() *
int **read**(byte buf[], int startingByte, int numBytesToRead) *

java.io.StringBufferInputStream

Description   This class is a String buffer that may be used as an input stream.
Parent Class   InputStream

CONSTRUCTORS

StringBufferInputStream(String str)

VARIABLES

buffer   protected String: The data buffer.
count   protected int: Number of characters to use in this buffer.
pos   protected int: Current position in the buffer.

METHODS

int **available**()   int **read**()
int **read**(byte buf[], int startingByte, int numBytesToRead)   void **reset**()
int **skip**(long nBytesToSkip)

* Throws IOException if an I/O error occurs.

LANG

java.lang.Cloneable (Interface)

Description   Objects must implement this interface if they wish to have a clone method.

Parent Class   Object

java.lang.Runnable (Interface)

Description   This interface is used by objects that want to execute code when they are active. Also, a class that implements Runnable and is not a Thread can run by passing itself as the target when instantiating a Thread instance.

Parent Class   Object

See Also   Thread

METHODS

run   abstract void run()

This method is called when a runnable object is activated.

java.lang.Class

Description   This **final** class is not modifiable at runtime, but it may be used to gain useful information about a Class. At runtime, every class has an associated class object descriptor, containing information about the class.

Parent Class   Object

See Also   ClassLoader

CONSTRUCTORS

None

VARIABLES

None

METHODS

forName	static Class forName(String className)
	Returns the runtime Class descriptor for the given *className*. Throws a ClassNotFoundException if this Class could not be found.
getClassLoader	ClassLoader getClassLoader()
	Returns the ClassLoader of this Class or a null if this Class has no ClassLoader.
getInterfaces	Class[] getInterfaces()
	Returns an array of interfaces implemented by this Class or an array of 0 length if the Class does not implement any interfaces.
getName	String getName()
	Returns the name of this Class.
getSuperClass	Class getSuperClass()
	Returns the superclass of this Class.
isInterface	boolean isInterface()
	Returns true if this Class is an interface, false otherwise.
newInstance	Object newInstance()
	Returns a new instance of this Class. Throws an InstantiationException if you try to instantiate an interface or an abstract Class. Throws an IllegalAccessException if the Class is not accessible.
toString	String toString()
	Returns a String showing the name of the Class or Interface with the text "Class" or "Interface" prepended.

java.lang.ClassLoader

Description	This **abstract** class can be used to define a means of loading Java classes into the runtime system. The default mechanism for loading classes is by reading them as files from the directory specified by the CLASSPATH environment variable. It does not use a class loader. However, classes could be loaded from some other source, perhaps a network. Classes loaded from a network are an array of bytes. In this case, a ClassLoader can be used to notify the runtime system to convert this array of bytes into an instance of a Class.
Parent Class	Object
See Also	Class

CONSTRUCTORS

ClassLoader()   Protected: Creates a new class loader and initializes it.

VARIABLES

None

METHODS

defineClass   protected final Class defineClass(byte data[], int startIndex, int length)

Returns an instance of Class created from an array of bytes specified by *data*, *startIndex,* and *length*. The class must be resolved before it can be used. Throws ClassFormatError if data does not contain a valid class.

findSystemClass protected final Class findSystemClass(String className)

Loads and returns the system Class specified by *className*. System classes are those using Java's default loading scheme (i.e., no ClassLoader). Throws NoClassDefFoundError if the class is not found.

loadClass   protected abstract Class loadClass(String className, boolean resolve)

This method must be defined in a subclass of ClassLoader. It is called by the Java runtime environment and should return the resulting class for the specified *className* or null if it was not found. If *resolve* is true, it should also resolve the class.

resolveClass   protected final void resolveClass(Class className)

Resolves classes referenced by the specified Class *className*. Before classes can be used they must be resolved. Class names referenced by the resulting Class are resolved by calling loadClass().

java.lang.Object

Description   This class is the root of the class hierarchy. It is the final parent of every Java class. All Object methods are available to every class, and are frequently overridden by child classes.

Parent Class   Not Applicable

CONSTRUCTORS

Object()   Creates a new Object.

VARIABLES

None

METHODS

clone   protected Object clone()

Creates a clone of this Object by creating a new instance, then executing the copy method. Throws an OutOfMemoryError if there is not enough memory for this operation.

equals   boolean equals(Object obj2)

Returns true if this Object is equivalent to Object *obj2*. This method is used when an Object is stored in a Hashtable. You should override this to define "equivalance" for your classes.

finalize   protected void finalize()

Called when this object is garbage collected. Throws Throwable.

getClass   final Class getClass()

Returns the Java runtime class descriptor for this Object.

hashCode   int hashCode()

Returns the hash code for this Object. Note that every Java Object has a hash code and that a hash code is usually different for different Objects. You should override this to define how your Objects get hashed.

notify   final void notify() *

Notifies a single waiting Thread of a condition change in another Thread. This can only be called from a synchronized method.

notifyAll   final void notifyAll() *

Notifies all waiting Threads of a condition change. This can only be called from a synchronized method.

toString   String toString()

Returns a String showing the value of this Object. You should override this to define the important text information for your classes.

wait   final void wait([int milliseconds]) *

Causes a Thread to wait until it is notified or until an optionally specified *milliseconds* timeout has elapsed. This can only be called from a synchronized method.

wait   final void wait(int milliseconds, int nanoseconds) *

Causes a Thread to wait until it is notified or until a specified *milliseconds* and *nanoseconds* timeout has elapsed. This can only be called from a synchronized method.

* Throws InternalError if the current Thread is not the owner of the Object's monitor.

java.lang.Process

Description	This **abstract** class is returned by the exec methods in the Runtime class.
Parent Class	Object
See Also	Runtime

CONSTRUCTORS

None

VARIABLES

None

METHODS

destroy, exitValue, getErrorStream, getInputStream, getOutputStream, waitFor
All of these methods are abstract in this class.

java.lang.Runtime

Description	This class gives you access to runtime functionality using a system independent interface. This includes some methods useful for debugging.
Parent Class	Object
See Also	System, Process

CONSTRUCTORS

None

VARIABLES

None

METHODS

exec   Process exec(String cmd [, String env[])) *

Starts a process and passes the command *cmd* to it. Optionally, an environment array *env* may be specified. It returns a reference to the appropriate subclass that "encapsulates" it.

exec   Process exec(String cmdArray[] [, String env[])) *

Starts a process and passes the command *cmdArray[0]* to it along with any command line arguments. Optionally, an environment array *env* may be specified. It returns a reference to the appropriate subclass that "encapsulates" it.

exit   void exit(int exitCode)

Exits the Java runtime with the specified *exitCode*.

freeMemory   long freeMemory()

Returns the estimated total number of free bytes in system memory.

gc   void gc()

Executes the garbage collector.

getLocalizedInputStream InputStream getLocalizedInputStream(InputStream in)

Returns a localized input stream that will convert any input from the local format specified input stream *in* to UNICODE format.

getLocalizedOutputStream OutputStream getLocalizedOutputStream(OutputStream out)

Returns the localized output stream that will convert any output from the UNICODE specified output stream *out* to the local format.

getRuntime   static Runtime getRuntime()

Returns the runtime.

load   synchronized void load(String fileName)

Loads a dynamic library, given a complete file name *fileName*.

loadLibrary   synchronized void loadLibrary(String libName)

Loads a dynamic library with the specified library name *libName*.

runFinalization   void runFinalization()

Calls the finalization methods of all Objects pending finalization. Since finalization methods are called asynchronously by a finalization Thread, it is usually not necessary to call this method.

totalMemory   long totalMemory()

Returns the total number of bytes in the system's memory.

traceInstructions   void traceInstructions(boolean trace)

Enables tracing of instructions when *trace* is true, else disables it.

traceMethodCalls   void traceMethodCalls(boolean trace)

Enables tracing of method calls when *trace* is true, else disables it.

* Throws IOException if an I/O error occurs.

java.lang.SecurityManager

Description   This **abstract** class can be subclassed to create a security policy. It provides a means to check on actions. For example, when a SecurityManager is set, Socket and ServerSocket classes invoke the checkAccept(), checkConnect(), checkListen(), etc., before doing things. Also, it enables you to retrieve and inspect the current classloader.

Parent Class	Object
See Also	System.getSecurityManager(), System.setSecurityManager()

CONSTRUCTORS

SecurityManager()   Protected

Creates a new SecurityManager. Throws SecurityException if the SecurityManager cannot be created.

VARIABLES

None

METHODS

checkAccept   void checkAccept(String host, int port) *

Checks to see if a socket connection has been accepted by the specified *host* and *port*.

checkAccess   void checkAccess(Thread thd) *

Thread.checkAccess() invokes this to check to see if the specified Thread *thd* is allowed to modify the Thread group.

checkAccess   void checkAccess(ThreadGroup tg) *

ThreadGroup.checkAccess() invokes this to check to see if the specified Thread group *tg* is allowed to modify this group.

checkConnect   void checkConnect(String host, int port) *

Checks to see if a socket has connected to the specified *host* and *port*.

checkConnect   void checkConnect(String host, int port, Object context) *

Checks if the current execution context and the specified *context* are both permitted to connect to the specified *host* and *port*.

checkCreateClassLoader   void checkCreateClassLoader() *

Checks to see if the ClassLoader has been created.

checkDelete   void checkDelete(String file) *

Checks if the specified *file* may be deleted.

checkExec   void checkExec(String cmd) *

System and Runtime exec() invoke this to check to see if the system command *cmd* is executed by secure code.

checkExit   void checkExit(int exitStatus) *

System and Runtime exit() invoke this to check to see if the system has exited the Java runtime with an exit code.

checkLink	void checkLink(String lib) *
	System and Runtime load() invoke this to check to see if the specified linked library *lib* exists.
checkListen	void checkListen(int port) *
	Checks to see if a server socket is listening to the specified local *port*.
checkPackageAccess	void checkPackageAccess(String package)
	Checks to see if an applet can access the specified *package*.
checkPackageDefinition	void checkPackageDefinition(String package)
	Checks to see if an applet can define classes in the specified *package*.
checkPropertiesAccess	void checkPropertiesAccess() *
	Checks to see who has access to the System properties.
checkPropertyAccess	void checkPropertyAccess(String key [, String def]) *
	Checks who has access to the System property specified by *key*. Optionally, a default value *def* may be specified to return if *key* is not defined.
checkRead	void checkRead(FileDescriptor fd) *
	Checks if an input file with the specified system dependent file descriptor *fd* is available.
checkRead	void checkRead(String file) *
	Checks to see if an input file with the specified system dependent file name is available.
checkRead	void checkRead(String file, Object context) *
	Checks if the current execution context and the specified *context* are both permitted to read the specified *file*.
checkSetFactory	void checkSetFactory()
	Checks to see if an applet can set a network object factory.
checkTopLevelWindow	boolean checkTopLevelWindow(Object window)
	Returns true if the specified top-level *window* can be created by the caller with no restrictions. Returns false if a top-level window can be created but should have a visual warning. The method should throw a SecurityException to not allow creation at all.
checkWrite	void checkWrite(FileDescriptor fd) *
	Checks if an output file with the specified system dependent file descriptor *fd* gets created.
checkWrite	void checkWrite(String filename) *
	Checks to see if an output file with the specified system dependent *filename* gets created.

classDepth	protected int classDepth(String className)
	Returns the position of the stack frame containing the first occurrence of the class *className*.
classLoaderDepth	protected int classLoaderDepth()
	Returns the position of the stack frame containing the first occurrence of the loaded class.
currentClassLoader	protected ClassLoader currentClassLoader()
	Returns the current ClassLoader on the execution stack.
getClassContext	protected Class[] getClassContext()
	Returns the context of this Class.
getInCheck	boolean getInCheck()
	Returns true if there is a security check in progress.
getSecurityContext	Object getSecurityContext()
	Returns an Object which may be used to perform some security checks later on the current execution environment.
inClass	protected boolean inClass(String name)
	Returns true if the specified *name* is in this Class.
inClassLoader	protected boolean inClassLoader()
	Returns true if the current ClassLoader is not equal to null.

* Throws SecurityException if a security error occurs.

java.lang.String

Description	This class encapsulates constant character Strings. The String's value cannot be changed after creation; however, because String Objects are immutable, they can be shared. Strings are more efficient than StringBuffers and should be used when possible.
Parent Class	Object
See Also	StringBuffer

CONSTRUCTORS

String()	Creates a new String that is empty.
String(StringBuffer strBuf)	
	Creates a new String with the contents of the specified StringBuffer *strBuf*.
String(String str)	Creates a new String that is a copy of *str*.
String(char ch[] [, int startIndex, int numChars]) *	
	Creates a new String from an array of characters *ch[]* or optionally from a subarray of characters *ch[]* beginning at *startIndex* with a

length of *numChars*. Note: The String contains a reference to the character array, so the character array should never be changed after the String is created.

String(byte ascii[], int hiByte [, int startIndex, int numBytes]) *

Creates a new String from an array of bytes *ascii[]* or optionally a subarray of bytes *ascii[]* beginning at *startIndex* with a length of *numBytes*. The *hiByte* of each UNICODE character should usually be specified as 0.

* Throws StringIndexOutOfBoundsException if startIndex and numBytes or numChars are invalid.

VARIABLES

None

METHODS

charAt   char charAt(int index)

Returns the character at the specified *index*.

Throws StringIndexOutOfBoundsException if *index* is larger than the number of characters in this String.

compareTo   int compareTo(Sting str2)

Returns 0 if the String *str2* equals this String. Returns a negative number if *str2* is lexically less than this String and returns a positive number if *str2* is lexically greater than this String.

concat   String concat(String str)

Returns a String concatenation of String *str* to the end of this String.

copyValueOf   static String copyValueOf(char ch[] [, int index, int count])

Returns a String that references a copy of the specified character array *ch[]* optionally starting at *index* and containing *count* number of characters. This creates a new array and copies the characters into it.

endsWith   boolean endsWith(String suffix)

Returns true if this String ends with *suffix*, otherwise false.

equals   boolean equals(Object obj2)

Returns true if the Object *obj2* equals this String (i.e., if the Object has the same characters and length as the String).

equalsIgnoreCase   boolean equalsIgnoreCase(Object obj2)

Same as equals, only case insensitive.

getBytes

void getBytes(int srcStartIndex, int srcEndIndex, char dest[], int destIndex)

Copies the characters from *srcStartIndex* to *srcEndIndex* from the String to a character array *dest* beginning at *destIndex*.

getChars

void getChars(int srcStartIndex, int srcEndIndex, char dest[], int destIndex)

Copies the characters from *srcStartIndex* to *srcEndIndex* from the String to a character array *dest* beginning at *destIndex*.

hashCode

int hashCode()

Returns a hash code for this String.

indexOf

int indexOf(int ch [, int index])

Returns the index of first occurrence of character *ch* from the beginning or optionally starting at location *index*. Returns -1 if it is not found.

indexOf

int indexOf(String str [, int index])

Returns the index of first occurrence of substring *str* from the beginning or optionally starting at location *index*. Returns -1 if it is not found.

intern

String intern()

Returns a String that is equal to the current String but from a unique String pool.

lastIndexOf

int lastIndexOf(int ch [, int index])

Returns the index of first occurrence of character *ch,* searching backwards from the end or from the optional location *index*. Returns -1 if it is not found.

lastIndexOf

int lastIndexOf(String substr [, int index])

Returns the index of first occurrence of substring *substr* searching backwards from the end or from the optional location *index*. Returns -1 if it is not found.

length

int length()

Returns the number of 16-bit UNICODE characters in the String.

regionMatches

boolean regionMatches([boolean ignoreCase,] int thisIndex, Sting str2, int str2Index, int numChars)

Returns true if the region of this String beginning at *thisIndex* matches the specified region of String *str2* beginning at *str2Index* where *numChars* is the number of characters to match. The search is case insensitive if the optional *ignoreCase* is set to true.

replace

String replace(char oldChar, char newChar)

Returns a String where *newChar* has replaced all occurrences of *oldChar* in this String.

startsWith	boolean startsWith(String prefix [, int startingChar])
	Returns true if this String contains *prefix* at the beginning or optionally at location *startingChar*.
substring	String(int startIndex [, int endIndex])
	Returns the substring *substr* of this String from *startIndex* to the end of this String or optionally to, but not including, *endIndex*.
toCharArray	char[] toCharArray()
	Returns an array of characters converted from this String.
toLowerCase	String toLowerCase()
	Returns this String converted to lowercase.
toString	String toString()
	Returns this String itself.
toUpperCase	String toUpperCase()
	Returns this String converted to uppercase.
trim	String trim()
	Returns this String with leading and trailing whitespace removed.
valueOf	static String valueOf(boolean b)
	static String valueOf(char ch)
	static String valueOf(int i)
	static String valueOf(long l)
	static String valueOf(float f)
	static String valueOf(double d)
	static String valueOf(Object obj)
	Returns a String representing the specified type or Object.
valueOf	static String valueOf(char ch[] [, int index, int count])
	Returns a String that is equivalent to the specified character array *ch[]* or optionally a substring of the specified character array *ch[]* starting from *index* with a length of *count*. Note: This just points the String to the correct position in character array — no copy is made.

java.lang.StringBuffer

Description	This **final** class encapsulates a growable buffer for characters. It is mainly used to create dynamic Strings. The compiler uses a StringBuffer to implement String concatenation (i.e., "+").
Parent Class	Object
See Also	String

CONSTRUCTORS

StringBuffer([int length])

Creates a new empty String buffer with an optional initial *length*.

StringBuffer(String str)

Creates a new empty String buffer with the specified initial value *str*.

VARIABLES

None

METHODS

append
synchronized StringBuffer append(boolean b)

synchronized StringBuffer append(char ch)

synchronized StringBuffer append(int i)

synchronized StringBuffer append(long l)

synchronized StringBuffer append(float f)

synchronized StringBuffer append(double d)

synchronized StringBuffer append(String str)

synchronized StringBuffer append(Object obj)

Returns the StringBuffer with the specified data type appended at its end.

append
synchronized StringBuffer append(char ch[][, int index, int count])

Returns the StringBuffer with an array of characters *ch[]* appended to the end of it or optionally a subarray of characters *ch[]* starting at *index* and with a length of *count* appended to the end of it.

capacity
int capacity()

Returns the total current capacity of the String buffer.

charAt
synchronized char charAt(int index) *

Returns the character at the given *index* where *index* is from 0 to length()-1.

copyWhenShared
void copyWhenShared()

Copies the buffer value if it is being shared.

ensureCapacity
synchronized void ensureCapacity(int minCapacity)

Guarantees that the capacity of the buffer is at least equal to the specified *minCapacity*.

getChars
void getChars(int srcStartIndex, int srcEndIndex, char dest[], int destIndex) *

Copies the characters from *srcStartIndex* to *srcEndIndex* from the String to a character array *dest* beginning at *destIndex*.

insert	synchronized StringBuffer insert(int index, boolean b) **
	synchronized StringBuffer insert(int index, char ch[]) **
	synchronized StringBuffer insertChar(int index, int ch) **
	synchronized StringBuffer insert(int index, int i) **
	synchronized StringBuffer insert(int index, long l) **
	synchronized StringBuffer insert(int index, float f) **
	synchronized StringBuffer insert(int index, double d) **
	synchronized StringBuffer insert(int index, String str) **
	synchronized StringBuffer insert(int index, Object obj) **

Returns the StringBuffer with the specified data inserted at position *index*.

length   int length()

Returns the number of 16-bit UNICODE characters in the String buffer.

setCharAt   synchronized void charAt(int index, char newCh) **

Sets the character at the *index* to be *newCh*.

setLength   synchronized void setLength(int newLength) *

Sets the length of the String to *newLength*. If the length is reduced, characters are lost, and if the length is extended, the new characters are initialized to 0.

toString   synchronized String toString()

Returns a String showing the data in the buffer.

* Throws StringIndexOutOfBoundsException if an invalid index or length is specified.

** Throws ArrayIndexOutOfBoundsException if an invalid index is specified.

java.lang.System

Description   This **final** class gives you access to system functionality using a system independent interface. This includes standard input and output streams. Unlike most classes, you do not instantiate the System class to use it (nor can you instantiate it).

Parent Class   Object

See Also   Runtime

CONSTRUCTORS

None

VARIABLES

err	static PrintStream: Standard error stream used to print error messages.
in	static InputStream: Standard input stream used to read in data.
out	static PrintStream: Standard output stream used to print messages (i.e., System.out.println("Hello"))

METHODS

arraycopy

static void arraycopy(Object src, int srcIndex, Object dest, int destIndex, int length) *,**

Copies an array from *src* starting at *srcIndex* and of length *length* to *dest* starting at *destIndex*. You must have previously allocated memory for the destination array.

currentTimeMillis

static long currentTimeMillis()

Returns the current time in milliseconds from 00:00:00 UTC, 1-January-1970. Also see java.util.Date for other time methods.

exit

static void exit(int status)

Exits the runtime environment specifying an exit *status* code. A status code of 0 means success.

gc

void gc()

Runs the garbage collector. Since the garbage collector automatically runs when the system is idle, it is not usually necessary to call this method.

getProperties

static String getProperties()
Returns the System properties.

getProperty

static String getProperty(String key[, String def])

Returns the System property indicated by the specified *key* and optional *def*.

getSecurityManager static SecurityManager getSecurityManager()

Returns the System security interface.

load

static void load(String pathName) ***

Loads a dynamic library, given a file with a complete *pathName*.

loadLibrary

static void loadLibrary(String libraryName) ***

Loads a dynamic library, given its *libraryName*.

runFinalization

static void runFinalization()

Runs the finalization methods of any Objects pending finalization. Since finalization methods are called asynchronously by a finalization Thread, it is usually not necessary to call this method.

setProperties

static void setProperties(Properties props)

Sets the System properties to *props*.

setSecurityManager static void setSecurityManager(SecurityManager sec)

>Sets the System security. This can be set only once and will throw a SecurityException if already set.

* Throws ArrayIndexOutOfBoundsException if copy causes an access of data outside array bounds.

** Throws ArrayStoreException if source and destination array types do not match.

*** Throws UnsatisfiedLinkError if the specified file or library does not exist.

java.lang.Thread

Description	The Thread object is the basis of multithreaded programming. See Chapter 14 for a detailed explanation of threads.
Parent Class	Object
See Also	ThreadGroup, Runnable

CONSTRUCTORS

Thread()

>Creates a new Thread. You must override the run() method to do anything.

Thread([ThreadGroup group,] Runnable target)

>Creates a new Thread that invokes the run() method on the specified *target* Object. You may optionally specify a ThreadGroup *group* for this Thread.

Thread([ThreadGroup group,] String name)

>Creates a new Thread with the specified *name*. You may optionally specify a ThreadGroup *group* for this Thread.

Thread([ThreadGroup group,] String name, Runnable target)

>Creates a new Thread with the specified *name* and applies the run() method to the specified *target* Object. You may optionally specify a ThreadGroup *group* for this Thread.

VARIABLES

MIN_PRIORITY	static int: The minimum priority for a Thread.
NORM_PRIORITY	static int: The normal priority for a Thread.
MAX_PRIORITY	static int: The maximum priority for a Thread.

METHODS

activeCount   static int activeCount()

>Returns the number of active Threads in this Thread's ThreadGroup.

checkAccess	void checkAccess()

Checks whether the current Thread is allowed to modify this Thread; throws SecurityException if not allowed to modify this Thread's ThreadGroup.

countStackFrames	int countStackFrames()

Returns the number of stack frames in this Thread. The Thread should be suspended when this is called or it will throw an IllegalThreadStateException.

currentThread	static Thread currentThread()

Returns the currently executing Thread.

destroy	void destroy()

Immediately destroys this Thread. Use this only as a last resort.

dumpStack	static void dumpStack()

Prints a stack trace for the current Thread.

enumerate	static int enumerate(Thread threadArray[])

Copies references to every active Thread in this Thread's group into an array *threadArray[]*. Returns the number of Threads put into the array.

getName	final String getName()

Returns this Thread's name.

getPriority	final int getPriority()

Returns this Thread's priority.

getThreadGroup	final ThreadGroup getThreadGroup()

Returns this Thread's ThreadGroup.

interrupt	void interrupt()

Send an interrupt to this Thread.

interrupted	static boolean interrupted()

Returns true if this Thread has been interrupted, otherwise it returns false.

isAlive	final boolean isAlive()

Returns true if this Thread has been started; otherwise it returns false.

isDaemon	final boolean isDaemon()

Returns true if this Thread is a daemon Thread; otherwise it returns false.

isInterrupted	static boolean isInterrupted()

Returns true if another Thread has been interrupted, otherwise false.

join	synchronized void join()
	Waits indefinitely for this Thread to die.
join	synchronized void join(int milliseconds[, int nanoseconds])
	Waits for this Thread to die or until the specified timeout number of *milliseconds* and optional *nanoseconds* expires.
resume	final void resume()
	Resumes this Thread's execution if it has been suspended.
run	void run()
	This method is the body of the Thread and is called after the Thread is started. You must either override this method by subclassing class Thread, or create the Thread with a target that implements Runnable.
setDaemon	final void setDaemon(boolean state)
	If *state* is true, this Thread is marked as a daemon Thread (a background Thread); otherwise it is marked as a user Thread. The Thread must be currently inactive to use this method or it will throw an IllegalThreadStateException. Java will exit if there are only daemon Threads left running in the system.
setName	final void setName(String newName)
	Sets the Thread's name to *newName*.
setPriority	final void setPriority(int newPriority) *
	Sets the Thread's priority to *newPriority*. This must be in the range from MIN_PRIORITY to MAX_PRIORITY or an IllegalArgumentException is thrown.
sleep	static void sleep(int milliseconds[, int nanoseconds])
	Causes this Thread to sleep for the specified number of *milliseconds* and optional number of *nanoseconds*.
start	synchronized void start()
	Starts this Thread immediately causing the run() method to be called. Throws an IllegalStateException if this Thread was already started.
stop	final void stop()
	Stops this Thread by throwing a new instance of ThreadDeath to it.
suspend	final void suspend()
	Suspends this Thread's execution.
yield	static void yield()
	Causes this Thread to yield, allowing other Threads to execute.

java.lang.ThreadGroup

Description	The Thread group can contain several Threads as well as other Thread groups. A Thread is able to access its Thread group, but it cannot access the parent of its Thread group.
Parent Class	Object
See Also	Thread

CONSTRUCTORS

ThreadGroup(String grpName)

Creates a new ThreadGroup with the specified *grpName*. Its parent is the parent of the currently running Thread.

ThreadGroup(ThreadGroup parent, String grpName)

Creates a new ThreadGroup with the specified ThreadGroup *parent* and ThreadGroup name *grpName*. Throws NullPointerException if the specified ThreadGroup *parent* equals null.

VARIABLES

None

METHODS

activeCount   synchronized int activeCount()

Returns the estimated number of active Threads in this ThreadGroup.

activeGroupCount   synchronized int activeGroupCount()

Returns the estimated number of active groups in this ThreadGroup.

checkAccess   final void checkAccess()

Checks to see if the current Thread is allowed to modify this group. Throws SecurityException if it is not allowed to access this ThreadGroup.

destroy   final synchronized void destroy()

Destroys this ThreadGroup, but does not stop the Threads in it. Throws an IllegalThreadStateException if this ThreadGroup is not empty or does not exist.

enumerate   int enumerate(Thread list[] [, boolean recurse])

Copies references of every active Thread in this ThreadGroup into the specified array *list[]*. The activeCount() method can give you an estimate of how big to make this array. This method recurses by default; however, *recurse* may be specified as false to prevent this from happening.

enumerate int enumerate(ThreadGroup list[] [, boolean recurse])

Copies references of every active ThreadGroup in this ThreadGroup into the specified array *list[]*. The activeGroupCount() method can give you an estimate of how big to make this array. This method recurses by default; however, *recurse* may be specified as false to prevent this from happening.

getMaxPriority final int getMaxPriority()

Returns the maximum priority of the group. All Threads in this group must have a priority lower than or equal to this priority.

getName final String getName()

Returns the name of this ThreadGroup.

getParent final ThreadGroup getParent()

Returns the parent of this ThreadGroup.

isDaemon final boolean isDaemon()

Returns true if this ThreadGroup is a daemon ThreadGroup.

list synchronized void list()

Lists this ThreadGroup for debugging.

parentOf final boolean parentOf(ThreadGroup grp)

Returns true if this ThreadGroup is a parent of ThreadGroup *grp*, else returns false.

resume final synchronized void resume()

Resumes all Threads in this group and its subgroups.

setDaemon final void setDaemon(boolean daemon)

Changes the daemon status of this group to *daemon*. True means "a daemon ThreadGroup," which is automatically destroyed when empty.

setMaxPriority final void setMaxPriority(int priority)

Sets the maximum priority of the group to *priority*. This does not affect Threads already in this group.

stop final synchronized void stop()

Stops all Threads in this group and its subgroups.

suspend final void suspend()

Suspends all Threads in this group and its subgroups.

toString String toString()

Returns a String describing this ThreadGroup.

uncaughtException void uncaughtException(Thread thread, Throwable exception)

Called when a *thread* in this ThreadGroup exists because an *exception* was not caught.

java.lang.Throwable

Description	This Class signals that an exceptional condition occurred. It provides standard methods (i.e., messages, stack traces) for objects that are thrown. All objects that can be thrown must be subclasses of Throwable.
Parent Class	Object
See Also	Error, Exception

CONSTRUCTORS

Throwable() Creates a new Throwable with no message. The stack trace is filled in automatically.

Throwable(String message)

Creates a new Throwable with the specified *message*. The stack trace is filled in automatically.

VARIABLES

None

METHODS

fillInStackTrace Throwable fillInStackTrace()

Fills in the execution stack trace. Returns itself for convenient rethrows.

getMessage String getMessage()

Returns the message of the Throwable.

printStackTrace void printStackTrace([PrintStream prt])

Prints the Throwable's stack trace. An optional PrintStream *prt* may be specified.

toString String toString()

Returns a String describing this Throwable.

Other Classes in java.lang:

java.lang.Boolean

Description	This class encapsulates a boolean.
Parent Class	Object

CONSTRUCTORS

Boolean(boolean state)

> Creates a Boolean object with the specified *state*.

Boolean(String state)

> Creates a Boolean object with the specified *state* represented by a String. If the *state* equals "true" then the Object will be true; otherwise, it will be false.

VARIABLES

TRUE	final static boolean: A boolean constant.
FALSE	final static boolean: A boolean constant.

METHODS

boolean **booleanValue**()	
boolean **valueOf**(String str)	boolean **equals**(Object obj)
int **hashCode**()	
static boolean **getBoolean**(String propName)	String **toString**()

java.lang.Character

Description	This class encapsulates a character.
Parent Class	Object

CONSTRUCTORS

Character(char value)

> Creates a Character object with the specified *value*.

VARIABLES

MIN_RADIX	final static int: Minimum radix for String conversion.
MAX_RADIX	final static int: Maximum radix for String conversion.

METHODS

boolean **equals**(Object obj)	
int **hashCode**()	char **charValue**()
static char **forDigit**(int digit, int radix)	static boolean **isDigit**(char ch)
static boolean **isLowerCase**(char ch)	static boolean **isSpace**(char ch)
static boolean **isUpperCase**(char ch)	static char **toLowerCase**(char ch)
static char **toString**()	static char **toUpperCase**(char ch)

java.lang.Compiler

Description   This class adds support for compiling Java classes.
Parent Class   Object

CONSTRUCTORS

None

VARIABLES

None

METHODS

static Object **command**(Object obj)

static boolean **compileClasses**(String str)

static void **disable**()

static boolean **compileClass**(Class class)

static void **enable**()

java.lang.Double

Description   This class encapsulates a double.
Parent Class   Number

CONSTRUCTORS

Double(double value)   Creates a double object with the specified *value*.

Double(String value) *   Creates a Double object with the specified *value* represented by a String.

VARIABLES

MIN_VALUE	final static double: Minimum value for a double.
MAX_VALUE	final static double: Maximum value for a double.
NEGATIVE_INFINITY	final static double: Negative infinity.
NaN	final static double: Not a number.
POSITIVE_INFINITY	final static double: Positive infinity.

METHODS

static long **doubleToLongBits**(double valToConvert)

boolean **equals**(Object obj)

int **hashCode**()

static boolean **isInfinite**(double valToTest)

static boolean **isNaN**(double valToTest)

double **doubleValue**()

float **floatValue**()

int **intValue**()

boolean **isInfinite**()

boolean **isNaN**()

static double **longBitsToDouble**(long bitsToConvert)   long **longValue**()

String **toString**()   Static String **toString**(double d)

static Double **valueOf**(String str) *

* Throws NumberFormatException if the String does not contain a parsable double.

java.lang.Float

Description   This class encapsulates a float value.

Parent Class   Number

CONSTRUCTORS

Float(float value)

Float(double value) Creates a Float object with the specified *value*.

Float(String value) * Creates a Float object with the specified *value* represented by a
String.

VARIABLES

MIN_VALUE	final static float: Minimum value for a float.
MAX_VALUE	final static float: Maximum value for a float.
NEGATIVE_INFINITY	final static float: Negative infinity.
NaN	final static float: Not a number.
POSITIVE_INFINITY	final static float: Positive infinity.

METHODS

double **doubleValue**()   boolean **equals**(Object obj)

static long **floatToIntBits**(float valToConvert)   float **floatValue**()

int **hashCode**()   int **intValue**()

static float **intBitsToFloat**(int bitsToConvert)   boolean **isInfinite**()

static boolean **isInfinite**(double valToTest)   boolean **isNaN**()

static boolean **isNaN**(double valToTest)   long **longValue**()

static String **toString**(float f)   static String **toString**(float val)

String **toString**()   static Float **valueOf**(String str) *

* Throws NumberFormatException if the String does not contain a parsable float.

java.lang.Integer

Description   This class encapsulates an integer.

Parent Class   Number

CONSTRUCTORS

Integer(int value)   Creates an integer object with the specified *value*.

Integer(String str) * Creates an integer object with the specified String *str*.

VARIABLES

MIN_VALUE   final static int: Minimum value for an integer.

MAX_VALUE   final static int: Maximum value for an integer.

METHODS

double **doubleValue**()

static Integer **getInteger**(String propName)

static Integer **getInteger**(String propName, int val)

static Integer **getInteger**(String propName, Integer val)

long **longValue**()

static int **parseInt**(String str, int radix) *

String **toString**(int i)

static Integer **valueOf**(String str, int radix) *

boolean **equals**(Object obj)

float **floatValue**()

int **hashCode**()

int **intValue**()

static int **parseInt**(String str) *

String **toString**()

String **toString**(int i, int radix)

static Integer **valueOf**(String str) *

* Throws NumberFormatException if the String does not contain a parsable integer.

java.lang.Long

Description   This class encapsulates a long value.

Parent Class   Number

CONSTRUCTORS

Long(long value)   Creates a long object with the specified *value*.

Long(String str) *   Creates a long object with the specified String *str*.

VARIABLES

MIN_VALUE   final static long: Minimum value for a long.

MAX_VALUE   final static long: Maximum value for a long.

METHODS

double **doubleValue**()

static Long **getLong**(String propName)

static Long **getLong**(String propName, long val)

static Long **getLong**(String propName, Long val)

boolean **equals**(Object obj)

float **floatValue**()

int **hashcode**()

int **intValue**()

long **longValue**()

static long **parseLong**(String str,int radix) *

static String **toString**(int i)

static Long **valueOf**(String str, int radix) *

static long **parseLong**(String str) *

String **toString**()

static String **toString**(int i, int radix)

static Long **valueOf**(String str) *

* Throws NumberFormatException if the String does not contain a parsable long.

java.lang.Math

Description	This class contains a math library.
Parent Class	Object

CONSTRUCTORS

None

VARIABLES

E	final static double: E = 2.7182818284590452354
PI	final static long: PI = 3.1415926535897932846

METHODS

static int **abs**(int a)

static float **abs**(float a)

static double **acos**(double a)

static double **atan**(double a)

static double **ceil**(double a)

static double **exp**(double a)

static double **log**(double a) *

static long **max**(long a, long b)

static double **max**(double a, double b)

static long **min**(long a, long b)

static double **pow**(double a, double b) *

static double **rint**(double a)

static long **round**(double a)

static double **sqrt**(double a) *

static long **abs**(long a)

static double **abs**(double a)

static double **asin**(double a)

static double **atan2**(double a, double b)

static double **cos**(double a)

static double **floor**(double a)

static int **max**(int a, int b)

static float **max**(float a, float b)

static int **min**(int a, int b)

static float **min**(float a, float b)

static double **random**()

static int **round**(float a)

static double **sin**(double a)

static double **tan**(double a)

* Throws ArithmeticException if a<0 in log and sqrt and if a=0, b<=0 or a<=0 and b is not a whole number in pow.

java.lang.Number

Description	This class is an **abstract** class, subclassed by scaler number wrapper objects such as Double, Float, Integer, and Long.
Parent Class	Object

CONSTRUCTORS

Number()	Creates a Number object.

VARIABLES

None

METHODS

abstract double **doubleValue()**	abstract float **floatValue()**
abstract int **intValue()**	abstract long **longValue()**

NET

java.net.ContentHandlerFactory (Interface)

Description	This interface defines a way to create instances of ContentHandler (notice that ContentHandler does not have a constructor). In other words, this interface specifies a factory for ContentHandler instances.
Parent Class	Object
See Also	ContentHandler, URLStreamHandler

METHODS

createContentHandler abstract ContentHandler createContentHandler(String mimeType)

Returns a new ContentHandler with the specified *mimeType* to read an object from a URLStreamHandler.

java.net.SocketImplFactory (Interface)

Description	This interface defines a way to create instances of SocketImpl (notice that SocketImpl does not have a constructor) that allow Socket instances to define their policies. In other words, this interface specifies a factory for SocketImpl instances.
Parent Class	Object

| See Also | Socket, ServerSocket, SocketImpl |

METHODS

createSocketImpl   abstract SocketImpl createSocketImp()
Returns a new SocketImpl object.

java.net.URLStreamHandlerFactory (Interface)

Description	This interface defines a way to create instances of URLStreamHandler (notice that URLStreamHandler does not have a constructor). In other words, this interface specifies a factory for URLStreamHandler instances.
Parent Class	Object
See Also	URLStreamHandler, URL

METHODS

createURLStreamHandler abstract URLStreamHandler createURLStreamHandler()
Returns a new URLStreamHandler object.

java.net.ContentHandler

Description	This class allows you to convert data from a URLConnection to an Object. You should never call ContentHandlers directly; instead you should invoke URL.getContent() or URLConnection.getContent().
Parent Class	Object
See Also	URL, URLStreamHandler, URLConnection

CONSTRUCTORS

None

VARIABLES

None

METHODS

getContent   abstract Object getContent(URLConnection urlCon)
Returns an Object created from an input stream positioned at the beginning of the Object's representation. The stream is obtained from the urlConnection *urlCon*. Throws IOException if an I/O error occurs.

java.net.DatagramPacket

Description	This **final** class encapsulates a datagram packet containing packet data, packet length, internet address, and port.
Parent Class	Object
See Also	DatagramSocket

CONSTRUCTORS

DatagramPacket(byte data[], int length [, inetAddress address, int port])

Creates a DatagramPacket to receive Datagrams. The number of bytes to read is specified by *length* and the received packet data is placed in *data[]*. Optionally, a destination *address* and *port* may be specified.

VARIABLES

None

METHODS

getAddress	InetAddress getAddress()
	Returns an InetAddress object for the DatagramPacket.
getData	byte[] getData()
	Returns the data in this DatagramPacket.
getLength	int getLength()
	Returns the length of this DatagramPacket.
getPort	int getPort()
	Returns the port used by this DatagramPacket.

java.net.DatagramSocket

Description	This **final** class encapsulates a datagram socket.
Parent Class	Object
See Also	DatagramPacket

CONSTRUCTORS

DatagramSocket([int port])

Creates a DatagramSocket. When an optional local *port* is specified a security check is also performed. Throws SocketException if there is a problem.

VARIABLES

None

METHODS

close	synchronized void close()
	Closes this DatagramSocket.
finalize	protected synchronized void finalize()
	Called when this object is garbage collected.
getLocalPort	int getLocalPort()
	Returns the local port to which this DatagramSocket is connected.
receive	void receive(DatagramPacket pkt) *
	Receives the specified DatagramPacket *pkt*. This blocks until input is available. When received the Datagram will contain the sender's address and port in addition to the data and its length.
send	void send(DatagramPacket pkt) *
	Sends the specified DatagramPacket *pkt* to the destination address.

* Throws IOException if an I/O error occurs.

java.net.InetAddress

Description	This **final** class encapsulates Internet addresses and is used to obtain information such as host name and port address. This class does not have a public constructor—you must use the getByName(), getLocalHost() or getAllByName() method to instantiate an object.
Parent Class	Object
See Also	Socket

CONSTRUCTORS

None

VARIABLES

None

METHODS

equals	boolean equals(Object obj2)
	Returns true if this InetAddress and the specified InetAddress *obj2* have the same Internet address.

getAddress	byte[] getAddress()
	Returns the raw IP address in network byte order; in other words, the most significant byte is first.
getAllByName	static synchronized InetAddress getAllByName(String hostName) *
	Returns an array of all InetAddress objects for the given *hostName*.
getByName	static synchronized InetAddress getByName(String hostName) *
	Returns an InetAddress object for the given *hostName*.
getHostName	String getLocalHostName()
	Returns the host name for this InetAddress.
getLocalHost	static InetAddress getLocalHost() *
	Returns an InetAddress object for the local host.
hashCode	int hashCode()
	Returns a hash code for this InetAddress.
toString	String toString()
	Returns a String showing the IP address for this InetAddress.

* Throws UnknownHostException if the address is unknown.

java.net.ServerSocket

Description	This class encapsulates a server socket. You must use SocketImpl to implement the actual Socket operation policies. For this reason, you are able to change socket implementations, depending on the type of firewall used, by setting the SocketImplFactory. See Chapter 15 for usage examples.
Parent Class	Object
See Also	Socket, SocketImpl, InetAddress

CONSTRUCTORS

ServerSocket(int port[, int time]) *

Creates a server socket and binds it to the specified *port*. If the *port* is 0, an anonymous port is used. Optionally, the amount of *time* to listen for a connection may be specified.

VARIABLES

None

METHODS

accept	Socket accept() *
	Returns a connection on a new socket. The original server socket is still around to listen for new connections.
close	void close() *
	Closes the connection.
getInetAddress	InetAddress getInetAddress()
	Returns the address to which this Socket is connected.
getLocalPort	int getLocalPort()
	Returns the port to which this Socket is connected.
setSocketFactory	static synchronized void setSocketFactory(SocketImplFactory sIFact) *
	Sets the system's server SocketImplFactory *sIFact*. Throws SocketException if the factory is already defined.
toString	String toString()
	Returns a String showing this Socket address and port.

* Throws IOException if an I/O error occurs.

java.net.Socket

Description	This **final** class encapsulates a client socket. A socket is the basis for network abstraction of input/output. Where it makes sense, sockets behave like files or devices. They can be used with the standard input and output streams. You must use the SocketImpl class to implement the actual Socket operation policies.
Parent Class	Object
See Also	ServerSocket, SocketImpl, InetAddress

CONSTRUCTORS

Socket(String hostName, int port[, boolean isStream]) *

> Creates a Socket and connects it to the specified *hostName* and *port*. It is a stream Socket if *isStream* is missing or true, otherwise it is a datagram Socket.
>
> Throws UnknownHostException if the host is not found.

Socket(InetAddress address, int port[, boolean isStream]) *

> Creates a Socket and connects it to the specified Internet *address* and *port*. It is a stream Socket if *isStream* is missing or true, otherwise it is a datagram Socket.

VARIABLES

None

METHODS

close	synchronized void close() *	
	Closes this Socket.	
getInetAddress	InetAddress getInetAddress()	
	Returns the address to which this Socket is connected.	
getInputStream	InputStream getInputStream() *	
	Returns an InputStream for this socket.	
getLocalPort	int getLocalPort()	
	Returns the local port to which this Socket is connected.	
getOutputStream	OutputStream getOutputStream() *	
	Returns an OutputStream for this Socket.	
getPort	int getPort()	
	Returns the remote port to which the socket is connected.	
setSocketImplFactory	static synchronized void setSocketImplFactory(SocketImplFactory sIFact)	
	Sets the system's client SocketImplFactory *sIFact*. Throws SocketException if the factory is already defined.	
toString	String toString()	
	Returns a String showing this Socket's address and port.	

* Throws IOException if an I/O error occurs.

java.net.SocketImpl

Description	This **abstract** class implements the actual socket operation policies for the Socket and ServerSocket classes. It must be subclassed to provide an actual implementation.
Parent Class	Object
See Also	Socket, ServerSocket, SocketImplFactory

CONSTRUCTORS

None

VARIABLES

address	protected InetAddress: The address to which the socket is connected.
fd	protected int: The file descriptor associated with the socket.

localport	protected int: The local port to which the socket is connected.
port	protected int: The remote port to which the socket is connected.

METHODS

accept	protected abstract void Socket accept(SocketImpl sock) *
	Returns a new connection to the socket in the *sock* argument.
available	protected abstract int available() *
	Returns the number of bytes available before blocking occurs.
bind	protected abstract void bindToPort(InetAddress addr, int port) *
	Binds the socket to address *addr* and a known *port*.
close	protected abstract synchronized void close() *
	Closes the connection.
connect	protected abstract void connect(String host, int port) *
	Connects the socket to the specified *host* and *port*.
connect	protected abstract void connect(InetAddress address, int port) *
	Connects the socket to the specified *address* on the specified *port*.
create	protected abstract void create(boolean isStream) *
	Creates a socket that is a stream socket if *isStream* is true, else it is a datagram (connectionless) socket.
getFileDescriptor	protected FileDescriptor getFileDescriptor()
	Returns a FileDescriptor for the socket.
getInetAddress	protected InetAddress getInetAddress()
	Returns an InetAddress for the socket.
getInputStream	protected abstract InputStream getInputStream() *
	Returns an InputStream for the socket.
getLocalPort	protected int getLocalPort()
	Returns a LocalPort for the socket.
getOutputStream	protected abstract OutputStream getOutputStream() *
	Returns an OutputStream for the socket.
getPort	protected int getPort()
	Returns a Port for the socket.
listen	protected abstract void listen(int time) *
	Specifies the amount of *time* the socket will listen for connections.
toString	String toString()
	Returns a String showing the socket address and port.

* Throws IOException if an I/O error occurs.

java.net.URL

Description	This **final** class encapsulates a Uniform Resource Locator. Once this object has been created, its fields cannot be changed.
Parent Class	Object
See Also	URLConnection, URLStreamHandler

CONSTRUCTORS

URL([URL context,] String urlSpec) *

Creates a URL from unparsed absolute *urlSpec* or optionally, creates the URL from the unparsed, relative *urlSpec* and the *context* specified.

URL(String protocol, String host, [int port,] String file) *

Creates an absolute URL from the specified *protocol*, *host*, and *file* connected to. The host's *port* may optionally be specified. If omitted, the port will default to the standard port for the specified protocol.

* Throws MalformedURLException if an invalid or unknown protocol is found.

VARIABLES

None

METHODS

equals	boolean equals(Object obj2)
	Returns true if this URL and *obj2* reference the same remote object
getContent	Object getContent()*
	Returns contents of this opened connection.
getFile	String getFile()
	Returns the file name.
getHost	String getHost()
	Returns the host name.
getPort	int getPort()
	Returns the port number, or -1 if not set.
getProtocol	String getProtocol()
	Returns the protocol name.
getRef	String getRef()
	Returns a subpart of the resource (e.g., a hypertext reference inside an HTML document).

hashCode	int hashCode()
	Returns a hash code for this URL.
openConnection	URLConnection openConnection() *
	Returns a URLConnection object that has a connection to the remote object referred to by the URL.
openStream	InputStream openStream() *
	Opens an input stream.
sameFile	boolean sameFile(URL url2)
	Returns true if this URL and *url2* reference the same remote object, but not necessarily the same part of that object.
setURLStreamHandlerFactory	static synchronized void setURLStreamHandlerFactory (URLStreamHandlerFactory urlFac)
	Sets the URLStreamHandler factory to *urlFac*. Throws an Error if this factory is already defined.
toExternalForm	String toExternalForm()
	Returns a String containing the fully qualified URL information.
toString	String toString()
	Returns a String showing URL information.

* Throws IOException if an I/O error occurs.

java.net.URLConnection

Description	This **abstract** class encapsulates an active connection to an object represented by a URL.
Parent Class	Object
See Also	URL, URLStreamHandler

CONSTRUCTORS

URLConnection(URL url)**protected**

Creates a connection to the specified URL *url*.

VARIABLES

allowUserInteraction	protected boolean: The flag determining if the user is allowed to interact.
connected	protected boolean: The flag determining if URL is connected.
doInput	protected boolean: The flag determining if URL may be used for input.
doOutput	protected boolean: The flag determining if URL may be used for output.

ifModifiedSince	protected long: Some protocols support fetching only when the object is newer than some time. This field may be set/gotten to define this time.
url	protected URL: The Uniform Resource Locator.
useCaches	protected boolean: The flag determining if caches are used when possible.

METHODS

connect   abstract void connect() *

Makes the URL connection for this Object. You must set various options (such as setDefaultUseCaches) before making the connection.

getAllowUserInteraction boolean getAllowUserInteraction()

Returns the current value of the allowUserInteraction flag. If true, then the user is able to interact with the URL connection.

getContent   Object getContent() *,**

Returns the object referred to by this URL. The instanceof operator may be used to determine what type of object was returned.

getContentEncoding String getContentEncoding()

Returns the content encoding or null if unknown.

getContentLength   int getContentLength()

Returns the content length or -1 if unknown.

getContentType   String getContentType()

Returns the content type or null if unknown.

getDate   long getDate()

Returns the sending date or 0 if unknown.

getDefaultAllowUserInteraction static boolean getDefaultAllowUserInteraction()

Returns the default value of the allowUserInteraction flag. See getAllowUserInteraction for an explanation.

getDefaultRequestProperty static String getDefaultRequestProperty(String keyword)

Returns the value associated with the *keyword* (e.g., accept) of the default general request property.

getDefaultUseCaches boolean getDefaultUseCaches()

Returns the default value of the UseCaches flag.

getDoInput   boolean getDoInput()

Returns true if this URL connection may be used for input.

getDoOutput   boolean getDoOutput()

Returns true if this URL connection may be used for output.

getExpiration long getExpiration()

Returns the expiration date or 0 if unknown.

getHeaderField String getHeaderField(String name)

Returns a header field by name, null if unknown.

getHeaderField String getHeaderField(int n)

Returns the value for the *n*th header field, null if there are fewer than *n* header fields.

getHeaderFieldDate long getHeaderFieldDate(String name, long default)

Returns a header field given its *name* and *default* (the value it returns if it cannot find the field) or null if not known. For example, getHeaderFieldDate("expires", 0) is the same as getExpiration().

getHeaderFieldInt int getHeaderFieldInt(String name, int default)

This works the same as above, except the value will be parsed and returned as an integer.

getHeaderFieldKey String getHeaderFieldKey(int n)

Returns the key for the *n*th header field.

getIfModifiedSince long getIfModifiedSince()

Returns the last modification time that was set.

getInputStream InputStream getInputStream() *,**

Returns an InputStream that reads from this object. When required, protocol implementors should implement this.

getLastModified long getLastModified()

Returns the last modified date or 0 if unknown.

getOutputStream OutputStream getOutputStream() *,**

Returns an OutputStream that writes to this object. When required, protocol implementors should implement this.

getRequestProperty String getRequestProperty(String keyword) ***

Returns the value associated with the *keyword* of the general request property.

getURL URL getURL()

Returns the URL for this connection.

getUseCaches boolean getUseCaches()

Returns true if the connection is using caches, else it returns false.

guessContentTypeFromName protected static String guessContentTypeFromName(String name)

Returns a guess of the content type of an object based upon the extension of the specified *name*.

guessContentTypeFromStream protected static String guessContentTypeFromStream(InputStream inStrm)

Returns a guess of the content type of an object based upon the contents of a stream *inStrm*. The stream must support marks. As an example, if the first four bytes in the stream are "GIF8", this method might return "image/gif".

setAllowUserInteraction void setAllowUserInteraction(boolean allowInteraction) ***

Sets the current value of the allowUserInteraction flag before actually connecting. If *allowInteraction* is true, then the user is able to interact with the URL connection.

setContentHandlerFactory static synchronized void setContentHandlerFactory (ContentHandlerFactory fact)

Sets the ContentHandler factory to *fact*. Throws Exception if the factory has already been defined.

setDefaultAllowUserInteraction static void setDefaultAllowUserInteraction(boolean allowDefInteraction)

Sets the default value of the allowDefaultUserInteraction flag for all instances of URL connection. If *allowDefInteraction* is true, then the user is able to interact with the URL connection by default.

setDefaultRequestProperty static void setDefaultRequestProperty(String keyword, String value)

Sets the default value of a general request property. A new URLConnection is initialized with the specified *keyword* and *value*.

setDefaultUseCaches void setDefaultUseCaches(boolean useCache)

If *useCache* is true, all the new URLConnections that are created will by default use whatever caches they can, else they will ignore all caches. The default is part of the static state of all URLConnections.

setDoInput void setDoInput(boolean doInput) ***

If *doInput* is true, then this URL connection can be used for input. Set before connecting.

setDoOutput void setDoOutput(boolean doOutput) ***

If *doOutput* is true, then this URL connection can be used for output. Set before connecting.

setIfModifiedSince void setIfModifiedSince(long ifModifiedSince) ***

Set *ifModifiedSince* to define a reference time. This is useful because some protocols can skip fetching unless the object is newer than a given time.

setRequestProperty void setRequestProperty(String key, String value) ***

Sets a general request property given a *key* and *value*.

setUseCaches void setUseCaches(boolean useCache) ***

If *useCache* is true, the connection will use whatever caches it can, else it will ignore all caches. The default is true. Set before connecting.

toString String toString()

Returns a String showing information about the URL connection.

* Throws IOException if an I/O error occurs.

** Throws UnknownServiceException if the protocol does not support the requested service.

*** Throws IllegalAccessError if this method is invoked after connect().

java.net.URLEncoder

Description	This class changes Strings of text into an x-www-form-url encoded format.
Parent Class	Object

CONSTRUCTORS

None

VARIABLES

None

METHODS

encode static String encode(String string)

Returns an x-www-form-url encoded String converted from the specified *string*.

java.net.URLStreamHandler

Description	This **abstract** class encapsulates URL stream openers. Subclasses should be able to create streams for particular protocol types.
Parent Class	Object
See Also	URL, URLConnection, URLStreamHandlerFactory

CONSTRUCTORS

None

VARIABLES

None

METHODS

openConnection	protected abstract URLConnection openConnection(URL url)
	Opens an input stream to the object referred to by the specified *url*. Throws an IOException if there is an error.
parseURL	protected void parseURL(URL url, String urlSpec, int start, int end)
	Parses the string *urlSpec* from *start* (just past the ":" - if present) to *end* (the last position to stop parsing at, or the position of the "#" character, if present) into URL *url*.
setURL	protected void setURL(URL url, String protcol, String host, int port, String file, String ref)
	Calls the specified *url's* set method with the specified parameters. The URL set method is not public, so this is the only way for a URLStreamHandler to modify the URL's fields.
toExternalForm	protected String toExternalForm(URL url)
	Returns a String containing the fully qualified URL information.

UTIL

java.util.Enumeration (Interface)

Description	This interface specifies a set of methods that may be used to iterate through a set of values. The values may be traversed only once (there is no previousElement method).
Parent Class	Object
See Also	Hashtable, Vector

METHODS

hasMoreElements	boolean hasMoreElements()
	Returns true if more elements exist in the enumeration.
nextElement	Object nextElement()
	Returns the next element in the enumeration. Throws NoSuchElementException if there are no more elements.

java.util.Observer (Interface)

Description	This interface allows classes to be observable by instances of class Observer.
Parent Class	Object
See Also	Observable

METHODS

update	abstract void update(Observable obsList, Object objArg)
	This method is called when the observers in the observable list *obsList* need to be updated with the *objArg* being notified.

java.util.BitSet

Description	This class implements a set of bits. This set will automatically grow in chunks of 64 bits as needed.
Parent Class	Object
Implements	Cloneable

CONSTRUCTORS

BitSet([int nBits])   Constructs an empty set of bits or a set of bits with size *nBits*.

VARIABLES

None

METHODS

and	void and(BitSet set2)
	Logically ANDs this BitSet with another *set2* and puts the result in this set.
clear	void clear(int bit)
	Clears the bit at position *bit*.
clone	Object clone()
	Returns a clone of this set of bits.
equals	boolean equals(Object set2)
	Returns true if all of the bits in this BitSet and the specified BitSet *set2* are identical (e.g., 00111 = 111).
get	boolean get(int bit)
	Returns the bit value at position *bit*.

hashCode	int hashCode()
	Returns a hash code for this BitSet.
or	void or(BitSet set2)
	Logically ORs this BitSet with another *set2* and puts the result in this set.
set	void set(int bit)
	Sets the bit value at position *bit*.
size	int size()
	Returns the current capacity of this set.
toString	toString()
	Returns a String showing the bits (e.g., "{0, 1, 0}").
xor	void xor(BitSet set2)
	Logically XORs this BitSet with another *set2* and puts the result in this set.

java.util.Date

Description	This class encapsulates a date. With this class you can obtain and manipulate the date without any concern for which system it is running on. All date fields are correctly normalized. For example, the 32nd of October is interpreted as the 1st of November.
Parent Class	Object
See Also	java.lang.System contains some other time methods.

CONSTRUCTORS

Date([long time])	Constructs a Date for today's date and the current time or for the specified *time* in milliseconds since 1970.
Date(String date)	Constructs a date for the specified String *date* according to the parse() syntax.
Date(int year, int month, int dayOfMonth [,int hour, int minute])	
	Constructs a date for the specified *year*, *month*, and *dayOfMonth* where *year* is after 1900, *month* between 0 and 11, and *dayOfMonth* between 1 and 31. Optionally, *hour* and *minute* may be added where *hour* is between 0 and 23 and *minute* is between 0 and 59.
Date(int year, int month, int dayOfMonth, int hour, int minute, int second)	
	Constructs a date for the specified *year*, *month*, *dayOfMonth*, *hour*, *minute*, and *second* where *second* is between 0 and 59.

VARIABLES

None

METHODS

after   boolean after(Date date2)

Returns true if this date is after *date2*.

before   boolean before(Date date2)

Returns true if this date is before *date2*.

equals   boolean equals(Object date2)

Returns true if this date and *date2* are identical.

getDate   int getDate()

Returns the day of the month between 1 and 31.

getDay   int getDay()

Returns the day of the week between 0 and 6.

getHours   int getHours()

Returns the hour between 0 and 23.

getMinutes   int getMinutes()

Returns the minutes between 0 and 59.

getMonth   int getMonth()

Returns the month between 0 and 11.

getSeconds   int getSeconds()

Returns the seconds between 0 and 59.

getTime   long getTime()

Returns the time in milliseconds since 1970.

getTimezoneOffset   int getTimezoneOffset()

Returns the current time zone offset in minutes for this locale.

getYear   int getYear()

Returns the year after 1900.

hashCode   int hashCode()

Returns a hash code for this Date.

parse   static long parse(String strTime)

Returns the time value given a string representing a time *strTime*. It accepts many syntaxes, including the IETF standard date syntax: "Sat, 20 Feb 1971 15:30:00 GMT".

setDate   void setDate(int date)

Sets the date to the specified *date*.

setHours   void setHours(int hours)

Sets the hours to the specified *hours*.

setMinutes	void setMinutes(int minutes)
	Sets the minutes to the specified *minutes*.
setMonth	void setMonth(int month)
	Sets the month to the specified *month*.
setSeconds	void setSeconds(int seconds)
	Sets the seconds to the specified *seconds*.
setTime	void setTime(long time)
	Sets the *time* in milliseconds since 1970.
setYear	void setYear(int year)
	Sets the year to the specified *year*.
toGMTString	String toGMTString()
	Returns this Date as a String, using the Internet GMT conventions.
toLocaleString	String toLocaleString()
	Returns this Date as a String, using the locale conventions.
toString	String toString()
	Returns this Date as a String, using the UNIX ctime conventions.
UTC	static long UTC(int year , int month, int day, int hours, int minutes, int seconds)
	Returns the Coordinated Universal Time value from the specified parameters.

java.util.Dictionary

Description	This **abtract** class is the parent of Hashtable, which maps keys to values.
Parent Class	Object
See Also	Hashtable

CONSTRUCTORS

None

VARIABLES

None

METHODS

elements	abstract Enumeration elements()
	Returns an enumeration of the elements in this Dictionary.

get	abstract Object get(Object key)
	Returns the object associated with the specified *key* in this Dictionary.
isEmpty	abstract boolean isEmpty()
	Returns true if there are no elements in this Dictionary.
keys	abstract Enumeration keys()
	Returns an enumeration of this Dictionary's keys.
put	abstract Object put(Object key, Object value)
	Puts the specified *value* into this Dictionary, using the specified *key*.
remove	abstract Object remove(Object key)
	Removes the element associated with the specified *key*.
size	abstract int size()
	Returns the number of elements in this Dictionary.

java.util.Hashtable

Description	This class implements a Hashtable, which uses a unique key to access data placed in the table. The key can be any object as long as it implements the hashCode() and equals() methods. All Hashtables will automatically grow when full.
Parent Class	Dictionary
Implements	Cloneable
See Also	Dictionary

CONSTRUCTORS

Hashtable()	Constructs a new and empty Hashtable with a default capacity and load factor.
Hashtable(int initialCapacity[, float loadFactor])	
	Constructs a new and empty Hashtable with the specified *initialCapacity* in buckets and optional *loadFactor*. The loadFactor is a unit between 0 and 1 that defines the threshold for rehashing the hash table into a larger one. Throws IllegalArgumentException if either argument is less than or equal to 0.

VARIABLES

None

METHODS

clear	synchronized void clear()
	Clears this Hashtable of all its elements.
clone	synchronized Object clone()
	Creates a clone of this Hashtable. Clone makes a shallow copy; in other words, the keys and elements themselves are NOT copied.
contains	synchronized boolean contains(Object lookingFor)
	Returns true if the specified object *lookingFor* is an element of the Hashtable; however, for increased performance, use containsKey when possible. Throws NullPointerException if *lookingFor* is null.
containsKey	synchronized boolean contains(Object findKey)
	Returns true if the specified object *findKey* is defined in the Hashtable.
elements	synchronized Enumeration elements()
	Returns an Enumeration of the elements.
get	synchronized Object get(Object key)
	Returns the Object associated with the specified *key* or null if the key is not defined in the Hashtable.
isEmpty	boolean isEmpty()
	Returns true if the Hashtable has no elements.
keys	synchronized Enumeration keys()
	Returns an Enumeration of this Hashtable's keys.
put	synchronized object put(Object key, Object element)
	Put the specified *element* into the Hashtable using the *key* specified. Neither the key nor the element may be null. Returns the old value of the given *key* or null if one did not exist. To retrieve the element, invoke a get() with the same key. Throws NullPointerException if the value of *element* is null.
rehash	protected void rehash()
	Rehashes the content of the table into a larger one. This method is automatically called when the Hashtable's size exceeds its threshold.
remove	synchronized Object remove(Object key)
	Removes the element corresponding to the specified *key* or does nothing if the *key* does not exist. Returns the value of the given *key* or null if the key did not exist.
size	int size()
	Returns the number of elements in this Hashtable.
toString	String toString()
	Returns the String showing this Hashtable.

java.util.Observable

Description	This class should be subclassed by Objects that wish to be observed. An Observable object may have multiple observers. Whenever its instance changes, it notifies all its observers by calling the update() method of all the observers in its list. These observers must implement Observer.
Parent Class	Object
See Also	Observer (Interface)

CONSTRUCTORS

None

VARIABLES

None

METHODS

addObserver	synchronized void addObserver(Observer obs)
	Adds an Observer *obs* to the list of observers.
clearChanged	protected synchronized void clearChanged()
	Clears an observable change.
countObservers	synchronized int countObservers()
	Returns the number of observers.
deleteObserver	synchronized void deleteObserver(Observer obs)
	Deletes an Observer *obs* from the list of observers.
deleteObservers	synchronized void deleteObservers()
	Deletes all observers from the list of observers.
hasChanged	synchronized boolean hasChanged()
	Returns true if an observable change has occurred.
notifyObservers	void notifyObservers()
	Notifies all Observers if an observable change occurs.
notifyObservers	synchronized void notifyObservers(Object arg)
	Notifies all Observers of the specified *arg* observable change that occurred.
setChanged	protected synchronized void setChanged()
	Notes an observable change.

java.util.Properties

Description	This class implements a Hashtable that can be saved to and loaded from a stream. If a property is not found, the list containing defaults is searched.
Parent Class	Hashtable
See Also	Dictionary

CONSTRUCTORS

Properties([Properties defaults])

Constructs an empty property list. Optionally, the Properties *defaults* may be specified.

VARIABLES

defaults protected Properties: The list of property defaults.

METHODS

getProperty String getProperty(String key [, String defaultValue])

Returns a property with the specified *key*. If the *key* is not found in this list, then the default's property list will be searched. Returns null or the specified *defaultValue* if not found.

list void list(PrintStream out)

Lists properties to PrintStream *out*, useful for debugging.

load synchronized void load(InputStream in)

Loads properties from the specified InputStream *in*.

propertyNames Enumeration propertyNames()

Enumerates all the keys for these Properties.

save synchronized void save(OutputStream out, String header)

Saves properties to an OutputStream *out* and writes a *header* at the top.

java.util.Random

Description	This class generates pseudo-random numbers that may be repeatable if the same seed is used.
Parent Class	Object
See Also	java.lang.Math's random() method.

CONSTRUCTORS

Random() Constructs a random number generator initialized with the current time. In other words, the stream of pseudo-random numbers will not be repeatable.

Random(long seed) Constructs a random number generator initialized with the specified *seed*. Use this when the stream of pseudo-random numbers requires repeatablity.

VARIABLES

None

METHODS

nextDouble double nextDouble()

Returns a pseudo-random, uniformly distributed double value between 0.0 and 1.0.

nextFloat float nextFloat()

Returns a pseudo-random, uniformly distributed float value between 0.0 and 1.0.

nextGaussian synchronized double nextGaussian()

Returns a pseudo-random, normally distributed double value with mean 0.0 and standard deviation 1.0.

nextInt int nextInt()

Returns a pseudo-random, uniformly distributed int value.

nextLong long nextLong()

Returns a pseudo-random, uniformly distributed long value.

setSeed void setSeed(long seed)

Sets the seed of the random number generator using the specified *seed*.

java.util.Stack

Description This class provides an easy way to create and use a vectored stack. A stack is a last-in first-out data structure, meaning that objects can only be added or deleted from the top of the list.

Parent Class Vector

See Also Vector

CONSTRUCTORS

Stack() Creates a Stack.

VARIABLES

None

METHODS

empty	boolean empty()
	Returns true if this Stack is empty.
peek	Object peek() *
	Returns a reference to the Object at the top of this Stack.
pop	Object pop() *
	Pops an Object off of this Stack.
push	Object push(Object obj)
	Pushes an Object onto this Stack and returns the same item.
search	int search(Object obj)
	Returns the distance Object *obj* is from the top of this Stack or -1 if it was not found.

* Throws EmptyStackException if the stack is empty.

java.util.StringTokenizer

Description	This class provides a means for simple linear tokenization of a string. The default delimiter is a whitespace, but a different one may be specified at creation time or on a per token basis.
Parent Class	Object
Implements	Enumeration
See Also	java.io.StreamTokenizer

CONSTRUCTORS

StringTokenizer(String str [, String delimiter])

> Creates a StringTokenizer on the specified input string *str*, using the default delimiter set ("\t\n\r" and whitespace) or the specified *delimiter* set.

StringTokenizer(String str, String delimiter, boolean returnTokens)

> Creates a StringTokenizer on the specified input string *str*, using the specified *delimiter* set. If *returnTokens* is true, delimiters will be returned as tokens, else they will be skipped.

VARIABLES

None

METHODS

countTokens   int countTokens()

Returns the number of tokens in the string with the current delimiter set. This is the number of times nextToken() may be invoked before a NoSuchElementException is generated.

hasMoreElements   boolean hasMoreElements()

Returns true if the Enumeration has more elements.

hasMoreTokens   boolean hasMoreTokens()

Returns true if more tokens exist.

nextElement   Object nextElement() *

Returns the next element in the Enumeration.

nextToken   String nextToken([String delimiter]) *

Returns the next token of the string or, optionally, switches to the new *delimiter* set and then returns the next token. Note: The new delimiter set remains intact after the method is executed.

* Throws NoSuchElementException if there are no more tokens or elements.

java.util.Vector

Description   The Vector class implements a growable array. Each Vector maintains a capacity and a capacityIncrement. When a Vector grows beyond its capacity, it will grow in chunks the size of its capacityIncrement.

Parent Class   Object

Implements   Cloneable

See Also   Enumeration, Stack

CONSTRUCTORS

Vector()   Constructs an empty Vector.

Vector(int initialCapacity [, int capacityIncrement])

Constructs a Vector with a storage capacity of *initialCapacity* and an optional chunk size of *capacityIncrement*.

VARIABLES

capacityIncrement   protected int: The size of growth increment (chunk size). If 0, the capacity doubles when it needs to grow.

elementCount   protected int: The number of elements in the Vector.

elementData   protected Object: The data buffer where the elements are stored.

METHODS

addElement
final synchronized void addElement(Object obj)
Adds the specified Object *obj* to the end of this Vector.

capacity
final int capacity()
Returns the current capacity of this Vector.

clone
final synchronized Object clone()
Clones this Vector but not its elements.

contains
final boolean contains(Object element)
Returns true if the specified *element* is in this Vector.

copyInto
final synchronized void copyInto(Object objArray[])
Copies the elements of this Vector into the array specified by *objArray*.

elementAt
final synchronized Object elementAt(int index) *
Returns the element at the givin *index* of this vector.

elements
final synchronized Enumeration elements()
Returns an Enumeration of the elements in this Vector.

ensureCapacity
final synchronized void ensureCapacity(int minCapacity)
Ensures that this Vector has at least a capacity of *minCapacity*.

firstElement
final synchronized Object firstElement() **
Returns the first element in this Vector.

indexOf
final int indexOf(Object element)
Searches forward from the beginning, then returns the index of the specified *element* in this Vector or -1 if it was not found.

indexOf
final synchronized int indexOf(Object element, int startingIndex)
Searches forward from *startingIndex*, then returns the index of the specified *element* in this Vector or -1 if it was not found.

insertElementAt
final synchronized void insertElementAt(Object obj, int index) *
Inserts the specified Object *obj* at specified *index* position and reindexes this Vector.

isEmpty
final boolean isEmpty()
Returns true if this Vector contains no elements.

lastElement
final synchronized Object lastElement() **
Returns the last element in this Vector.

lastIndexOf
final int lastIndexOf(Object element)
Searches backward from the end, then returns the index of the specified *element* in this Vector or -1 if it was not found.

lastIndexOf
final synchronized int lastIndexOf(Object element, int startingIndex)
Searches backward from *startingIndex*, then returns the index of the specified *element* in the Vector or -1 if it was not found.

removeAllElements   final synchronized boolean removeAllElements()

Removes all elements in this Vector.

removeElement   final synchronized boolean removeElement(Object obj)

Removes the first occurrence of the specified Object *obj* from this Vector. Returns false if the object was not found and true if it was found and removed.

removeElementAt   final synchronized void removeElementAt(int index) *

Deletes the element at specified *index* position and reindexes this Vector.

setElementAt   final synchronized void setElementAt(Object obj, int index) *

Overwrites the element at specified *index* position with the given Object *obj*.

setSize   final synchronized void setSize(int newCapacity)

Sets this Vector's capacity size to *newCapacity*. If the size shrinks, the elements at the end of the Vector are lost.

size   final int size()

Returns the current number of elements in this Vector.

toString   final synchronized String toString()

Returns a String showing all the elements in this Vector.

trimToSize   final synchronized void trimToSize()

Trims this Vector's capacity to the current size. Future insertions will cause reallocation to occur.

* Throws ArrayIndexOutOfBoundsException if the index is invalid.

** Throws NoSuchElementException if the sequence is empty.

EXCEPTIONS   ERRORS

awt

AWTException   AWTError

io

EOFException
FileNotFoundException
InterruptedIOException
IOException
UTFDataFormatException

lang

ArithmeticException	AbstractMethodError
ArrayIndexOutOfBoundsException	ClassCircularityError
ArrayStoreException	ClassFormatError
ClassCastException	Error
ClassNotFoundException	IllegalAccessError
CloneNotSupportedException	IncompatibleClassChangeError
Exception	InstantiationError
IllegalAccessException	InternalError
IllegalArgumentException	LinkageError
IllegalMonitorState Exception	NoClassDefFoundError
IllegalThreadStateException	NoSuchFieldError
IndexOutOfBoundsException	NoSuchMethodError
InstantiationException	OutOfMemoryError
InterruptedException	StackOverflowError
NegativeArraySizeException	ThreadDeath
NoSuchMethodException	UnknownError
NullPointerException	UnsatisfiedLinkError
NumberFormatException	VerifyError
RuntimeException	VirtualMachineError
SecurityException	
StringIndexOutOfBoundsException	

net

MalformedURLException
ProtocolException
SocketException
UnknownHostException
UnknownServiceException

util

EmptyStackException
NoSuchElementException

Index

Books have a substantial influence on the destruction of the forests of the Earth. For example, it takes 17 trees to produce one ton of paper. A first printing of 30,000 copies of a typical 480-page book consumes 108,000 pounds of paper, which will require 918 trees!

Waite Group Press™ is against the clear-cutting of forests and supports reforestation of the Pacific Northwest of the United States and Canada, where most of this paper comes from. As a publisher with several hundred thousand books sold each year, we feel an obligation to give back to the planet. We will therefore support organizations that seek to preserve the forests of planet Earth.

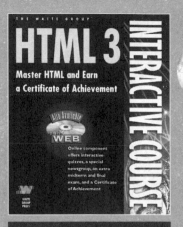
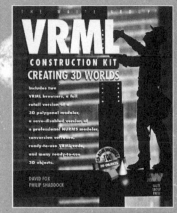

LIMITED WARRANTY

The following warranties shall be effective for 90 days from the date of purchase: (i) The Waite Group, Inc. warrants the enclosed disk to be free of defects in materials and workmanship under normal use; and (ii) The Waite Group, Inc. warrants that the programs, unless modified by the purchaser, will substantially perform the functions described in the documentation provided by The Waite Group, Inc. when operated on the designated hardware and operating system. The Waite Group, Inc. does not warrant that the programs will meet purchaser's requirements or that operation of a program will be uninterrupted or error-free. The program warranty does not cover any program that has been altered or changed in any way by anyone other than The Waite Group, Inc. The Waite Group, Inc. is not responsible for problems caused by changes in the operating characteristics of computer hardware or computer operating systems that are made after the release of the programs, nor for problems in the interaction of the programs with each other or other software.

THESE WARRANTIES ARE EXCLUSIVE AND IN LIEU OF ALL OTHER WARRANTIES OF MERCHANTABILITY OR FITNESS FOR A PARTICULAR PURPOSE OR OF ANY OTHER WARRANTY, WHETHER EXPRESS OR IMPLIED.

EXCLUSIVE REMEDY

The Waite Group, Inc. will replace any defective disk without charge if the defective disk is returned to The Waite Group, Inc. within 90 days from date of purchase.

This is Purchaser's sole and exclusive remedy for any breach of warranty or claim for contract, tort, or damages.

LIMITATION OF LIABILITY

THE WAITE GROUP, INC. AND THE AUTHORS OF THE PROGRAMS SHALL NOT IN ANY CASE BE LIABLE FOR SPECIAL, INCIDENTAL, CONSEQUENTIAL, INDIRECT, OR OTHER SIMILAR DAMAGES ARISING FROM ANY BREACH OF THESE WARRANTIES EVEN IF THE WAITE GROUP, INC. OR ITS AGENT HAS BEEN ADVISED OF THE POSSIBILITY OF SUCH DAMAGES.

THE LIABILITY FOR DAMAGES OF THE WAITE GROUP, INC. AND THE AUTHORS OF THE PROGRAMS UNDER THIS AGREEMENT SHALL IN NO EVENT EXCEED THE PURCHASE PRICE PAID.

COMPLETE AGREEMENT

This Agreement constitutes the complete agreement between The Waite Group, Inc. and the authors of the programs, and you, the purchaser.

Some states do not allow the exclusion or limitation of implied warranties or liability for incidental or consequential damages, so the above exclusions or limitations may not apply to you. This limited warranty gives you specific legal rights; you may have others, which vary from state to state.

SATISFACTION REPORT CARD

Please fill out this card if you wish to know of future updates to
Java Primer Plus, or to receive our catalog.

First Name: _____   Last Name: _____

Address: _____

Street: _____

City: _____   State: _____   Zip: _____

Daytime Telephone: (   ) _____

E-Mail Address: _____

Date product was acquired: Month _____   Day _____   Year _____   Your Occupation: _____

Overall, how would you rate *Java Primer Plus*?

☐ Excellent   ☐ Very Good   ☐ Good
☐ Fair   ☐ Below Average   ☐ Poor

What did you like MOST about this book? _____

_____
_____

What did you like LEAST about this book? _____

_____
_____

Please describe any problems you may have encountered with installing or using the disk: _____

_____

How did you use this book (problem-solver, tutorial, reference...)?

_____

What is your level of computer expertise?

☐ New   ☐ Dabbler   ☐ Hacker
☐ Power User   ☐ Programmer   ☐ Experienced Professional

What computer languages are you familiar with? _____

_____

Please describe your computer hardware:

Computer _____ Hard disk _____
5.25" disk drives _____ 3.5" disk drives _____
Video card _____ Monitor _____
Printer _____ Peripherals _____
Sound board _____ CD-ROM_____

Where did you buy this book?

☐ Bookstore (name): _____
☐ Discount store (name): _____
☐ Computer store (name): _____
☐ Catalog (name): _____
☐ Direct from WGP   ☐ Other _____

What price did you pay for this book? _____

What influenced your purchase of this book?

☐ Recommendation   ☐ Advertisement
☐ Magazine review   ☐ Store display
☐ Mailing   ☐ Book's format
☐ Reputation of Waite Group Press   ☐ Other

How many computer books do you buy each year? _____

How many other Waite Group books do you own? _____

What is your favorite Waite Group book? _____

_____

Is there any program or subject you would like to see Waite Group Press cover in a similar approach? _____

_____

Additional comments? _____

_____
_____

Please send to: **Waite Group Press**
                        200 Tamal Plaza
                        Corte Madera, CA 94925

☐ **Check here for a free Waite Group catalog**

STOP!